Social Mobility in Britain

INTERNATIONAL LIBRARY OF SOCIOLOGY
AND SOCIAL RECONSTRUCTION

Founded by Karl Mannheim

Editor: W. J. H. Sprott

A catalogue of the books available in the INTERNATIONAL LIBRARY OF SOCIOLOGY AND SOCIAL RECONSTRUCTION, and new books in preparation for the Library, will be found at the end of this volume.

SOCIAL MOBILITY
IN BRITAIN

EDITED BY D. V. GLASS

with contributions by

J. BERENT

T. BOTTOMORE

R. C. CHAMBERS

J. FLOUD

D. V. GLASS

J. R. HALL

H. T. HIMMELWEIT

R. K. KELSALL

F. M. MARTIN

C. A. MOSER

R. MUKHERJEE

W. ZIEGEL

ROUTLEDGE & KEGAN PAUL LTD

Broadway House, 68–74 Carter Lane

London

First published in 1954
by Routledge & Kegan Paul Limited
Broadway House, 68-74 Carter Lane
London, EC4V 5EL

Reprinted 1963, 1966, 1967, 1971

Reproduced and Printed in Great Britain by
Redwood Press Limited
Trowbridge & London

ISBN 0 7100 3327 3

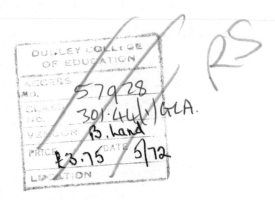

Preface

To anyone reading this book, it will be evident that the series of studies brought together here could not have been carried out save with the advice and help of many individuals and organizations—of colleagues, of Government Departments and, not least, of the large numbers of people who allowed themselves to be interviewed and questioned. Specific references to this help are given in the various chapters. It is only fitting, however, that speaking for my co-authors, I should draw attention in this preface to our most heavy obligations.

It was Professor T. H. Marshall who first presented, to the Social Research Division of the London School of Economics, a memorandum calling for a long-term programme of research into social selection and differentiation in Britain. The studies contained in this volume derive from his memorandum, the research itself having been made possible by a very generous grant from the Nuffield Foundation and subsequently by an additional grant from the Rockefeller Foundation. From its beginnings, the research has profited from the interest and advice of Professor Marshall, as also of Professor M. Ginsberg, who had himself previously undertaken the pioneer study of social mobility in England and Wales.

In its initial stages, the main inquiry was directed by Mr. D. Caradog Jones, who published, in the *British Journal of Sociology*, the first two reports on the results of the research. Unfortunately, he did not take part in the final analysis of the material. But our main studies have profited greatly from his experience and initiative.

After the retirement of Mr. Caradog Jones, the supervision of the central inquiry was carried on by Mr. John Hall. He was assisted by Miss B. Roxburgh who, though she resigned before the completion of the studies, contributed very substantially to the analysis presented in Chapters IV and VIII of the volume. Further considerable help was given by Dr. R. Mukherjee, especially in the measurement of mobility, and by Mr. W. Ziegel. Most useful advice on the measurement of mobility was also given by Mr. J. Durbin, Reader in Statistics, and by Mr: A. Stuart, of the Division of Research Techniques, both of them colleagues at the London School of Economics.

Our thanks are due to Dr. George North, Registrar General of England and Wales and Chairman of the Inter-Departmental Committee on Economic and Social Research, for his encouragement at a critical stage of our research. To Mr. L. Moss, Director of the Government Social Survey, we are much indebted for his own aid, as well as for that of his department, in carrying out our main sample investigation.

This preface also provides an opportunity to record our obligation to Professor Lancelot Hogben. Professor Hogben was not associated with our research and is in no way responsible for our faults. But our approach to the study of social selection and differentiation has clearly been influenced by the investigations which he promoted before World War II in the Department of Social Biology, the London School of Economics. It gives me great pleasure to acknowledge that fact, especially as I myself had the privilege of working in Professor Hogben's Department.

D. V. GLASS

London, May 1953

Contents

vii

see 291 first

Part deux

CONTENTS

PART I

I

Introduction

D. V. GLASS

THE studies brought together in this volume represent the first main
results of a programme of research now being carried out through
the Department of Sociological and Demographic Research of the
London School of Economics. The programme as a whole is concerned
with the processes of social selection and differentiation which are at
work in Britain, with the formation of social strata, and with the nature,
composition and functions of those strata. Such problems are central to
the study of social structure; they are of direct concern both for the
development of sociological theory and for the formulation of social
policy.

No research programme dealing with problems of this kind could aim
at being exhaustive. The field is vast, touching—at least at its edges—the
whole area of social relations. And the boundaries and content have
been changing as recent developments in economic and social policy
have affected the rôles of the different social institutions. Some delimita-
tion of scope was essential, even though it was obvious that there could
be no sharp demarcation and that to illuminate one sector would often
involve the study of other sectors.

As a starting-point it was proposed to focus upon the formation and
structure of the 'middle classes'. Much has been said in recent years
about the changing circumstances of this section of the community. But
in Britain, at least, the discussion has not generally been based upon
systematic, objective, prior study. Indeed, save in respect of their early
history the 'middle classes' of Britain have not been much exposed to
investigation.[1] The social reformers of the late nineteenth and early

[1] The most recent English study, R. Lewis and A. Maude, *The English Middle
Classes*, London, 1949, is an interesting and useful survey. Nevertheless, being
necessarily based upon what material was at hand, it inevitably contains very
large gaps, notably concerning the recruitment of the 'middle classes'.

twentieth centuries were understandably interested in the 'working class' and in the problems of poverty, and it became the custom for the local social survey—a major British contribution to empirical social research—to keep within those limits. There had long been concern with the professions, and the work of Carr-Saunders and Wilson has not been surpassed in Britain or in any other country.[1] But that work relates to the development of professional structure and codes, and to the place of professionalism in society, rather than to actual recruitment to the professions or to the extent to which, because the rise in the minimum educational requirements of the professions has been more rapid than the expansion of educational opportunities for the community as a whole, the supply of professional men has continued to come largely from the 'middle classes'. Similarly, there had been much interest in the general question of the selection of 'the nation's leaders', and its relationship to educational opportunities. But the level of interest before World War II was not high enough—or, perhaps, not of the kind—to provide the funds and collaboration indispensable for really comprehensive inquiries. The studies undertaken were thus inevitably limited in range and depth. Characteristically, lack of adequate social research did not prevent the passing of the 1944 Education Act, which, so far as social stratification is concerned, is probably the most important measure of the last half-century. Equally characteristically, however, no central provision was made to ascertain the social consequences of this great expansion of educational opportunity—its effects upon the existing 'middle classes', for example, or its rôle in the formation of new élites. Both in relation to the recent past and to the present, there is obviously more than enough scope for studies of the 'middle classes'.

Given the definition of the narrower province of inquiry, the 'middle classes', certain specific studies were relevant—such as the degree of self-recruitment of particular groups, and especially of the professions and the higher Civil Service; the factors affecting the prestige of 'middle-class' occupations in the community and the carry-over of occupational prestige into other realms of activity; differentiation within the 'middle classes'; and the nature and distinctiveness of 'middle-class' aspirations and ideals. But no less obviously studies of this kind would be truncated if confined to the 'middle classes'. The prestige of the professions and of other white-collar occupations cannot be considered without reference to a possible overall hierarchy of occupational prestige. Self-recruitment in the professions and the higher Civil Service would have little meaning

[1] A. M. Carr-Saunders and P. A. Wilson, *The Professions*, Oxford, 1933.

unless compared with self-recruitment in other occupational groups. Indeed, it was clear that the study of particular groups needed, as background, a *general* investigation of social status and social mobility in Britain. Hence it was upon this general investigation that first inquiries were focused. Later studies will deal specifically with the 'middle classes' as a whole or with subdivisions of them, such as the Higher Civil Service or the various professions. The present volume, however, is concerned with the *general* picture of social status and social mobility in Britain. The successive chapters, which examine various aspects of that general picture, aim to be self-contained and self-explanatory, and it is not, therefore, necessary to refer in detail to them here. But since the material on which the chapters are based derives from a series of studies —covering seven new field investigations—it is desirable to describe briefly the framework within which those studies were set. The description will also show, it is hoped, that though the sequence of the chapters may appear a little odd, it is not entirely capricious.

The core of the general investigation is the study of social mobility in Britain—of the extent of movement in social status or social position by individuals of diverse social origins. Such a study assumes a hierarchy of social status—that society is arranged in a series of layers—and that there are criteria which may be used to indicate the status level, or position in the hierarchy, of an individual or a group.[1] It needs no elaborate conceptual framework or tests of carefully formulated hypotheses to show that there are different levels of social status in contemporary Britain. What is more difficult is the choice of a criterion or criteria which will give at least a useful first approximation of the social status of an individual. In a society divided into a series of 'estates', the rank, privileges and contents of those 'estates' being defined by law, there should theoretically be no problem in identifying the position of an individual in the social hierarchy. But in contemporary society, the different levels are not so specified and the criteria chosen must reflect a customary rather than a legal structure. Earlier studies have often used occupation as an index of social status and there is much to be said for this. Certainly, groups constructed of occupations of presumed

---

[1] See T. H. Marshall, 'The nature and determinants of social status', *Year Book of Education, 1953*. On the literature on social stratification in general, see D. G. MacRae, 'Social stratification: a trend report and bibliography', *Current Sociology*, Vol. 2, No. 1, 1953–4; and H. W. Pfautz, 'The current literature on social stratification: critique and bibliography', *Am. J. Sociology*, January 1953. P. Sorokin, *Social Mobility*, New York and London, 1927, is still the only comprehensive study of social mobility.

similar status have shown consistent patterns in fertility and mortality as well as in the degree of self-recruitment. And this is not surprising for it is evident that, in our own society for example, occupation reflects the combined influence of a number of factors linked to social status. Moreover, there is an important advantage in using, as a first approximation, a single criterion, for the relationship and influence of other separate factors or determinants may then be examined separately. Available knowledge certainly gives strong support to the use of occupation as an initial index of social status in Britain, and it has been so used in the present research.

But in previous British studies, the classification of occupations in terms of social status was not based upon deliberate empirical research. The classification reflected the views of a small number of persons, themselves mainly 'middle class' in position. It was unlikely that this would greatly affect the ranking of occupations at the extreme ends of the scale. But in the middle ranges, in which in any case there would tend to be less agreement, 'middle class' bias of judgement might be significant. Moreover, in the most widely used classification, that of the Registrar General of England and Wales, manual occupations were divided up into categories of skill, though it cannot simply be assumed that skill and social status are perfectly correlated.[1]

Hence in order to use occupation as an index of social status, it was necessary to begin the general investigation of social mobility by a new empirical study (see Chapter II). The study was limited in scope and objective. Equating the social status of an occupation with the prestige it had in the community, the study aimed to discover if there was substantial agreement in the community as a whole on the position of various occupations in a hierarchy of social prestige—of occupations regarded as stereotypes, not as influenced by personal knowledge of individual, and possibly exceptional, cases. A wide measure of agreement was found—sufficient to justify the construction of a series of broad groups constituting a scale of prestige. Accordingly, the groups could then be used in the second main stage of the general investigation.

The second stage consisted in obtaining the life histories—in respect of social origins, education, occupation, marriage and fertility—of a random sample of 10,000 adults, the sample representing the adult

[1] For a discussion of the difficulties and anomalies in the Registrar General's classification, see the writer's note in *Population Studies*, December 1947, pp. 296–300. Some of the doubts raised there concerning consensus on the prestige of occupations have, in fact, been dispelled by the studies carried out subsequently.

civilian population of Great Britain. This was a very substantial task, and would have presented extremely serious difficulties if the work had fallen to an *ad hoc* group of untrained interviewers. Fortunately, however, with the help of the Inter-Departmental Committee on Economic and Social Research, and with the sponsorship of the Ministry of Labour, it was possible to make use of the services of the Government Social Survey. This organization gave valuable advice on the questionnaires and designed the sample; while, through its interviewers, the actual field work was carried out most effectively.

It was to the occupational data collected by this investigation that the prestige scale of occupations was applied. For the main purpose of the investigation was not to study occupations as such, but levels of social status. By using the prestige scale, even though it was a crude first approximation, it was possible to assign occupations to social status categories. And this having been done, a wide range of analyses could be undertaken. Thus it was possible to see whether there were consistent and significant differences between the levels of education attained by individuals whose fathers were at different levels of social status (Chapter V), and to examine the relationship between the social status of fathers and sons (Chapters VIII and IX). Similarly, the relationship between the social origins of brides and grooms could be studied (Chapter XII), and the influence on fertility of upward or downward social mobility.[1] These questions are discussed in detail in subsequent chapters and need not be elaborated here. It is, however, worth noting that, because of the nature of the sample investigation, the whole range of questions could be examined within a single framework, using common criteria and bases of classification. In dealing with the various aspects of social mobility, a common method of analysis was also developed and applied—a method which attempts to overcome some of the main difficulties involved in comparing the mobility of persons of different social origins, whether that mobility is considered in terms of occupational achievement or marriage.

Fitting into these two central studies, six more specialized inquiries were undertaken, dealing with particular aspects of the general question of social status and social mobility. One of these went beyond the simple prestige scale of occupations, to explore a wider range of attitudes to and determinants of social status, and to examine the relation between

[1] The study of the fertility aspect, carried out under the auspices of the Population Investigation Committee, has already been published. See J. Berent, 'Fertility and social mobility', *Population Studies*, March 1952.

7

social status and political opinions (Chapter III). Two studies are concerned with problems of educational selection. The main material on education—the material collected by the central sample investigation—relates to individuals who had passed through the school system before the 1944 Education Act had come into force. But some important social factors influencing selection and achievement in the new secondary school system are considered in the two additional studies (Chapters VI and VII). The remaining special studies are focused on particular aspects of social mobility. The basic collection of material on social mobility is analysed in terms of movements between broad status categories. This analysis is supplemented by a study of self-recruitment in four professions, a study based upon information relating to university students (Chapter XI). Similarly, social status, in the central investigation, is discussed in terms of occupation. But there are other possibilities of obtaining social prestige in the community, and it is important to know whether these are effective alternatives—in the sense that they are opportunities available to and used by individuals engaged in occupations of low prestige—or whether they reflect, and perhaps intensify, the prestige hierarchy of the world of employment. Leadership in voluntary associations is often regarded as offering an alternative basis of social prestige, and the two final studies examine the structure of voluntary associations from this point of view (Chapters XIII and XIV).

One difference between the central investigation and the more specialized inquiries should be emphasized. The central investigation relates to Great Britain as a whole, and is based upon a sample designed to represent the whole community. This approach was followed because of the need to obtain a valid, overall view against which subsequent local or sectional studies, dealing with specific topics in greater detail, might be set. The special inquiries are local in character, with two exceptions—the studies of self-recruitment in four professions, and of the leadership structure of three women's voluntary organizations—and are designed to illuminate certain problems from local materials, not to provide national generalizations. But the specialized studies fit into the same general framework and use the same broad classifications; the results are comparable between themselves and with those of the central investigation.

In the present volume the reports deriving from the two different types of studies have been so arranged as to group together chapters dealing with the same or similar topics, whatever the particular inquiry from which the material has been obtained. Since the central investigation covers a number of topics or, rather, aspects, the results are not presented in one block, but in several sections, interspersed with chapters reporting cognate results from the more specialized research. Part I of the volume consists of two chapters bearing upon social status; the first (Chapter II) concerns the prestige of occupations and the second (Chapter III) presents an analysis of attitude studies carried out in Greenwich and Hertford. Part II begins with a fairly detailed discussion of the basic sample investigation of 10,000 adults (Chapter IV), and then goes on to examine the relations between social origins and education. In Chapter V, this is done for the population which had passed through the school system before the 1944 Act came into force. Chapters VI and VII, however, relate to the new secondary school system, the first chapter reporting the results of an investigation carried out in London grammar and secondary modern schools, and the second consisting of a study of the attitudes to secondary education of the parents of all children who, in 1952, were passing through the secondary school selection process in south-west Hertfordshire. With this background analysis of social factors affecting educational selection, Part III then takes up the study of social mobility. Of the five chapters in this section, four make use of the material derived from the central sample investigation: Chapter VIII dealing with changes in social status between fathers and sons—that is, changes between two generations;[1] Chapter IX with changes in social status over three generations, between grandfathers, fathers and sons; Chapter X with the way in which the education affects the social mobility of individuals of different social origins; and Chapter XII with social mobility in marriage, or the extent of marriage between partners of different social origins as defined in terms of paternal occupation. Chapter XI, on the other hand, is based on information about the undergraduate students of four universities and examines the professional careers chosen by those students in relation to the specific professions of their fathers. Finally, Part IV, consisting of two chapters, is concerned with the extent to which leaders in voluntary associations are recruited from those groups of people who, in terms of occupation (their own or their husbands'), already have high social status. Chapter XIII summarizes the results of two inquiries conducted in a small country town—one giving a relatively superficial view of the social status make-up of all the relevant voluntary associations, and the other studying a few 'critical' associations more closely.

[1] The methods used to measure mobility are discussed in detail in Appendices 1 and 2 to Chapter VIII.

9

Chapter XIV, the last in the volume, looks rather at the national picture and in somewhat more qualitative terms, and examines three associations restricted very largely to women, the W.V.S., the Women's Institutes and the Red Cross.

The previous discussion aimed to show that the various chapters in this volume, though covering a wide range of topics and deriving from a series of investigations, are linked together and fit into a common framework of research, focused on social status and social mobility in Great Britain. To say this, however, by no means implies that the picture presented is complete,[1] or that the actual research itself is free from limitations or defects. Each chapter draws attention to deficiencies of approach or material, and either explicitly or implicitly suggests ways in which subsequent inquiries might be improved. There is no need to repeat those suggestions here. But there are, in addition, certain general questions which should be considered in this introduction in order to prevent later misunderstanding.

It should in the first place be emphasized that the research is concerned with social status or social prestige, and not with social class in the classical sense of the term. This does not mean that the studies do not throw light on problems of social class. But the approach is rather different, and many topics which would be looked for in a report on 'class structure' are not dealt with at all here.

Secondly, the studies in this volume are rather formal and quantitative; the subtleties of social relationships have not generally been examined. This limitation springs from the need to establish an order of priority in developing systematic research into problems which, as occurs so often in sociology, have hitherto been treated largely on an *ad hoc* basis. In such circumstances, however valuable individual studies may be, the separate studies are either not additive, or at best the process of addition is both difficult and precarious. We may contrast the situation here with that in demography. In the latter field of study there has, of course, been a powerful element of good fortune—namely, that by the middle of the nineteenth century the concern of the community with records of birth and death had been recognized and to a substantial extent accepted. But it was the early demographers themselves who

---

[1] The chapters in this volume do not exhaust the material collected by the various inquiries. There will be additional reports on the process of educational selection, under the 1944 Education Act, in London, Hertfordshire, and Middlesbrough. And the central sample investigation will be used in studying the social mobility of families, as distinct from that of individuals. Further analyses of social status aspects of marriage will also be published.

10

insisted upon the need for an overall view, and it has been against the increasingly detailed overall picture provided through the machinery of the State that particular studies have since been developed. No demographer going into an area which lacked census and vital statistics would suggest studying the more subtle influences on fertility before he had obtained at least a reasonable estimate on the level of fertility, and its variation over time and between groups in the country chosen. Even then it would still be necessary to distinguish the influence of 'mechanical' factors, for differences in total reproductivity may be due to differences in the extent of marriage, or in the numbers of children born to marriages, or to both factors working in combination. The same kind of requirements apply to the study of social mobility. We need to know, as a first guide, how much mobility there is in the community as a whole; whether it has been rising or falling; what differences there are in the degree of self-recruitment between the various social strata; and with what primary objective characteristics mobility or immobility is most closely associated. To answer these questions inevitably means a rather statistical physiology. But without it, there will be little guidance for more subtle inquiries.

This kind of first approach is even more necessary when, as is clearly to be desired, international comparisons are made. It is, of course, true that we already know something of the differences in social stratification between various countries. In one sense we usually know a good deal more than we realize; unfortunately, we rarely take the trouble to codify our existing knowledge and see what emerges and what major gaps are evident. But in the international, as in the national scene, the available information is drawn from a large number of unconnected studies, so that the results do not fit together. There are, for example, sample studies carried out in the U.S.A., France and Italy which may be used to estimate the degree of social mobility in those three countries.[1] But the comparison between the estimates is crude because the samples were designed on different bases and because the investigators posed the problem in varying terms. Hence though we may infer from other studies that the individual manual worker in the three countries differs in his view of the desirability of upward social mobility—that, for example, the French syndicalist may regard such personal mobility as being 'treason' to his class, whereas for the American worker the idea of

---

[1] An interesting attempt to compare France and the U.S.A. has been made by N. Rogoff, 'Social stratification in France and the United States', *Am. J. Sociology*, January 1953. See also Chapter VIII, Appendix 3, in the present volume.

11

upward movement is part of the accepted set of aspirations in his society —we cannot say whether such differences actually affect the rigidity of the social structure. Or to take another example, we might infer, from what has been written on the social history of Western countries, that there would be strong similarities in the hierarchy of prestige of occupations in the various contemporary industrial societies. Until very recently, this could not be verified from available empirical research; prestige studies were confined to the U.S.A. and, even so, were not comparable between themselves. Now, however, the application of a more formal approach—even though the approach is still very imperfect —is beginning to yield interesting results for a number of countries, and may help to throw light both on similarities and on differences in occupational prestige, and suggest lines for more sensitive and profitable inquiry.[1]

The question of carrying out comparative studies of social stratification and social mobility in a number of countries has been taken up by the International Sociological Association. Reports on available information have been prepared, and new empirical research is being initiated.[2]

[1] See A. A. Congalton, 'Social grading of occupations in New Zealand', *Brit. J. Sociology*, March 1953; and R. Taft, 'The social grading of occupations in Australia', *Brit. J. Sociology*, June 1953. There is, of course, no question here of recommending the indiscriminate use of a single list of occupations in various countries as a means of 'discovering' the hierarchies of occupational prestige. The approach would inevitably be broader and more complex. Nevertheless it would be advantageous to include in each list certain common, key types of occupations— e.g. professions, managerial, routine non-manual and skilled manual. As is also made clear in Chapter II of the present volume, the simple ranking of occupations is insufficient, even in a national inquiry. And for international comparisons, the provision of a common scale of distance (e.g. a percentile scale of prestige) is almost indispensable. In using occupational classifications for measuring social mobility, it is, of course, also valuable to have functional classifications—e.g. those based upon differences in the length of training or degree of skill, or distinguishing such categories as managerial, executive, clerical, manual, etc. But without reference to the social status attached to such categories of employment in the given societies, indices of self-recruitment or mobility will lose much of their significance.

[2] See *First International Working Conference on Social Stratification and Social Mobility*, International Sociological Association, August 1951. The first reports on past research into stratification and social mobility, which are being published in *Current Sociology*, are those by D. G. MacRae, already referred to; by the late Professor L. Wirth, on the U.S.A.; by Professor C. Boalt, on Sweden; and by Professor K. Odaka, on Japan. At the time of writing, new empirical research is being undertaken in the Netherlands, Japan and Denmark.

It has been argued by one critic of the I.S.A. proposals for comparative research, that to begin by attempting to construct occupational prestige scales implies a fundamentally conservative view of social structure. (A. Touraine, 'Rapport sur la préparation en France de l'enquête internationale sur la stratification et la mobilité sociales', mimeographed report to the I.S.A.) But this is to misunderstand both the

But when the results of the present inquiry were being analysed, no strictly comparable material could be found for other countries. Nor were there earlier inquiries for Britain, the results of which could be drawn upon to establish historical trends, though there are unpublished official records which we hope to use subsequently for such purposes.

The absence of other comparable inquiries itself imposes a limitation on the value of the present studies, for they are confined within a narrow band of time and space. We cannot, for example, see the effects on the recruitment of industrial and commercial leaders, of the shift from partnership to joint-stock enterprise. In looking at the changes in social mobility resulting from increasing State provision of education, we are in the main limited to the period spanned by the Education Acts of 1870 and 1902. Nor can we tell with real precision whether the degree of self-recruitment found in the various strata in Britain for the recent past differs significantly from that obtaining in other Western countries—whether our society is more rigid than, for example, that of the U.S.A. Not until the results of similar research in other countries are available, and until repeat studies are done in Britain in the future, will it be possible fully to appreciate the relevance of the present inquiries.

Since external comparisons are so restricted at present, we have tried to extend the range of internal comparison, especially in relation to trends in social mobility. Thus the central sample investigation was not confined to one age group of the population, though such a limitation would have increased the statistical efficiency of the inquiry. Instead, all adult age groups were covered and the results have been analysed by decades of birth of the individuals interviewed, so as to make it possible to see if the level of mobility differs significantly between the various birth cohorts. This is a method of analysis used in other fields of inquiry; in studying fertility trends, for example, this approach is made necessary because in many countries fertility censuses, which ask each married, widowed or divorced woman to state the total number of live-born children she has had, are taken at rather widely separated intervals of time. But the use of information relating to old people almost inevit-

---

intention and the technique of the research. There is certainly no intention of constructing a continuum if none exists; on the contrary, to find that, in a particular country, no single scale existed would itself be of very great interest. And even to find sufficient agreement, by sample inquiries, on a single scale would not necessarily suppose a continuum within which one stratum moved imperceptibly into another. The use of a percentile or equivalent scale of distance and the analysis of the different degrees of self-recruitment of the various categories would, in fact, throw light upon the existence of sharp divisions between the various strata.

13

ably entails some kind of bias. In fertility censuses, the oldest marriage cohorts are over-weighted by women who married at the younger ages, as well as by women of the 'middle classes', for in both cases it is those women who are most likely to survive until the date of the census. There may, in addition, be some correlation between total fertility and the chances of survival beyond the end of the reproductive period—that is, of women marrying in a given year those who died just after their fiftieth birthday may have been less fertile, perhaps for physiological reasons, than those who survived until they were 75 years of age. And it is the latter women who will be included in the census. Undoubtedly, there are biases of this order involved in using the data of the sample investigation into social mobility, though there is not yet sufficient evidence to allow us to say, as may be said in studying fertility trends, how those biases distort the results.

Ideally, the investigation of social mobility, like that of fertility, should be forward-looking, not backward-looking in design. The Netherlands, for example, has a system of continuous vital registration. When a man marries, a special 'family card' is started for him and his wife, and on that card is entered every vital event occurring thereafter to the couple and to any children they may have. Hence, at least in theory, it is possible to ascertain, without bias, the fertility of women who married in a particular year; for the cards for all such women will be available, whatever their age at marriage or death.[1] A modification of this system would provide an equally undistorted view of social mobility, solving many of the problems discussed by Dr. Mukherjee later in this volume.[2] But it is most unlikely that such a system would be acceptable here, or, for that matter, in many other countries. At the same time, some of the chief difficulties of analysis would be reduced if future investigations of the backward-looking variety were carried out regularly and at intervals of not more than, say, fifteen or twenty years.

[1] The Statistics Committee of the Royal Commission on Population favoured the establishment of a comparable system of vital registration in Britain, though recognizing that there were many practical difficulties.

[2] See Appendix 2 to Chapter VIII. The defect of the Netherlands 'family card' for the study of social mobility is in the recording of occupation. There is no provision for the regular recording of changes in occupation. But if the 'family card' data were linked with the censuses, and if the new cards established for children when they themselves marry were linked by a serial reference to the original family card, the information would be practically complete, and the basic study of mobility could be carried out without any further questioning of the people concerned. The Swedish continuous registration system, with its combination of 'church book' and 'tax assessment' records, provides for regular reporting of occupation, but has no linked 'family card'.

Indeed, information on many of the factual questions could easily, and with justification, be collected by the normal periodic censuses, especially if, as is to be hoped, future censuses adopt sampling techniques in gathering or tabulating their basic data.[1] The use of the censuses would also allow much larger samples to be provided and greatly enhance the value of the analysis.

The background of general limitations needs to be borne in mind when considering the actual studies brought together in the present volume. No detailed account of those studies will be given here, for it is the purpose of this introduction to introduce the main contents of the volume, not to be a substitute for them. But a note on the findings will serve both to show the points at which further research is needed, and to lead to a more general consideration of the problem of social mobility and social stratification in Britain.

Making the note as short as possible, it may be put in the following terms. Before the 1944 Education Act came into operation, the level of education obtained by an individual depended closely upon the social status of his (or her) father; social status being measured in terms of the father's occupation.[2] Our survey of the educational experience of the adults interviewed in 1949 is incomplete in that no information on 'measured intelligence' was—or could be—obtained. The results of

[1] Justifiably, because so far as long-term social policy is concerned, it is certainly not less important to know the parental occupations of the population than whether they have a piped water supply or a separate bathroom. And easily, for many of the questions to which answers would be needed were already asked at the 1951 census of Great Britain. Thus the 1951 census schedule asked questions on fertility (the question would need to be extended to cover marriages of completed fertility) and education (the question would need no modification; in its 1951 form it was scarcely of use for any purpose, for it asked only the age at which full-time education was completed and, even so, was not required to be answered by married women unless they were gainfully employed). With these modifications and with the addition of a question on the occupation of the father of each person enumerated, an enormous amount of valuable basic information would be made available. The use of the census as a means of providing this information—preferably on a sample basis, comparable with the 1 per cent sample of the 1951 census—would make possible a much more detailed study of occupational self-recruitment, a matter of immediate practical, as well as of long-term theoretical, interest. It is, for example, of direct practical concern to know how far coal-miners are themselves the sons of coal-miners and hence to what extent, given present incentives, the future size of the coal-mining labour force will depend upon local fertility, mortality and out-migration.

[2] And also, of course, on father's income, though income and social status were correlated. This does not, however, mean that there was no opportunity for 'working class' children to acquire secondary education. See, for example, the discussion on p. 20 of this chapter.

15

other inquiries make it clear, however, that quite apart from the extent to which I.Q. differences are influenced by the cultural loading of the tests and hence by social and cultural differences between the various social strata in Britain,[1] I.Q. as such is by no means a sufficient explanation of educational differences within the 1949 adult population.[2] Crude economic, together with more subtle social and cultural, factors account for the major differences. And though between the two World Wars there was an unprecedented expansion in the opportunities for secondary and university education, the discrepancies in educational opportunity as between individuals of different social origins had by no means been eliminated. Nor have they disappeared under the new system of secondary education for all. The more obvious inequalities have been removed by the abolition of fees in secondary schools belonging to the new State system, by the use of standardized procedures for selecting children for grammar schools, and by the much more generous provision of scholarships to the universities. But the public boarding schools are still independent and, in general, are inaccessible to working-class children. Moreover, even within the State system parental attitudes and aspirations, clearly related to social status and perhaps heavily conditioned by the education of the parents themselves, affect a child's chances of entering a grammar school, and further influence his level of achievement within that school. To make fully effective the thesis of the 1944 Education Act—equality of educational opportunity—even within the State system of secondary education, will require closer co-operation

[1] See the discussion in Chapter VI of the present volume. See also J. D. Nisbet, 'Level of national intelligence', *Nature*, 15 November 1952; and *ibid.*, 'Family environment and intelligence', *Eugenics Review*, April 1953.

[2] We may, for example, compare the social status distribution of those eleven-year-old children tested in Scotland in 1947 who scored sixty points or more in the group intelligence tests (see [J. Maxwell], *The Social Implications of the 1947 Scottish Mental Survey*, London, 1953, p. 45), with the social status distribution of those adults who, according to our central sample investigation, had had a university education. The social status classification was not the same for both inquiries, but there is sufficient similarity to justify a comparison by broad groups. The Scottish children scoring sixty or more points represented the top 6·3 per cent of all test scores. In social status, 36·2 per cent of these children had 'non-manual' fathers, and 63·8 per cent 'manual'. For England and Wales, our sample showed, by contrast, that of all male subjects with university qualifications, 72·7 per cent had 'non-manual' fathers and 27·3 per cent 'manual'. (In grouping the Scottish data, the non-manual weekly wage-earner has been put under the broad 'manual' category, in order to make the classification comparable with that used in our central sample investigation.)

For an interesting attempt to compare occupational mobility and measured intelligence in the U.S.A., see C. A. Anderson, J. C. Brown, and M. J. Bowman, 'Intelligence and occupational mobility', *Journal of Political Economy*, June 1952.

between teachers and parents, and probably a more sympathetic relationship between teachers and their pupils of diverse social origins.

For the adults surveyed in 1949, educational level is not only related to social origins but also to achieved social status, as measured in terms of the occupations the individuals themselves had obtained. This is scarcely surprising; the increasing educational requirements of the developing professions and of the upper branches of governmental and industrial administration have made university education a technical as well as a cultural necessity for occupations of high social prestige. Two facts are of importance, however. First, in the period before the 1944 Education Act, social origins and education tended to reinforce each other, and thus acted cumulatively to produce a close association between the social status of father and son. This was especially so for the higher levels of social status—for the occupations for which university education was indispensable, or at least highly desirable. The rise in the educational requirements of such occupations kept pace with, and perhaps in some cases even outpaced, the expansion of opportunities to enter a university.[1] Secondly, though education was a powerful factor in the achievement of high social status, it was not sufficient in itself. Men with university education *and* relatively high social origins were more likely to reach the upper levels of social status than other men with a comparable education but lower social origins. Having a father of relatively high social status thus provided a double premium.

It is desirable, in view of the reference in the preceding paragraph to the association between the social status of fathers and sons, to explain very briefly how that association has been measured. In studying social mobility, it is not sufficient to know that, say, 50 per cent of the men now engaged in skilled manual or routine non-manual employment had fathers who were in the same occupational category, or that 48·5 per cent of·the men in the professional and administrative *cadres* had fathers

---

[1] This happened as regards the Civil Service, with the introduction of the open competition system of entry. Thomas Farrer, Permanent Secretary of the Board of Trade, pointed out in 1873 that the new system of selection demanded 'an expensive education in high subjects in early years, which only the rich can afford'. And the MacDonnell Commission of 1912–14 argued that only if there were equality of educational opportunity would the *carrière ouverte aux talents* be a possibility. See J. D. Kingsley, *Representative Bureaucracy*, Yellow Springs, Ohio, 1944, pp. 76 and 98.

It is also possible that, in the inter-war period, the increasing entry of university graduates into industry and commerce began to block the possibilities of promotion of individuals who started at the bottom and who, early in the century, might have had some prospect of rising to the administrative level.

17

in those grades. Some standard or norm must be applied before we can say whether the two percentages indicate a closely similar or a widely different degree of self-recruitment. The norm chosen in the present studies postulates a random association between the occupations of fathers and sons—that, irrespective of social origin, each son has the same chance as any other son of entering any of the various levels of social prestige. The way in which this norm is applied may be illustrated by the example of the sons of skilled manual workers. In our main sample investigation, 1,510 of the 3,497 men interviewed were the sons of skilled manual workers, while at the same time 1,429 of the 3,497 men were themselves engaged in skilled manual employment. Given a random association between the occupations of fathers and sons, the number of sons of skilled manual workers who would themselves be in the same occupational category is $(1,510/3,497) \times 1,429$, or 617. In fact, however, 714 of the sons of skilled manual workers were in the same category as their fathers, and what we have termed the 'Index of Association', measuring the relationship between the actual and the expected numbers, is $(714/617)$, or $1\cdot16$. The comparable index for the men whose fathers were in professional or administrative employment is $13\cdot16$, and the two indices are widely different, showing a much higher degree of self-recruitment in the upper levels of social prestige. If the parental-filial association were random, the indices in both cases would be $1\cdot0$, for the actual and expected numbers would be the same. The problems involved in using the 'Index of Association', of relating actual to expected numbers, are discussed in a later chapter.[1] Here, however, it is relevant to emphasize two points. First, the use of random association as a norm in constructing the index implies no value judgements and makes no suggestions as to the practicability of achieving so high a level of mobility in contemporary Britain or in any other country. The sole purpose of the norm is to allow a valid comparison of the extent of self-recruitment in different strata and periods of time. Secondly, the index does not explain why actual mobility is less than what would be expected on a random basis, or how far actual mobility is limited by specific factors. Part of that explanation is given in other chapters in this volume. But much more research will be required if a full appreciation of the actual constraints on mobility is to be obtained.

What the present research shows, however, is that measured in terms of the relation between actual and expected numbers of men who are in the same occupational categories as their fathers, the highest rigidity is

[1] See Chapter VIII, and Appendices 1 and 2 to that chapter.

found in the professional and high administrative *cadres*, and the least in the skilled manual and routine non-manual category. The latter category is, in fact, in a kind of valley, the rigidity increasing on each side, though far more in the upper than in the lower status categories. Taking, for example, those men in the basic sample investigation who were born in the period 1900–9—and they are not untypical of the whole sample—the indices of self-recruitment, calculated in the way described previously, are 15·1 for the professional and high administrative category, 1·2 for the skilled manual and routine non-manual, and 2·6 for the unskilled manual category.

The same technique of analysis has also been applied to the data on marriage collected by the basic sample investigation, in order to see how far there is social mobility within marriage. Here, too, characteristic patterns of association have been found between brides and grooms in respect of social origins and educational level. On both counts, there has been substantial assortative mating. As in the case of social status measured in terms of occupations, there is most exclusiveness in the marriages of individuals whose fathers were in the professional, managerial and executive grades, and least in the marriages of the sons and daughters of skilled manual and routine non-manual workers. For the former group, the index measuring the ratio of actual to expected numbers of marriages in which brides and grooms had the same social background is 6·6, while it is only 1·2 for the latter, taking into account all periods of marriage covered by the sample. Exclusiveness as regards the educational level of brides and grooms is, as might be expected, highest for individuals with a university or professional education, and lowest for individuals who, in the period before the 1944 Act, had only an elementary education. On the other hand, educational exclusiveness has diminished during the present century, whereas there has been little apparent change in the selective force of social origins. There is now rather more marriage than formerly between partners of unequal educational backgrounds.

A rather different aspect of social mobility is examined by the last two studies included in the volume—namely, how far leadership in voluntary associations is focused on individuals who already have high social status in terms of their occupations. If there were no such concentration, we should be able to point to a genuine alternative means of obtaining prestige, a means whereby individuals in low status employment might find scope for self-expression and prestige in other community activity. The two studies do not, however, suggest a full alternative route to positions of prestige. In the analysis of the three national women's organizations there is evidence of an increased proportion, in recent years, of working-class women in positions of leadership. Some part of this change has been due to external circumstances—to the disappearance of the squire's lady from the village scene, or to the impoverishment of the parson's wife—and some part to positive action taken by the organizations to provide leaders more widely representative of the various social strata. Similarly, the investigation of an extensive range of voluntary organizations in a small country town shows that between the manual workers and the uppermost levels of status, there is a broad band from which leaders are chosen without reference to their particular position in the prestige hierarchy. Nevertheless, it is clear from both studies that manual workers have little share in leadership, and that it is individuals at the top of the occupational hierarchy who constitute the primary source of leaders for the various voluntary organizations. To that extent, therefore, the leadership of voluntary associations duplicates the hierarchy of occupational prestige rather than providing an alternative to it.

It should be remembered, in considering the implications of these results, that the summary has inevitably done some injustice to the position in Britain. The fact that a high degree of self-recruitment has been found in the upper status levels does not mean that British social structure is an inflexible one. On the contrary, the specific studies suggest that there is more flexibility in Britain than in France or Italy and undoubtedly reveal a good deal of upward and downward movement in social status between generations. Thus, again taking the men born in the period 1900–9, 46 per cent of those whose fathers had been in the upper occupational categories—professional, high administrative, managerial and executive—fell in social status; while of those men whose fathers had been semi-skilled or unskilled manual workers, 53 per cent achieved a higher status than their fathers'. For such individuals there was a genuine change in social status, even though, in terms of the norm of random expectation, the degree of self-recruitment was widely different for the two groups. There is also clear evidence of the reality of the expansion in educational opportunity prior to 1944. Taking, for example, as an indication the extent to which the sons of skilled manual and routine non-manual workers went to grammar schools or their equivalent, there was a rise from 2·2 per cent for those born before 1890 to 10·7 per cent for those born in the period 1920–9. In addition, there is some suggestion that, for the generation born in 1920–9, there may be a significant, though probably not a very large; fall in the degree of self-recruitment. Nevertheless the general picture so far is of a rather stable social structure, and one in which social status has tended to operate within, so to speak, a closed circuit. Social origins have conditioned educational level, and both have conditioned achieved social status. Marriage has also to a considerable extent taken place within the same closed circuit. Leadership in voluntary organizations again reflects the hierarchy of occupational prestige.

But this outline necessarily describes a situation unaffected by the 1944 Education Act. So far, the influence of that Act has been only upon boys and girls passing through the educational system. Not for another forty years or so shall we be able to see how this new, far more revolutionary expansion of educational opportunity has altered the degree of social mobility in the community. That there are likely to be substantial changes is, however, already indicated. There are still obvious imperfections in the operation of the Act. Evidence presented in this volume shows that among the 'grammar marginals'—the children on the borderline of acceptance by a grammar school—the chances of getting into a grammar school lie in favour of 'middle-class' children. Perhaps this occurs because the phrase 'capacity to profit' from a grammar school education is interpreted with insufficient sympathy, teachers knowing, as appears to be the case at present, that 'middle-class' children have the aspirations and background which will make it easier for them than for 'working-class' children to assimilate the school values and objectives, and that because of their parents' aspirations, 'middle-class' children are less likely to be 'premature leavers'. But such difficulties will probably be overcome with time. It is at least already evident that, proportionately, far more 'working-class' children are now going to grammar schools and are thus overcoming the first hurdle in the path to university or professional education and to occupations of relatively high social status.[1] Even assuming, however, that the now visible defects in the secondary school selection process are removed, that grammar school pupils of all social origins are enabled to make a successful adjustment to their school objectives and curricula, and that the road to the universities is widened to take all those students with a capacity to

---

[1] The continuing research into education and social mobility in south-west Hertfordshire—Chapter VII of the present volume represents only a preliminary report on one section of this research—shows that between the 1930's and 1951 the proportion of children of manual workers in the total annual entry to grammar schools rose from about 15 per cent to 43 per cent.
The results of the 1952 selection process shows that, in south-west Hertfordshire

profit from university education, there still remain certain basic problems which need to be considered. And at this point, I should like to step outside the frame of the studies contained in the present volume and put forward personal views which are explicitly 'loaded' in that they have a value basis.

First, though the 1944 Education Act will no doubt greatly increase the amount of social mobility in Britain, there is an upper limit to that increase which the Act itself imposes by leaving the independent public school system substantially intact. Public schools may, and some do, accept pupils who have emerged through the ordinary Local Education Authority selection process. In the main, however, entry to the public boarding schools will depend not only on 'talent' or 'measured intelligence' but also on parental wealth. And though the relative prestige of the public boarding schools may well diminish, it is not likely to dis-

---

at least, I.Q. was clearly the primary consideration in selecting pupils for grammar schools. This is evident from the table below.

S.W. HERTS. I.Q. AND ENTRY TO GRAMMAR SCHOOLS IN 1952

Father's Occupation	Percentage of Pupils with I.Q. of 112 or over	Percentage of Pupils awarded Grammar School Places
Managerial and professional	52·9	50·9
Clerical—higher and lower grades	45·8	38·3
Supervisory and miscellaneous	21·8	22·9
Skilled manual	17·2	16·9
Semi-skilled and unskilled manual	13·7	12·3

The research also shows, however, that looking at the selection process in 1952, and analysing the children by paternal occupation, 'within each occupational group the parents of those children who were subsequently allocated to the Grammar Schools . . . differ quite markedly from other parents . . . in their interest in education, their attitudes to education, and their aspirations for their children. They have a better knowledge of the selection procedure; they have paid more visits to the child's primary school; they are more likely to have met the child's Class Teacher and Head Teacher, and to have discussed the child's secondary education with them. They are more likely to have given general consideration to the child's secondary education, and to appreciate that the move from the primary school may greatly influence the child's future. They are far more likely to have expressed a strong preference for the Grammar School as against other forms of secondary education, to prefer a higher school-leaving age, to want their children to have some form of post-secondary education or training, and to hope they will take up occupations of higher status than their own.' (From an unpublished interim report by Mrs. J. Floud and Dr. F. M. Martin.)

What we do not know is how far these differences in parental aspirations and pressures influence the I.Q. results of the children in question. The work of Professor Vernon and others has shown the effect of 'coaching' on I.Q. results. The possible influence of other environmental factors needs much closer examination.

appear. So far as education is concerned, the public boarding schools have a great deal to offer. And the products of those schools are, as was pointed out by Norwood, consistent in character and dependable. Moreover, there is the importance of accent. As Norwood made clear, there is no doubt of the social status indications of accent in speech, of the way in which, to cite his examples, an individual's social background is judged by his pronunciation of 'strange change' or 'round the town'.[1] Given these facts, and given also the fact that products of the public boarding schools are now well represented in positions of authority and eminence in various branches of life, it is hardly an accusation of bias to suggest that such individuals may give some preference, in appointments conferring or promising high social status, to other individuals who, to adopt a genetic term, belong to their own social isolate. In an overheard conversation between two temporary civil servants, one complained that 'the old school tie no longer counts for anything'. But that was in war-time, and at the point at which it had become almost preferable to try the untried. In less desperate days, the untried has fewer attractions and the consistent and dependable product is a more natural choice. So long as the public boarding schools in particular remain outside the State system of secondary education, the 1944 Act cannot fulfil the explicit intention of the White Paper on *Educational Reconstruction*, to provide equality of educational opportunity.[2] And the inequality is likely to cut across the line of social mobility, blocking ascent to, and limiting descent from, the upper reaches of social status.

Secondly, leaving aside the whole question of the public schools, there are even more serious problems within the State system itself. These problems derive from the curious belief of the Norwood committee that children could be divided into three types, each type requiring a different kind of secondary education and, to some extent, a different school-leaving age.[3] The legislators did not, fortunately, enshrine this superstition in an Act of Parliament. Nevertheless the belief

---

[1] C. Norwood, *The English Tradition of Education*, London, 1929, pp. 130–2, wrote: 'The schools are successful, because on the whole they do what they profess to do: they "deliver the goods". They impart a character which is consistent, and can be trusted.' He also added, 'Other less praiseworthy reasons for the success of these schools are that they confer a social badge, and they give easy rights of entry to circles which people do as a matter of fact very much desire to enter'.

[2] *Educational Reconstruction*, Cmd. 6458, 1943, p. 3.

[3] H. C. Dent, *Secondary Education for All*, London, 1949, pp. 9–11, draws attention to the similarity between these three types and the threefold division of secondary education proposed by the Schools Inquiry Commission in their 1868

has been widely translated into practice in the distinction between grammar, technical and modern secondary schools. The separation between the three types of school is not, of course, supposed to be definitive; a process of osmosis is allowed, pupils who subsequently disclose abilities different from those exhibited in the selection examination being transferred to the category of school better suited to them. But the transfer is itself only an acknowledgement of the practical deficiencies of the selection procedure. If the procedure were perfect, then, given the tripartite secondary school system, no further transfer would be necessary. The nearer the process approaches perfection, the more sharply will children be divided, at the age of 11 years, into groups which will receive educations fitting them for different kinds of future occupations, occupations which, if present attitudes persist, will lie at different levels of the scale of social prestige.[1] Given the diminishing importance of economic and social background as a determinant of the type of secondary education a child receives, social mobility will increase, and probably increase greatly. There will no doubt be increasing differentiation, as regards future social status, between children whose fathers belong to a particular occupational stratum, and decreasing differentiation between children whose fathers belong to different occupational strata. The question to be answered, however, is whether the increased social mobility achieved in this way will be an unmixed blessing. And to answer this question we must consider the reasons for encouraging relatively high social mobility in a society.

There are two primary reasons for wishing to see the possibility of high social mobility in a community. First, in order to increase economic and social efficiency, since with a fluid social structure there is more likelihood that positions requiring high ability will in fact be held by individuals who possess high ability. A fluid social structure is also, on

---

Report. But those latter recommendations were based on the existing social structure and not on a belief of the existence of three different types of pupil. The Commission said: 'Much of our evidence tends to show that social distinctions in education cannot at present be altogether ignored. . . . It would be better that such distinctions, as far as education is concerned, at any rate in day schools, should disappear; but an attempt to obliterate them by superior authority might both do mischief and fail of its object.' See J. W. Adamson, *English Education, 1789–1902*, Cambridge, 1930, p. 269. For the Norwood Committee discussion, see *Curriculum and Examinations in Secondary Schools*, London, 1943, pp. 2–4 and ch. 3.

[1] One of the questions which requires study is how far the increased and specialized educational opportunities, coupled with increased educational requirements of the high status occupations, will result in lower occupational mobility *within* a generation while promoting higher social mobility *between* generations.

that account, more capable of adapting itself to internal and external change. Secondly, from the point of view of the individual, social mobility should ensure that there are fewer square pegs in round holes, and the existence of opportunity to rise in status will in any case provide an incentive for the fuller utilization of a person's capacities. There may, as a consequence, be less feeling of personal frustration and a greater possibility of social harmony. Indeed, even if there is little actual opportunity to rise in social status, the belief in a myth of opportunity may produce similar results; and perhaps part of the pride which Americans feel in their 'open' society derives more from the image of nineteenth-century U.S.A. than from any exceptional present reality. Certainly it is one of the postulates of a democratic and egalitarian society that ability, whatever its social background, shall not be denied the chance to fulfil itself. This is not to say that social mobility is free from disadvantages. For those who fall in social status, the sensation of being *déclassés* is scarcely a comfortable one. Concern to ensure a rise, or at least to prevent a fall, in status is part of the 'anxiety neurosis' so evident in 'middle-class' parents' aspirations for their children and in the willingness of the parents to make very substantial sacrifices so long as those children can obtain the kind of education which connotes relatively high future status. In addition, actual movement itself may, save in special circumstances, distort or destroy kinship associations, with possible personal and social deprivation. We need to encourage mobility for the advantages it offers to individuals and to society; but we also need to avoid, as far as possible, such disadvantages as may follow from having a social structure in which the status relationships between individuals in successive generations will be far less stable than at present or during the past half-century.

The 1944 Act will do much to enable ability to fulfil itself. But the working out of the Act through the threefold system of grammar, technical and modern secondary schools will by no means minimize the disadvantages of the new unstable relationships between successive generations. On the contrary, the more efficient the selection procedure, the more evident those disadvantages are likely to become. Outside of the public schools, it will be the grammar schools which will furnish the new *élite*, an *élite* apparently much less assailable because it is selected for 'measured intelligence'.[1] The selection process will tend to reinforce the prestige of occupations already high in social status and to

[1] It should be emphasized that the present sponsors of the tripartite secondary school system are proposing to give to the grammar schools a rôle which they

25

divide the population into streams which many may come to regard—indeed, already regard—as distinct as sheep and goats. Not to have been to a grammar school will be a more serious disqualification than in the past, when social inequality in the educational system was known to exist. And the feeling of resentment may be more rather than less acute just because the individual concerned realizes that there is some validity in the selection process which has kept him out of a grammar school. In this respect, apparent justice may be more difficult to bear than injustice.

Assuming that we do not wish to sponsor a modern version of inculcating a sense of 'my station and its duties' in the various sections of the population, there are two major possibilities of reducing the sense of frustration or grievance which may otherwise accompany the new social mobility. First, it does not follow that an *élite*, even if selected for 'measured intelligence', need be so distant in social prestige from the rest of the population as has been the case in the past or as may be the case if present trends continue. In the nineteenth century, in order to minimize the cost of public education, the State took action which resulted in lowering the prestige of school-teaching as compared with that of other professions. It is not difficult to envisage deliberate public and private action which would, conversely, help to raise the prestige of, say, skilled manual work relative to non-manual occupations. Secondly, employment in occupations requiring high ability and long training and carrying high social status need not be the only means of gaining social prestige; there are other ways of serving the community and there should, correspondingly, be other paths to social prestige.[1]

---

did not really aim to play prior to the 1944 Act. The pre-World War II grammar schools did not concentrate on the education of an *élite*. The range of I.Q. among grammar school pupils was wide, and so was the range of interests and ultimate occupations. It should also be pointed out that in Scotland, with a traditionally more open social structure and wider educational opportunities, the grammar school was, in reality, comprehensive in type, and still is today. That is also true of many of the public boarding schools.

[1] These questions, which have a direct bearing upon problems of recruitment and incentive in industry, require further study, and it would be out of place to discuss here the various factors which are involved. On the first question, however, it is evident that recent developments may help to narrow the gap in prestige between non-manual and manual occupations. The levelling of incomes may tend in that direction. Social security legislation and the maintenance of full employment in industry may also do so directly, as well as indirectly, by promoting—as appears to be the case since World War II—the increased entry of grammar school leavers into technical, industrial employment, as the unemployment risks

Action in these two directions would lie largely outside the educational system. But the nature of the educational framework has an important bearing upon the possible success of this other action. To separate children into three distinct streams during the formative years is to reduce the chances of bringing them together again in adult life. And with the present prestige ranking of different types of occupation, it is difficult to envisage effective 'parity of esteem'—at least in the near future—between the grammar, technical and modern schools which are intended to supply recruits for these different occupations. Hence, though by itself the comprehensive type of secondary school may not contribute directly to the solution of the social problems which have been discussed, it would at least provide the background against which effective subsequent action might be developed. It is true that many educationists have, on 'educational' grounds, spoken against the comprehensive school. But even if their arguments are well founded— and I very much doubt if the last word has been said on the subject—the social aspects and consequences of an educational system are not less important than the pedagogic. R. A. Butler was undoubtedly right when he said that education cannot by itself create the social structure of a country. Nevertheless it is a contributory and reinforcing factor and, as such, cannot be left out of account.[1] What we wish to do in the field of education should not, and cannot, be kept apart from our broader social objectives—from our ideas of the kind of society we wish to see develop. There was certainly no such separation in the past. In the early nineteenth century, public education was sometimes feared for the unrest it might provoke among the population. The Bishop of London reported, in 1803, 'men of considerable ability say that it is safest for both the Government and the religion of the country to let the lower classes remain in that state of ignorance in which nature has originally placed

in such occupations diminish and as the apprenticeship hurdles are surmounted. Much more could be done by comparable social and economic action, and much could also be done to raise the prestige of manual occupations by conferring symbols of status on representatives of such occupations—by ensuring, for example, a much larger representation of manual workers in official ceremonies.

[1] Mr. Butler made this statement in discussing the question of the public schools. (See H. C. Dent, *The Education Act, 1944*, London, 1944, p. 58 ; *Hansard*, 28 March 1944, Vol. 398, No. 54, cols. 1302–3.) He explicitly admitted, however, the contributory influence, saying, 'It can very considerably influence it and I believe the fact that we have got priority for this great Bill will very much influence the world in which we hope to live in the future. But I have to take the world as I find it, and the economic arguments . . . affect the structure of our society and our democracy even more than do the poor efforts of a Minister of Education.'

them'.[1] Later, education came to be regarded as a means of social control, as a bulwark of private property and public order.[2] We have travelled a long way since then. The White Paper on *Educational Reconstruction*, in speaking of the need for equality of educational opportunity and also for diversity to suit various talents, emphasized that 'such diversity must not impair the social unity within the educational system which will open the way to a more closely knit society and give us strength to face the tasks ahead'.[3] If that is our view, we must not 'take the world as we find it' and ground our educational system in the existing social structure. In the schools, as in the wider society of which they are a part, we must deliberately make that closer community; it will not create itself.

[1] N. Hans, *Comparative Education*, London, 1949, p. 133.

[2] Norwood, *op. cit.*, p. 171, expressed a similar view: 'Incomplete as it is, elementary education has been a steadily civilizing agency. It has, I think, been the main influence which has prevented Bolshevism, Communism, and theories of revolt and destruction from obtaining any real hold upon the people of this country.'

[3] *Educational Reconstruction*, p. 3.

II

The Social Grading of Occupations

C. A. MOSER AND J. R. HALL

Introduction

T HE material presented in this chapter derives from an inquiry into the social grading of occupations. A more extensive report on certain aspects of this inquiry has already appeared elsewhere.[1] The main sections of that report are summarized here, however, because it is upon the results of the inquiry into occupational grading that the social status classification used in subsequent chapters is based. In turn, it is this classification which forms an essential part of the analysis of social mobility, the subject with which this book as a whole is concerned.

The earlier report on the social grading of occupations made use of one particular statistical approach. Since its publication it has been possible to analyse the material in a somewhat different way, and the results of this second approach are also given in the present chapter.

The concept of social status, basic to all the studies contained in this book, assumes that the community consists of strata arranged in the form of a hierarchy. The individual strata may shade into each other, both the characteristics and limits of the individual strata being uncertain.[2] But to discern and measure the extent of movement within the hierarchy it is essential to locate a number of arbitrary but realistic boundaries, their nature and position varying according to the criteria of social status used.

In the attempt to assign social status, both objective and subjective

---

[1] John Hall and D. Caradog Jones, 'The social grading of occupations', *Brit. J. Sociology*, Vol. 1, No. 1, March 1950.

[2] But there may also be sharp breaks between the strata, and the use of a prestige scale may in fact help to show such breaks. Indeed, the use of prestige scales might also show the existence of different ranking universes—i.e. universes not forming part of a common continuum.

criteria are relevant: income, occupation, education and material possessions; self-assessed status, participation in certain social activities and relationships, and the status judgements of others, being some of the criteria.

Theoretically, the range of possible criteria of social status is very wide. The difficulty of selection is, however, reduced by a number of practical considerations. There is, first, the need to choose criteria about which reasonably accurate information can be obtained and which lend themselves to classification. Secondly, there is a high degree of interrelationship between many of the criteria. In addition, in certain types of study—and the investigations with which this symposium is concerned are examples—there is an advantage in deliberately selecting one major criterion in order to see how far it is correlated with other characteristics of status.

In the present study, occupation is the criterion used in constructing a classification of social status. Though clearly not the only important criterion which might have been selected, it is a particularly useful one because it is linked to economic status and to educational background. It is therefore correlated with the 'pattern of living' of an individual. Moreover, as is shown in Chapter III, it is one of the aspects of social status which springs most readily to mind when people try to assess the position of an individual in the social hierarchy. Educational background is also frequently reported as a related factor. But since an essential part of the aim of the present series of studies is to examine the link between status origins and education on the one hand, and between education and status achievement on the other, education as such has not been taken into account in the initial construction of status groupings.

In order to use occupation as a basis of classification, and in order especially to apply it to the results of the random sample inquiry designed to provide background information for the whole investigation of social selection and differentiation discussed in the introductory chapter, some agreed grouping of occupations in terms of social status or prestige is necessary. Several occupational classifications already exist, including those of the Registrar-General, the Population Investigation Committee and the Social Survey. For various reasons, none of these was entirely suited to our purpose and accordingly the following sevenfold classification (referred to henceforth as the 'Standard Classification') was prepared with the object of distinguishing between occupations in terms of their social prestige.

30

Standard Classification

1. Professional and High Administrative;
2. Managerial and Executive;
3. Inspectional, Supervisory and other Non-Manual, Higher Grade;
4. Inspectional, Supervisory and other Non-Manual, Lower Grade;
5. Skilled Manual, and routine grades of Non-Manual;
6. Semi-skilled Manual;
7. Unskilled Manual.

Category 1 includes all occupations calling for highly specialized experience, and frequently the possession of a degree or comparable professional qualification necessitating a long period of education and training. Category 2 includes those responsible for initiating and/or implementing policy, e.g. personnel manager, headmaster (elementary school), whilst those in category 3 do not have such responsibility but may have some degree of authority over others, e.g. police inspector, assistant teacher (elementary school). In category 4, authority over others is restricted, but the nature of the job itself involves a measure of responsibility, e.g. costing clerk, relieving officer.

The distinction between skilled, semi-skilled and unskilled is sometimes difficult to draw. Skilled work implies special training or apprenticeship, and responsibility for the process on which the individual is engaged. Where no special skill or responsibility is involved, but the individual is doing a particular job habitually and usually in association with a certain industry or trade, it is rated as semi-skilled. Unskilled work requires no special training and is general in nature rather than associated with a particular industry.

A large number of occupations were graded on this sevenfold basis. But as the classification was to be used in assessing social mobility in terms of occupational achievements, it was essential to see whether this *a priori* scale was in keeping with actual attitudes towards the relative social status of occupations. Indeed, this raised the whole question of whether there is any general agreement in the community on the social prestige of occupations, including occupations other than those of which people have personal knowledge or experience. In other words, does the term 'social status', when applied to occupations, have any generally accepted meaning, and if so, what kind of scale or hierarchy is indicated.

31

THE SOCIAL GRADING OF OCCUPATIONS

Part I: The Original Inquiry

To answer these questions public opinion was tested as to the relative social prestige of a number of key occupations.[1] These were selected from an original list of 138 (which had been grouped by five independent judges into nine grades) ranging from professions demanding exceptional qualifications to general labouring requiring no skill or training. To make it easier to gain the co-operation of a sample of the general public, the number of occupations included in the inquiry was limited to thirty. A Pilot Study (P) was carried out with the co-operation of the Association of Adult Education Tutors. Individuals taking part were asked to rank the selected occupations in relation to each other according to their social standing in the community and were asked to think not of exceptional individuals, but of the average type of person engaged in each occupation. The sex, age, and occupational status (according to the Standard Classification) of those persons who completed forms were also recorded to permit some study of difference of opinion in terms of these variables. For this more detailed treatment, however, further material was required and a General Inquiry (G) was undertaken. Those co-operating included members of the National Amalgamated Union of Life Assurance Workers, the National Association of Local Government Officers, the Civil Service Clerical Association, the Trades Union Congress, as well as a further group from the Association of Adult Education Tutors. Contact was made through the Central Office of each of these organizations with branch secretaries, scattered throughout the country, who had indicated that their branches were willing to take part in the inquiry.

Table 1 shows how the returns submitted in the Pilot and General inquiries were distributed according to the sex, age and occupational status of those completing them.

The Pilot survey produced 343 returns, and the General Inquiry 1,056. The totals for the latter in Table 1 do not add up to this number as, in some instances, the age or status category was not recorded. As only 55 forms were returned from persons in categories 6 and 7 in both the Pilot and General inquiries, these two classes were combined.

Everyone who took part in the inquiry was asked first, to assign each

[1] The occupations selected, and the instructions to those co-operating in the inquiry are shown in the Appendix to the original article. For a critical survey of studies of occupational prestige, see A. F. Davies, 'Prestige of occupations', *Brit. J. Sociology*, June 1952. See also H. H. Hyman, 'The psychology of status', *Archives of Psychology*, No. 269, 1942.

occupation to one of five social grades, these not being defined other than that A was to be the highest and E the lowest; and then to arrange the occupations in descending status order within each grade. In this way all thirty occupations were ranked in relative order of social status or prestige. The 'tying' of occupations judged to be of equal status was explicitly permitted. The individual rankings of each of the thirty occupations were then listed and the median and quartile judgements for each occupation determined.

Table 1

PERCENTAGE DISTRIBUTION BY SEX, AGE AND STATUS CATEGORY OF PERSONS TAKING PART IN THE PILOT (P) AND GENERAL (G) INQUIRIES

Standard Classificat'n	Males		Females		Age Group	Males		Females	
	P	G	P	G		P	G	P	G
1	14	24	6	9	15–29	17	18	{57	38
2	12	17	12	16	30–39	39	34		25
3	16	17	32	22	40–49	24	24	{43	22
4	13	15	19	14	50+	20	24		15
5	38	23	28	35					
6, 7	7	4	3	4					
Percentage	100	100	100	100	Percentage	100	100	100	100
Number in sample	219	710	124	281	Number in sample	219	749	124	302

For the General sample, twenty sets of median male judgements were obtained based on four age groups and five categories of the Standard Classification (omitting categories 6 and 7).[1] The arithmetic means of these twenty median judgements, for each occupation, were then obtained. They are shown in column 3 of Table 2. A similar process was followed for the Pilot inquiry (taking males and females together and including all status categories), and the results are shown in column 4 of Table 2. The mean readings for individual occupations in the two lists are very close, and the order in which the thirty occupations are judged to be graded relative to one another is identical.

[1] Of the persons who completed forms, relatively few had occupations falling into Categories 6 and 7 of the Standard Classification. To maximize the number, the results (for such persons) from both the Pilot and General Inquiries were pooled; and the median and quartile judgements were obtained for each of the thirty occupations. The occupations ranked in order according to the median judgements were then compared with the ranking recorded in Table 2 for males of Classes 1 to 5. There was a large measure of agreement between the two sets of results.

THE SOCIAL GRADING OF OCCUPATIONS

In column 2 of Table 2 is recorded the Standard Classification to which we had originally allocated each of the occupations covered by the experiment. This may be compared with the occupational ranking

Table 2

SOCIAL GRADING IN THE PILOT (P) AND GENERAL (G) INQUIRIES
RELATED TO STANDARD CLASSIFICATION

1 Occupation	2 Standard Classification	3 A.M. of Group Judgements Males Cl. 1–5 (G)	4 Males and Females Cl. 1–7 (P)
Medical Officer	1	1·3	1·4
Company Director	1	1·6	1·2
Country Solicitor	1	2·6	2·8
Chartered Accountant	1	3·2	3·6
Civil Servant (Exec.)	2	6·0	5·9
Business Manager	2	6·0	6·0
Works Manager	2	6·4	6·2
Nonconformist Minister	2	6·4	6·3
Farmer	1	7·3	7·9
Elementary School Teacher	3	10·8	10·4
Jobbing Master Builder	3	11·4	11·2
News Reporter	3	11·8	11·2
Commercial Traveller	3	12·0	12·6
Chef	4	13·8	14·2
Insurance Agent	4	14·6	14·8
Newsagent and Tobacconist	4	15·0	15·6
Policeman	5	16·1	15·5
Routine Clerk	5	16·1	16·1
Fitter	5	17·6	16·3
Carpenter	5	18·6	17·4
Shop Assistant	5	20·2	20·2
Bricklayer	5	20·2	20·4
Tractor Driver	6	23·0	22·8
Coal Hewer	5	23·2	23·0
Railway Porter	7	25·3	24·8
Agricultural Labourer	6	25·5	25·5
Carter	6	25·8	26·2
Barman	7	26·4	26·2
Dock Labourer	7	27·0	27·0
Road Sweeper	7	28·9	29·2

derived from the General Inquiry (being based on a greater number of returns than the Pilot). Only three occupations fall out of the order suggested by the Standard Classification, namely farmer, coal hewer, and railway porter. The Standard Classification would place the farmer

34

in category 1, but the empirical judgement associates him with those occupations allocated to category 2. Similarly, the coal hewer and railway porter are ranked empirically with those whom we would place in category 6, though in the Standard Classification the former was placed in category 5 and the latter in category 7. These differences, however, are not great. The more marked deviation of the farmer may be due to the difficulty which townspeople, who form the bulk of our sample, encounter in attempting a status judgement of a rural occupation. However, in the light of this inquiry, the relative ranking of these three occupations in the Standard Classification was duly modified.

The inferences to be drawn from the data summarized in Table 2 are, first, that the general public ranked the thirty occupations in the inquiry, in terms of social status, in much the same order as that adopted in the Standard Classification; secondly, that there seems to be a common standard of judgement in our sample as to the social grading of occupation.

In the original paper, which reported on this investigation, attention was drawn to the jump in the value of the median (derived from the General Inquiry) between occupations which had been allocated to category 1 and those allocated to category 2 of the Standard Classification. There are similar lines of division between occupations attributed to category 2 and category 3, and between occupations classified in 6 and 7. The gaps between categories 3 and 4 and between 4 and 5 are less marked, whilst the gap is least between categories 6 and 7. Such differences must, however, be treated with reserve.[1] The gaps may in part be produced by the method of treating occupations ranked as socially equal.[2] They may also be partly the result of the fact that persons co-operating in the inquiry were asked to group occupations into five grades before ordering them *within* grades, and to the constraint on the experiment imposed by this restriction.

As already indicated, comparisons were made between the rankings by different age, sex, and occupational groups. The judgement of men, when analysed by age and occupational status, showed only slight variations. Similarly, very small differences were found as between men and women. The slight differences discovered by these comparisons were largely confirmed by the further study of the material now to be des-

---

[1] Tests for the significance of such differences were discussed by A. Stuart, 'An application of the distribution of the ranking concordance coefficient', *Biometrika*, Vol. 38, June 1951.

[2] See Appendix to original article in *Brit. J. Sociology*.

cribed. Consequently, a discussion of their nature is deferred until later in this chapter.

Two main conclusions were drawn in the original study. First, there did not appear to be any major difference of opinion, among those tested, as to the social grading of the selected occupations. Secondly, the ordering of occupations in the Standard Classification and the undirected judgements of the samples of the public indicated that the proposed Standard Classification 'was not out of touch with the opinion of the man in the street'. It cannot, however, be assumed that there are significant and abrupt gaps in status between the standard categories. The divisions drawn between grades should be regarded merely as arbitrary but convenient boundaries.

Part II: Comments on the Original Inquiry

An examination of certain methodological features of the original inquiry may be useful as an aid to the planning of future research in this field. In addition, such an examination, by indicating the nature and basis of the Standard Classification, may help to prevent it from being used indiscriminately and without a sense of its purpose and limitations.

A feature of earlier studies of the prestige of occupations has been the unrepresentativeness of the samples of rankers, investigators rarely going far beyond the circle of their university associates. The sample in our inquiry, though much more widely based, is still not very satisfactory. The distribution of rankers according to the Standard Classification is shown in Table 3.

Table 3

DISTRIBUTION OF RANKERS GRADED ACCORDING
TO THE STANDARD CLASSIFICATION (P AND G)

Occupational Category	Percentage
1	17
2	16
3	19
4	15
5	29
6, 7	4
	100

The sample was thus 'top-heavy' and to that extent unrepresentative of the total population. A sample representative of the whole population is not, of course, a prerequisite of an occupational ranking study; on occasions it may be more valuable to confine the inquiry to samples of particular sections of the population. The ranking population to be covered must, however, be carefully defined and the sample selected so as to represent this particular population correctly and without bias. The sample in the original inquiry was drawn from an arbitrary selection of organizations, and even within those organizations its representativeness was affected by the extent of non-co-operation by members.

An occupational ranking study can cover only a limited number of occupations, for otherwise the burden on rankers would become intolerable. In the present case, thirty occupations were included, these being selected from an original list of 138. With such a relatively small number of occupations, it is important that they are selected so as to cover the range both of occupational prestige and types of occupation as well as possible. In addition, the relative importance of the occupation in the community, in terms of the numbers employed, should not be neglected. Although the occupations included in the experiment covered only some 10 per cent of the working population, they did represent a wide range of prestige.

The modified Standard Classification has been used in subsequent studies to grade occupations other than the thirty included in the final list, and a word of explanation and caution is necessary regarding this generalization. The original thirty occupations have been used as 'reference points' in relation to which a considerable number of additional occupations have been scaled. Such a process is justifiable as long as it is realized that the generalization of the scale does not rest upon the judgements of the 1,400 rankers taking part in the original experiment. The ordering of the additional occupations is a product only of the opinion of those few individuals who collaborate in grading this wider occupational range, and who make implicit and explicit generalizations from the particular occupations covered by the original inquiry.

Part III: Further Analysis of the Material

It has already been suggested that at least one characteristic of the prestige scale of occupations derived from the inquiry may be the result of the instructions given to the individuals who took part in the experiment. These individuals were asked to begin by allocating the separate occupations to five grades, A, B, C, D and E. The object of this instruction was twofold: first, to facilitate the task of ranking; and secondly, to provide five categories, the content of which might be compared with that of the five 'classes' customarily used by the Registrar-General of England and Wales. In effect, however, this procedure also imposed a set of constraints on the freedom of individuals undertaking the ranking, and may thus have contributed to the artificial bunching of occupations and to the breaks in the scale noted above.

The effect of this fivefold grid cannot now be eliminated from the ranking; it can, however, be 'by-passed' by employing a different method of analysis. This has been attempted in two stages. First, an analysis was made, for each occupation, of the distribution of rankings over the five grades. Secondly, the use made of the opportunity to tie occupations judged as of equal social status was studied. These analyses, between and within the five grades, were only two of many possible ways of further studying the material. No other analyses were attempted, however, partly because the hand tabulation involved would have been too laborious and partly because it was felt that the nature of the sample did not justify too refined an analysis.

1. *The Distribution over the Five Grades*

It should be said at once that the results of this new analysis do not contradict those already published, but rather support the earlier conclusions.

The five grades, A to E, into which, as a first step, rankers were asked to place occupations, were not defined except that A was to be regarded as the highest and E as the lowest in prestige. In theory, there was nothing to prevent anyone from placing all thirty occupations into one grade. In fact, most rankers used all five grades, the overall distribution being:

	A	B	C	D	E	
Percentage	16	19	25	21	19	100

Too much significance should not be attached to the pleasant normality of this distribution as, in order to ease their task, rankers were advised to start by placing those occupations judged to be highest and lowest in A and E respectively and then to work towards the middle grade. This may have influenced the distribution and turned C into a kind of residual grade. There were no differences in this overall spread as between the sexes or occupational categories of the participants in the inquiry.

38

Table 4 gives the distribution for each of the thirty occupations:

Table 4

PERCENTAGE OF SAMPLE PLACING OCCUPATIONS INTO EACH OF THE
FIVE INITIAL GRADES

Occupation	A	B	C	D	E
Medical Officer of Health	89	10	1	—	—
Company Director	87	12	1	—	—
Country Solicitor	74	24	2	—	—
Chartered Accountant	66	31	3	—	—
Civil Servant (Exec.)	34	53	12	1	—
Nonconformist Minister	32	54	12	2	—
Business Manager	28	62	10	—	—
Works Manager	28	59	12	1	—
Farmer	21	58	19	2	—
Elementary School Teacher	3	38	54	5	—
Jobbing Master Builder	2	35	54	9	—
News Reporter	2	33	58	7	—
Commercial Traveller	1	23	61	14	1
Chef	1	21	56	21	1
Insurance Agent	—	13	60	25	2
Newsagent and Tobacconist	—	10	59	29	2
Policeman	1	8	55	34	2
Routine Clerk	—	6	54	37	3
Fitter	—	6	43	44	2
Carpenter	—	3	34	59	4
Shop Assistant	—	1	27	62	10
Bricklayer	—	2	19	61	18
Tractor Driver	—	1	10	58	31
Coal Hewer	—	2	10	44	44
Railway Porter	—	—	3	30	67
Barman	—	—	2	29	69
Agricultural Labourer	—	1	5	23	71
Carter	—	—	2	24	74
Dock Labourer	—	—	2	14	84
Road Sweeper	—	—	1	4	95

A wide measure of agreement is recorded for occupations ranked at the extreme ends of the scale. In the case of four occupations—Medical Officer of Health, company director, dock labourer and road sweeper— more than four-fifths of the sample agree on the grades to which they shall be allocated. The 'modal' grade is fairly clearly indicated for most occupations. For about half the occupations at least 60 per cent of the sample agree as to the grade, A, B, C, D or E, to which to allocate the occupation. Considering that the groups were not defined and that rankers were asked for their relative, rather than their absolute, ranking the extent of agreement seems very high.

The striking exceptions are the fitter and the coal hewer, for each of which a wide dispersion of judgement is shown (a dispersion which persists throughout age, sex and occupational groups). Other occupations with relatively wide dispersion are civil servant, minister, elementary school teacher, jobbing master builder, policeman and clerk. Some of these are 'broad' occupations in that they genuinely spread over a wide social range. Others, notably the minister, may show a wide spread because they are occupations for which material rewards and traditional social prestige are at variance. The spread in ranking in such cases indicates that different rankers may employ different criteria as a basis for their judgement. It is in these marginal, typically middle-range occupations, rather than in the occupations at the end-points of the scale, that the sociologist is most interested. In order to study them detailed knowledge about individual rankers and their criteria of ranking is essential.

The original inquiry was not designed for such detailed investigation, but it is possible to split up the sample by the occupational grade of the rankers. Accordingly, for each occupation the distribution over the five grades has been analysed according to the occupational category of the ranker.[1] Table 5A, which relates to the ranking of the Medical Officer, is typical of the distribution for the other highly ranked occupations, company director, solicitor and chartered accountant.

Table 5A

PERCENTAGE OF RANKERS (IN EACH OCCUPATIONAL CATEGORY)
ALLOCATING MEDICAL OFFICER OF HEALTH TO THE GRADES A TO E

Occupational Category of Rankers	A	B	C	D	E	Total
1	93	6	1	—	—	100
2	92	8	—	—	—	100
3	87	13	—	—	—	100
4	87	12	1	—	—	100
5	85	12	3	—	—	100
6, 7	78	18	4	—	—	100

There is a strong tendency for more people in the higher occupational grades to place the Medical Officer of Health in the highest grade. Exactly the same applies to the other three occupations mentioned. Further, the type of distribution shown in this table is not confined to occupations at the top of the scale. Throughout the entire range of

[1] Owing to lack of space only a few of the resultant tables can be given.

occupations, rankers in the higher occupational grades tend to show less variability in judgement in placing occupations than those in the lower occupational grades. On the other hand this may reflect the tendency of those in lower occupational grades to downgrade occupations of higher prestige than their own.

The road sweeper may be taken as an example of the other extreme of the scale.

Table 5B

PERCENTAGE OF RANKERS (IN EACH OCCUPATIONAL CATEGORY)
ALLOCATING ROAD SWEEPER TO THE GRADES A TO E

Occupational Category of Ranker	A	B	C	D	E	Total
1	—	—	—	1	99	100
2	—	—	—	2	98	100
3	—	—	—	2	98	100
4	—	—	1	5	94	100
5	—	—	1	6	93	100
6, 7	—	—	2	11	87	100

Again, there is a greater measure of agreement among the higher groups. Or, alternatively, there is a higher average prestige given to the road sweeper by rankers in the lower occupational grades.

Finally, Tables 5C and 5D show the distributions for the two occupations, the rankings of which are most widely dispersed, namely, the fitter and the coal hewer.

Table 5C

PERCENTAGE OF RANKERS (IN EACH OCCUPATIONAL CATEGORY)
ALLOCATING FITTER TO THE GRADES A TO E

Occupational Category of Ranker	A	B	C	D	E	Total
1	—	2	35	61	2	100
2	—	6	44	49	1	100
3	—	5	44	50	1	100
4	—	4	46	50	—	100
5	1	7	44	46	2	100
6, 7	1	11	57	30	2	100

In both cases, category 1 rankers give a substantially different ranking from the rest of the participants in the inquiry.

As for the remainder of the occupations, we can only summarize our general impressions. Throughout, variability of ranking is higher among the lower occupational grades, a conclusion already noted in the earlier paper. There is no systematic evidence to show that rankers grade their

41

own occupations, or even occupations in their own social neighbour-hood, higher than the average. On the whole, the analysis has provided us with relatively few large or systematic differences. It has, however, suggested certain principles for future research which will be mentioned in the last section of this chapter.

Table 5D

PERCENTAGE OF RANKERS (IN EACH OCCUPATIONAL CATEGORY)
ALLOCATING COAL HEWER TO THE GRADES A TO E

Occupational Category of Ranker	A	B	C	D	E	Total
1	—	1	8	39	52	100
2	—	1	10	45	44	100
3	—	1	9	43	47	100
4	—	1	11	51	37	100
5	—	3	13	41	43	100
6, 7	—	7	11	48	33	100

2. *The Ties*

Rankers were given the following instruction: 'If you judge two or more occupations to be on the same social level, please label them with the same number.' A glance at a selection of the forms suggested that ample use had been made of this opportunity and that the nature of the ties themselves might justify study. The problem of ties had not been ignored in the original paper. The 'Statistical Note' appended to it described the different statistical methods of dealing with ties in a ranking. The point to be stressed now is that if tying took place on any extensive scale, it is of sociological interest and should be subjected to separate study. This may be illustrated by an extreme case. Suppose that 99 out of 100 rankers tie all 30 occupations, whilst the 100th submits a straight ranking. The final ranking of the 100 rankers will be that of the 100th man. Though statistically unexceptionable, this is not a conclu-sion which would be acceptable sociologically. The problem may be looked at from another angle. Suppose that 90 per cent of the rankers place occupation A equal to occupation B, that 6 per cent place A above B and 4 per cent B above A. In the final scale A would appear above B. Once again, the conclusion is statistically correct but sociologically misleading in view of the fact that the vast majority of rankers were unable to distinguish between the two occupations.

A tie may mean several things. It may mean that the ranker has judged two or more occupations as being socially equal; that owing to un-

42

familiarity or ignorance, he is unable to distinguish between them (an index of uncertainty); or it may simply indicate a lack of interest. The first two factors are of particular importance and it would be useful to distinguish between them and to study these two kinds of tie. In the present inquiry nothing more than an overall examination of the incidence of tying is possible.

The analysis of the amount of tying may proceed in several ways, no one way being very satisfactory when used by itself.

(i) The *number of ranks* distinguished on the average out of the possible 30 may be analysed. If all occupations are tied, the fraction would be 1/30, if none are tied 30/30. This is perhaps the best simple index of the amount of tying. But it tells us nothing about the number of ties, whether they are small or large ties, or how many occupations are involved in them altogether.

(ii) A simple analysis of the *number of ties* can be made. There is one difficulty here. Consider the following ties:

Occupation A = Occupation B
    ,,   C =   ,,   D
    ,,   E =   ,,   F = Occupation G

To call this a total of three ties ignores the fact that the three-way tie itself implies three pairs of two-way ties. It is not satisfactory simply to count the number of ties, ignoring their 'size', or to sum all ties, splitting multiples into their respective two-way ties. The latter method fails to distinguish between

$$A = B = C \text{ and } A = B, C = D, E = F$$

both of which contribute three ties to the total.

(iii) Finally, the *number of occupations* involved in ties, on the average, may be counted. This might appear the obvious method, but again it is unsatisfactory by itself. Thus, if a ranker has 18 occupations involved in ties, this may mean that he judges all these 18 as equal to each other, or that he has nine two-way ties, or any of the other combinations which may differ in their sociological implications.

The Amount of Tying

The main results have been prepared largely in terms oɪ (i) and (iii) above, and are given in Tables 6 and 7.

These figures show very clearly the great amount of tying. On the average only 61 per cent of the possible ranks were distinguished, that is to say about 18 out of 30. This analysis of the original data therefore reveals a very considerable inability on the part of the rankers to distinguish between the prestige levels of occupations. Certain other features of the table are also of interest. Women seem slightly more likely to tie than men, old people than young. These age and sex differences are not, however, substantial. Nor are there appreciable differences between the social categories of rankers (leaving aside the lowest group whose very small numbers make this figure of doubtful validity). The differences in the amount of tying within the given grades A to E are considerable. In the middle (residual) grade it is very much higher than in the outside grades.

Table 6

PERCENTAGE OF POSSIBLE 30 RANKS DISTINGUISHED BY RANKERS
(ACCORDING TO THEIR AGE, SEX AND STATUS CATEGORY; AND ACCORDING
TO GRADE OF OCCUPATION RANKED)

(a) By age of Rankers		(b) By sex of Rankers		(c) By status category of Rankers		(d) By grade of occupation ranked	
	%		%		%		%
15–29	64	M	62	1	62	A	65
30–39	62	F	59	2	63	B	64
40–49	58			3	62	C	56
50 +	58			4	61	D	59
				5	60	E	63
				6. 7	53		

One interesting question is whether rankers in the upper occupational grades are more prone to tie occupations far removed from their own and vice versa. An analysis along these lines showed no systematic differences and, in fact, what evidence there is points in the opposite direction. The differences are small, however, and should not be regarded as significant until tested by further research.

The Size of Ties

Sixty per cent of the ties are two-way ties, 25 per cent are three-way and the remainder involve more than three occupations each.

Number of Occupations Involved[1]

On the average, 19 out of the total 30 occupations on a schedule were involved in ties. The distribution was as follows:

[1] The results under this head are calculated for males only, trial comparisons indicating little difference between the sexes.

44

Table 7

PERCENTAGE OF RANKERS TYING VARIOUS
NUMBERS OF OCCUPATIONS

No. of Occupations tied	Percentage of Rankers
0	6
2–9	10
10–14	8
15–19	22
20–24	30
25 +	24
	100

The distribution for the different age groups and for the social categories show few large differences. As so often with the analysis of the results of this study, we gain the impression that we are dealing with a relatively homogeneous ranking universe.

Table 7 shows that only 6 per cent of the male rankers distinguished 30 different ranks and that about one-quarter of the rankers had less than 15 occupations involved in ties. At the other end of the scale, we see that no less than 24 per cent of the rankers tied at least 25 of the 30 occupations (in 12 cases, all 30 occupations were involved in ties, not of course necessarily all tied to each other).

The amount of tying raises doubts as to the value of a simple uni-dimensional ranking scale showing occupations as necessarily above or below each other. It should, however, be emphasized that the presence of the ties does not seem to have affected the rank order to any extent (as is clear by a comparison of Tables 2 and 4). But this may be a characteristic of the present survey only and cannot be assumed to apply to all comparable studies.

Which Occupations are Tied?

It would be useful to know which occupations tend to be tied most frequently, whether different types of rankers tend to tie certain occupations, whether clusters of occupations tend to be tied and so forth. Future research should attempt to answer these questions. In the present inquiry, hand tabulations on these lines would have been forbiddingly laborious. A rough survey of the material showed that the occupations most frequently involved in ties were carpenter, fitter, clerk, coal hewer, commercial traveller, insurance agent, policeman and bricklayer, while those least frequently involved were company director, barman, Medical

Officer of Health, farmer, minister and road sweeper. This list suggests that the most frequently tied occupations are also the ones with the highest ranking variability. Notable exceptions to this tendency are the farmer and the minister, both of which are seldom tied but nevertheless display high variability of ranking.

3. *Conclusions*

The main results obtained from two further analyses of the original material have been described. These results, and especially those regarding the ties, have left many questions unanswered and have indicated certain problems as worthy of further examination. In particular, no elaborate statistical tests have been attempted in view of the nature of the sample, and although many of the results are suggestive, we do not wish to claim statistical significance for them. Some methodological problems inherent in any study of social prestige, together with suggestions for future research, are discussed below.

Part IV: Future Research

The statement that in Britain occupation holds a central position as a means of facilitating the investigation of social status cannot be seriously challenged. Occupation is closely related to many of the objective and subjective factors influencing the problem, though knowledge of the nature of these relationships is· imperfect in the absence of specific inquiry.

A social ranking of occupations cannot be made simply in terms of a single criterion such as income, working conditions, responsibility, educational standards or any other single objective characteristic; social status involves associational, prestige, and allied matters. An ordering of occupations resulting from the summation of all relevant factors is a subjective concept and it is the attempt to measure and scale this quality which presents most of the obstacles to research in this field.

The separate factors which together determine social status may be primarily objective in character. But the judgement of the 'weight' to be assigned to each factor, and in consequence the rank to which an occupation is assigned, are subjective. Further, the 'weight' ascribed to a given factor by different rankers is likely to vary according to the ranker's background, experience and outlook.

The study of occupational prestige may have two main purposes. First, an occupational classification, if correlated with social prestige, would facilitate the study of social differentiation and selection—the purpose of the original inquiry. Secondly, the nature of subjective evaluations may be discerned through study of the relationship between occupational status judgements and the backgrounds of rankers differentiated in terms of age, education and other appropriate variables.

With these purposes in mind the following considerations may be useful for future research.

1. It is essential that the population to be sampled be clearly defined in relation to the purpose of the inquiry, and that the sample drawn represent this population correctly.

2. Future ranking studies should, where possible, be based on proper experimental designs. In particular, past studies have been limited to short lists of occupations to ease the burden on rankers, and have thus suffered in loss of generality. The need for short lists of occupations is lessened by modern developments in the theory of experimental design. Some methods directly applicable to occupational ranking studies are discussed in a recent paper.[1]

3. (a) The sex, age, occupation, education, social background, self-assessed status and other relevant characteristics of rankers should be recorded.

(b) Information is needed concerning the basis of ranking. What criteria have been employed by individual rankers? Do these criteria vary as between rankers from different social strata? On what knowledge and information are the judgements based? In order to record these details, and to ensure adequate response, personal interviews would be necessary. Final rankings could then be analysed according to the criteria employed.

4. The practicability of using the method of paired comparisons should be further explored.[2] The technique secures maximum discrimination, in so far as only two occupations are involved in any one judgement. The obvious limitation is that only a very few occupations can be included; even with 30 occupations, a total of 435 comparisons would be involved. It may, however, be possible to confine judgements to critical or close occupations. The use of paired comparisons *in conjunction* with straight ranking might well be worth considering, the former being confined to judgements of occupations close to each other.

---

[1] J. Durbin, 'Incomplete blocks in ranking experiments', *Brit. J. Psychology* (Statistical Section), Vol. 4, Part 2, June 1951, p. 85.
[2] See, for example, W. Coutu, 'The relative prestige of twenty professions', *Social Forces*, May 1936.

5. Experiments to test the effects of particular technical approaches might be undertaken.

(a) The sample of rankers could be split into two identical halves, the tying of occupations judged as socially equal being encouraged in one group but not the other.

(b) Similarly, the effect of constraints could be examined. Equivalent samples might be used to study the effect of allocating occupations to status groups of various types (such as the fivefold grading in the original inquiry), these samples being compared with a control group to which no constraints are applied.

(c) Rankers in the original study were asked to grade the 30 occupations in relation to each other in the order which they felt people in general would rank them. An interesting comparison might be made by asking one group to rank according to these terms, and an identical group to rank the occupations according to their own personal opinion. These various problems could, of course, be examined in an experiment designed on a factorial basis.

Three basic problems remain to be considered. First, the original inquiry produced a scale which summarized and averaged the relative ranking judgements of all those taking part. In such a process, status judgements of occupations familiar and unfamiliar are given equal weight. A person's judgement of two occupations may depend on his own social status, on particular chance encounters with or knowledge of persons in these occupations and on other factors.

However, it is the totality of such judgements, some based on knowledge, others on uncertainty, which make up social status distinctions and prejudices. All these judgements were relevant to the purpose of the original inquiry, but in future work it may not always be desirable to add together in one scale judgements of such varying nature.

Several types of judgements can be distinguished; first, the relative grading of occupations of which the ranker has personal knowledge; secondly, the judging of occupations, one of which is familiar and the other less familiar; and finally, the relative ranking of two occupations, neither of which is well known to the ranker. All such judgements may be further influenced by the ranker's own status position and his distance from or proximity to the occupations being judged. These considerations will also affect the problem of tying.

This has two implications for future research. The sample of rankers must be split, for purpose of analysis, into as many groups as possible, for the more homogeneous—with reference to relevant variables such as those mentioned above—these groups can be made, the more will be learnt from the experiment. Also, as has already been suggested, every effort should be made to discover on what criteria *individual* rankers have in fact based their judgements.

The second problem is related to the first, namely whether rankers should be asked to grade a list in which all types of occupation, for example, agricultural, professional, commercial, are included. It is likely that rankers have difficulty in making some judgements, and when asked to rank a chef against a commercial traveller, or a minister against a works manager would prefer to say that they are not comparable. In the original inquiry, many of the ties may be hidden 'non-comparable' judgements. Occupations might be grouped into meaningful strata according to their nature, ranking being undertaken within these strata. The various scales might be linked up, for instance by ranking or tying from one scale to another, or by the use of paired comparisons.

This problem was recognized during preliminary work on the social grading of occupations, and a number of individuals engaged in certain professions or industry were asked to grade the occupations coming within their own specialized field of knowledge and experience. The professions of medicine, the Church, law, accounting, the civil service, engineering, building, are smoe of the twenty occupations so graded. But the process was not entirely satisfactory, for several of those collaborating found difficulty in selecting occupations within their own profession directly comparable to those in the grading of the educational profession, submitted as a guide.

Finally, there is a problem central to research into social status, though not dealt with in the present inquiry. That is the problem of measuring the social distance between two occupations whose relative status is being judged, or between two occupational strata which are being considered from the same point of view. Two individuals may rank occupation A below occupation B. But the order BA would give no clue to the differences in distance which might underlie the two judgements.

One possible solution lies in the use of a scale which can be divided into a fixed number of units irrespective of the number of occupations to be ranked. For instance, a 100-point scale might be used to rank twenty-five to thirty occupations. Judges would then rank the chosen occupations in two : ways in relation to each other, and in terms of their relative position within the social range represented by the scale. This would permit the measurement of the distance between any two occupations.[1] But certain difficulties would still exist, the most important being that the scales may themselves be ranked on different levels, and cover differing ranges of prestige, the upper and lower limits being given different prestige values by different rankers. Here, again, the problem might be overcome by the use of a number of key occupations, common to each scale, whose relative positions would offer some measure of the effective range which the ranker had in mind. Such a device would facilitate the combination, into one vertical scale, of the separate occupational groups mentioned above. But this approach is by no means simple, and its development would demand careful experimentation.

In summarizing the results of this discussion, we should point out that, although the various limitations and defects of the present inquiry as a general study of the social prestige of occupations have been emphasized, it is no less important to stress the fact that the inquiry had a limited and specific objective. It was designed as the first stage in an investigation of social mobility in England and Wales. For that purpose, it was necessary to ascertain whether there is sufficient agreement among the public that occupations differ in social prestige, as well as on the relative prestige of different occupations. The inquiry has certainly shown a substantial measure of public agreement as to the prestige of various occupations—and, indeed, has indicated that in the sample studied opinions on prestige are largely independent of the sex, age or occupation of the observer. Moreover, the results very largely confirm the broad status hierarchy envisaged by the Standard Classification, drawn up in advance of the empirical investigation. Hence that Standard Classification, modified to take account of certain differences shown up by the inquiry, may justifiably be used in measuring social mobility—that is, in the sense that movement towards category 1 may be regarded as upward social mobility, and movement towards category 7 as downward mobility. The measure is one of direction only, and even so is crude. Movement within a category cannot be measured; a more elaborate and subtle inquiry would be needed for that purpose. And it is clear that the demarcation between two contiguous grades is by no means precise. For this reason, as well as for purely statistical reasons, it was frequently found necessary to compress the Standard Classification into five or, on occasion, into three categories, as will be seen in subsequent chapters. Nevertheless, even the use of three or four broad categories may produce interesting and relevant results.

[1] Studies on these lines are being undertaken in the Netherlands.

III

Some Subjective Aspects of Social Stratification

F. M. MARTIN

THIS chapter is not designed to provide a tight link between the previous discussion of the social grading of occupations and the subsequent concrete analysis of social mobility. Instead, the main purpose here is to explore more widely the nature of social status and social class as seen in subjective terms, and to examine the relation between subjective and objective determinants. To this end, the chapter reports some of the findings of another investigation—an investigation carried out separately, though conceived within the framework of the study of social selection and differentiation referred to in the introduction. At the same time, some of the questions considered here have a direct bearing upon the use of occupation as an index of status, while others point clearly to the importance attached by individuals to education as a correlate of status and as a means of providing upward social mobility.

There has been relatively little systematic empirical study of such questions as the relation between objective social location and subjective, self-evaluated status; or of the range of popular conceptions of the nature of social classes; or of the criteria of class membership. Hence it seemed more appropriate to follow a frankly exploratory approach, using the method of the sample interview survey and relying fairly heavily upon open-ended questions, than to attempt to formulate precise hypotheses which might then be subjected to rigorous empirical tests.

The survey was carried out in September–October 1950, in two districts—Greenwich and Hertford. In both these areas, a good deal of background information was available—in Greenwich, in particular, that being so, for a research team of the London School of Economics had conducted an inquiry into political behaviour in that district. Each

51

district had in its favour, from our point of view, a fairly heterogeneous social composition, while at the same time the small, compact county and market town and the sprawling, variegated metropolitan borough presented some interesting contrasts.

In each district, a stratified sample of subjects was drawn from the Electoral Registers.[1] The two districts were each divided into three areas, of high, low and intermediate average rateable value respectively, and sampling fractions were adjusted so as to give a sample of equal size in each area. The criterion of rateable value turned out, in Greenwich at any rate, to be an imperfect one,[2] for many of the larger houses had been requisitioned by the local authority. Nevertheless, the number of subjects other than manual workers who were drawn into our sample, though rather smaller than we had hoped, was still far in excess of what would have been found in an unstratified random sample.[3]

For each district 510 names (3 × 170) were drawn, together with a list of substitutes one-third of the length of the original list. Substitutes were interviewed where original subjects had died, had moved to another address, were ill, were likely to be away from the district for some time, or, in a few cases, where persistent call-backs had failed to find the original subject at home. In the case of a refusal, no substitute was used, so that the size of the sample was correspondingly reduced.

Table 1

SUMMARY OF INTERVIEWING RESULTS

	Greenwich		Hertford		Total	
	N	%	N	%	N	%
Original subjects interviewed	395	77·4	371	72·7	766	75·1
Substitutes interviewed	65	12·8	68	13·3	133	13·0
	460		439		899	
Refusals	50	9·8	71	14·0	121	11·9
Sample drawn	510 : 100·0		510 : 100·0		1020 : 100·0	

[1] The Electoral Register was chosen rather than the more up-to-date National Register because it lent itself more readily to stratification by streets or areas. The advantages and disadvantages of the available sampling frames are discussed in P. G. Gray and T. Corlett, 'Sampling for the Social Survey', *J. Roy. Stat. Soc.* (Series A), Vol. 113, 1950.

[2] The difficulty might have been partly overcome had the criterion been rateable value per head rather than rateable value per dwelling.

[3] M. Benney and P. Geiss ('Social class and politics in Greenwich', *Brit. J. Sociology*, Vol. 1, 1950) in a 1/60 sample from the Greenwich Electoral Register, secured 19 subjects in the professional and managerial range, out of a total of 715 (2·7 per cent), as against 13·5 per cent in the present inquiry; similarly, 15·2 per cent of their sample fall into the 'salaried' category, compared with our 22·2 per cent.

Tables 1 and 2 give details of the substitution and refusal rates, and of the composition of the effective sample by age and sex. The two districts are fairly closely balanced in respect of age structure; the Greenwich sample included a somewhat higher propoition of younger subjects, while in Hertford we drew rather more subjects over 50 years of age. In both districts, women formed the majority of the sample; in Hertford, however, their numerical superiority was rather less pronounced.

Tables 2A and 2B

COMPOSITION OF EFFECTIVE SAMPLE

(a) By Age:

Age Groups	Greenwich N	Greenwich %	Hertford N	Hertford %	Total N	Total %
21–30	93	20	61	14	154	17·1
31–40	128	28	115	26	243	27·0
41–50	105	23	107	24	212	23·6
51–60	64	14	90	21	154	17·1
61+	66	14	65	15	131	14·6
Age not given	4	1	1	—	5	0·6
	460 :	100·0	439 :	100·0	899 :	100·0

(b) By Sex

	Greenwich N	Greenwich %	Hertford N	Hertford %	Total N	Total %
Male	200	43·5	205	46·7	405	45·0
Female	260	56·5	234	53·3	494	55·0
	460 :	100·0	439 :	100·0	899 :	100·0

When all the interviewing was completed, 90 schedules were taken at random (1 in every 10), and the replies to each of the open-ended questions were extracted. These were used as the material for constructing a series of categories into which, it was hoped, it would be possible to fit without artificial constraint the open responses on the remaining schedules. This procedure was quite effective, and it was necessary to add further categories in the course of coding for only one or two questions.

Occupational Status and Subjective Status

Interviewers were instructed to obtain from each subject sufficient information about his occupation to permit the subject to be allocated to one of the grades of the classification given in Chapter II; only two cases had to be discarded because the information available was inadequate. Married women were classified according to the occupations of their husbands, and unmarried women living with their parents according to their fathers' occupations; a female subject's own occupation was recorded only if she was unmarried and living away from her parents. One modification was introduced into the classification, and undoubtedly increased its usefulness in the present inquiry. The occupations listed under category 5 include both skilled manual work and weekly paid non-manual jobs (e.g. routine clerk, typist, telephone operator). It was thought very probable that there would be important socio-psychological differences between these two groups, and they were, therefore, separated out in our analysis. The routine non-manual workers were put into a new category, which was called 4a, so that the sevenfold classification was transformed into an eightfold.

Table 3

RELATION OF SUBJECTIVE STATUS TO OCCUPATIONAL GRADE

Percentage assessing self as

Occupational Grade	District	Lower	Poor	Working	Lower Middle	Middle	Upper Middle	Professional	Upper	Don't Know	Don't Belong	N (=100%)
1	Greenwich	—	—	6	3	55	12	18	3	3	—	31
	Hertford	—	—	3	—	81	8	8	—	—	—	36
2	Greenwich	—	—	3	—	82	3	3	—	6	3	31
	Hertford	—	—	4	4	75	2	13	—	2	—	46
3	Greenwich	—	2	22	6	64	2	—	—	4	—	51
	Hertford	3	—	12	10	71	—	4	—	—	—	67
4	Greenwich	4	2	37	4	41	—	2	—	10	—	51
	Hertford	—	—	32	11	49	3	3	1	1	—	79
4a	Greenwich	9	9	33	6	43	—	—	—	—	—	33
	Hertford	5	2	31	7	48	—	—	—	7	—	42
5	Greenwich	10	5	56	1	25	1	—	—	1	1	156
	Hertford	4	9	47	2	33	—	—	—	4	1	127
6	Greenwich	4	7	61	—	24	—	—	—	4	—	54
	Hertford	14	7	44	—	25	—	—	—	3	7	28
7	Greenwich	6	12	62	—	10	—	—	—	4	6	52
	Hertford	15	—	70	15	—	—	—	—	—	—	13

A second index secured was the subject's own estimate of his social location. Early in the interview he was asked: 'How many social classes would you say there are in this country?' 'Can you name them?' 'Which of these classes ao you belong to?' The expectation underlying the use of an index of subjective status was simply that an individual's beliefs and ideas would be functionally related, not only to his objective social situation, but also to his own definition of that situation. Accordingly, the subjective index was regarded as a means of sub-classifying respondents who were stratified in the first instance by the relatively objective criterion of occupation.

The relationship between occupational grade and subjective status, as set out in Table 3, is itself of some interest. The number of subjects not able or not prepared to assess their own status was remarkably small. Although they were, so to speak, thrown back on their own resources, and not provided with any check-list, 96·1 per cent of the sample attempted a self-assessment. Four out of five of these assessments (79·1 per cent of the entire sample) are accounted for under the headings 'Working Class' and 'Middle Class' (36·6 per cent and 42·5 per cent respectively); and although 80 subjects (9 per cent) assessed themselves as 'Lower Class' or 'Poor', these may be regarded as different from the self-assessed working class in name only, since none of them, in naming the classes they supposed to exist, specified a working class in addition to their own. The proportion of persons allocating themselves to a specific sub-section of the middle class was surprisingly small—3·9 per cent to the lower middle class, 1·4 per cent to the upper middle class, and 2·5 per cent to the professional class—especially since the sample included an unusually high proportion of subjects in the higher occupational grades. The term 'Professional Class', it would seem, is used synonymously with 'Upper Middle Class'. Only two subjects described themselves as belonging to the upper class.

Occupational grades are shown to be clearly differentiated in terms of self-evaluated status. There is within each district a gradual and consistent reduction, as we pass down the occupational scale, in the percentage of self-allocations to one form or another of the middle class, the extreme values being 88 per cent and 10 per cent in Greenwich and 97 per cent and 15 per cent in Hertford. The marked reductions that appear in the transition from category 4a to category 5 were to be expected, for this is the conventional line of demarcation between manual and non-manual occupations; less obvious is the falling off between categories 3 and 4. There is a corresponding increase in the percentage of self-allocations to the working class from 6 per cent and 3 per cent of the professional group in Greenwich and Hertford respectively to 80 per cent and 85 per cent of the unskilled workers. Examining the table from a slightly different point of view, we can say that the nearest approach to unanimity in self-assessment is displayed by the extreme groups in the occupational scale, with divergence becoming progressively more marked as the middle of the scale is approached. In both districts, the self-evaluations of the lowest grade of non-manual employees (4a) are almost evenly divided between 'Working Class' and 'Middle Class'.

Certain differences between the two districts stand out unmistakably. In the small county town, there is, compared with the metropolitan borough, a considerably stronger tendency to cling to middle-class status; manual workers are more likely to think of themselves as middle class, and clerks, tradesmen, supervisors and technicians are very much less likely to assess themselves as working class. The differences in the distribution of self-assessments both within and between the districts are brought out more clearly by Table 4, which compresses the material of Table 3.

Table 4

RELATION OF SUBJECTIVE STATUS TO OCCUPATIONAL CATEGORY (GROUPED)

Occupational Categories	District	Lower, Poor, Working %	Lr. Middle, Middle, Upper Mid. %	Don't Know Don't Belong %	No. (=100%)
1, 2	Greenwich	5	89	6	62
	Hertford	4	95	1	82
	TOTAL	4	93	3	144
3, 4, 4a	Greenwich	38	57	5	135
	Hertford	27	71	2	188
	TOTAL	32	65	3	323
5	Greenwich	72	26	2	156
	Hertford	61	34	5	127
	TOTAL	67	30	3	283
6, 7	Greenwich	76	17	7	106
	Hertford	71	22	7	41
	TOTAL	75	18	7	147

This table suggests that a grouping of our subjects into five categories, based on a combination of the two indices of status, is the most useful for further analysis. One category contains the subjects in the professional and managerial grades, who are virtually unanimous in their self-ratings. The salaried grades are divided in a ratio of about 2 : 1 between middle and working class, and accordingly form two groups; while the two remaining categories are made up of manual workers, of whom about three-quarters assess themselves as working class and about one-quarter as middle class. More precisely:

Group	Occupational Categories	Subjective Status	
A	1 and 2	Middle Class	N = 133
B	3, 4 and 4a	Middle Class	N = 210
C	3, 4 and 4a[1]	Working Class	N = 108
D	5, 6 and 7	Middle Class	N = 111
E	5, 6 and 7	Working Class	N = 300

The grouping chosen gives us an opportunity to examine some of the primary characteristics of the 'deviants'—that is, the manual workers whose subjective status is middle class, and the black-coated employees who assess themselves as working class. Table 5 shows the composition

Table 5

PRIMARY CHARACTERISTICS OF 'DEVIANT' GROUPS

AGE DISTRIBUTION	Age Groups				
	21–30	31–40	41–50	51–60	60+
	%	%	%	%	%
Group C	13	28	21	22	16
Groups B and C	16	26	22	22	14
Group D	18	35	18	15	14
Groups D and E	20	31	20	15	14

SEX DISTRIBUTION	Male	Female
	%	%
Group C	58	42
Groups B and C	45	55
Group D	32	68
Groups D and E	44	56

DISTRICT	Greenwich	Hertford
	%	%
Group C	50	50
Groups B and C	41	59
Group D	47	53
Groups D and E	59	41

FATHER'S OCCUPATIONAL CATEGORY	Father's Occupation Manual
	%
Group C	45
Groups B and C	31

	Father's Occupation Non-Manua
	%
Group D	19
Groups D and E	14

[1] Except for six cases from Grades 1 and 2.

57

of Group D in terms of age, sex, district and father's occupational category, as compared with the composition of the total sample of manual workers—i.e. Groups D and E combined—and the composition of Group C in comparison with Groups B and C combined.

Age does not appear to be a differentiating factor; the age composition of each of the deviant groups is almost identical with that of the occupational sample from which it is drawn. It is interesting, however, to note the appreciable sex difference; women, it seems, are considerably more disposed than men to upgrade themselves into the middle class and less likely to allocate themselves to the working class—a finding which confirms the common observation that status-consciousness is more pronounced among women.

Subjective assessments of status involve some reference to the individual's family background as well as to his present occupational level; but in this instance, common observation is not the most reliable guide to its direction of operation. While it is true that Group D contains a slightly higher proportion of subjects whose father's occupational status was higher than their own, there is no corresponding tendency for those subjects who have surpassed their parents in terms of occupational status to reject their class of origin, and to identify themselves particularly strongly with their new social stratum. Indeed, the reverse of this process is very evident, those who have been mobile out of the manual working group being particularly likely to claim membership of the working class.

Differential Social Perspectives

The great majority of our subjects thought in terms of a three-class system, and most of them described these classes by the same set of names—upper, middle and working. But could we assume that these names had the same significance for all who used them? To speak of these classes was to refer implicitly to a mental map of the social scene. But was it always substantially the same map? Were the boundary lines separating the regions always drawn with the same degree of clarity and precision, or were they sometimes—either among a particular group of respondents, or in respect of a particular division—vague and uncertain? Might it not be the case that for some of our informants the boundaries had been shifted so as to increase or diminish the territory of a particular region? And would all subjects, whatever their own vantage point, think of all the regions primarily in terms of the same attributes? Social class terminology is all too often used as if such a congruence of social perspectives did in fact exist; yet the questions posed above have only to be set out for the possibility of wide divergences to become apparent. As a first step towards the clarification of these questions, each respondent was asked:

'What sort of people belong to the same class as yourself?' and 'What sort of people belong to the other classes you have mentioned?'

It was hoped that rather ambiguously expressed questions would enable our subjects to answer within their habitual frames of reference —would put them in a position where the subjective map was the only guide to a reply.

Tables 6 to 8 show, for each group, the incidence of different frames of reference and of certain specific descriptions.

Table 6

MEMBERSHIP OF THE WORKING CLASS

Frames of Reference	Profess. Mid. (A) %	Salaried Mid. (B) %	Salaried Wkg. (C) %	Manual Mid. (D) %	Manual Wkg. (E) %
Occupation:	73	71	78	32	76
Labourers, unskilled workers	16	31	—	22	2
Manual workers, Factory workers, Artisans	39	34	19	10	27
Manual workers plus minor non-manual	18	5	38	—	29
'Everyone who works for a living'	—	1	21	—	18
Income or standard of living	5	9	11	22	10
Education	7	5	2	3	—
Mobility	1	—	—	3	—
Moral or evaluative	10	9	2	22	2
Unclassifiable or working class not specified	4	6	7	18	12
N (=100%)	133	210	108	111	300

It will be seen that about three-quarters of the subjects, in every group but one, describe the working class primarily in occupational terms; there are, however, some significant variations in the type of occupation specified. The less skilled and least esteemed kinds of work are scarcely ever mentioned by the self-rated working class itself; on the other hand, descriptions of the working class as consisting of 'dustmen', 'road-sweepers', 'navvies' and so on—a description which may be said to

Table 7

MEMBERSHIP OF THE MIDDLE CLASS

Frames of Reference	Profess. Mid. (A) %	Salaried Mid. (B) %	Wkg. (C) %	Manual Mid. (D) %	Wkg. (E) %
Occupation :	66	74	46	59	50
	—	—	—	—	—
Professional, Managerial, Business owners	42	32	38	10	26
Tradesmen, Clerical, Supervisors	13	24	5	8	20
All other than manual workers	7	9	3	3	3
'Everyone who works for a living'	4	9	—	38	1
	—	—	—	—	—
Income or standard of living	8	5	16	10	13
Education	7	2	—	2	—
Mobility	1	—	3	3	1
Moral or evaluative	3	6	2	10	6
Unclassifiable or middle class not specified	15	13	33	16	30
N (=100%)	133	210	108	111	300

Table 8

MEMBERSHIP OF THE UPPER CLASS

Frames of Reference	Profess. Mid. (A) %	Salaried Mid. (B) %	Wkg. (C) %	Manual Mid. (D) %	Wkg. (E) %
Lineage[1]	49	37	22	20	16
Occupation :	13	18	17	14	16
	—	—	—	—	—
Industrialist	6	6	9	3	10
Professional	4	9	4	10	4
Industrialist and Professional	3	3	4	1	2
	—	—	—	—	—
Income or standard of living	18	31	38	43	44
Education	4	3	—	—	1
Moral or evaluative	2	3	2	5	6
Unclassifiable or not specified	14	8	21	18	17
N=(100%)	133	210	108	111	300

[1] E.g. 'The aristocracy', 'members of old, titled familes', 'the landed gentry'.

maximize social distance—are given quite often by subjects who regard themselves as middle class, particularly if they are below the professional level in occupational status.

By contrast, the working class tends to extend its frontiers either so as explicitly to include clerks, shop assistants and so on, or else, more vaguely, to embrace 'everyone who works for a living'. Definitions such as these are particularly frequent among that section of the self-assessed working class which is made up of non-manual workers; nearly two-thirds of all their definitions of the working class fall under these headings. Within the other 'deviant' group—the manual workers, self-rated as middle class—there is a unique distribution of what we have rather broadly called 'frames of reference'. References to occupation occur in only one in three of their answers; these references are generally derogatory, and never include any suggestion that non-manual employees may belong to the working class. References to income or standard of living occur more frequently than in any other group, and generally picture the working class as existing on the borders of poverty. Also frequent, and often rather colourful, are what are here described as moral or evaluative references; laziness, lack of ambition, and irresponsibility are the qualities most often attributed to the working class.

Table 7 leaves one with the not unexpected impression that the concept of the middle class is relatively vague and ill-defined. There is a reduction in the percentage of occupational definitions, and an increase in definitions of a vagueness that defies attempts at classification; one-third of the working-class subjects could not give even the simplest description of the members of the middle class. References to income or standard of living as a way of characterizing the middle class are more likely to be made by those who do not consider themselves members of that class, though suggestion that the middle class is primarily an 'income-bracket' are rarely made; indeed, it is interesting to see how few people, in plotting their map of all the classes, make explicit use of a simple income scale. Evaluative definitions of the middle class emphasize either respectability and integrity or snobbery and pretensions to superiority, according to the status of the respondent. Within the range of occupational definitions, professional and managerial grades are specified most frequently by subjects who are themselves of professional status, and clerical work and shopkeeping most frequently by Group B. The 'middle-class' manual workers rarely mention specific occupations. As will be shown below, their tendency is to elevate the professions to the upper class. It is interesting to see that their most popular definition

61

of the middle class is identical with one that the 'working-class' manual workers quite often use in describing the working class—'everyone who works for a living'. The frequency with which this is put forward as a description of the membership of the middle class strongly suggests that when a manual worker assesses himself as middle class he is not merely asserting his personal superiority; he carries with him a large proportion of his compeers, and in so doing, he shifts the boundaries of the classes.

When we are examining the 'public images' of the middle and the working class, we can say that we are concerned with the way in which two broad groups, sub-divided according to certain criteria, perceive each other. But when we turn to the upper class, we can deal only with the way in which it is seen 'from outside'; the present sample does not, unfortunately, permit us to examine either the self-image of the upper class (however this may be defined) or its picture of other classes. Within the sample, however, we find that two-thirds of all descriptions of the upper class are accounted for by two frames of reference, but that their respective frequencies within the five groups are inversely related. Group A, for example, is most likely to think of the members of the upper class in terms of their social prestige or familial status; they are the old landowning families, the hereditary aristocracy, or simply 'Society'. But descriptions of this kind become progressively less frequent as we move towards Group E, falling from 49 per cent of the total to 16 per cent. Meanwhile references to income increase from 18 per cent to 44 per cent among the manual (working-class) group; the members of the upper class come to be thought of more and more as 'people with private incomes'. They are sometimes called simply 'the rich' or the 'very rich', though precise limits are scarcely ever stated. Most often, however, it is the source of their income to which reference is made; they are 'people who don't need to work for a living'.

An additional series of questions was inserted into this section of the interview. It was hoped that these questions would help to amplify the spontaneous descriptions of the middle class—would show, even where occupation was not specified as the primary criterion, what the occupational composition of that class was held to be. The informant was handed twelve cards, each bearing the name of an occupation, and was asked:

'About which of these jobs would you say that people doing them belong, on the whole, to the middle class?'

Table 9 shows the percentage of subjects in each group who allocated each of the twelve occupations to the middle class.

Although several occupations had been included because of their 'marginal' character, the differences of opinion which emerged were more striking than had been anticipated. Works manager, for example, is the only occupation which is allocated to the middle class by more than 50 per cent of each group, although *every* occupation is so allocated by a majority of at least one group. Even if the ratings of the two 'deviant' groups are excluded from consideration, we still find a majority vote in each of the three remaining groups for only four occupations.

Table 9

FREQUENCY WITH WHICH OCCUPATIONS ARE ALLOCATED TO THE MIDDLE CLASS

Occupations	Profess. Mid. (A) %	Salaried Mid. (B) %	Wkg. (C) %	Manual Mid. (D) %	Wkg. (E) %
1. Barrister	78	58	66	35	60
2. Doctor (General Practitioner)	88	73	72	43	74
3. Works Manager	82	88	57	61	69
4. Foreman	34	53	13	75	24
5. Chargehand	19	38	12	65	15
6. Wages Clerk	43	62	19	70	24
7. Typist	47	67	14	71	24
8. Tobacconist	56	75	39	72	54
9. Saleswoman (Department Store)	56	66	23	75	32
10. Shop Assistant	26	38	12	59	10
11. Radio Mechanic	26	45	12	70	15
12. Bus Driver	9	24	5	60	7
N (=100%)	133	210	108	111	300

This table should leave us in no doubt that the relationship between occupational status and social class self-rating—and, in particular, apparent discrepancies—must be interpreted with considerable care. It is clear, for example, that when manual workers describe themselves as middle class, they generally extend this description—as was suggested above—to most other manual workers of a status similar to their own, group them together with supervisors and the lower ranks of the black-coated, and tend to place the professions in the upper class. These non-manual employees on the other hand, whose subjective status is working class—who have, as it were, excluded themselves from the middle class—have downgraded the other clerks and typists with themselves; their standards for admission to the middle class are very high, and seem to be satisfied only by people of professional or managerial status. In other words, their refusal to draw a clear line of distinction between themselves and industrial workers is not necessarily to be interpreted as a demonstration of a new class allegiance.

If we compare Groups A and B, we find the group of higher occupational status consistently more exacting in its standards of judgement; there is usually a difference of 18 per cent to 20 per cent in the proportion of subjects admitting a particular occupation to the middle class. The greater leniency of the subjects in the lower occupational grades needs little comment. Neither group, however, sets standards as high as do the working-class manual workers, whose ratings are only slightly more lenient than those of the non-manual working-class group. The barrister, the doctor, and the works manager receive a majority vote— although there is a definite tendency to place the barrister in the upper class; the tobacconist is admitted, though by a very narrow margin. But there is a refusal to concede any claims to middle-class status by clerks, typists, supervisors and shop assistants, although it is interesting to see that the saleswoman in the department store tends here, as in other groups, to receive a middle-class rating more often than any other marginal occupation.

We have a situation, then, in which the 'pure samples' of each class are striving to extend their frontiers at each other's expense. We can do no more than speculate as to the interpretation of this finding; but it seems likely that it represents on the one hand a genuine decline, in the eyes of the working class, of the prestige of the minor non-manual occupations, rather subtly coloured by a slightly resentful attitude, which, in the course of the interviews, found expression in occasional spontaneous exclamations such as: 'They're no better than we are!' In the middle class, on the other hand, the tendency towards an attitude of exclusiveness conflicts with, and is partially overcome by, a perhaps defensive tendency to minimize the size and importance of the working class by restricting its membership.

As for the two groups in which there appears to be a difference between occupational and subjective status, this part of the interview material gives added weight to the suggestion that their departure from the patterns of self-rating characteristic of their respective occupational groups may not necessarily indicate a conflict of loyalties, or gross contradictions of status, but should be seen rather as an attempted redrawing of class boundaries.

Patterns of Aspiration

The present study was not concerned with the facts of social mobility, which are reported elsewhere in this symposium, but rather with opinions relating to the facts, and with aspirations and expectations, which the facts might or might not warrant.

Tables 10A and 10B

PERSONAL MOBILITY

(*a*) DESIRE FOR OWN BUSINESS

		Percentage replying		
		'*Yes*'	'*No*'	'*Don't Know*'	$N (=100\%)$
Profess.	Mid. (A)	48	50	2	48
Salaried	Mid. (B)	57	41	2	103
Salaried	Wkg. (C)	57	43	—	70
Manual	Mid. (D)	54	46	—	59
Manual	Wkg. (E)	58	38	4	230

(*b*) POSSIBILITY OF OWN BUSINESS

		Percentage replying		
		'*Yes*'	'*No*'	'*Don't Know*'	$N (=100\%)$
Profess.	Mid. (A)	52	48	—	23
Salaried	Mid. (B)	30	64	6	59
Salaried	Wkg. (C)	15	85	—	40
Manual	Mid. (D)	22	72	6	32
Manual	Wkg. (E)	15	81	4	133

Virtually all our subjects had completed their own education and had embarked on some definite occupation; it was improbable that many of them would experience any dramatic change of social status. Advancement might come about, however, either through promotion within their present or some other employment, or, perhaps, if they were to embark on some independent enterprise. Our questioning about personal mobility was restricted to this latter type, which seems to involve a more clearly marked change of status (compare, for example, the varying valuations by working-class subjects of the status of tobacconists and foremen respectively). Two questions were put, wherever they were appropriate: 'Would you (your husband) like to own your (his) own business at some time in the future?' and, where the answer was affirmative: 'Do you think you stand a reasonable chance of getting a business of your own?' As Tables 10A and 10B show, quite half of each group would have liked this measure of independence and (for most of them) social advancement. But there is no confusing of the probable with the desirable; in fact, very few expect to be able to make this move. At least four-fifths of the working-class sub-samples did not think that they had a reasonable chance of 'starting on their own'; and it was only in Group A, where the question often referred to private professional practice, that as many as half of those who wished to give up the status of employee thought that they might be able to do so. If we take those answering 'Yes' to both these questions, and express their number as a percentage of those to whom the first question was put, we find that 25 per cent of the professional or managerial subjects both wished to embark on some independent enterprise and thought that their chances of doing so were 'reasonable'. The proportion among the salaried employees is 14 per cent, but only 9 per cent where their subjective status is working class; among the working-class manual workers it is 9 per cent, rising to 12 per cent among the manual workers whose subjective status is middle class.

Table 11

OWN CHILD'S OPPORTUNITIES OF SOCIAL MOBILITY, COMPARED WITH OTHER CHILDREN

		'Better'	'As Good'	'Not as Good'	D.N.A. D.K.	N
		%	%	%	%	(=100%)
Profess.	Mid. (A)	13	75	2	10	134
Salaried	Mid. (B)	9	75	3	13	209
Salaried	Wkg. (C)	14	66	10	10	108
Manual	Mid. (D)	8	85	2	5	111
Manual	Wkg. (E)	5	82	9	4	300

Most of the questions on mobility, however, referred to the subjects' children, and here we find a very different picture. The subjects were asked, for example, how they thought their children's chances of 'moving up in the world' compared with those of most other children. Those respondents who had no children, or whose families were grown up, were invited to give a hypothetical answer—to say what they thought their children's chance would be, if they had any at the present time. Table 11 shows that only 2 per cent or 3 per cent among the middle-class groups thought their children's chances of mobility inferior to those of most other children, while among the working-class subjects the proportion is still no higher than 9 per cent or 10 per cent.

Obviously, no very far-reaching conclusions can be drawn from these figures alone.

In the first place, working-class self-respect leans heavily upon the creed of 'being as good as anyone', a complex sentiment which combines a claim for equality of rights with a denial that social inferiority connotes an intrinsic inferiority. Even if we feel justified in assuming, none the less, that these answers are in the main realistic, we should still be uncertain whether the reference groups on which our subjects' replies were implicitly based were the same in all cases. Some unambiguous confirmation is required; and it is amply provided by the replies of the sample to the question whether their children's chances of moving up in the world were as good as, not as good as, or better than their own chances had been. No fewer than 88 per cent of Group E are convinced that their children have a better chance of social advancement than they themselves had, and only 2 per cent think their children's chances poorer than their own. The proportion answering 'Better' decreases to about two-thirds and one-half among the salaried and professional middle-class groups respectively; but even in the latter group there are only 16 per cent who think their children's opportunities less favourable than their own had been.

Table 12

CHILDREN'S OPPORTUNITIES OF MOBILITY AS COMPARED WITH PARENTS

		Percentage replying				
		'Better'	*'As Good'*	*'Not as Good'*	*'D.K.'*	*N (=100%)*
Profess.	Mid. (A)	49	30	16	5	133
Salaried	Mid. (B)	68	18	4	10	210
Salaried	Wkg. (C)	83	12	3	2	108
Manual	Mid. (D)	80	14	1	5	111
Manual	Wkg. (E)	88	8	2	2	300

Table 13

REASONS GIVEN FOR CHILDREN'S SUPERIOR OPPORTUNITIES

	Profess.	*Salaried*		*Manual*	
	Mid. (A)	*Mid. (B)*	*Wkg. (C)*	*Mid. (D)*	*Wkg. (E)*
	%	%	%	%	%
Improved educational standards	20	26	31	34	36
Improved educational opportunities	36	44	44	40	37
Welfare services, family allowances	—	1	5	2	5
Incomes higher, unemployment lower	4	1	2	—	3
Improved occupational opportunities	4	8	7	5	7
Parents' position better	27	15	3	10	6
Miscellaneous	9	5	8	9	6
N = (100%)	66	142	89	88	264

The explanations given by those who had answered 'Better' are of considerable interest. About three-quarters of the answers in every group except Group A referred to changes in the educational system. Among manual workers, improvements in teaching methods and general educational standards are mentioned almost as often as improved opportunities for obtaining higher education. These former changes are less often specified by Groups A and B—whose own early educational experiences may perhaps have been rather more fortunate. At the same time, the latter groups more frequently draw attention to improvements in their own status as a means of furthering their children's progress.

More detailed information on the levels of aspiration of the different groups is provided by Table 14, which summarizes replies to the question: 'Up to what age would you like to see your children continue full-time education?'

Table 14

PREFERRED SCHOOL-LEAVING AGE FOR OWN CHILDREN

		14–15	16–17	18–19	20+	D.K.	Mean
		%	%	%	%	%	Age
Profess.	Mid. (A)	8	13	36	40	3	18·8
Salaried	Mid. (B)	11	42	20	24	3	17·5
Salaried	Wkg. (C)	16	33	33	14	5	17·1
Manual	Mid. (D)	30	32	24	11	3	16·7
Manual	Wkg. (E)	27	38	18	11	6	16·6

While there is a positive correlation between the status of each group and its average preferred school-leaving age, it should be noted that most members of the manual groups would prefer to see their children reach a level of education superior to their own. Practically everyone in Groups D and E left school at 14; but two-thirds would prefer their children to remain at school at least until the age of 16. Only 11 per cent of the manual workers, however, as against 40 per cent of Group A, suggest an age which implies a desire for university education or its equivalent; and only 18 per cent (or 24 per cent of the manual middle-class group) mention an age corresponding to higher school certificate standard, compared with 36 per cent of the professional and managerial group. In short, while a majority of the manual workers would wish to see their children reach an educational standard higher than their own, their level of aspiration tends to remain fairly modest. The salaried groups aim somewhat higher, 44 per cent and 47 per cent suggesting ages of 18 and above, but still well below the level set by the professional and executive groups.

The distribution of preferences in respect of sons' occupations, which is analysed in Table 15, corresponds closely to the distribution of suggested school-leaving ages. It is difficult, however, to bring the two sets of answers precisely into line, for the second question evoked a significantly higher proportion of noncommittal answers; in each group there was a minority who firmly refused to express any preference, asserting that they would never do anything to impede their children's free choice of occupation. There is some reason to believe that this attitude—which, incidentally, seems to be rather more prevalent among the non-manual groups—cannot always be taken at its face value, as a declaration of intention; that it is something of a stereotyped response, which may not reflect the actual practice of those concerned. Even to favour the extension of one's children's education to any point beyond the legal minimum is, by implication, to push the desired range of occupations above a certain minimum level and hence to restrict the lower end of choice.

Table 15

PREFERRED OCCUPATION FOR SON

	Profess. Mid. (A)	Salaried Mid. (B)	Salaried Wkg. (C)	Manual Mid. (D)	Manual Wkg. (E)
	%	%	%	%	%
Professions	60	45	35	26	22
Independent business	7	4	7	1	3
Clerical	1	2	4	5	9
Skilled trade, craft	1	11	20	31	38
Farming	2	4	5	6	3
Forces	4	5	1	6	4
Miscellaneous	1	2	1	2	3
'Free choice'	17	20	16	12	9
D.K.	7	7	11	11	9
N (=100%)	98	166	82	86	223

But it would have required more intensive and more individualized interviewing than was possible in the present survey to clarify the implications of this answer, and we have no choice but to exclude these respondents from consideration. If we confine ourselves to the aspirations of those subjects who gave a positive answer we still find very marked inter-group differences. In Group A, for example, a preference for one or other of the professions was expressed in three-fifths of all the answers given. At the other extreme, little more than one-fifth of the manual workers would have chosen an occupation of professional level for their sons; their most common preference is for some skilled trade or craft—for an occupation which stands high in the hierarchy of manual work, but which does not involve too marked a change of status.

69

Among the professional group, only 1 per cent or 2 per cent suggested as desirable occupations for their sons anything that implied a significant loss of status. Groups B and C again have an intermediate position, but differ slightly from each other. Among those whose subjective status is middle class, the professions are mentioned less frequently than in Group A, and the proportion favouring manual trades increases from 1 per cent to 11 per cent; in the self-rated working-class category, the proportion rises still further to 20 per cent, while references to the professions are correspondingly reduced from 45 per cent to 35 per cent. It is perhaps surprising that types of occupation other than these two are so infrequently suggested. Even in Groups A and C, independent business does not account for more than 7 per cent of all answers, and in other groups it is even less popular; while clerical work, which finds only a single sponsor in Group A, is still not favoured by more than 9 per cent of Group E.

It may be profitable, at this point, to reconsider the material just discussed in the light of a recent American research finding. In a discussion of the problems arising in a situation where access to culturally approved goals is restricted by the existing social structure, Robert Merton[1] remarks 'As is well known, many parents confronted with personal "failure" or limited "success" may mute their original goal-emphasis, and may defer further efforts to reach their goal, attempting to reach it vicariously through their children. . . . We have found among both Negroes and Whites that the lower the occupational level of the parents, the larger the proportion having aspirations for a professional career for their children.' Merton does not present any statistics but it is evident that his findings and our own fall in exactly opposite directions. The most plausible explanation of this difference would be in terms of cultural variations between the two countries. As Merton points out, '. . . Societies do differ in the degree to which the folkways, mores and institutional controls are effectively integrated with the goals which stand high in the hierarchy of cultural values. The culture may be such as to lead individuals to centre their emotional convictions about the complex of culturally acclaimed ends, with far less emotional support for prescribed methods of reaching out for these ends.' But while 'contemporary American culture appears to approximate the polar type in which great emphasis upon certain success-goals occurs without equivalent emphasis upon institutional means', the balance, in British culture,

[1] R. K. Merton, 'Social structure and anomie', *Social Theory and Social Structure*, Free Press, 1949.

is to some extent redressed. Success-goals are rather less heavily and less universally emphasized, and there is a correspondingly greater stress on the institutionalized norms. We may thus reasonably expect to find, for example, that the mode of adaptation which Merton calls ritualism, which involves an abandonment or drastic scaling-down of the cultural goals together with a close adherence to the institutional norms, recurs more frequently and is, on the whole, less unfavourably regarded than in America. We might also anticipate that an inability to 'get ahead in the world' would be less likely to be interpreted as a *personal* failure, damaging to self-esteem. In brief, we should not be justified in assuming that parents of a low occupational level *necessarily* felt a compensating need to displace their unfulfilled strivings on to their children. And, as a corollary, we might expect to find that within a group of relatively low status, high aspirations for their children were voiced more often among those who did have a sense of personal dissatisfaction than among the others.

Two questions which were put to our subjects may provide a very rough indication of job-dissatisfaction; these were: 'Is the job you are now doing the kind of work you originally wanted to do?' and 'Do you feel that your present job gives you a fair chance to make use of your abilities?' Replies are summarized in Tables 16 and 17, and show clear but by no means dramatic inter-group differences. The claim to be doing the work of their choice is most common among those of Group A (68 per cent) and least frequent in Group E (50 per cent); the second largest percentage difference is between the two groups of manual workers. We do not find—as we might well expect to find if Merton's analysis were immediately applicable to British society—even as many as half our manual workers reporting frustrated ambitions. Similarly, although none of the other groups in answer to the second question shows the same level of satisfaction as the professional and executive group, nine out of ten of whose members believe that their work gives them a reasonable chance to utilize their abilities, we do find the same view expressed by seven out of ten in both groups of manual workers. But our principal task is to examine the relationship between aspirations for children and work satisfaction. This can be done by dividing the manual workers into two groups, irrespective of subjective status— those who would prefer a non-manual occupation for their children, and the rest—and comparing them in respect of the two available indices. As Table 18 shows, both types of dissatisfaction are found almost twice as frequently in the group with high aspirations for its sons as in the

71

group which does not aim above the level of manual work; the evidence for the projection of thwarted ambitions seems clear.

Table 16

DOES PRESENT WORK REPRESENT SUBJECT'S ORIGINAL CHOICE?

		Doing job originally wished %	Not doing job originally wished %	'D.K.' %	N (=100%)
Profess.	Mid. (A)	68	30	2	118
Salaried	Mid. (B)	62	35	3	186
Salaried	Wkg. (C)	59	38	3	99
Manual	Mid. (D)	65	35	—	103
Manual	Wkg. (E)	50	48	2	284

Table 17

DOES PRESENT WORK PROVIDE AN OPPORTUNITY TO USE ABILITIES?

		Reasonable chance to use abilities %	Not reasonable chance to use abilities %	'D.K.' %	N (=100%)
Profess.	Mid. (A)	90	9	1	118
Salaried	Mid. (B)	78	20	2	186
Salaried	Wkg. (C)	75	24	1	100
Manual	Mid. (D)	69	25	6	101
Manual	Wkg. (E)	69	27	4	284

Table 18

MANUAL WORKERS' PREFERRED OCCUPATIONS FOR SONS, IN RELATION TO EXPRESSED DISSATISFACTION

	Not doing job originally wished %	Not able to use abilities %	N (=100%)
Manual workers preferring professional, business, or clerical work for son	63	36	103
Other manual workers	35	19	206

A comparison of the reasons brought forward in support of their specific occupational aspirations for their children reveals fairly typical differences between the groups. Monetary attractions are mentioned most frequently by the working-class groups (27 per cent and 29 per cent) and least often by Group A (13 per cent). The two other middle-class groups (salaried and manual respectively) occupy an intermediate position, with 21 per cent and 20 per cent referring to income as the principal advantage; the difference between these and the working-class groups of equivalent occupational status are suggestive, though too small to be statistically significant. In the same way, stability of employment or security of tenure is mentioned by 14 per cent of the manual workers in explanation of their choice, but by only 5 per cent of the professional group. On the other hand, 22 per cent of the professional group explain their preferences in terms of the intrinsically interesting or satisfying features of the work, as against 5 per cent and 9 per cent of the working-class groups and 7 per cent of the middle-class manual workers, while 15 per cent of the professional group, in comparison with 3 per cent and 5 per cent of the manual workers, are most concerned to see their sons continue a family tradition in their work. Answers which justify a particular occupational choice in terms of social usefulness are given by 15 per cent of Group B, compared with 12 per cent of the middle-class manual workers and 7 per cent or 8 per cent of the other groups. It is very doubtful, however, whether these differences are sufficiently large to justify more than casual speculation. Other answers are distributed fairly evenly; the status or prestige of an occupation does not receive explicit mention by more than about 5 per cent of each group, while about 15 per cent explain that the occupations that they have suggested represent the personal choice of their children, or that their children have at least displayed a marked aptitude for such work.

Table 19

OCCUPATIONAL ADVANTAGES (SON)

	Profess. Mid. (A)	Salaried Mid. (B)	Wkg. (C)	Manual Mid. (D)	Wkg. (E)
	%	%	%	%	%
Interest, Satisfaction	22	16	5	7	9
Social usefulness	8	15	8	12	7
Family tradition	15	10	8	3	5
Status	5	4	5	6	4
Security, Stability	5	8	10	14	14
Choice, Aptitude	17	11	15	14	14
Income	13	21	27	20	29
Miscellaneous	12	9	15	18	11
D.K.	3	6	5	6	7
N (=100%)	74	122	60	66	181

Sharply contrasted attitudes are indicated by the answers to the question: 'What things help a man to move up in the world?' The prevalence of the ideology of self-help among the non-manual groups is illustrated in Table 20. Hard work and strength of character are men-

73

tioned by 41 per cent of Group A, ambition and the desire to succeed by 12 per cent, personality by 20 per cent, and intelligence by 27 per cent; the corresponding proportions of Group E are 28 per cent; 6 per cent; 10 per cent and 17 per cent. Under most of these headings the three intermediate groups come very close together, with a rather wider gap on either side. The references to personality need a word of explanation, as the word was not used in the comprehensive sense usual in psychological literature. In this context, it denotes certain easily perceptible, though not necessarily superficial, features of the individual's make-up— the capacity to make a good immediate impression, to adapt quickly to different people, to convey a sense of warmth and acceptability. As part of the vocabulary of social mobility, it probably belongs essentially to the middle decades of the twentieth century, and its use here is reminiscent of Riesman's recent emphasis on the growth of 'other-direction' in the urban middle classes.[1]

Table 20

FACTORS ASSOCIATED WITH MOBILITY

	Profess. Mid. (A) %	Salaried Mid. (B) %	Salaried Wkg. (C) %	Manual Mid. (D) %	Manual Wkg. (E) %
Education; training	22	32	33	33	43
Hard work; character	41	37	36	35	28
Self-confidence	3	8	3	4	6
Influence; contacts	8	12	4	5	16
Ambition	12	9	6	8	6
Money	5	4	5	5	12
Personality	20	18	19	14	10
Sociability	4	3	6	1	4
Ability: intelligence	27	22	15	12	17
Politeness	4	2	2	1	1
Good upbringing	5	3	4	5	3
Luck	4	9	8	4	3
Miscellaneous	5	8	8	12	7
Don't know	2	2	6	5	5
N (=100%)	133	210	108	111	300

(Percentages add to more than 100, as most subjects gave more than one answer.)

The reduced emphasis in the lower status groups on psychological characteristics is balanced by a higher respect for the role of education and training; these factors are mentioned by 43 per cent of Group E, as against 22 per cent in Group A, and 33 per cent in all other groups. The only other factors which are mentioned more frequently in Group E

[1] See D. Riesman et al., The Lonely Crowd, Yale University Press, 1950.

than elsewhere are 'influence' (16 per cent) and money (12 per cent). References to the latter do not exceed 5 per cent in any other group, but belief in the importance of influence varies somewhat; it is mentioned by 4 per cent of the salaried middle-class group, by 8 per cent of the professional group and only 4 per cent and 5 per cent of Groups C and D respectively. Other items than these are mentioned very rarely, and the differences are never significant.

Some of the findings reported in this chapter merit further research, and it is hoped that two problems, in particular, will receive attention in the near future. Further studies of the evaluation of occupations are clearly required; these might be designed so as to clarify the relationship between rank-ordering and social class rating, and might well be supplemented by a direct attempt to assess the criteria upon which such judgements are based. For while the prestige ranking of occupations seems scarcely to be affected by the occupational status of the ranker, it is evident that opinions as to the occupational composition of social classes are deeply and consistently influenced by both the accorded and the subjective status of the respondent. The related problem of educational and occupational aspiration levels is being studied in some detail in a separate inquiry into educational selection and social mobility; it has been possible, in the population selected for study, to relate the stated ambitions of parents to other socio-cultural data.[1] The relationship between such aspirations and the eventual achievement of the children concerned is also being studied, and will be described fully in a forthcoming volume.[2]

[1] An analysis of material derived from this part of the inquiry is given in Chapter VII of the present volume.
[2] It may be useful to provide a brief note on the bearing of this study on the findings reported by Centers in *The Psychology of Social Classes* (Princeton University Press, 1949).
Directly relevant to the present inquiry is Centers's treatment of class identification or subjective status. Centers regards this as the best estimate of a person's class, in spite of the fact that when objective stratification position is partialled out, most of the correlations involving class identification shrink to very small magnitudes. We have proceeded on the assumption that although subjective status may be a useful variable, a group composed of individuals who in fact occupy very different positions on the social scale cannot reasonably be regarded as homogeneous simply because all describe themselves as belonging to the middle class. We have therefore tried throughout to hold occupational status constant, in order to ascertain the independent influence of subjective identification. Centers also makes no attempt to investigate the meaning of his subjects' statements about class membership. Our own findings show clearly that conceptions of the nature and range of the class to which the subject allocates himself vary systematically with the subject's occupational level.

PART II

IV

A Description of a Sample Inquiry into Social Mobility in Great Britain

D. V. GLASS AND J. R. HALL

Introduction

I T was explained in Chapter II that the study of the social prestige of occupations reported there was undertaken to provide a grouping which might be used in a new investigation of social mobility in Britain. The purpose of the present chapter is to give an account of the nature of that investigation. The results are not given here; they are analysed and interpreted in other chapters which deal with specific aspects of the question of social mobility.[1] But before presenting those results it is necessary to show from what kind of inquiry they derive.

When the programme of research into social selection and differentiation was first drawn up, it was clear that most of that programme would demand new empirical studies. This was particularly the case as regards the direct measurement of social mobility and of its trend during the past two or three generations. There had been a few pioneer studies.[2] But there had not previously been in Britain—or, for that matter, in any

---

[1] See Part IV.
[2] The pioneer studies in Britain are those by Professor M. Ginsberg, 'Interchange between social classes', *Economic Journal*, December 1929; and D. Caradog Jones, ed. *The Social Survey of Merseyside*, Vol. 2, ch. 4, London, 1934. The former was not based upon a representative sample, and the latter related exclusively to Liverpool and was confined to the study of sons still living with their fathers and thus rather young. Neither inquiry dealt with the problem of the difference between individual and communal movement. It may be added, however, that very few other studies have considered that problem, perhaps the most interesting being N. Rogoff, 'Recent trends in urban occupational mobility', in P. K. Hatt and A. J. Reiss, Jnr., eds. *Reader in Urban Sociology*, Glencoe, Illinois, 1951, pp. 406–420; N. Rogoff, 'Les recherches américaines sur la mobilité sociale', *Population*, October–December 1950. See also T. Geiger, *Soziale Umschichtungen in einer Dänischen Mittelstadt*, Copenhagen, 1951.

other country—a systematic inquiry so designed that the results could be regarded as giving a valid description of the position in the community as a whole. A valid, generalized description was, however, essential, not only for itself, but also as a background for more detailed studies of particular sections of the social structure. Hence, having arrived at a fairly useful prestige grouping of occupations, the next main task was to carry out an investigation planned to show the amount and direction of social mobility in the community as a whole. A sample investigation, involving interviews, was the only effective way to obtain the information required. The practical task was thus twofold: to prepare a suitable questionnaire and to construct a suitable sampling design. Each of these questions is discussed in some detail below. But before moving to that discussion, it is only proper that full acknowledgement be made to the governmental organizations which made it possible for the inquiry to be carried out. Through the Inter-Departmental Committee on Economic and Social Research, and with the sponsorship of the Ministry of Labour, it was possible to make use of the services of the Government Social Survey. The latter organization gave considerable help in the preparation of the final interview schedule, designed the sample, and, through its interviewers, most successfully carried through the field work. Without the collaboration of the Government Social Survey it would have been extremely difficult to undertake a national inquiry based upon a stratified random sample, the only practical form of sampling satisfactory for the purpose of the research.

The Questionnaire

The questions contained in the interview schedule are reproduced in Appendix 1. As the schedule was intended for use by professional interviewers, it contains many abbreviations, the meaning of which may not be immediately apparent. In the present discussion, therefore, it is simpler to list the various types of questions under a number of main headings.

To begin with, it should be noted that the questionnaire was directed to 'adults' (men or women), defined, because of the way in which the sample was drawn, as persons aged 18 years or over. The individuals actually drawn in the sample will be referred to as the 'subjects', and they were asked to give certain information concerning themselves and their parents. When the subject was married, widowed or divorced, questions were asked concerning the spouse, children and father-in-law. In addition, if the subject was a married, widowed or divorced man, he was asked to give certain information concerning each of his brothers. The full list of questions is rather extensive, for the inquiry was designed as a multi-purpose one. In the first place, the Ministry of Labour, which took part in the inquiry, was interested in various aspects of industrial and occupational mobility. Secondly, our own inquiry into social mobility covered the interests of two associated research groups at the London School of Economics, one of which was concerned with fertility differences between social status categories and with relationships between fertility and social mobility. The final questionnaire represents a compromise in the sense that, in order to avoid an impossibly long interview, many relevant but secondary questions had to be omitted. The questions actually asked are considered below under five heads.

I. General Classification Questions. Each subject drawn in the sample was asked:

1. Year of birth.
2. Place of birth.
3. Sex.
4. Marital condition (single, married, widowed, etc.). If the subject was married or widowed (or divorced) he or she was asked:
5. Whether married more than once.
6. Year of last (or present) marriage.
7. Number of children born alive to last (or present) marriage. If the subject had children, the following additional questions were asked:
8. Sex of first-born and last-born.
9. Year of birth of first-born and last-born.
10. Year of death of first-born and last-born, if either or both had died.

The year of birth of the subject was asked so that the sample might be divided into birth cohorts, and the information thus used to give an indication of changes over time—that is, over generations of birth. This division has been applied throughout to the fertility data, to the information on education and employment, and also on the status of the subject's father, obtained from the subsequent questions. The data on first- and last-born children were intended to be used, in combination with corresponding material on education and employment, for a study of the relative influence on social mobility of position within family.

II. Education. The following information was obtained for the subject, the subject's husband or wife, and the first- and last-born children of the subject:

1. Type of primary school.
2. Type of secondary school.

3. Method of obtaining secondary education—free or fee payer.
4. Examinations passed at secondary stage—school certificate, higher school certificate, university scholarship.
5. Further education—full-time, part-time or none.
6. Type of further education—commercial, technical, teacher-training, university, other.
7. Whether education had been completed by the time of interview.
8. Qualifications or degrees obtained—university, professional, miscellaneous.

The questions on education make it possible, when the sample is classified by date of birth, to give an historical survey of the accessibility of primary, secondary and further education to the population as a whole, to show the differences in accessibility as between males and females and, in conjunction with the subsequent data on the occupation of the subject's father, as between the different social strata. Many other cross-tabulations are also possible, and some of them will be referred to later.

It should be explained that in obtaining the information on secondary education it was necessary to take into account the fact that whereas the subjects would have gone through the pre-World War II educational system, some of their children would be enrolled in a system modified by the 1944 Act. The categories used in coding this information obtained through the sample survey reflect these changes in the structure of State education. Thus secondary education has been classified as Secondary Day A, Secondary Day B, and Secondary Boarding. Secondary Day A covers normal post-primary education up to the age of 15 at present, and mainly up to 13 or 14 in the past. It includes the secondary modern and secondary technical schools under the post-war system. But for subjects who went through the older system, it covers the senior departments of elementary schools, the central schools (administered under the elementary code) which admitted pupils on a selective basis, and the junior technical schools, admission to which was also selective. The category Secondary Day B covers subjects who had attended grammar schools and also those who had been day pupils at the independent public schools, while the Secondary Boarding category covers subjects who had been boarders at public, private or grammar schools. The distinction between the Secondary Day B and Boarding categories is primarily one of educational costs. Nevertheless it is very largely also a distinction of social prestige within the field of education, for such of the subjects who went to the major public schools are almost exclusively

82

entered under Secondary Boarding, and few who had been to other types of boarding school would be found in that category.

III. Occupation. Questions on occupation were asked in respect of the subject, his or her first- and last-born children, the subject's wife (or husband), the subject's father and the father-in-law. The questions were:

1. Precise description of occupation (e.g. if a clerk, what type of clerk).
2. Industry, trade or profession.
3. Position, rank or grade in employment (e.g. foreman, manager, etc.).
4. Whether paid weekly or less frequently (that is, distinguishing between wage-earning and salaried).
5. Whether employer, self-employed, or employee.
6. If in control of others, numbers controlled.
7. If operative, whether skilled, semi-skilled or unskilled.

The overlapping in the questions results from the fact that two different types of occupational classification were involved—one customarily used by the Government Social Survey, and the other the sevenfold classification derived from the previous study of the social prestige of occupations. For the latter classification it was desired to obtain as precise as possible a description of the position of the person concerned in the occupation in which he was engaged. In practice, it was found that information on the degree of skill in operative employment was often inconsistent with information given elsewhere in the schedule. Hence for this part of the classification it was necessary to depend upon the answers to preceding questions and to information concerning formal apprenticeship, as recorded in the later part of the questionnaire.

The point of time to which the occupational data refer varies with the individual in respect of whom the question was asked. For the subject and his children, the questions refer to the time of interview—or, if the person concerned was unemployed, retired or dead, to the last main occupation. In the case of a married woman, the occupation at the time of marriage was requested, though in allocating women to social status categories the occupation of their husband or father was used. This was done because, with the still limited employment opportunities for women—that is, especially in professional and administrative rôles—occupation is not a satisfactory index of social status for women in our society. For the father and father-in-law of the subject, the last main occupation was asked. The subject was also asked certain supplementary questions on occupation, which will be referred to later.

The information on occupation, translated into status categories, was basic to the inquiry into social mobility. Coupled with the answers given to other questions on the schedule, a very wide range of relevant tabulations was made possible, bearing upon such questions as inter-marriage; fertility differences between status categories (and by educational difference within a given status category); and many tabulations concerned with the influence of parental social status on the education of subjects, as well as with the relation between the education and the ultimate social status of the subjects themselves.

IV. Additional information obtained if the subject was a married or widowed (or divorced) man. The subject in question was asked to state the total number of brothers he had (or had had) and, for each brother, to tell the interviewer:

1. Year of birth.
2. Year of marriage.
3. Marital condition at the time of interview.
4. Year of death.
5. Year of wife's death.
6. Occupation at the time of interview (at death, if dead; or at wife's death if wife died before him).
7. Number of live-born children.

The questions in this section were designed to deal with a particular aspect of the relation between fertility and social mobility—in this case, the analysis of mobility with reference to the size of family from which the subject came, as well as according to his social origins. The results may also be used for a more detailed study of the importance of position in family and for examining the mobility of families as units, in contrast to the more customary study of the movement of individuals.

V. Occupational changes during the subject's lifetime. Each subject was asked the following questions in respect of the first job he had held, and also for every remembered change in occupation, grade within occupation, industry or town in which he was employed:

1. The place of work.
2. Occupation and grade within it.
3. Industry.
4. Method of entering occupation.
5. Reasons for entering occupation.
6. Age at entry into occupation.
7. Age on leaving occupation.
8. Whether any systematic training for occupation had been received.

These questions aimed primarily to provide information for the Ministry of Labour. But the answers are also of direct use for the study of social mobility. The information on job changes (after translation into the sevenfold prestige classification) makes it possible to construct 'profiles' of the social status of each subject during his lifetime. This is of interest in itself, and it is also of special value in comparing the achievements of two generations, one of which is old enough to have experienced its full chances of social promotion, while the other is still young enough for further movement. In this respect, occupational profiles, describing the status of subjects at the ages of 20, 25, 30, 35 and 40 years, are equivalent in the study of social mobility to the use of segmental analysis (involving the date of birth of each child born) in the study of fertility.

It would, of course, be too much to hope for perfection in a new questionnaire of the kind discussed. Inevitably there were omissions, in spite of repeated scrutiny. And the need to meet the minimum requirements of three organizations meant that the interests of each had to some extent to suffer. Had the schedule been designed solely to clarify the relationship between social mobility and fertility, for example, the questions on family size would have undoubtedly asked for the date of birth of each child. If social mobility alone were the focus of the investigation, it would have been useful to ask for the occupations of the maternal and paternal grandfathers of the subject, in order both to extend the time scale of the study and to throw some light on what may be regarded as 'crucial' status categories—categories not necessarily high in the status scale but nevertheless of more than average importance in facilitating upward movement in the next generation. It would also have been of interest to deal separately with, and to ask additional questions of, those subjects born in rural areas—to see when and why they moved to cities, and at which points in the social hierarchy they entered the urban framework. But in spite of these limitations, it is clear that the questionnaire actually used covers many questions not previously studied in Britain, and makes possible an extensive study of the complex problem of social mobility.

The Sample

Because the Ministry of Labour sponsored the inquiry, and was itself directly interested in certain sections of the questionnaire, the Social Survey undertook the whole of the field work involved. The sampling design, too, was of the type normally used by the Social Survey for its national investigations—a two-stage, stratified random sample of persons aged 18 years and over, drawn in June and August 1949, from the 'live' cards maintained in the various local offices of the National Registration system.[1]

A sample of this kind is not ideal for the purpose of studying social mobility. The difficulty with such a random sample is that persons in the higher status categories, being selected in proportion to their presence in the population, are bound to constitute small numbers. The whole set of so-called 'middle-class' categories, covering the range from clerical to administrative and professional groups, will comprise only about a third of the adult population. The analysis of the data for these higher prestige groups is thus necessarily limited. Had cost been unimportant, a more efficient sample could have been constructed, in which the number of persons was the same in each status category, that number being determined by the requirements of the full statistical analysis to which the material was to be subjected. But such a sample would have been extremely expensive. Since the National Registration cards gave no indication of social status, it would have been necessary to begin with a much larger screening sample than that ultimately required, the final sampling fraction being determined after persons originally drawn had been asked for information on their occupation and perhaps also on other characteristics. This was impracticable. Failing this, and bearing in mind the need to have results which would give a valid description of the British community as a whole, the Social Survey sample was the best alternative.

The sample constructed was one of 10,000 adult civilians aged 18 years and over, living in England, Wales and Scotland. Those to be interviewed were selected from the local files of the National Register, which gave the current address, age or date of birth, nationality and National Registration number of the population of Great Britain and the Isle of Man.[2] A two-stage stratified random sample design was used. The first-stage units were local government administrative districts. These were stratified by civil defence regions (of which one was Greater London, discussed separately below), and within each region by urban and rural districts. The urban districts of each region were listed in descending order of their population, and districts of over 140,000 population were allocated a proportion of the 10,000 interviews according to the overall sampling fraction in relation to their population. Some

---

[1] For a more detailed description of the sampling techniques employed by the Social Survey, see P. G. Gray and T. Corlett, 'Sampling for the Social Survey' *J.R.S.S.*, Vol. CXIII, Part 2, 1950.

[2] Identity cards, the basis of the continuous National Register, have since been given up. An extremely valuable sampling frame has thereby been lost.

23 per cent of the sample, therefore, consisted of a single-stage stratified random sample of the populations of large towns.

The urban areas of less than 140,000 were listed in descending order of their population and grouped in strata according to their population size. Each stratum was then allocated a number of interviews proportional to the total population in the stratum. For reasons of cost and administration it is convenient to have some thirty interviews in each district. Accordingly, a number of districts were selected at random from each stratum, the number selected being dependent upon the number of interviews allocated to the stratum. The districts having been selected, a systematic sample was taken within each district by drawing cards at constant intervals throughout the register. The sample from rural areas was selected in exactly the same fashion as described in the preceding paragraph.

A slightly different procedure was adopted in the treatment of Greater London. The number of interviews allocated to this area was divided between three special regions of approximately equal populations. Districts within each special region were then arranged according to rateable value per head of the population, this range then being divided into strata of approximately equal population size. Districts in which the interviewing was to be undertaken were then selected at random from each stratum, the list of persons being obtained by systematic sampling within each district.

Interview Results

Interviewing of the persons drawn in the sample took place in June and August 1949. It is not usually possible to find every person drawn in a sample, and it is therefore not surprising that completed interviews were obtained for 9,296 persons, instead of the 10,000 originally aimed at for Great Britain. Indeed, a response rate of 93 per cent is unusually high for inquiries of this kind; save in special circumstances, the response rate for a random sample investigation rarely runs above about 85 per cent. It is, however, necessary to look rather more closely at the make-up of the 9,296 completed interviews.

The practice of the Social Survey, at the time the investigation into social mobility was being undertaken, was to aim at completing interviews for the whole of the original sample but also to allow substitutions for those persons who could not be found or would not co-operate. The substitutes were drawn by a process of sampling exactly the same as that by which the original sample was obtained. But this is not necessarily the most satisfactory procedure, for there is no guarantee that the substitutes will co-operate or that, if they do, they will constitute effective replacements for the individuals missed on the first round.[1] This is more especially so of substitutes for refusals; there is no doubt a larger element of chance in the occurrence of no-contacts, in which case substitution may provide equivalent individuals.

For the original 10,000 sample for Great Britain, 7,751 completed interviews were obtained, the balance consisting of 341 refusals and 1,908 no-contacts, a total of 2,249 missing. Substitutes were then selected, and a further 1,545 interviews completed. For the balance of 704 substitutes the questionnaires could not be filled, either because the individuals could not be found, or because they refused to answer the questions. At the end of the interviewing, there were only 704 persons in respect of whom the required information had not been collected. But because substitutes had been used, the figure of 93 per cent, mentioned above, cannot be taken as measuring the response to the investigation. The true response must have been lower than that. At the same time it is very probably higher than 77·5 per cent—the substitutes must have been effective replacements for some of the original no-contacts.

Some evidence in support of this last statement may be found by comparing, for a series of characteristics, the individuals in the original sample for whom completed questionnaires were obtained with the substitutes who were successfully interviewed. This has been done for the England and Wales sample, comprising 6,914 original and 1,357 substitute interviews, a total of 8,271. No significant differences were found between substitutes and originals with regard to age or marital status, status category of subject's father (either for male or female subjects), or of subject. The differences in primary and secondary education were not significant for males, but they were statistically highly significant[2] for females, suggesting that the females in the substitute group may have been drawn from slightly higher status occupations within the given status categories, or that the aspirations of their parents were slightly more 'middle class' in character than those of the parents of the original sample. The evidence is very limited, however, and does not lead to any greater precision in estimating the true, final response rate. And the analysis of the original and substitute cases does

[1] See D. V. Glass and E. Grebenik, 'The Family Census: a preliminary report', *Reports and Selected Papers of the Statistics Committee* (Papers of the Royal Commission on Population, London, 1950, p. 89).

[2] Significance at the 1 per cent level is referred to as 'highly significant', and at the 5 per cent level as 'significant'.

not in itself indicate whether the results of the final, composite sample accurately reflect the position for the country as a whole.

It is, of course, obvious that when a sample inquiry is undertaken to collect information not otherwise available, not a great deal can be done to compare the new results with independent data which might serve as external measures of reliability. This is the case for most of the information collected by the sample investigation described here. There is a good measure of agreement between the sample estimates, presented in the following chapter, of the proportions of elementary school pupils who proceeded to secondary schools and such estimates as can be derived from official statistics. But the latter estimates have a margin of indeterminacy, so that the comparison is somewhat loose.[1] There is also extremely good agreement between the sample averages of size of completed families for broad social status groups and the comparable averages given by the Family Census of 1946.[2] But for the rest, direct national comparison is practicable only for age and marital composition, and the relevant data are given below. The discussion refers only to the results for England and Wales, estimates of age and marital composition in combination not being published for Scotland.[3]

1. *Age Composition*

The comparison here is between the sample results, relating to a point of time just past mid-year 1949, and the Registrar-General's estimate for 31 December 1949. This estimate was chosen, rather than the mid-year estimate, because the year-of-birth classification of the sample would thereby fully agree with that of the Registrar-General. The selection of the December estimate also meant, however, that the sample no longer referred to a population aged 18 years or more, but one aged 18½ years or over, and interpolations had accordingly to be made in the Registrar-General's estimates, no doubt increasing the margin of error. It should

[1] Life-table calculations, based on the not fully satisfactory annual statistics of the Board of Education for the years 1931–8, suggest that the probability of an ex-elementary schoolboy reaching a secondary school was between about 13·5 per cent and about 17·9 per cent, the difference depending upon the definitions of 'ex-elementary schoolboy' and 'secondary school'. Allowing for the margin of error in these calculations, the results agree fairly well with the finding of the present investigation, namely that of elementary schoolboys born in the period 1920–9, some 16·2 per cent obtained secondary education.

[2] See D. V. Glass and E. Grebenik in the forthcoming *Final Report on the Family Census*, Chapter 6.

[3] The question of bias is, however, further discussed in the main chapters on social mobility.

also be noted that whereas the sample excludes both the armed forces and the merchant navy, the Registrar-General's estimates excludes only the former.

Table 1

AGE DISTRIBUTION OF SAMPLE

Age (Years)	Nos. in Sample	Males Nos. if Sample had same distribution as R.G.'s estimate end 1949	Nos. in Sample	Females Nos. if Sample had same distribution as R.G.'s estimate end 1949
18½–19	59	89	135	108
20–29	800	796	1019	841
30–39	800	809	971	833
40–49	776	821	874	856
50–59	556	610	646	721
60 and over	712	760	923	1027

The χ^2 test indicates that the differences between the sample results and the official estimates are highly significant statistically. There are too few men and women aged 18½ and under 20 years in the sample. There are also too many women aged 20 and under 40 years and too few in the 50 years and over group. Altogether, there are too many women in the sample. These differences result from a combination of factors. For the youngest age group the problem arises partly in interviewing, for it is especially difficult to contact young, unmarried people. But it is not unlikely that the National Registration files were in error. It is known that a few of the persons drawn in the sample were less than 18 years of age and, since the age of 18 was the transition age in the registration system, errors in the other direction are not inconceivable. For the other discrepancies the problems of making contact must be the primary explanation. Women are more likely to be at home than men, and women aged 20 to 40 years are, because they tend to have young children, more likely to be found at home than older women.

2. Age and Marital Composition

The only relevant material available for comparison is the Registrar-General's provisional estimate for mid-year 1949, and this estimate is given in the table on the opposite page, subjects born after 1930 being omitted.

A number of highly significant differences are apparent, differences which to some extent illustrate the problem of interviewing in a random sample inquiry. Both single men and women are under-represented in the sample, reflecting the difficulty of contacting them,[1] while married women aged 20 to 40 are over-represented, there being a greater likelihood of interviewing women with young children.

Table 2

AGE AND MARITAL STATUS IN THE SAMPLE

MALES

	Single		Married, Widowed or Divorced	
Age (Years)	Nos. in Sample	Nos. if R.G.'s distribution applied	Nos. in Sample	Nos. if R.G.'s distribution applied
20–29	397	462	403	352
30–39	100	113	700	664
40–49	62	69	714	705
50–59	37	47	519	522
60 and over	53	62	659	648
	FEMALES			
20–29	356	328	663	557
30–39	100	129	871	734
40–49	111	145	763	741
50–59	104	114	542	629
60 and over	146	165	777	891

To conclude the discussion, the following points may be made. Because of the use of substitutes in the sample investigation, the true response rate cannot be calculated, though it must lie between the limits of 77·5 per cent and 93 per cent. Whatever the actual figure may be, it is clear that there is some bias in the age and marital composition of the final sample as compared with the official estimates, but whether that bias is likely seriously to affect the analysis is doubtful. In the first place, the analysis reported in the subsequent chapters largely ignores the age group of under 20 years because of the small numbers. This removes one important contribution to the bias. Secondly, the analysis is carried out in terms of birth (or age) cohorts. The overweighting of certain age groups at the expense of others does not, therefore, influence the results of the various calculations undertaken. There still remains the question of bias within age groups—for example, the under-representation of the unmarried in a given age group. With a very large sample, this source of bias might have been largely removed by reweighting within age

[1] It should, however, be added that errors in marital status classification are also a possibility in the sample results. The R.G.'s estimates are based upon official statistics of marriages and dissolutions. In a sample investigation, however, it is not unlikely that some women will describe themselves as married even though they may be single or divorced. In so far as this is the case, the 'genuine' error in the sample results will be correspondingly reduced.

groups.[1] But with the relatively small numbers in the present sample, the effects of such a process would be slight. At the same time, the actual method of analysis adopted may provide a partial correction by removing one possible contribution to this bias. It is almost always found in voluntary sample investigations that the response rate is lower for the 'middle class' than for the 'working class' groups. Since age at marriage is higher for the 'middle-class' groups, their under-representation may be associated with, and contribute to, the bias against the unmarried in the younger age groups. And in so far as this is true, the analysis of the sample results by status category and birth cohort—and this is the basic form of analysis used in studying the degree and direction of social mobility—would tend to counteract this type of bias. In sum, therefore, though the sample is by no means perfect, the bias involved is not likely to be crucial and is to a substantial extent counteracted by the method of analysis. Certainly the results for two important characteristics— fertility and attainment of secondary education—do not appear to have been affected to any considerable extent.

The Status Composition of the Sample

Details of the composition of the sample are given in subsequent chapters—especially in Chapter V and in Part III—in connection with the various analyses carried out. It may nevertheless be of interest to show, in summary form, the percentage distribution of male subjects in Great Britain by status categories—using the sevenfold classification discussed in Chapter II—and by date of birth. The results are presented in Table 3, a brief description of the separate categories being given below for reference.

1. Professional and high administrative.

2. Managerial and executive.

3. Inspectional, supervisory and other non-manual (higher grade).

4. Inspectional, supervisory and other non-manual (lower grade).

5. Skilled manual and routine grades of non-manual.

6. Semi-skilled manual.

7. Unskilled manual.

---

[1] E.g. by a process of random rejection or duplication of punched cards for given age groups. This was done in the Indianapolis inquiry into family planning. It was also applied to the Family Census cards to compensate for local variations in the response to the investigation.

A discussion of these distributions, and a comparison of the results of the sample inquiry with those of the 1951 census will be found in Chapter VIII.

Table 3

GREAT BRITAIN: MALE SUBJECTS CLASSIFIED BY PRESENT SOCIAL STATUS (PERCENTAGES)

Date of Birth of Subjects	Social Status Categories of Subjects							
	1	2	3	4	5	6	7	Total
Before 1890	4·3	3·5	9·3	13·1	35·8	16·1	17·9	100·0
1890–99	3·1	5·7	12·1	13·4	35·4	16·3	14·0	100·0
1900–09	2·8	6·7	11·0	15·2	37·5	16·2	10·6	100.0
1910–19	2·6	4·2	10·6	14·5	42·0	15·2	10·9	100·0
1920–29	2·1	2·6	6·3	7·4	53·2	18·6	9·8	100·0
All dates	2·9	4·5	9·8	12·7	41·2	16·5	12·4	100·0

APPENDIX 1

As the questionnaire used in the sample investigation discussed in Chapter IV provided the data from which Chapters V, VIII, IX, X and XII derive, it is desirable to show the full list of questions covered. Accordingly the list is reproduced below. In essence this list is the equivalent of the original questionnaire, the contents of which are Crown Copyright. A few minor modifications have been made—either spelling out in full certain abbreviations which would not be immediately clear, or altering the layout in order to facilitate reproduction in the present volume. The original questionnaire was in mimeographed form, on foolscap-size sheets.

EDUCATION AND EMPLOYMENT INQUIRY

Subject
- (i) Year of birth ....
- (ii) Birthplace ....
- (iii) *Sex:* Male ....
  - Female ....
- (iv) *Status:* Single ....
  - Married ....
  - Widowed, etc. ....

IF MARRIED OR WIDOWED ASK (v) ONWARDS
- (v) *Married before:* Yes ....
  - No ....
- (vi) Year of last marriage.............
- (vii) No. of children born alive (last marriage) ....

IF CHILDREN, ASK (viii) ONWARDS

	1st born	*Last born*
(viii) *Sex:* Male	....	
Female		....
(ix) Year born	....	
(x) Year died	....	

(sideways, left) Questions 2 (a) to (g) to be completed for subject's father and for father of husband or wife of subject.

1. EDUCATION

(a) *Schools attended* (i) Elementary or primary / Private or prep.
  (ii) Secondary Day—A / Secondary Day—B / Secondary Boarding / No secondary education

(b) *If Elementary to Secondary*
  Free/spec. place in secondary
  Not free or special place

(c) *Exams passed* (i) School Cert. passed / School Cert. failed / School Cert. not sat
  (ii) HSC/Univ. Schol. gained / HSC/Univ. Schol. failed / HSC/Univ. Schol. not sat

(d) *Further Education* (i) None / Full-time / Part-time
  (ii) None / Commercial / Technical / Teachers Training (Non-Univ.) / University / Other

(e) *Education complete?*
  (i.e. no intention of obtaining further education)
  Yes
  No

(f) *Qualifications, Degrees*
  None
  University
  Professional
  Miscellaneous

2. OCCUPATION

(a) Precise Occupation

(b) Industry/Trade/Profession

(c) Position/Rank/Grade

(d) *Paid weekly?* Yes / No

(e) *If Operative* Skilled / Semi-skilled / Unskilled

(f) *Employee/Employer?* Employee / Employer / Self-employed

(g) If in control of others (direct or indirect) state numbers controlled

(sideways, right) Questions 1 (a) to 2 (g) to be completed for subject, wife or husband of subject, and first-born and last-born children of subject.

94

3. OCCUPATIONS, INDUSTRIES, CHANGES OF TOWN

(a) Where did you first start work?

(b) What was your first occupation (job)?
    (i) Town/district
    (ii) County
    (iii) Occupation and grade
    (iv) Industry
    (v) Method of entering occupation
    (vi) Reasons for entering
    (vii) Age entered
    (viii) Reasons for leaving
    (ix) Age left
    (x) Did you have any training for the job?
        Apprenticeship/articles
        Other systematic training
        None
    (xi) Was it the job you wanted to do or not? If not, what did you want to do? If not, why did you want to do the other job?

(c) What other kinds of work have you done since then?
    Prompt in periods: Up to 1918,
    1919 to 1931
    1932 to 1939
    1940 to June 1945
    1945 to May 1949

Make an entry where subject has:
    (i) changed occupation
    (ii) changed grade.
    (iii) changed industry
    (iv) changed town

For each entry, ask:
    (i) Town/district
    (ii) County
    (iii) Occupation and grade
    (iv) Industry
    (v) Method of entering occupation
    (vi) Reasons for entering
    (vii) Age entered
    (viii) Reasons for leaving
    (ix) Age left
    (x) Did you have any training?
        Systematic training
        None

[Repeat for each change in occupation, grade, industry or town.]

TO ALL STILL IN EMPLOYMENT, ASK QUESTION 4 ONWARDS. TO THOSE NOT EMPLOYED, GO ON TO QUESTION 19

4. Has the work you have done so far fitted in with what you have wanted to do?
    Yes, completely ....
    Yes, to some extent ....
    No ....
(a) If NO or TO SOME EXTENT what would you have liked to do?
    Occupation..............................
    Industry ....
(a) (i) Why did you want to do this job?
    (ii) What stopped you from doing this job?

5. Health plays a large part in what people can do. Would you say that up to now you have had:
    Good health ....
    Moderate health ....
    Bad health ....

6. Do you suffer from any injury or incapacity which might limit the kinds of job you can do?
    Yes ....
    No ....

7. Have you been away from work through illness or injury in the last three months?
    Yes ....
    No ....
(a) If YES, how many days in Jan., Feb., and March?
    Jan. .... Feb. .... March ....
                           Total ....

CHANGES OF JOB (I.E. FIRM)

8. When did you last change your job (i.e. firm)?
    Month ....
    Year ....

IF CHANGED SINCE JAN. 1945 ASK QUESTIONS 9–18

IF NOT CHANGED SINCE JAN. 1945 GO ON TO QUESTION 19

9. How many times have you changed your job in each year since June 1945 up to May 1949?

        June '45–May '46 ....

        June '46–May '47 ....

        June '47–May '48 ....

        June '48–May '49 ....

10. Were the wages, hours and conditions in your last job good, bad, or neither good nor bad?

                    Good Bad Neither

    Wages ....

    Hours ....

    Conditions ....

11. On the whole did you like or dislike your last job?

        Liked it ....

        Disliked it ....

        Neutral ....

  (*a*) Why do you think this?

12. Exactly why did you leave your last job?

13. How did you get your present job?

        Employment exchange ....

        Appointments office ....

        Private employment agency ....

        Friend, etc. ....

        Other means ....

14. Why did you take your present job?

15. Did you expect it to be different from your last job in any way? In what way?

16. Are wages, hours and conditions good, bad or neither good nor bad in your present job?

                    Good Bad Neither

    Wages ....

    Hours ....

    Conditions ....

17. On the whole do you like it or dislike it?

        Like it ....

        Dislike it ....

        Neutral ....

  (*a*) Why do you think this?

18. Have you any ideas about changing your present job?

19. TO ALL MARRIED OR WIDOWED MEN: How many brothers have you had (alive or dead)? ....

For each brother give following details:

(a) Year of brother's birth
(b) Year of brother's marriage
(c) No. of brother's children born alive
(d) Year of brother's death
(e) Year of brother's wife's death
(f) Brother's occupation

<table>
<tr><td>Delete if brother married more than once</td><td>(i) IF BROTHER NEVER MARRIED:
Present occupation or occupation at death</td></tr>
<tr><td></td><td>(ii) IF BROTHER AND HIS WIFE BOTH ALIVE AT PRESENT
Present occupation</td></tr>
<tr><td></td><td>(iii) IF BROTHER DIED BEFORE HIS WIFE
Occupation at death of brother</td></tr>
<tr><td></td><td>(iv) IF BROTHER'S WIFE DIED BEFORE BROTHER
Brother's occupation at death of wife</td></tr>
</table>

(g) Brother's present status

Brother	Year born	Year married	No. of children born alive	Year brother died	Year brother's wife died	Occupation (see notes)	Brother's present status		
							Sin.	Mar.	Wid.
1st									
2nd									
3rd									
4th									
5th									
6th									

CLASSIFICATION 2

(i) Interviewer ....
  Authorization No. ....

(ii) Town/District ....

(iii) Region ....

(iv) Urban ....
  Rural ....

(v) No. of years lived in town/district ....

(vi) Original interviewed ....
  Original not interviewed (non-contact) ....
  Substitute interviewed ....
  If original not interviewed give full reason

(vii) May we call back in six months' time?
  Yes ....
  No ....

(viii) Serial No. on original address list ....

(ix) Subject
  Working ....
  Not working ....

(x) Subject's wife/husband
  Working ....
  Not working ....

(xi) Total wage-earners in family
  Males ....
  Females ....
  Total ....

(xii) Total in family
  Males ....
  Females ....
  Total ....

(xiii) Where living
  With parents ....
  Own home ....
  Lodgings ....
  Hostel ....
  Boarder ....

(xiv) House type
  Dwellinghouse ....
  Block flat ....
  Rooms in house ....
  Other ....

(xv) Ownership of house
  Own (incl. buying) ....
  Rented Furnished ....
  Rented Unfurnished ....
  Tied House ....

IF SUBJECT MARRIED: HUSBAND/WIFE'S

(xvi) Year of birth ....
(xvii) Year of death ....

97

V

The Educational Experience of the Adult Population of England and Wales as at July 1949

JEAN FLOUD

Introduction

T HIS chapter presents a description and analysis of the educational experience of the adult population of England and Wales as sampled for the purposes of the inquiry in July 1949. This is not entirely unknown territory. But the results of the sample survey make it possible to be precise where before, even with the aid of the statistical material in the annual and other reports of the Board of Education, only the roughest of estimates could be put forward. Moreover, since the individuals in the sample have been classified according to the occupational status of their fathers, far more light can be thrown than has hitherto been possible on the distribution of educational opportunity as between social strata defined with reference to this criterion of status.

The material yields a picture of the achievement up to the outbreak of World War II (the numbers in the youngest age groups in the sample do not permit of generalization) of the English system of public education. This may be taken as having been launched in 1870 when the principle of compulsory attendance (though with certain exceptions) at elementary schools up to the age of 13 was first introduced. Needless to say, quantitatively insignificant developments, however important in themselves (e.g. in the field of technical education at the secondary level) are not reflected in the material, and naturally, no hint is given of the great variations in the content and quality of the national education, either over time or as between different regions. What is given, however, is an accurate picture of the extent to which men and women aged 18 and over in July 1949, grouped broadly into a number of strata with reference to the social status of their fathers, were exposed to the various stages of the educational process. This is of value both in itself and as a base against which to measure developments reflected in material of a similar comprehensive kind which it is hoped will be collected from time to time in the future.

Great changes occurred in the development of the system of public education after 1900. The leaving age in elementary schools was raised generally from 13 to 14 years and the system of half-time attendance was abolished. A large number of central schools with a leaving age of 15 years was established, as well as many junior technical schools, junior commercial schools and junior art departments. And the system of secondary (grammar) education was created, embodying arrangements on a fairly large scale for admitting children judged to be suitable, regardless of the means of their parents. The school life of every child in the country was lengthened by at least a year and that of a fair-sized minority by three or four years.

The far-reaching effects of these changes may be studied from many points of view. In this survey they have been considered in their relation to social mobility; the object was to study their effect on the chances of movement up or down the social scale as indicated by the nature and extent of occupational selection and mobility at various points of time. Between the wars, as a result of technological and organizational changes in industry, education rose to a position of prime importance as an agency of occupational and hence of social selection. Schooling and employment became very closely correlated, and inequalities of educational opportunity, whether affecting different geographical areas or different strata of the population, took on a heightened significance.

In considering educational developments from this point of view, we must emphasize from the start that there is in this country an independent as well as a publicly provided system of schools and that the distinction between the two is at the heart of our class structure, being both cause and effect of many of its characteristic features.

The *independent system* comprises schools which are private or proprietary on the one hand, and schools on the other which are public in the sense that they are maintained by endowment and governed under trust. Independent schools catering for children between the ages of 5 and 11, or right through the period of compulsory attendance, are generally speaking 'private' in the sense of proprietary. Those catering for children between the ages of 8 to 13, though also proprietary, fall mainly within the class known as 'preparatory' schools, since their pupils in the main proceed to independent secondary (for the most part, boarding) schools of the so-called 'public' type.

The 'private' schools corresponding to the publicly maintained primary schools cannot be said to form an independent school system. They are an adjunct to the public system, catering for people of moderate, if not modest, means who wish to buy for their children real or supposed educational or social advantages not provided free in the public system. The number of such schools is not known, there being as yet no regulation for the registration, licensing or inspection of independent schools in this country.[1]

An independent school system is, however, formed by the 'preparatory' schools (8 to 13 years) and the independent 'public' schools (13 to 19 years) which they feed. Not all of these are boarding schools, but the socially more important of them are.

As regards *the publicly provided system*, a word is necessary about the educational classification used in the inquiry.[2] Children today attend primary (formerly 'public elementary') schools from the age of 5 to 11 years, and thereafter, one of three types of secondary school—a secondary 'modern' (formerly 'senior elementary' or sometimes 'central'), secondary 'grammar' (formerly 'secondary' and sometimes 'high') or secondary 'technical' (formerly 'junior technical') school. This logical division of the educational process has however only come into general educational use in Britain since 1944 (though it was formulated by the Hadow Report in 1926, and further developed in 1938 by the Spens Report of the Consultative Committee of the Board of Education). Underlying the official adoption of the division since the 1944 Education Act is the embodiment in the Act, after twenty years or more of campaigning, in particular by the Labour Party, of the policy of 'secondary education for all' and the abolition of the traditional division between a more or less self-contained system of elementary education and another somewhat less self-contained but superior and still insulated system of secondary education along 'grammar' and academic, as against 'modern' or practical, lines.

Virtually none of the subjects of the inquiry have enjoyed the implications of this reclassification of schools, though for convenience they

---

[1] The many different types of school not in receipt of grants from public funds were enumerated in the Report of the Departmental Committee on Private Schools (1932) and it was estimated that some 350,000 children of 5–14 were then attending 'private' schools. The Education Act, 1944, Part III, makes provision for the compulsory registration, inspection and licensing of independent schools, but no date for the commencement of this part of the Act has so far been specified by the Minister.

[2] Cf. Chapter IV, p. 82.

are classified as having attended 'secondary modern' or 'secondary grammar' schools. In fact, before 1944 only those who attended grammar schools regarded themselves, and were generally accepted as having had, properly speaking, a secondary education at all. They were a select minority; and the great majority who failed to win their way on examination at 11+ into the secondary schools 'stayed on' in the senior departments of the elementary schools until they reached the leaving age of 14. A few were selected for admission to the central schools (administered under the elementary code) with a leaving age of 15 and a vocational, usually commercial, bias in the work of the last year, and at the age of 13 a few more for admission to junior technical schools also with a leaving age of 15. But the great majority of those in the group 'secondary modern' had 'only an elementary education'. Admittedly, the publication and wide public welcome of the Hadow Report in 1926 gave a great impetus to what was known as 'reorganization' (viz. the separation off, where possible into a separate building with separate staff and specially designed curriculum, of the senior departments of the elementary schools) and this gave birth to the great body of valuable experimentation round the concept of a 'modern', as distinct from a 'grammar' and academic curriculum. But the process of reorganization was sporadic—considerable progress was made between 1926 to 1930, only to be greatly slowed down by the economy measures introduced following the world economic crisis. In any case, there never developed in the public, or even in the professional, mind anything remotely resembling parity of esteem between the avowedly secondary education given in the 'secondary' schools, and the post-primary, only nominally secondary education given within the elementary system. The junior technical schools fought their way to recognition as offering a valuable alternative type of secondary education for children of a supposedly practical turn of mind, but their numbers were very small indeed and the secondary schools continued to recruit the best in terms of I.Q. and attainment of the 11+ age group (so far as this was yielded by the selection tests) and to develop experimental curricula (engineering and commercial sixth forms) to cater for those who would enter the practical occupations.

In short, for the subjects of this inquiry, as far as the publicly provided system was concerned, there was in fact only one form of accepted secondary education available, namely that provided in the high-prestige grammar schools.

The practical significance of all these educational-cum-social distinctions is clearly revealed in the material here presented, which makes it possible to trace the separate origins and fates of children educated in the various types of school: in preparatory and public schools with their high prestige and social influence; in 'private' schools catering for those who, whilst disdaining the publicly provided system at least at the primary level, do not aspire to the independent preparatory and public schools; in the secondary schools for the minority within the publicly provided system; and in the elementary schools with their senior departments for the rest. The basic distinction was, of course, as between children whose parents were able to pay fees for their schooling and those whose parents could not do so. This is a distinction which, as will be seen, held despite all official attempts to overcome it (and no doubt still holds, since though fees were abolished in 1945 in all maintained and aided secondary schools, the dual system will persist, with most of its social implications unaffected, so long as fees continue to be charged in schools not on the Ministry's Grant List).

Independent Schools

1. 'Private' Schools

The inquiry has afforded some interesting information on the use made of independent schools for children at the primary stage. 3·6 per cent of the boys in the sample and 6·6 per cent of the girls (Table 1, footnote)[1] attended so-called 'private' schools, i.e. proprietary, but not 'preparatory' for the independent public schools. Just under 20 per cent of these boys and rather less than a third of the girls (Table 5) had no secondary education other than that provided within the public elementary system, i.e. they went on to the senior departments of the old elementary schools, or, in a very small number of cases not shown separately in the table, to a central or technical school. But the great majority of children whose primary education was received in independent schools of one sort or another proceeded to secondary grammar and boarding schools, not necessarily, though no doubt normally, as fee-payers. Thus as a group their chances of obtaining a secondary education were far higher than those of the corresponding group who received their primary education in the elementary schools. But their achievements hardly justified this disparate opportunity. A very high proportion of those proceeding to secondary grammar and boarding schools from

[1] Unless otherwise stated all references are to tables included in Appendix I.

102

independent primary schools did not sit their school certificate examination (Table 12, 63·2 per cent as against 53·3 per cent of ex-elementary pupils), which is to say they failed to complete their secondary school course in the 'approved' manner. A substantially higher proportion (Table 13, 36·1 per cent of the men and 39·4 per cent of the women) than of their counterparts from the elementary schools (22 per cent men and 32 per cent women) attained full-time further education, in particular at the universities. But part-time courses were not followed to anything like the same extent as by ex-elementary pupils and, consequently, as a group the pupils from independent primary schools include a larger proportion of individuals with no further education whatsoever.

Parents in status category 2 are shown (Table 2) to be most inclined to send their children to 'private' schools without following this with secondary education (4 per cent of the boys and 11·3 per cent of the girls from families in this grade attended independent primary schools but did not proceed to grammar or boarding schools at the secondary stage), though in the case of girls the tendency is present also in categories 1 (7·2 per cent), and 3–4 (4·9 per cent). However, the popularity of 'private' schools has shown a marked decline with the development of the public elementary schools away from their original association with charitable relief, disciplining of the poor and education in elementary personal hygiene. The figures given in Table 6 cover 'preparatory' as well as 'private' schools. There is no reason to assume any decline in the popularity of the former over the period covered by the table since their fortunes have kept pace with those of the independent public schools they feed. The decline in the proportion shown 'attending independent primary schools' may thus be attributed to the waning importance of the 'private' primary school in the face of the developing public elementary system. The proportion of girls attending 'private' schools has always been strikingly higher than the proportion of boys (Table 6 shows it to have been at most periods almost double) particularly in the upper status categories (Table 3).

2. Preparatory and 'Public' Schools

The social significance of the preparatory and 'public' schools, known to be out of proportion to the numbers passing through them, can hardly emerge from the present material. It is, however, amply attested by special studies of the educational antecedents of leading personalities in business, administration and the professions. Nevertheless, the present inquiry does yield systematic information concerning the populations attending the various types of secondary school, and their respective chances of obtaining a university education.[1] Table 6 shows that the proportion of boys attending secondary boarding schools has scarcely changed over the whole period, remaining around 2 per cent, but that there has been a marked decline (from 4·4 per cent to 2·2 per cent) in the proportion of girls attending these schools. This latter fact reflects the expansion and greatly improved standing of the far less expensive local secondary schools for girls which catered, at the end of the period, for twice as high a proportion as at the beginning (17·8 per cent as against 8·6 per cent). The proportion of boys attending local secondary schools nearly trebled itself over the period, but this was to a greater extent than in the case of girls at the expense of the secondary modern rather than the boarding schools.

However, the independent schools, accessible to only a fraction of the population, are of much less importance to the understanding of trends in social mobility in the inter-war years than is the pre-1944 secondary school system.

The Public Secondary School System

The public secondary school system owes its origin to the 1902 Education Act, which built on the foundation of inadequate and ill-distributed local provision of endowed grammar schools. Many of the more successful experiments in secondary education which had been launched within the old elementary system were incorporated into the new secondary system, and this provision, particularly in 'new' areas, was supplemented with a great number of new schools provided and maintained wholly from public funds.

In 1907, the introduction of arrangements for the award of a proportion of places in the secondary schools free to children judged suitable on the basis of an examination at 11+, opened the doors to a socially much more diverse population. Theoretically, any child worthy of a place need not be denied access to a secondary school. It was never the official intention to make secondary education selective of the highest working-class ability, but to open the secondary schools to children of all classes on equal terms. In their Annual Report for 1909–10, the Board of Education state that objection had been taken by some school authorities to the rule on which the Board from the first insisted that holders of free places must as far as possible be put on the same footing

[1] See p. 113.

with ordinary fee-paying pupils and no conditions as to fitness, progress or attendance be attached to them that did not apply equally to fee-paying pupils. 'This objection when examined', the Report remarks, 'is found to be based on the view that the full access to the benefits of secondary education which it was the object of the free-place regulations to secure throughout the country either is, or should be confined as regards the poorer classes to boys and girls of exceptional ability and used as a means of enabling them to transfer themselves, or as it is often called "rise" into a different social class. This is not the Board's object. Their object was that the education provided in public secondary schools . . . should be open to children of all classes as nearly as possible upon equal terms.' Again, in their Report for 1912–13, in the course of an historical survey of the period 1902–12, it is stated, 'As originally conceived, the Free Place regulations were not framed with the intention of instituting a scholarship system for the intellectual élite of the elementary schools. The intention was rather to bring the advantages of higher education so far as the limited funds of the Board of Education would permit within reach of children of the poorer classes and to place them on the same footing as pupils whose parents were in a position to pay the school fees.' There is no suggestion, in the official declarations of policy around 1911, that the impact of such a policy on the composition of the secondary schools was realized. Indeed, it was expressly stated in the Annual Report for 1909–10 that 'a progressive increase from year to year in the proportion of free-place holders to the total number of pupils in the school' was never intended.

In fact, as this inquiry shows, no more than 12·1 per cent (Table 1) of the adult population in 1949 had been through the secondary schools; and even as late as 1938 the proportion of those children in the elementary schools eligible by age for a secondary education who obtained admission to the secondary schools was estimated to be still only 14·3 per cent.[1] The number of places in the secondary schools, in spite of great expansion, always lagged far behind the public demand, which was stimulated by the knowledge that on admission to a secondary school largely depended a child's chances of leaving the ranks of the wage workers and obtaining a secure, clean and therefore 'respectable' job, and even more so his likelihood of gaining a university education and entrance to one of the professions. The competition for places was therefore severe, and what was intended as a qualifying test of attainment and general suitability for admission to a secondary school soon became

[1] Cf. *Statistics of Public Education for the year 1937–8*, Table 41.

105

throughout the country a competitive examination, though the intensity of the competition varied from area to area and even annually within the same area according to the number of places available.

Nevertheless, the existence of a substantial educational and social ladder from the elementary school to the secondary school has been popularly taken for granted. The well-known increase in the proportion of secondary school pupils drawn from the elementary schools (which reached 70 per cent to 80 per cent in the youngest age groups, Table 8) and holding free or special places (65 per cent, Table 10), has been taken as confirmation of the democratization of the educational system. But these figures cannot be taken by themselves to mean that elementary school pupils as a group had high chances of a secondary education. Their chances obviously depended on the total number of secondary school places available. Moreover, after 1900, the public elementary school enjoyed a waxing popularity, particularly for boys, even among parents in the upper social grades. Table 4 shows that just on 80 per cent of the girls and 90 per cent of the boys in the 1920–9 birth cohort from families in the first four status categories received their primary education in elementary schools. In all but the 'worst' districts these schools rapidly passed the stage when middle-class parents and, in particular, lower middle-class parents were unwilling on cultural or hygienic grounds to risk sending their children to them. And even if it was intended subsequently to send a child to a secondary school as a fee-payer, there was some incentive to place him first in a primary school where the teaching was designed to meet the requirements of the selection examination. It is important to remember this 'improved' social composition of the elementary schools when considering statements about the effectiveness of the educational ladder which base themselves solely on figures showing the increasing proportion of ex-elementary pupils in secondary schools and universities. It does not follow that such children or students all come from the 'poorer' social strata. In 1938 as many as 25·4 per cent of ex-elementary school pupils admitted to the secondary schools paid full fees and another 9·2 per cent part fees.[1]

It is true that over the period 1900–40 the proportions of children coming from status categories 5, 6 and 7 who achieved a secondary education increased substantially. The proportion of *girls* from category 5 who attended secondary grammar schools was almost trebled and the proportion of *boys* was multiplied by approximately $2\frac{1}{2}$ in the case of categories 6–7, and almost quintupled in the case of category 5

[1] Cf. *Statistics of Public Education for the year 1937–8*, Table 42.

(Table 7). But all categories show a marked increase, and at the end of the period a boy in categories 1–3 still had more than four times, and a girl almost three times as high a chance as one in category 5 of obtaining a secondary education in a grammar school. A boy from categories 1–3 still had more than five times and a girl more than seven times as high a chance as one in categories 6–7 of obtaining a secondary education in a grammar school; and it must be remembered that the higher status categories also made use of the independent boarding schools. The greatest reduction in the differential advantage as regards secondary education of a child from categories 1–3 was made in respect of boys from category 5. The odds against them were reduced from 12 to 1 in the case of the earliest cohort, to 4 to 1 in the case of the latest. Nevertheless, we must remember that only 10·7 per cent of even the latest cohort of boys from category 5 obtained a secondary education as compared with 54·2 per cent of those from categories 1–3 (45·7 per cent of which attended secondary grammar schools and 8·5 per cent secondary boarding schools, Table 7).

This inequality in the educational chances of children from families in the different status categories accounts for the fact, shown in column 6 of Table 9, that not only a child's chances of getting to a secondary school at all, but also his chances of doing so *as a holder of a free or special place* were startlingly higher the higher his place in the social hierarchy—more than six times as great if he came from categories 1–3 rather than categories 6–7. Column 6 of Table 9 is a much more significant expression of the social rôle of the secondary schools than column 5, which merely shows that in so far as children in the lower categories reached secondary schools they did so for the most part as holders of free or special places; or than Table 10, which merely shows a steady and substantial increase, amounting to a significant majority in the later cohorts, in the proportion of secondary school pupils holding free or special places.

The common impression that the secondary schools were 'flooded' by children of working-class origin is, of course, accounted for by the size of the various occupational groups in the population. Even where the chances of children reaching secondary schools were low—as was the case of the children of skilled workers—the *absolute* numbers of such children found in the secondary schools were substantial. Indeed, in absolute numbers the largest single group of individuals achieving secondary education were those whose fathers were in status category 5 (Table 9, column 2), though categories 1–4 still provided almost twice as many secondary school pupils as categories 5–7. But the increasing intake, between the wars, of children from the lower status categories into schools which, whatever their exact social composition (this of course varied widely from area to area), traditionally served mainly middle-class social groups, grew up with a distinctive middle-class tradition and were staffed largely by teachers of corresponding outlook and aspirations, presents a fascinating problem in the study of social mobility and assimilation.

The undoubted failure of the Board's original policy of placing secondary education within the reach of children from all social classes on equal terms may be considered from many points of view, among which not the least important is the purely educational, though this cannot be dealt with here. The socio-economic aspect—the refusal of free places offered to the able children of poor parents, as well as the markedly different rates of success in the selection examination as between children from poorer and better-off districts—began to cause concern at an early date,[1] since these factors gravely impeded the effectiveness of the policy even on the limited scale on which the funds of the Board permitted it to be applied. The crude economic burden on parents, ably analysed by Dr. Leybourne White in her *Education and the Birth-rate* (London, 1940), was acknowledged by the Board. But it was never successfully offset by the small maintenance grants, primarily intended to provide out-of-pocket expenses (uniform, books, etc.) in the years spent at school after the age of compulsory attendance, and not to meet the major burden of the foregone earnings of adolescents. Parents had either to have sufficient means (i.e. to be in occupational categories well above the lowest) or to be unusually ambitious and willing to make sacrifices for their children if advantage was to be taken of even free secondary education. Unfortunately, there is no direct evidence as to trends in the rates of refusal of free places offered. But there can be little doubt that the situation was much worsened by the impact of the world economic depression in the thirties on families in the lower status categories, particularly categories 6 and 7. The Depression, moreover, was responsible for a change of official policy in the award of free places to secondary schools, arresting the previously steady growth in the proportion of those children in the schools for whom no fees at all were paid.

---

[1] There are frequent references to both factors in the important series of inquiries made by H.M. Inspectors between 1902 and 1939 into the selection of children for secondary education in different areas (access to the reports of these investigations was kindly given by the Ministry of Education).

In 1933, following the report of the May Committee, the Board initiated economy measures involving cessation of building, reduction of staff and salaries, increases in fees, lowering of the income level of eligibility for the maintenance grants available to children remaining at school after the age of compulsory attendance, and the conversion of free places into 'special' places, i.e. the assessment of liability for fees for competitively awarded places according to means. The result was to widen the gap between the demand for and supply of places in the schools and to increase the sacrifices demanded of those parents in the lower status categories whose children might be offered secondary education.

The introduction of the Special Place Regulations in 1933 gave rise to fears[1] that parents of moderate means, i.e. the lower middle-class groups—would be the sufferers. It was argued that the democratic influence in local education departments would see to it that working-class parents were properly cared for (and in fact the regulations were often interpreted liberally by local authorities and the Board did not raise objections). In its Annual Report for 1934, however, the Board had no difficulty in showing that parents of moderate means were better able to obtain cheap secondary education for their children under the new arrangements. The fact that in 1933 the number of 'special' places assessed to carry no fees was very little below the 1932 figure of free places (1,085 fewer, a reduction of only 1·8 per cent in the 1932 total) was also taken to mean that there was no significant worsening of the position of poorer parents. But this does not appear to have been the case. An analysis of the composition of the total secondary school population from year to year[2] shows that the proportion of children in the schools who were totally exempt from payment of fees had increased from 24 per cent in 1907, before the inception of the official free-place awards, to 50 per cent in 1932 after which it diminished. By 1938 it was down to 46·9.[3] This of course implied a corresponding decline until 1933, and an increase thereafter, in the fee-paying group. But after the introduction of special places in 1933, this fee-paying group was only

[1] Cf. Reports of the Annual Conferences of the Incorporated Association of Head Masters, 1933 and 1934.
[2] Figures are available in the Annual Reports of the Board of Education for all years between 1907 and 1938 except 1913–15 inclusive.
[3] This decline took place despite the fact that free place holders are well known to have had on the average a longer school life than other categories of pupils, so that, other things remaining equal, there is a tendency for them in time to form an increasing proportion of the total secondary school population.

partly composed of children whose parents paid full fees for their education. After 1933 there were children holding special places assessed at reduced fees, and the proportion of these part-fee payers to the total secondary school population rose steadily from 3·6 per cent in 1933 to 9·7 per cent in 1938, whilst the proportion of full-fee payers (i.e. 'ordinary' fee-payers plus a small number of special place holders paying full fees) declined steadily from 47 per cent in 1933 to 43·4 per cent in 1938.[1] To a substantial extent, therefore, the new group of 'part-fee' payers represented a transfer from the group of full-fee payers, and the impact on fee-paying pupils of increased fees after, 1933 was in this way mitigated by official subsidy.

At the same time the competitive position of children from poorer families deteriorated, and this may be seen by examining the annual entry to secondary schools (Appendix 2, Table 2). There was a sharp rise after 1933 in the proportion of the annual vacancies in secondary schools open to competition. The proportion in 1932 was 51·6 per cent and by 1938 it had risen to 69·3 per cent. But the proportion of places awarded annually free of fees rose only slightly over the period 1933–8; there was very little change either in the proportion of places awarded in competition but assessed to carry full fees. However, the proportion of places *partially* exempt from fees rose over the period from approximately 8 per cent of the annual total of special places awarded to 10 per cent and absorbed almost the whole of the increased numbers of places open to competition. The proportion of places allocated annually to 'ordinary' (non-competitive) fee-payers fell in striking fashion from 48·5 per cent in 1932 to only 30·7 per cent in 1938, and it was this group which must have been the main beneficiary of the special place arrangement introduced in 1933. The Board were correct in claiming that parents of moderate means were actually assisted to obtain secondary education for their children. But children from the lower income groups were unable to compete successfully for the increased number of places thrown open to competition, all of which went to fee-payers of one category or another.

There is no reason to suppose that the conditions of selection were changed in 1933, so that the worsened relative position of these poorer children is on the face of it attributable to an increased refusal rate resulting from the combined effects of the economic depression and the introduction of less generous terms governing the award of free places and maintenance allowances.

[1] Appendix 2, Table 1.

The rôle of the 1933 regulations needs to be borne in mind when interpreting the sample survey data on the development of opportunities for secondary education. The survey results are summarized in Table 7, which shows the trend over time in the proportions of boys and girls drawn from various status categories, who achieved secondary education. The numbers in respect of status categories 6–7 are very small, save for the most recent cohort, and fluctuate rather widely. But for the remaining categories the data show movements entirely in keeping with the preceding discussoin. For boys, there was an immediate response to the launching of the new secondary school system in 1902 and the sharp upward trend in the proportion of boys entering secondary schools from all occupational groups is broken only for the cohort of 1900–9, reflecting the impact of World War I on that group. The effect of the Depression and of the 1933 special place regulations is clearly indicated in the check on the upward trend of the proportion of boys from status category 5 entering the secondary schools. Whereas there was no increase in the proportion of boys from this category as between the cohorts of 1910–19 and 1920–9 (boys born during the latter period would be entering secondary school in 1931–40), there was an increase in the proportion of those from status category 4 and a substantial increase in those from categories 1–3.

Not until after 1920 was there any notable increase in the proportion of girls attending secondary schools. Between 1920 and 1930, however —that is, between the birth cohorts of 1900–9 and 1910–19—there was a great increase, most marked for girls from categories 1–3. The rate was not maintained after 1930; there was even a drop in the proportion of girls from categories 1–3 who entered secondary schools, attributable at least partly to official measures of retrenchment affecting the recruitment and payment of teachers. The Depression and the special place regulations, however, left less mark on the recruitment to secondary schools of girls from the lower status categories than of boys. This is to be expected since employment prospects for secondary school boys were much more seriously affected than those for secondary school girls and there was a tendency for boys to try to get into employment as soon as possible (though some measure of success was achieved by the official campaign to persuade those already in secondary schools to lengthen their stay in the hope of an improvement in employment prospects).[1]

One of the avowed deficiencies of the English system of secondary

[1] Cp. Reports of the Annual Conferences of the Incorporated Association of Head Masters, 1934–5.

education between the wars was its lack of diversity. Only a minority of children achieved a secondary education and there was little range or variety of type in the secondary education they achieved. In spite of experiments in the curricula of individual schools, which attempted to provide for pupils with different interests and aspirations, secondary schools in general gave a distinctly academic turn to all aspects of the curriculum. With the expansion of the system, however, they necessarily came to harbour an increasing number of children whose aptitudes and aspirations were only accommodated with difficulty in this generally academic mould. This is reflected in Table 11 which shows the extent to which secondary school pupils completed their course in the accepted fashion by taking their first school examination. The proportion of children gaining their school certificate more than doubled as between the birth cohorts of 1900–9 and 1920–9 (Table 11). However, the proportion of secondary school pupils who sat the examination remained surprisingly low. Over half of even the select group of ex-elementary pupils in the maintained grammar schools failed to obtain their school certificate, though they were notably more successful in this respect than the ex-independent school pupils; 41·7 per cent of ex-elementary pupils obtained their school certificate as against only 33 per cent of ex-independent primary school pupils (Table 12).

Further Education

The survey provides information as to the extent to which further education, particularly university education, was attained by individuals of different schooling and drawn from different status categories.

We may deal first with the further education of the two groups who received their primary education in independent and public-elementary schools respectively. Neither group, as has been shown above, had a high success rate in the school certificate examination; it is, therefore, not surprising to find a high proportion (35·2 per cent of the men and 44·1 per cent of the women, Table 13) even of the selected group of ex-elementary secondary pupils achieving no further education at all. The proportion of ex-independent school secondary pupils who terminated their education at school is higher (44·3 per cent of the men and 48·2 per cent of the women), but of the members of this group who went on to further education, a greater proportion did so to full-time courses (36·1 per cent men and 39·4 per cent women) than of those proceeding to further education from the ex-elementary group (only 22 per cent

112

men and 32 per cent women)—a reflection of their superior chances of obtaining a university education. Thus, Table 18 shows that boys born before 1909 who received their primary education in an independent school had eleven times and girls fourteen times as great a chance as their fellows from the elementary schools of obtaining a university education. It is of more interest, however, to examine the extent to which the considerable expansion of university provision in the early years of the century affected this inequality in the chances of the two primary school populations. It can be seen from Table 18 that the proportion of *girls* reaching universities from both elementary and independent primary schools doubled over the period ending in 1949, when the youngest of those born between 1910–29 were entering universities. Yet the differential chances of the two groups were hardly changed. Thus, ex-independent school girls born between 1910 and 1929 still had as many as twelve times as great a chance as ex-elementary school girls born in the same period of reaching a university. The proportion of *boys* from elementary schools who reached university more than doubled over the period whilst the proportion of those from independent primary schools increased by only two points. Yet boys born between 1910 and 1929 who attended independent primary schools retained more than five times as great a chance of reaching a university as boys in the same birth cohort from elementary schools.

Although more than 40 per cent of university students in 1938–9 began their education in elementary schools,[1] the chances in the period between the wars of ex-elementary pupils achieving a university education, relative to those of the independent school population, remained small. Table 18 likewise shows that secondary boarding school pupils (boys and girls) born before 1910 had more than twice as great a chance of reaching a university as those educated in secondary grammar schools. For *boys* born between 1910 and 1929, however, the superior

---

[1] The Reports of the University Grants Committee show the following trend in the percentage of full-time graduating and diploma students entering universities in England and Wales for the first time, with homes in the U.K. and who began their education in a public elementary school:

1938–9	1945–6	1946–7	1947–8	1948–9
42·01	53·35	55·2	57·64	59·62

It is important in interpreting these figures to bear in mind the improved social composition of the public elementary school mentioned above (p. 106). The much greater absolute size of the secondary grammar school population as compared with that of the secondary boarding schools also helps to account for the preponderance of ex-elementary pupils in the universities despite their inferior chances of attaining a university education.

I

113

chances of boarding school pupils are improved—they had more than three times as great a chance of reaching a university as their fellows from the secondary grammar schools whose relative chances (contrary to what is probably the prevailing opinion of the trend in educational development in this country) were thereby diminished. In the case of *girls* the proportion reaching universities from secondary grammar schools rose over the period by just under 3 points and that of those from secondary boarding schools by just under 4 points. This represented a small improvement in the relative chances of those educated in grammar schools; the superior chances of boarding school pupils born before 1910—more than double those of grammar school pupils—were reduced to rather less than double for those born between 1910–29.

We may now turn to the question of the relative chances of individuals coming from families in the different status categories of obtaining a university education. Though the numbers in the sample are small, the differences shown in Table 19 are statistically significant. The very small proportion of *boys* born before 1910 reaching universities from families in status categories 6–7 was doubled for the later birth cohort and the girls, unrepresented in the earlier period, contributed 0·2 per cent of their number in the later birth cohort. There was very little increase in the proportion from category 5—less than 1 point in the case of boys and none at all in the case of the girls. However, the proportion of boys from categories 3–4 was almost trebled and that of girls almost doubled over the period; double the proportion of girls in the later birth cohort reached universities from categories 1–2, and there was an increase of 7 points in the proportion of boys drawn from these categories. Thus notwithstanding the increased proportions of boys and girls from lower status categories reaching the universities, the same failure of university expansion to improve their relative prospects is evident. *Boys* from categories 1–2, born before 1910, had thirteen times as great a chance of attaining a university education as those from categories 5–7; for those born between 1910 and 1929 the differential was the same. This also applies to the *girls*, a differential of 60 to 1 as between categories 1–2 and 5–7 for those born before 1910 was unchanged for those born between 1910 and 1929.

It is noteworthy that even for individuals *within* the higher status categories there are differential chances of obtaining a university education according to the type of secondary school attended. Thus it can be seen from Table 20 that not only have the prospects of *boys* from categories 1–4 improved for the later birth cohorts, but they have improved more for those with boarding school education than for those educated in secondary grammar schools, the former more than doubling their chances of a university education and the latter multiplying theirs by something less than $1\frac{1}{2}$. In the case of *girls*, the position is reversed; the chances of those from families in categories 1–4 with a grammar school education have more than doubled for those in the later birth cohort, whilst the chances of those with a secondary boarding education are less than half as great again. It is probable, however, that these figures merely reflect in another form the superior chances of children from families in categories 1–2 obtaining a university education, since the *boys* in these categories attend boarding schools in large proportion whilst there has been a marked decline made in the use of secondary boarding schools for *girls* in the higher status categories, and an increase in their attendance at secondary grammar schools (Table 7).

The attainment of formal qualifications, preferably professional, represents much the most significant avenue of mobility for children from families in the lower status categories who are unlikely to have the resources and personal connections which would enable them to rise in industry or commerce by other means. It is of interest therefore to examine more particularly the light thrown by the survey on the further education and success in obtaining qualifications of individuals from status category 5—those from categories 6 and 7 whatever their schooling being evidently least likely to be successful in this respect. Although as has been said above, children from families in category 5 form the largest single group in the secondary grammar schools, individuals achieving secondary grammar or boarding school education constitute only a small minority (8 per cent, Table 2) of the category as a whole. In the case of the large majority of girls from category 5 families who did not reach the secondary grammar schools but remained in the secondary modern schools for their secondary education, and who achieved much less further education of any sort than the boys with similar schooling, a surprisingly high proportion (4·4 per cent, Table 14) attained full-time further education. This does not apply to boys, who undertook part-time courses to a much greater extent than the girls (24·1 per cent as against 10·8 per cent, Table 14), and is no doubt accounted for partly by the frequency with which girls attend short, but full-time commercial courses, and partly by the contribution which this status category must have made to the central and junior technical schools, from which teachers' training colleges in part re-

115

cruited their students. However, despite their greater tendency to undertake some sort of further education, individuals from category 5 were notably less successful than those from category 3 in translating it into formal qualifications, professional or otherwise. The proportion of individuals with qualifications is markedly smaller in the lower status categories as might be expected, and the proportion within the qualified minority, of holders of 'miscellaneous', socially less valuable, qualifications, is markedly greater (Table 15).

Table 15 summarizes trends in the development of different types of further education in England and Wales. The well-known influx of women into commerce is clearly indicated. Before the launching of the new secondary school system in 1902 the main avenue to secondary education for girls was through teacher-training, and this type of further education predominates amongst the women of the earlier cohorts of the sample. Thereafter the position was reversed and the main avenue to teaching was through the secondary schools. Despite fluctuations in official policy relating to the teaching profession, the relative importance of this form of further education (i.e. teacher-training) declined heavily in favour of commercial courses which, in the more recent cohorts, absorbed some 60 per cent of all those undertaking further education. The attraction of commerce has never been as strong for boys. The proportion of boys undertaking commercial courses of further education varied only slightly from 21·9 per cent in the case of earlier cohorts to 28·3 per cent in the case of the group born 1910–19. Thereafter the impact of World War II showed itself in a decline to 15·4 per cent, while the proportion of those taking technical courses increased to 67·8 per cent.

Summary and Conclusion

The economic vicissitudes of the inter-war years were mainly responsible for the limited application of the policy of the 'educational ladder'. It is not generally appreciated, however, that even in its limited application the policy did not in fact result in an unqualified improvement in the relative educational prospects of children drawn from families in the lower status categories of the population. There were more places in the secondary grammar schools and the universities to compete for and a far wider circle of competitors at the end than at the beginning of the period covered by this survey, so that the contribution of the lower categories to the grammar schools and universities naturally increased. It is evident from the material here presented, however, that the chances of success

116

in the competition remained weighted and, indeed, in the course of time became in some respects more heavily weighted, according to the nature of the schooling at each stage—whether in the independent or the publicly maintained school system—and according to the status category of the family of the pupils concerned. The following two tables summarize the educational experience of the sample population with reference to these two factors.

The very large majority of the children educated in independent primary schools have always received a secondary education (i.e. have proceeded either to secondary grammar or to boarding schools, Table 1 overleaf, column 7), whereas no more than a minority of ex-elementary school children ever attained this degree of education (column 5); the proportion of boys and girls born before 1910 who proceeded from elementary schools to secondary schools was slightly more than doubled for those born 1910–29, but the figures, even for the latest birth cohort —1920–9—remained below 15 per cent (Table 1 below, column 5). The proportion of ex-elementary pupils who attained a university education, even after trebling itself as compared with those born before 1910, for those born 1910–29 remained very small (Table 1 below, column 11); though it is noteworthy that, in so far as *boys* from the elementary schools get to the secondary schools, they reach universities in hardly smaller numbers proportionately than those from the independent primary schools. Thus 14·7 per cent of the elementary and 89·1 per cent of the independent primary school pupils in the later birth cohort were educated to secondary level, and the corresponding proportions reaching the universities from each primary school population were 3 per cent and 15·6 per cent respectively (i.e. approximately one-fifth of the secondary educated amongst them in each case). This does not apply to the *girls*. Only one-seventeenth of the secondary educated ex-elementary pupils amongst them reached universities, whereas one-ninth of those proceeding to secondary schools from independent primary schools did so. However, as can be seen from columns 16–19 of the table, the boarding school pupil had always a much higher chance of a university education than the grammar school pupil and their differential advantage actually increased over time. It is noteworthy that a small number of pupils who failed to reach either a secondary grammar or a secondary boarding school nevertheless proceeded to a university. They have been excluded from Table 17 but are shown separately in Table 19 as having attended 'secondary modern' schools. In some cases this must mean a selective central or junior technical school, and in others the senior

1. DISTRIBUTION OF EDUCATIONAL OPPORTUNITY IN RELATION TO PREVIOUS SCHOOLING IN ENGLAND AND WALES [1]

Date of Birth	Primary Education			Secondary Education in Relation to Primary Education (i.e. Secondary Grammar or Boarding Schools)					
				Pupils originating from:					
	Elementary	Independent Primary	Total[1]	Elementary Schools	%	Independent Primary Schools	%	Total[1]	%
	(1)	(2)	(3)	(4)	(5)	(6)	(7)	(8)	(9)
MALES									
Before 1910	1875	133	2044	132	7·0	104	78·2	241	11·8
1910–29	1501	64	1600	221	14·7	57	89·1	281	17·6
FEMALES									
Before 1910	2145	258	2444	115	5·4	165	64·0	282	11·5
1910–29	1807	139	1989	221	12·2	107	77·0	330	16·6

[1] The totals include cases in respect of which information on primary education was not given.

Date of Birth	University Education in Relation to Primary Education						University Education in Relation to Secondary Education					
	Students originating from:						Students originating from:					
	Elementary Schools	%	Independent Primary Schools	%	Total	%	Secondary Grammar Schools	%	Secondary Boarding Schools	%	Total	%[1]
	(10)	(11)	(12)	(13)	(14)	(15)	(16)	(17)	(18)	(19)	(20)	(21)
MALES												
Before 1910	22	1·2	18	13·5	40	2·0	18	9·0	8	19·0	26	10·8
1910–29	45	3·0	10	15·6	55	3·4	29	11·4	11	30·6	40	14·3
FEMALES												
Before 1910	7	0·3	11	4·3	18	0·7	8	3·9	7	8·9	15	5·4
1910–29	12	0·7	12	8·6	24	1·2	20	6·7	4	12·5	24	7·3

[1] Students with undefined secondary education excluded from the total here. A small number of university students in both birth cohorts originated from the so-called 'secondary modern' schools (Table 20). These have also been excluded. They no doubt were the products, for the most part, of selective central and junior technical schools which were included in the category 'secondary modern', though a number must have reached the university from the senior departments of the elementary schools via adult education classes and evening courses at polytechnics and similar institutions.

Column (5): percentage of column (4) to column (1).
Column (7): percentage of column (6) to column (2).
Column (9): percentage of column (8) to column (3).
Column (17): percentage of column (16) to pupils of cohort who attended secondary grammar schools.
Column (19): percentage of column (18) to pupils of cohort who attended secondary boarding schools.
Column (21): percentage of column (20) to pupils of cohort who attended secondary grammar and boarding schools.

Column (11): percentage of column (10) to column (1).
Column (13): percentage of column (12) to column (2).
Column (15): percentage of column (14) to column (3).

119

2. DISTRIBUTION OF EDUCATIONAL OPPORTUNITY IN RELATION TO SOCIAL ORIGINS IN ENGLAND AND WALES

Date of Birth	Total Subjects of Known Status	Pupils originating from status categories: 1–4				
		Secondary Education		University Education		
		No. who attended Secondary Grammar or Boarding Schools	Percentage col. 2 to col. 1	No. who went to a University	Percentage col. 4 to col. 1	
	(1)	(2)	(3)	(4)	(5)	
MALES						
Before 1910	663	179	27·0	29	4·4	
1910–29	449	175	38·9	40	8·5	
FEMALES						
Before 1910	776	199	25·6	16	2·1	
1910–29	526	188	35·7	21	4·0	

120

Pupils originating from status categories: 5–7

Date of Birth	Total Subjects of Known Status	Secondary Education		University Education	
		No. who attended Secondary Grammar or Boarding Schools	Percentage col. 7 to col. 6	No. who went to a University	Percentage col. 9 to col. 6
	(6)	(7)	(8)	(9)	(10)
MALES					
Before 1910	1256	50	4·0	11	0·9
1910–29	1045	99	9·8	15	1·4
FEMALES					
Before 1910	1537	54	3·5	2	0·1
1910–29	1372	127	9·3	3	0·2

departments of elementary schools followed by work as evening students in adult educational classes or at polytechnics and similar institutions.

An analysis of the educational experience of the various status categories of the population (Table 2 above) enables us to make this general picture of the distribution of educational opportunity more precise. Thus although Table 1 above shows that some 15 per cent of ex-elementary pupils proceeded to secondary schools, by no means all of these were drawn from families in categories 5–7. Only one-tenth of the individuals in categories 5–7 received a secondary education as compared with one-third of those in categories 1–4. Despite, however, the adverse effect on their prospects of the economic depression of the thirties and the consequent economy measures of the Board of Education, the chances of children from families in categories 5–7 reaching the secondary grammar schools were multiplied 2½ times for those born between 1910 and 1929 as compared with those born earlier, and since in the case of *boys* this improvement was also reflected in the proportions from these categories going to the universities, the educational ladder, though a slender one, was for them a reality.

The Education Act, 1944, has formally abolished the policy of the 'educational ladder', introducing instead the policy of 'secondary education for all'. This involves, apart from increasing the provision, introducing a greater variety of forms of secondary education—and in such a way as to induce the public to attribute more or less equal standing to each. The difficulties of implementation are great and meantime the familiar competition for places in grammar schools and universities remains intense. Much work has still to be done to reduce the odds against individuals from families in the lower status categories of the population in so far as these are attributable to more or less crude economic factors. Nevertheless, to the extent that it is implemented at all, the new policy will have an important effect on the social structure of this country. Secondary schools between the wars were relatively exclusive, and this fostered the development and perpetuation of a specialized and in this sense narrow tradition of secondary education. The restrictive effect on occupational and social mobility of this narrow scope and maldistribution of educational opportunity is analysed elsewhere. It may, however, be remarked here in conclusion that changes in the twentieth century in industrial and economic organization have rendered obsolescent traditional methods of industrial recruitment and of selection for occupational and social mobility. Entry into industry or commerce from the elementary school and the gradual acquisition of specialized skill as apprentice or 'on the job', the accumulation of small capital and the working up of a small concern into a large one, are now overshadowed as methods of advance by the acquisition of formal educational and professional qualifications. Education, at least to the secondary level, has long been almost indispensable even in the lower ranks of industry and commerce, and some form of further education a prerequisite for individual advance. The educational system has thereby become the primary agency of occupational and social selection, and the results of the inquiry presented in this chapter make clear the limited fashion in which it functioned in this respect in the inter-war years. The 1944 Act, however, provides a framework of reform. It constitutes a promise of change in the nature and distribution of educational opportunity which, if it materializes, will almost certainly be accompanied by considerable changes both in the social hierarchy of occupations and in the degree of mobility within and between occupations.

APPENDIX 1

Table 1

PERCENTAGE DISTRIBUTION OF ATTENDANCE AT VARIOUS TYPES OF PRIMARY
AND POST-PRIMARY SCHOOLS

	Primary School Attended		
Sex	*Elementary*	*Independent*	*Total*
	%	%	%
Males	94·5	5·5[1]	100·0 (3665)
Females	90·9	9·1[1]	100·0 (4539)
Total	92·5	7·5	100·0 (8204)

	Secondary School Attended			
Sex	*Modern*	*Grammar*	*Boarding*	*Total*
	%	%	%	%
Males	85·4	12·7	1·9	100·0 (3672)
Females	85·9	11·6	2·5	100·0 (4512)
Total	85·6	12·1	2·3	100·0 (8184)

[1] These figures include both independent 'preparatory' boarding schools and local 'private' schools. An estimate of the use made of the latter can be obtained by subtracting the percentage shown as having attended secondary boarding schools (who for the most part will have attended preparatory schools at the primary stage) from the figure here shown.

Thus: Males   5·5% − 1·9% = 3·6%
         Females 9·1% − 2·5% = 6·6%

Table 2

PRIMARY AND SECONDARY SCHOOLING IN RELATION TO STATUS CATEGORY
OF FATHER

| Schools Attended | Status Category of Father | | | | | |
	1 %	2 %	3 and 4 %	5 %	6 and 7 %	Total %
Males						
Elementary: Modern	27·5	47·7	77·5	91·7	95·2	84·7
Elementary: Grammar or Boarding	26·0	25·8	16·7	6·3	4·0	9·9
Independent: Grammar or Boarding	45·7	22·5	4·6	1·0	0·7	4·4
Independent: Modern	0·8	4·0	1·2	1·0	0·1	1·0
Total	100·0 (127)	100·0 (151)	100·0 (863)	100·0 (1483)	100·0 (827)	100·0 (3451)
Females						
Elementary: Modern	23·2	46·5	72·1	89·7	96·3	83·5
Elementary: Grammar or Boarding	14·4	18·3	12·7	6·7	2·4	7·7
Independent: Grammar or Boarding	55·2	23·9	10·3	2·0	0·3	6·0
Independent: Modern	7·2	11·3	4·9	1·6	1·0	2·8
Total	100·0 (125)	100·0 (159)	100·0 (1000)	100·0 (1821)	100·0 (1042)	100·0 (4147)
Males and Females						
Elementary: Modern	25·4	47·2	74·6	90·6	95·8	84·0
Elementary: Grammar or Boarding	20·2	21·9	14·5	6·5	3·1	8·
Independent: Grammar or Boarding	50·4	23·2	7·7	1·5	0·5	5·3
Independent: Modern	4·0	7·7	3·2	1·4	0·6	2·0
Total	100·0 (252)	100·0 (310)	100·0 (1863)	100·0 (3304)	100·0 (1869)	100·0 (7598)

125

Table 3

PRIMARY SCHOOLING IN RELATION TO STATUS CATEGORY·OF FATHER

Primary School Attended	Status Category of Father						
	1 %	2 %	3 %	4 %	5 %	6 and 7 %	Total %
Males							
Elementary	53·5	73·7	91·3	96·0	97·9	99·2	94·6
Independent	46·5	26·3	8·7	4·0	2·1	0·8	5·4
Total	100·0 (127)	100·0 (152)	100·0 (355)	100·0 (530)	100·0 (1527)	100·0 (850)	100·0 (3541)
Females							
Elementary	36·4	65·3	79·5	88·3	96·4	98·7	91·2
Independent	63·6	34·7	20·5	11·7	3·6	1·3	8·8
Total	100·0 (129)	100·0 (167)	100·0 (420)	100·0 (607)	100·0 (1905)	100·0 (1104)	100·0 (4332)
Males and Females							
Elementary	44·9	69·3	84·9	91·9	97·1	98·9	92·8
Independent	55·1	30·7	15·1	8·1	2·9	1·1	7·2
Total	100·0 (256)	100·0 (319)	100·0 (775)	100·0 (1137)	100·0 (3432)	100·0 (1954)	100·0 (7873)

Table 4

ATTENDANCE AT PUBLIC ELEMENTARY SCHOOLS OVER TIME IN RELATION
TO STATUS CATEGORY OF FATHER

| | Status Category of Father | | | | | |
| | 1–4 | | 5 | | 6–7 | |
Date of Birth	Total primary school population	% elementary school pupils	Total primary school population	% elementary school pupils	Total primary school population	% elementary school pupils
MALES						
1889 or earlier	251	84·1	279	97·9	144	97·2
1890–99	189	84·7	219	98·2	128	99·3
1900–09	249	88·0	338	97·4	162	99·5
1910–19	241	88·7	347	98·0	178	100·0
1920–29	219	89·1	318	98·4	221	99·6
FEMALES						
1889 or earlier	308	70·1	362	94·7	197	95·5
1890–99	214	77·1	263	95·8	129	100·0
1900–09	250	83·7	389	95·7	198	99·0
1910–19	271	79·3	414	97·8	233	99·6
1920–29	251	79·7	415	97·2	305	99·4

Table 5

POST-PRIMARY SCHOOLING OF PUBLIC ELEMENTARY AND INDEPENDENT
PRIMARY SCHOOL PUPILS RESPECTIVELY

Schools Attended		Males %	Females %	Total %
Elementary	Secondary Modern	89·3	91·2	90·3
	Secondary Grammar or Boarding	10·7	8·8	9·7
		100·0	100·0	100·0
		(3433)	(4076)	(7509)
Independent	Secondary Modern	19·1	32·0	27·7
	Secondary Grammar or Boarding	80·9	68·0	72·3
		100·0	100·0	100·0
		(199)	(407)	(606)

127

Table 6

ATTENDANCE AT VARIOUS TYPES OF PRIMARY AND POST-PRIMARY SCHOOLS
OVER TIME

Date of Birth	Primary Schools			Secondary Schools			
	Elementary %	Independent %	Total %	Modern %	Grammar %	Boarding %	Total %
MALES							
1889 or earlier	91·8	8·2	100·0 (706)	89·4	8·3	2·3	100·0 (702)
1890–99	93·8	6·2	100·0 (550)	86·1	12·1	1·8	100·0 (554)
1900–09	94·6	5·4	100·0 (770)	88·3	9·6	2·1	100·0 (771)
1910–19	95·7	4·3	100·0 (791)	83·7	14·5	1·8	100·0 (792)
1920–29	96·1	3·9	100·0 (789)	80·9	17·5	1·6	100·0 (794)
1930	96·6	3·4	100·0 (59)	74·6	23·7	1·7	100·0 (59)
Total	94·5	5·5	100·0 (3665)	85·4	12·7	1·9	100·0 (3672)
FEMALES							
1889 or earlier	85·2	14·8	100·0 (921)	87·0	8·6	4·4	100·0 (909)
1890–99	90·2	9·8	100·0 (641)	88·8	8·1	3·1	100·0 (640)
1900–09	92·8	7·2	100·0 (871)	89·4	8·4	2·2	100·0 (865)
1910–19	92·4	7·6	100·0 (965)	83·6	14·9	1·5	100·0 (953)
1920–29	93·3	6·7	100·0 (1007)	82·8	15·4	1·8	100·0 (1010)
1930	92·5	7·5	100·0 (134)	80·0	17·8	2·2	100·0 (135)
Total	90·9	9·1	100·0 (4539)	85·9	11·6	2·5	100·0 (4512)

Table 7

DISTRIBUTION OF PUPILS IN ATTENDANCE AT VARIOUS TYPES OF POST-PRIMARY SCHOOL OVER TIME, ACCORDING TO STATUS CATEGORY OF FATHER

(a) SECONDARY MODERN SCHOOL

Date of Birth	Males				Females			
	Status Category of Father							
	1–3 %	4 %	5 %	6–7 %	1–3 %	4 %	5 %	6–7 %
1889 or earlier	67·6 (145)	90·3 (103)	97·9 (277)	96·5 (145)	62·2 (167)	85·6 (139)	95·0 (359)	97·9 (192
1890–99	55·3 (112)	83·5 (79)	95·4 (218)	97·6 (131)	63·2 (125)	87·5 (88)	96·2 (262)	100·0 (130)
1900–09	64·5 (121)	87·4 (127)	93·0 (339)	98·7 (161)	66·2 (133)	88·0 (117)	93·3 (386)	99·0 (196)
1910–19	55·6 (135)	77·4 (106)	89·9 (346)	95·5 (180)	49·6 (141)	81·5 (130)	88·6 (411)	96·9 (225)
1920–29	45·7 (118)	74·3 (105)	89·0 (317)	90·6 (224)	50·4 (135)	78·2 (119)	86·1 (417)	95·0 (303)

(b) SECONDARY GRAMMAR SCHOOL

Date of Birth	Males				Females			
	Status Category of Father							
	1–3 %	4 %	5 %	6–7 %	1–3 %	4 %	5 %	6–7 %
1889 or earlier	23·4	7·8	2·2	3·5	22·8	11·5	3·9	1·6
1890–99	38·4	13·9	4·1	2·3	24·0	10·2	3·4	—
1900–09	26·4	10·2	6·8	1·2	24·8	11·1	5·4	1·0
1910–19	35·5	20·7	10·1	4·4	43·3	17·7	11·2	3·1
1920–29	45·7	25·7	10·7	8·9	38·5	21·8	13·2	5·0

(c) SECONDARY BOARDING SCHOOL

Date of Birth	Males				Females			
	Status Category of Father							
	1–3 %	4 %	5 %	6–7 %	1–3 %	4 %	5 %	6–7 %
1889 or earlier	9·0	1·9	—	—	15·0	2·9	1·1	0·5
1890–99	6·3	2·5	0·5	—	12·8	2·3	0·4	—
1900–09	9·1	2·4	0·3	—	9·0	0·9	1·3	—
1910–19	8·9	1·9	—	—	7·1	0·8	0·2	—
1920–29	8·5	—	0·3	0·4	11·1	—	0·7	—

Note. Figures in brackets in section (a) give the total numbers in each birth cohort on which the percentages in all three sections of Table 7 are based.

Table 8

DISTRIBUTION OF SECONDARY GRAMMAR AND BOARDING SCHOOL PUPILS
ACCORDING TO PRIMARY EDUCATION OVER TIME

Date of Birth	Males			Females		
	Inde-pendent %	Ele-mentary %	Total %	Inde-pendent %	Ele-mentary %	Total %
1889 or earlier	63·9	36·1	100·0 (72)	71·8	28·2	100·0 (117)
1890–99	30·7	69·3	100·0 (75)	59·2	40·8	100·0 (71)
1900–09	39·3	60·7	100·0 (89)	42·4	57·6	100·0 (92)
1910–19	22·0	78·0	100·0 (127)	35·9	64·1	100·0 (156)
1920–29	19·2	80·8	100·0 (151)	29·7	70·3	100·0 (172)
Total	31·3	68·7	100·0 (514)	44·7	55·3	100·0 (608)

Table 9

DISTRIBUTION OF ATTENDANCE AT, AND OF FREE OR SPECIAL PLACE
HOLDERS IN, SECONDARY GRAMMAR SCHOOLS ACCORDING TO STATUS
CATEGORY OF FATHER

Status Category of Father	Total attending secondary schools (1)	Total attending secondary grammar schools (2)	% Col. 2 to Col. 1 (3)	Total secondary grammar pupils holding free or special places (4)	% Col. 4 to Col. 2 (5)	% Col. 4 to Col. 1 (6)
Males:						
1 and 2	283	115	43·8	33	28·7	12·4
3	356	83	23·3	42	50·6	12·0
4	526.	79	16·2	50	63·3	9·6
5	1,524	103	7·4	73	70·9	4·8
6 and 7	858	34	4·7	23	67·7	2·7
Females:						
1 and 2	298	87	33·2	32	36·8	11·6
3	418	116	28·7	49	42·2	11·9
4	607	82	15·0	31	39·0	5·4
5	1,899	142	8·3	98	69·0	5·2
6 and 7	1,086	28	2·8	17	60·7	1·6
Total:						
1 and 2	581	202	38·4	63	32·2	13·2
3	774	199	27·0	91	45·7	12·0
4	1,133	161	15·5	82	50·9	8·0
5	3,423	245	7·9	171	69·8	5·0
6 and 7	1,944	62	3·6	40	64·5	2·1

Table 10

DISTRIBUTION OF FREE OR SPECIAL PLACE HOLDERS IN SECONDARY
GRAMMAR SCHOOLS OVER TIME

Date of Birth		Total numbers attending sec. grammar schools (1)	Total free or special place holders (2)	% Col. 2 to Col. 1 (3)	% Col. 2 to Total subjects (4)
1889 or earlier	..	102	21	20·6	1·3
1890–1904	..	169	64	38·5	3·2
1905–19	..	321	169	52·7	6·5
1920 or later	..	316	207	65·5	10·3
Total	..	908	461	50·9	5·6

Table 11

SUCCESSES IN SCHOOL CERTIFICATE EXAMINATION OVER TIME

Date of Birth	Percentage of all ex-secondary grammar pupils with School Certificate		
	Males	Females	Total
1889 or earlier	2·53	2·49	2·51
1890–99	6·47	3·56	4·91
1900–09	6·18	3·66	4·85
1910–19	9·11	7·00	7·96
1920–29	11·38	10·12	10·67

Table 12

SUCCESS IN SCHOOL CERTIFICATE EXAMINATION IN RELATION TO SCHOOLING

Schools Attended	School Certificate			
	Obtained %	Failed %	Not sat %	Total %
Elementary: Secondary Modern	1·1	0·3	98·6	100·0 (6632)
Elementary: Secondary Grammar	41·7	5·0	53·3	100·0 (686)
Independent Primary: Secondary Modern	5·6	—	94·4	100·0 (160)
Independent Primary: Sec. Gram. or Boarding	33·0	3·8	63·2	100·0 (427)
Total	6·5	0·8	92·7	100·0 (7905)

Table 13

FURTHER EDUCATION IN RELATION TO SCHOOLING

Schools Attended	Sex	Further Education			Total %
		None %	Full time %	Part time %	
Elementary: Secondary Modern	M.	75·4	2·8	21·8	100·0 (3508)
	F.	84·9	4·3	10·8	100·0 (3717)
Elementary: Secondary Grammar or Boarding	M.	35·2	22·0	42·9	100·0 (364)
	F.	44·1	32·0	22·9	100·0 (349)
Independent Primary: Secondary Modern	M.	47·4	13·1	39·5	100·0 (38)
	F.	70·0	15·0	15·0	100·0 (127)
Independent Primary: Secondary Grammar or Boarding	M.	44·3	36·1	19·6	100·0 (158)
	F.	48·2	39·4	12·4	100·0 (274)

132

Table 14

FURTHER EDUCATION IN RELATION TO SCHOOLING AND STATUS CATEGORY OF FATHER

SCHOOLS ATTENDED

FURTHER EDUCATION

Status Category of Father	Elementary: Secondary Modern				Elementary: Secondary Grammar or Boarding				Independent Primary: Secondary Grammar or Boarding			
	None	Full	Part	Total	None	Full	Part	Total	None	Full	Part	Total
MALES												
1–4 %	69·6	5·1	25·3	100·0 (783)	34·4	23·1	42·5	100·0 (221)	40·9	40·2	18·9	100·0 (132)
5 %	73·8	2·1	24·1	100·0 (1375)	34·7	21·1	44·2	100·0 (95)	66·7	6·7	26·6	100·0 (15)
6–7 %	83·0	2·0	15·0	100·0 (800)	44·1	14·7	41·2	100·0 (34)				(6)
Total %	75·2	2·9	21·9	100·0 (2958)	35·4	21·7	42·9	100·0 (350)	45·1	35·9	19·0	100·0 (153)
FEMALES												
1–4 %	76·8	7·6	15·6	100·0 (832)	42·9	34·5	22·6	100·0 (177)	44·6	44·1	11·3	100·0 (213)
5 %	84·8	4·4	10·8	100·0 (1679)	41·2	33·6	25·2	100·0 (131)	51·4	29·7	18·9	100·0 (37)
6–7 %	91·2	2·0	6·8	100·0 (1041)	74·1	11·1	14·8	100·0 (27)				(3)
Total %	84·8	4·4	10·8	100·0 (3552)	44·8	32·2	23·0	100·0 (335)	46·2	41·5	12·3	100·0 (253)

Table 15

DISTRIBUTION OF VARIOUS TYPES OF FURTHER EDUCATION OVER TIME

FURTHER EDUCATION

Date of Birth	%	MALES					FEMALES					
		Comm.	Tech.	Univ.	Other[1]	Total	Comm.	Tech.	T.T.	Univ.	Other	Total
1889 or earlier	%	21·9	47·7	9·4	21·0	100·0 (128)	13·4	12·4	25·8	5·2	43·2	100·0 (97)
1890–99	%	23·3	51·1	8·3	17·3	100·0 (133)	32·6	13·1	10·9	5·4	38·0	100·0 (92)
1900–09	%	24·4	56·1	4·1	15·4	100·0 (221)	48·9	12·6	4·6	3·4	30·5	100·0 (174)
1910–19	%	28·3	54·9	7·3	9·5	100·0 (286)	45·9	12·0	5·6	4·3	32·2	100·0 (233)
1920–29	%	15·4	67·8	6·7	10·1	100·0 (298)	60·9	11·1	4·2	4·8	19·0	100·0 (289)
1930 or later	%	3·2	80·6	3·2	13·0	100·0 (31)	62·7	13·7	2·0	2·0	19·6	100·0 (51)
Totals	%	22·0	58·1	6·7	13·2	100·0 (1097)	47·3	12·1	7·4	4·4	28·8	100·0 (936)

[1] Includes for *males* only teacher training in addition to other.

Table 16

DISTRIBUTION OF INDIVIDUALS HOLDING VARIOUS TYPES OF QUALIFICATION
ACCORDING TO STATUS CATEGORY OF FATHER

Status Category of Father	Univ. %	Qualifications Prof. %	Misc. %	Total %	Percentage Of all Sub-jects with Qualifications
1	36·1	27·8	36·1	100·0 (72)	28·1 (256)
2	17·6	25·5	56·9	100·0 (51)	16·0 (319)
3	9·7	34·4	55·9	100·0 (93)	12·0 (775)
4	4·2	27·7	68·1	100·0 (94)	8·3 (1137)
5	1·8	22·8	75·4	100·0 (167)	4·9 (3432)
6 and 7	5·5	13·9	80·6	100·0 (36)	1·8 (1954)
				Total	6·5 (7873)

Table 17

UNIVERSITY EDUCATION IN RELATION TO PRIMARY AND SECONDARY EDUCATION OVER TIME

	University Education in Relation to Primary Education. Students originating from:						University Education in Relation to Secondary Education. Students originating from:					
Date of Birth	Elementary Schools	%	Independent Primary Schools	%	Total[1]	%	Secondary Grammar Schools	%	Secondary Boarding Schools	%	Total[2]	%
MALES												
Before 1910	22	1·2 (1875)	18	13·5 (133)	40	2·0 (2044)	18	9·0 (200)	8	19·0 (42)	26	10·8 (242)
1910–29	45	3·0 (1501)	10	15·6 (64)	55	3·4 (1600)	29	11·4 (255)	11	40·7 (27)	40	14·3 (282)
FEMALES												
Before 1910	7	0·3 (2145)	11	4·3 (258)	18	0·7 (2444)	8	3·9 (205)	7	8·9 (79)	15	5·3 (284)
1910–29	12	0·7 (1807)	12	8·6 (139)	24	1·2 (1989)	20	6·7 (297)	4	12·5 (32)	24	7·3 (329)

[1] The totals include cases in respect of which information on primary education was not given.

[2] Students whose secondary education was obtained in 'secondary modern' schools or was undefined have been excluded from the total here. The numbers reaching universities from 'secondary modern' schools are shown in Table 20. They were no doubt for the most part the products of selective central and junior technical schools though a number must have reached the university from the senior departments of elementary schools via the hazardous route of adult education and evening courses at polytechnic and similar institutions.

136

Table 18

UNIVERSITY EDUCATION IN RELATION TO STATUS CATEGORY OF FATHER
OVER TIME

Date of Birth		*Status Category of Father*				
		1–2	*3–4*	*5*	*6–7*	*Total*
MALES						
Before 1910	No. of subjects of known status origin	160	503	825	431	1919
	No. of such subjects reaching University	19	10	9	2	40
	Percentage of subjects reaching University	11·9	2·0	1·1	0·5	2·1
1910 to 1929	No. of subjects of known status origin	111	338	651	394	1494
	No. of such subjects reaching University	20	20	11	4	55
	Percentage of subjects reaching University	18·0	5·9	1·7	1·0	3·7
FEMALES						
Before 1910	No. of subjects of known status origin	174	602	1014	523	2313
	No. of such subjects reaching University	10	5	2	0	17
	Percentage of subjects reaching University	6·3	0·8	0·2	0·0	0·7
1910 to 1929	No. of subjects of known status origin	119	407	835	537	1898
	No. of such subjects reaching University	15	6	2	1	24
	Percentage of subjects reaching University	12·6	1·5	0·2	0·2	1·3

Table 19

UNIVERSITY EDUCATION IN RELATION TO STATUS CATEGORY OF FATHER AND SECONDARY EDUCATION OVER TIME

Date of Birth		Status Category of Father								
		1–4			5–7			Total		
		Sec. Mod.	Sec. Gram.	Ind. Bdg.	Sec. Mod.	Sec. Gram.	Ind. Bdg.	Sec. Mod.	Sec. Gram.	Ind. Bdg.
MALES										
Before 1910	No. of subjects of known status origin and sec. schooling.	488	134	37	1195	47	2	1683	181	39
	No. of such subjects reaching university.	6	15	8	8	3	0	14	18	8
	Percentage of subjects reaching university.	1·2	11·2	21·6	0·7	6·4	0·0	0·8	9·9	20·5
1910 to 1929	No. of subjects of known status origin and sec. schooling.	283	141	23	937	96	2	1220	237	25
	No. of such subjects reaching university.	6	23	11	9	6	0	15	29	11
	Percentage of subjects reaching university.	2·1	16·3	47·8	1·0	6·3	0·0	1·2	12·2	44·0

FEMALES									
Before to 1910									
No. of subjects of known status origin and sec. schooling.	570	139	60	1460	49	11	2030	188	71
No. of such subjects reaching university.	2	8	7	1	1	0	3	9	7
Percentage of subjects reaching university.	0·4	5·8	11·7	0·1	2·0	0·0	0·1	4·7	9·9
1910 to 1929									
No. of subjects of known status origin and sec. schooling.	336	161	26	1223	124	4	1559	285	30
No. of such subjects reaching university	0	17	4	0	3	0	0	20	4
Percentage of subjects reaching university.	0·0	10·6	15·4	0·0	2·4	0·0	0·0	7·0	12·3

APPENDIX 2

Table 1[1]

DISTRIBUTION OF PUPILS IN GRANT-EARNING SECONDARY SCHOOLS
IN RELATION TO FEES, 1933–8

	1933 %	1934 %	1935 %	1936 %	1937 %	1938 %
Free Place Pupils, and Special Place Pupils paying *no fees*	49·4	48·1	47·6	46·9	46·5	46·9
Special Place Pupils paying *part fees*	3·6	5·0	6·3	7·7	9·2	9·7
'Ordinary' Fee-payers and Special Place Pupils paying *full fees*	47·0	46·9	46·1	45·4	44·3	43·4
Total Fee-payers, all categories	50·6	51·9	52·4	53·1	53·5	53·1

[1] Compiled from figures given in the Annual Reports of the Board of Education.

Table 2[1]

ANNUAL ENTRY TO GRANT-EARNING SECONDARY SCHOOLS

	1932[2] %	1933 %	1934 %	1935 %	1936[3] %	1937 %	1938 %
Special Place Pupils:	51·6						
No fees		49·8	49·6	50·2	51·4	52·0	52·6
Part fees		8·1	9·1	9·3	9·6	10·3	9·9
Full fees		6·3	6·4	6·3	6·3	6·7	6·8
'Ordinary' fee-payers	48·4	35·8	34·9	34·3	32·7	31·0	30·7
Total	100·0	100·0	100·0	100·0	100·0	100·0	100·0
Total Special Places		64·2	65·1	65·7	67·3	69·0	69·3
Total fee-payers all categories	48·4	50·2	50·4	49·8	48·6	48·0	47·4

[1] Compiled from figures supplied in the Annual Reports of the Board of Education, 1932–38.

[2] Percentage of annual entry awarded *free* places. Special Place Regulations introduced 1933.

[3] Former upper limit on the award of special places in schools to 40 per cent of previous year's entry removed.

VI

Social Status and Secondary Education since the 1944 Act: Some Data for London

H. T. HIMMELWEIT

IN Britain, secondary education of the grammar school type provides the main avenue for upward social mobility for the children of the 'working class'. *Successful* attendance at a grammar school is becoming increasingly the necessary first qualification for entry into salaried occupations. Before the 1944 Education Act, the role of the grammar school in this respect was very limited because of the marked under-representation of children from the lower socio-economic groups.[1] But it is generally believed that recent educational and economic changes have considerably altered the social class composition of the grammar schools. The abolition of fees and the allocation of places on the basis of a standardized selection procedure should have led to more places being offered to children from the lower socio-economic groups. Further, because of full employment and the raising of the statutory school-leaving age to fifteen, it is probable that parents have become more ready to allow their children to accept a place in a grammar school.

In this chapter, some new data concerning the relationship of social status to secondary school education will be presented. The data were obtained in the Greater London area as part of a more comprehensive inquiry into the influence of social status upon the outlook, attitudes and behaviour of young adolescents.[2] Since the study was carried out in 1951, several years after the Education Act had come into force, the results may serve to throw light upon the way in which 'secondary education for all' has worked out in practice.

Questionnaires and tests, dealing with the boy's relationship to

[1] Cf. Chapter V.
[2] I should like to acknowledge the very able collaboration of E. Bene, A. H. Halsey, and A. N. Oppenheim, who acted as research assistants in this inquiry.

others, with his leisure interests, his vocational aspirations and his attitude to school were administered to over seven hundred young adolescent boys in grammar and secondary modern schools,[1] the two main types of secondary schools within the State system.

The study was restricted to one age-group; thirteen to fourteen-year old boys were chosen because at that age they are already sufficiently close to school-leaving to make questions both about school and about vocational aspirations meaningful to them. It is also the latest age at which secondary modern school boys can be tested as a group and at which one can be certain of obtaining a truly representative cross-section of the grammar school population. To ensure representativeness, all the boys in the third forms were tested.

Table 1

PERCENTAGE DISTRIBUTION OF SAMPLE BY TYPF OF SCHOOL AND SOCIAL STATUS GROUPS

Social Status of Pupils	Grammar School		Secondary Modern School		Total	
	%	(N)	%	(N)	%	(N)
Middle Middle	21·7	(72)	5·9	(23)	13·1	(95)
Lower Middle	26·5	(88)	13·7	(54)	19·6	(142)
Upper Working	37·0	(123)	38·4	(151)	37·8	(274)
Lower Working	14·8	(49)	42·0	(165)	29·5	(214)
Total	100·0	(332)	100·0	(393)	100·0	(725)

Each boy was assigned to a given social status group on the basis of his father's occupation, using the Hall-Jones scale of occupational prestige. But because of the limited numbers, a fourfold classification of status was adopted: the middle middle group (comprising in the main Hall-Jones categories 2 and 3); the lower middle group; and the upper and lower manual groups.[2] It must be emphasized that these divisions are relatively crude and that the groups adopted here are defined exclusively in terms of occupational prestige, thus leaving out of account the other important indices which may affect an individual's position in

[1] Allocation to these schools is made on the basis of an examination at the age of 11 +. The top 20 per cent of each age group, generally with I.Q.s of 115 and above, are offered places in the grammar school. The secondary modern schools cater for children of average and below average ability, the majority of whom take up manual work after leaving school.

[2] Only five boys in the sample came from the upper middle group (professional and business executive occupations). The upper manual group consists of sons of foremen and skilled manual workers, the lower of sons of semi-skilled and un-skilled workmen.

the social hierarchy. This should be borne in mind in connection with subsequent references in this chapter to 'working class' and 'middle class'; those terms are used as a convenient shorthand description, but they refer to groups defined in terms of occupational prestige and not to 'classes' in the classic sense of the word.

To move upwards in status, a working-class child must not only have the opportunity of attending a grammar school, but also pass its examinations. This chapter will therefore first consider the proportion of sons of manual workers in the sample who go to grammar schools, and then examine their performance and standing at such schools as compared with those of the sons of white-collar workers.[1]

Selection for Grammar School Education

In order to increase the range of geographic and social variation, the schools covered in this inquiry were chosen from two districts from the centre of London—one a predominantly working-class district in the East End (Schools A), the other a more 'mixed' district in the south-west of London (Schools B)—and from two rather more middle-class suburban districts (Schools C and D). Grammar and modern schools were drawn from the same or equivalent districts to permit a more systematic study of the effect of different school environments upon boys from similar socio-economic background coming from the same neighbourhood.

Table 2 shows the difference in social composition of the grammar and modern schools in these four districts. While we have no figures for these particular schools prior to the Education Act of 1944 from which to draw precise comparisons, there can be little doubt that the number of children from upper working-class homes in grammar schools has increased considerably. They constitute one-third of both grammar and modern school populations. By contrast, children from lower working-class homes, despite their numerical superiority in the population as a whole, continue to be seriously under-represented. They constitute only 15 per cent of the grammar school as against 42 per cent of the modern school sample. This under-representation, while most pronounced in the suburban districts, is also evident in the working-class district.[2]

[1] A fuller account of the inquiry will be found in separate publications: H. T. Himmelweit, A. H. Halsey, and A. N. Oppenheim, 'The views of adolescents on some aspects of the social class structure', *Brit. J. Sociology*, Vol. III, No. 2, June 1952; A. H. Halsey and L. Gardner, 'Social mobility and achievement in four grammar schools', *Brit. J. Sociology*, March 1953.

[2] The positive correlation between poverty and failure to gain entry into a

Table 2

PERCENTAGE DISTRIBUTION OF THE SOCIAL STATUS COMPOSITION OF THE
THIRD FORMS OF FOUR GRAMMAR AND FOUR MODERN SCHOOLS DRAWN
FROM THE SAME DISTRICTS IN THE GREATER LONDON AREA

Districts		Middle Middle	Lower Middle	Upper Working	Lower Working
A	Grammar School	7·2	25·5	46·9	20·4
	Modern School	2·2	14·3	45·0	38·5
B	Grammar School	18·0	33·7	34·8	13·5
	Modern School	0·0	6·7	34·7	58·7
C	Grammar School	33·3	21·8	29·9	14·9
	Modern School	7·2	12·4	37·1	43·3
D	Grammar School	34·5	24·1	34·5	6·9
	Modern School	6·7	20·0	42·2	31·1
	Total	21·7	26·5	37·1	14·8
		5·9	13·7	38·4	42·0

Because the schools selected were not a random sample of schools, no great stress should be placed upon the actual figures quoted. However, the very consistency of the trend, despite differences in the social composition of the districts from which the schools were drawn, suggests that these findings apply more generally. The figures show that in recent years the upper working class has become more adequately represented, but, given the social composition of the neighbourhoods served by the grammar schools, the middle class continues to be over-represented. It is unlikely that there are so few children from lower working-class homes in the grammar schools because parents refused the offer of a grammar school place. What is much more probable is that the performance of the children at the selection examination at the age of 11+ was such that only very few came within the top fifth of their age group which would qualify them for entry into the grammar school.[1] It might be argued, in turn, that this occurs because, in the lower working class, the number of boys of the requisite ability is small. But several facts speak against such an interpretation.

In the first place, previous research has shown that, except for the extremes of the occupational ladder, variations in I.Q. *within* occupa-

---

grammar school has been demonstrated by several writers; cf. Ruth Glass, *The Social Background of a Plan*, London, 1948, and C. Burt, *The Sub-Normal School Child*, Vol. II, London, 1950.

[1] The selection procedure used in allocating children to secondary schools consists of three tests: an intelligence test, and two tests of attainment, one in English and the other in arithmetic.

tional groups are generally greater than those *between* the groups.[1] Very large occupational groups like those to which semi-skilled and unskilled manual workers belong should, therefore, contain a larger absolute number of individuals of the requisite ability than some of the numerically much smaller middle-class occupational groups, despite the higher average intelligence level to be found among the latter.[2]

It is more likely that the children from the lower socio-economic groups do relatively less well on the tests of attainment which make up 66 per cent of the total marks.[3] Some indirect evidence in support of such a view was found in comparing the borderline cases in the two school populations. Although the majority of boys in the grammar school sample had significantly higher I.Q.s than those in the secondary modern school, there were some boys with identical intelligence test results who had nevertheless been assigned to different schools. Sixty-nine modern school boys constituted the sample of 'under-achievers' and 89 grammar school boys the sample of 'over-achievers'. It was found that over- and under-achievement were significantly related to social status; thus 55 per cent of the over-achievers came from the middle class and only 12 per cent from the lower working-class homes. In the case of the under-achievers, only 19 per cent came from the non-manual and 39 per cent from the manual groups.

Table 3

PERCENTAGE DISTRIBUTION OF SECONDARY SCHOOL SAMPLE SIZE OF FAMILY

	Working Class		Middle Class		Total		Total
	Small Family	Large Family	Small Family	Large Family	Small Family	Large Family	
Grammar School	62·9	37·1	67·9	32·1	65·4	34·6	100 (332)
Secondary Modern School	36·7	63·3	64·9	35·1	42·2	57·8	100 (393)

Secondly, it was found that in both the upper and lower manual groups, family size and ordinal position within a family were factors influencing a boy's chances of going to a grammar school. These were significantly greater for the boy from a small-size family (one- or two-child families) (p $\angle$ 0·003) and also for the eldest son, irrespective of the

[1] C. Burt, *op. cit.*, H. T. Himmelweit and J. Whitfield, 'Mean intelligence test scores of a random sample of occupations', *British Industrial Med.*, 1947, Vol. I.
[2] That is, assuming that intelligence is to some degree genetically determined.
[3] The correlations between intelligence tests and the tests of attainment were only of the order of 0·6.

number of his siblings. Since no such differences were found in the non-manual groups they require an explanation over and above that of the known negative correlation between I.Q. and family size.

A child, especially a young child, is likely to do better at school the more encouragement and help he receives from home. It is probable that such help is afforded more readily in small families and that for the first-born more ambitious plans are made, plans in which higher education is a necessary stepping-stone. In the middle class, however, scholastic achievement is of concern to all parents since higher education is valued as the necessary means, not only of getting on, but also of maintaining existing social status. Such differences in parental attitude towards education may well influence a child's attitude to school work and so affect his performance in the examination.

In addition, middle-class homes provide greater opportunities for extra-curricular learning. Davis's studies in the United States[1] suggest that verbal intelligence tests draw upon experiences with which a middle-class child would be more familiar than a working-class child. Since the majority of education authorities used verbal intelligence tests, the results for boys from the lower social groups may represent an underestimate of their effective or at least of their potential intelligence.

None of the facts presented here provides more than a hint as to the reasons for the differential performance of children from the various social classes. Nevertheless, the evidence does suggest that, although the main economic barriers may now have been removed, there are other, less tangible, barriers which affect a boy's chances of getting into a grammar school.

A Comparison of the Achievements and Aspirations of Middle and Working-class Grammar School Boys

In her analysis of educational mobility prior to 1940, Mrs. Floud drew attention to the fact that even among the selected grammar school population, the odds were heavily weighted against children from the lower status categories. Compared with children from the middle class, a disproportionately small number of working-class children obtained the school certificate—the first formal qualification—and an even smaller number proceeded to further education, leading to professional qualifications. Increasingly today, for the vast majority, a rise in social status is dependent upon the attainment of professional qualifications.

[1] A. Davis, *Social Class Influences upon Learning*, Harvard University Press, 1948.

Mere attendance at a grammar school ensures no more than entry into the lowest grades of clerical occupations, representing only a small step up the social scale for the son of a skilled workman. Moreover, before World War II a considerable number of grammar school pupils took up manual work on leaving school,[1] i.e. they retained, at least initially, their parental social status. In view of the academically orientated curriculum of the grammar school and of the fact that teachers judge the success of their school in terms of the size and activity of their sixth form, this tendency to leave school early connoted a failure of the educational system in this respect. The failure, due to an interplay of economic, historical and psychological factors, lay in not mobilizing to the full those resources of endeavour and ability among the working-class youth which enabled them in the first instance to succeed in the competitive examination at the age of 11+.

To what extent has this picture changed as a result of the Education Act of 1944? There are as yet no statistics available concerning the differential school-leaving record of children from the various social status groups. But in the course of the present inquiry it was possible to study the effect of social status upon scholastic performance and upon attitude to education at an earlier stage, i.e. two to three years after entry into the grammar school. The marked differences in academic attainments and in outlook to school life already shown at that age give little ground for supposing that the 'failure of the grammar school' has become a problem of the past.

Academic Record

There is no examination common to all grammar schools, prior to the school-leaving examination, which would make cross-school comparisons possible. The analysis of the scholastic performance of boys of different social status had, therefore, to be restricted to a comparison of the annual examination results within forms. Such small units make a statistical evaluation of the significance of differences meaningless, but the very consistency of the results leaves little doubt as to the likely outcome had the results of a common examination been available. Within each form, the social background of those who belonged to the five best and the five worst in the class was listed. Eleven such comparisons were made for each of the seven subjects common to the curricula of the four schools, and the results are presented in Table 4. Except for the pre-

[1] K. Lindsay, *Social Progress and Educational Waste*, London University Press, 1926, p. 3.

147

Table 4

PERFORMANCE OF SOCIAL STATUS GROUPS IN SEVEN SCHOOL SUBJECTS

School	Form	English	French	Maths.	Science	Geography	History	Art	M C	W C	*
A	1	M C	M C	M C	M C	W C	W C	M C	5	2	0
	2	W C	M C	M C	W C	M C	M C	M C	5	2	0
	3	*	W C	M C	*	W C	W C	M C	2	3	2
									12	7	2
B	1	W C	*	M C	W C	W C	W C	M C	2	4	1
	2	M C	W C	W C	M C	M C	M C	W C	4	3	0
	3	W C	W C	M C	M C	W C	W C	W C	2	5	0
									8	12	1
C	1	M C	M C	M C	M C	M C	M C	M C	7	0	0
	2	*	*	M C	M C	M C	M C	M C	5	0	2
	3	M C	*	*	W C	M C	M C	*	3	1	3
									15	1	5
D	1	M C	M C	W C	M C	*	M C	—	4	1	1
	2	M C	*	W C	W C	M C	M C	—	3	2	1
									7	3	2
Total	M C	6	4	7	6	6	7	6	42	23	10
	W C	3	3	3	4	4	4	2			
	*	2	4	1	1	1	0	1			

M C = Middle class has higher placing in examination.
W C = Working class has higher placing in examination.

* = Social classes have equal placing in examination.

148

dominantly working-class grammar school in the East End, a consistently higher percentage of children from middle-class homes was found among the top five and less among the bottom five. The rows across the bottom of the table show that the superiority of these children was fairly evenly spread over all subjects in the curriculum. Taking all four schools together, in no subject did the manual group attain the higher position.

Analysis of the data showed that this inequality of examination performance was not accounted for by differences in I.Q. To throw some light upon the problem, each form master was asked to indicate the boys who, in his opinion, were the five best and the five worst in the form with regard to a number of characteristics, namely, industriousness, sense of responsibility, interest in school affairs (extra-curricular activities), good behaviour, good manners and popularity with other boys. These characteristics were chosen as being likely to bring out differences in the evaluation of pupils from varying home backgrounds. The results were analysed on the lines of those on academic performance and are presented in Table 5. Throughout, without a single exception, middle-class pupils received a higher rating. The consistency of the findings, irrespective of the quality rated, is of interest. True, this may simply reflect the well-known 'halo effect' which so greatly influences ratings of apparently independent characteristics. Nevertheless, the results show that, in the teacher's view, the middle-class boy, taken all round, proves a more satisfactory and rewarding pupil. He appears to be better mannered, more industrious, more mature and even more popular with the other boys than his working-class co-pupil.

In the eyes of the teachers, therefore, the boy with a working-class background is not so well integrated into the school. It is difficult to estimate how far such evaluation is the result of genuine differences in behaviour and outlook on the part of the boys or to what extent it reflects differences in the teacher's attitudes to pupils coming from different social backgrounds. No generalization would be justifiable at this stage. But there is evident need for an investigation into the attitudes of grammar school teachers to the recent educational changes and to the resultant increase in the numbers of working-class boys among their pupils.

Given equal intelligence, and leaving aside the question of teacher's attitudes, differences in scholastic attainment may be due to differences in interest, in effort expended or in home facilities provided. Data on each of these aspects were obtained during the inquiry. On the whole,

Table 5

RATINGS BY FORM MASTERS OF CERTAIN PERSONALITY TRAITS OF PUPILS FROM DIFFERENT SOCIAL LEVELS

School	Form	Industriousness	Sense of Responsibility	Interest in School Affairs	Good Behaviour	Good Manners	Popularity with Peers
A	1	M C	M C	M C	M C	M C	M C
	2	*	*	M C	*	*	M C
	3	W C	W C	M C	M C	W C	W C
B	1	W C	M C	M C	*	*	M C
	2	M C	M C	W C	M C	M C	W C
	3	M C	*	M C	M C	M C	M C
C	1	M C	*	M C	*	M C	M C
	2	W C	M C	M C	M C	M C	M C
	3	*	W C	M C	W C	W C	W C
D	1	M C	M C	M C	*	M C	M C
	2	M C	M C	M C	W C	M C	M C
Total	M C	6	6	10	5	8	8
	W C	3	3	1	2	2	3
	*	2	2	0	4	1	0

M C = Middle class has higher rating.
W C = Working class has higher rating.
* = Social classes have equal rating.

150

the working-class boy considers school and progress at school of rather less importance than the middle-class boy. Thus in answer to the question 'How important do you think good marks at school are for getting on in the world later on?', 76 per cent of the middle-class boys thought them very important and only 24 per cent fairly or not very important; the corresponding percentages for the working-class boys were 63 per cent and 37 per cent respectively (p $\angle$ ·05).

Related to this estimate of the importance of school-marks is the concern that the boys feel about their own progress. In answer to the question 'How much do *you* worry about your school work compared with other boys?' 33 per cent of middle-class boys felt they worried more than other boys as compared with only 21 per cent for working-class boys (p $\angle$ ·01). When the replies were analysed by size of family of the respondent within a given social status group, the children from small families worried more than those from large families. This greater anxiety and concern on the part of children from the middle classes has been noted in the answers to most of the questions. It is of interest to relate these findings to Davis's theory concerning socialized anxiety.[1] When presented with a question requiring a decision as to whether they would refuse an invitation to a party in order to prepare for an examination or go to the party, 59 per cent of middle-class children chose to prepare for the examination compared with only 49 per cent in the working-class group.[2] Again within each social class, the children from a small family proved more concerned with school results than one from a large family.

Differences between the social status groups were also found with regard to interest in extra-curricular activities. Such participation is a further sign of the boy's integration into the school. Table 6 shows that fewer working-class boys were members of school clubs and societies; once more, the child from a small family tended to be more positive in that direction than a child from a large family.

When the non-members were asked to say why they did not belong to school clubs and societies, the working class, more frequently than the

[1] A. Davis, 'Socialization and adolescent personality', *Readings in Social Psychology*, eds. Newcomb and Hartley, New York, 1947.
[2] Suppose you planned to stay home one evening to work because you had an examination at school the next day. In the afternoon, you heard that two friends who had been away for a long time had just come back and were giving a party. What would you do?
    1. Study and not go to the party.
    2. Go to the party and hope that you would know enough to pass the examination.

middle class (42 per cent as compared with 24 per cent), answered that they were not interested (p $\angle$ ·01). This was especially true of the working-class children from large families (51 per cent). As our subjects were third-form boys, very few held official positions in school clubs and no significant differences between the groups were found. The boys' answers on interest in school affairs were confirmed by the ratings given by their form masters. In ten out of the eleven forms concerned, the middle-class group was given a higher rating.

Table 6

MEMBERSHIP OF SCHOOL CLUBS AND SOCIETIES

Social Status and Family-size Group	Members %	Non-Members %	Total %	(N)
Middle Middle	47·1	52·9	100	(70)
Lower Middle	38·8	61·2	100	(84)
Upper Working	27·0	73·0	100	(120)
Lower Working	31·9	68·1	100	(47)
Middle Class { Small Family	43·0	57·0	100	(103)
Middle Class { Large Family	41·2	58·8	100	(51)
Working Class { Small Family	34·2	65·8	100	(108)
Working Class { Large Family	18·6	81·4	100	(59)

An attempt is now being made to estimate the degree to which the parents of these boys show similar differences in attitude towards education and school work. Results are not as yet available, but some indirect evidence concerning parental interest in school and pressure for scholastic achievement were obtained by asking the boys about their parents' attitudes. A larger proportion of the middle-class group thought that their parents worried more than other boys' parents about their sons' progress at school. A consistent social class and family-size relationship was also found when the boys were asked if their parents had visited the school during the current session. Parents' visits increased with the social level of the family and decreased with the number of siblings. Middle-class parents were found more frequently to watch plays and sports (p $\angle$ ·05), showing by their attendance an interest in the extra-curricular activities of the school.

Differences in scholastic performance will also depend upon the degree of parental supervision of homework and upon the facilities provided. The number of children who admitted being helped by their parents was small, but within that small group, more middle-class children reported help with languages. These children were more often able to do their homework in a room on their own and tended more frequently to do homework during the holidays. Although the total amount of time they admitted spending on homework did not differ between the class, children from middle-class homes reported more supervision by their parents. Thus in answer to the question, 'Do your parents see to it that you finish your homework before you go out to play, or do they leave it to you to do it without being reminded?' a higher percentage of middle-class boys reported supervision by their parents. Within the working class, there was a significant difference between small and large families (44 per cent and 27 per cent respectively).

From these answers, therefore, it would appear that in a variety of ways middle-class parents show greater concern for their sons' scholastic progress and take more interest in the affairs of the school. The parents thus provide a greater motivation for their sons to do well at school.

One further sign of the child's integration into the school would be his willingness to accept the grammar school view of the value of further education and of the need to continue at school beyond the minimum school-leaving age. The boys were asked to underline the age at which, were they free to choose, they would like to leave school, and they were offered an age range from thirteen to eighteen years. The same question was put twice again, the boy being also asked to underline the age at which his father and mother would wish him to leave. The study now in progress will show how far the boys correctly assessed their parents' wishes. But the similarity of pattern presented by the data from the present inquiry for the boy's own wish and his estimate of his parents' wishes suggests that the boy feels supported in his attitude by his parents. A larger proportion of middle-class boys chose to stay beyond the age of sixteen and thus by implication to take up sixth-form work. As found in replies to earlier questions, the child from a small family within a given social class wanted to stay longer than the child from a large one.

The mean preferred age for leaving the grammar school was:

	Small Family	Large Family
(a) For the middle class	17·0 years	16·4 years
(b) For the working class	16·5 years	16·1 years

and the views attributed by these groups to their parents followed the same pattern.

These results are in line with the earlier age at leaving actually found for working-class boys. It is true that the economic incentives towards early leaving are greatest for a working-class boy, the majority of whose friends in the secondary modern schools will already be earning a wage. Nevertheless, the replies to the attitude questions described earlier suggest that the desire to leave school early may in part at least be due to the incomplete acceptance by the boys of the grammar school 'values'.

Vocational Aspirations

In our inquiry into social status differences in the outlook of young adolescents, the boys were asked a number of questions to bring out their views of the nature of social stratification in Britain. Comparison of their replies with those obtained for adults[1] showed a remarkable similarity and suggests that adolescents are aware of the prestige value of different occupations and of the factors associated with moving up in the world. The differences between the replies of the two broad status groups were not very marked; where they occurred, they were in the direction of greater 'sophistication' in the answers of middle-class boys. The working-class grammar school boy mentioned education as the second most important factor for upward mobility, and 78 per cent of them, as compared with 65 per cent of middle-class boys, regarded their chances of getting on in the world as better than those their fathers had had.

Both working- and middle-class young adolescents have a fairly realistic conception of the nature of the social hierarchy in Britain. Nevertheless, a number of working-class boys would like to leave school at an age which would make it difficult for them to obtain further education. Is it then that, 'with their eyes open', they want to go into occupations which carry little more prestige than those of their fathers, or is there an unresolved discrepancy between the desire for early school-leaving, which puts out of reach higher status occupations, and their vocational aspirations?

In a questionnaire which is described in greater detail elsewhere,[2] the boys were asked to name the job they would like to take up supposing they could be anybody, go anywhere or do anything (fantasy job). They were also asked to name the job they expected to get when they were grown up, and the job their fathers expected them to go into. In addition to naming the jobs, they were asked to evaluate, on a five-point scale, the prestige that these jobs carry. The scale ranged from 'Almost every-

[1] H. T. Himmelweit, A. H. Halsey and A. N. Oppenheim, 'The views of adolescents on some aspects of the social class structure', *Brit. J. Sociology*, June 1952.

[2] H. T. Himmelweit, A. H. Halsey, A. N. Oppenheim, *op. cit.*

Table 7

PERCENTAGE DISTRIBUTION OF BOYS WHO SHOW UPWARD SOCIAL STRIVING, BY TYPE OF SCHOOL AND SOCIAL CLASS, FOR EACH OF EIGHT DIFFERENT CRITERIA

OBJECTIVE

Occupations on which comparisons are based	Grammar								Modern							
	Middle Middle Class		Lower Middle Class		Upper Working Class		Lower Working Class		Middle Middle Class		Lower Middle Class		Upper Working Class		Lower Working Class	
	1	2+	1	2+	1	2+	1	2+	1	2+	1	2+	1	2+	1	2+
	%	%	%	%	%	%	%	%	%	%	%	%	%	%	%	%
Father's vs. Wish	44	0	45	28	6	75	16	84	40	0	20	30	4	36	51	40
Father's vs. Expected	48	0	31	19	6	61	34	63	14	0	17	8	2	8	65	12
Father's vs. Father's Wish	43	0	36	27	5	68	19	81	7	0	23	17	1	18	66	19
Expected vs. Wish	9	2	20	15	18	19	22	24	14	21	9	24	7	28	10	30

SUBJECTIVE

Occupations on which comparisons are based	Grammar								Modern							
	Middle Middle Class		Lower Middle Class		Upper Working Class		Lower Working Class		Middle Middle Class		Lower Middle Class		Upper Working Class		Lower Working Class	
	1	2+	1	2+	1	2+	1	2+	1	2+	1	2+	1	2+	1	2+
Father's vs. Wish	37	24	29	34	28	44	35	52	14	0	22	11	19	26	24	37
Father's vs. Expected	20	10	25	16	25	29	54	21	11	0	20	8	17	16	25	20
Father's vs. Father's Wish	30	11	39	20	32	29	39	36	6	0	26	8	18	14	26	31
Expected vs. Wish	15	26	28	20	27	20	23	26	0	0	18	13	15	17	15	21

The figures in the table show the percentage of each class group whose aspirations exceeded their father's or expected job by 1 scale interval; by 2 or more scale intervals.

For each type of discrepancy, the data both for the adult (Objective) and for the adolescent (Subjective) frame of reference are given.

155

one looks up to the persons who hold these jobs' to 'Hardly anybody looks up to the persons who hold these jobs'. The intermediary steps were: most people, many people, some people. Previously the boys had assessed their father's occupation on the same scale. These assessments will be described as 'subjective' ratings in contrast to the 'objective' ratings of the prestige value of the occupations, based on the Hall-Jones scale. A number of discrepancy scores were then computed: an 'objective' discrepancy score indicates the difference between the prestige levels of two occupations as judged by adult standards: a 'subjective' discrepancy score indicates the difference between the prestige levels as judged by the adolescents themselves. A measure of *expected social mobility* was obtained by determining the 'objective' discrepancy score between father's occupation and the job the boy expects to take up. Upward social mobility is denoted by a negative discrepancy score. Table 7 indicates the percentage in each social class group who have named occupations which are one or two grades above those of their fathers. Figures for the modern school have also been given to show the greater importance of school compared with social class in determining vocational expectations. Thus, many middle-class boys in the modern school expect to go in for jobs of lower social prestige than those listed by the lower working-class boys in the grammar school. Of all the groups, the working-class groups in the grammar school proved to be the most upwardly mobile both with regard to 'objective' and to 'subjective' ratings.

Figure 1 gives a graphic presentation of the various mean discrepancy scores. Across the centre of each quadrant in the graph, a line of 'zero discrepancy' indicates no change in prestige level. Points above indicate upward social strivings, points below downward mobility trends. For each social status group, the mean discrepancy score has been computed (taking into account both upward and downward mobility). These graphs show once more the aspiration to upward social mobility in the lower social class groups.

The most accurate measure of social striving, it was felt, would be obtained first, by relating subjective and objective ratings of expected and fantasy jobs to the ratings of the fathers' occupations, and secondly, by comparing the levels of expected and fantasy jobs. Some of the boys tended to list wish jobs of higher social status than the ones they expected to go in for (e.g. the draughtsman became an architect and the clerk an accountant). Others chose work quite different in type from their expected jobs (e.g. professional footballer and toolmaker). No

OBJECTIVE   SUBJECTIVE

FATHER'S JOB v WISH JOB

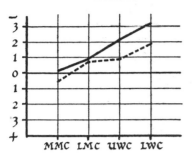
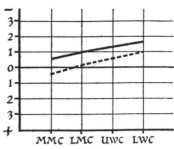

FATHER'S JOB v EXPECTED JOB

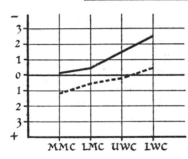
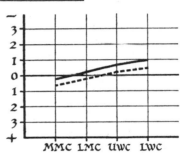

FATHER'S JOB v JOB WISHED BY FATHER FOR BOY

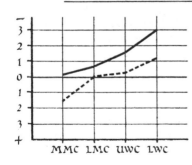
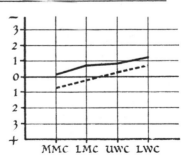

Fig. I.—Aspired and Expected Social Mobility. (Mean Discrepancy Scores obtained from objected and subjective assessments of occupations)

———— = Grammar School   - - - - - = Modern School
MMC = Middle Middle Class   UWC = Upper Working Class
LMC = Lower Middle Class   LWC = Lower Working Class

evidence of compensatory fantasy was found since the frequency of one or the other type of relationship between fantasy job and expected job did not differ for the various school and social class groups. The jobs chosen showed a wide range, with airplane pilots and positions in the entertainment world not unexpectedly receiving the most frequent mention. Clerical work, which the majority of grammar school boys in fact take up on leaving school, was hardly ever mentioned.

The occupational prestige questionnaire brought to light several interesting points. First, on the whole, the subjective evaluation did not differ markedly from the objective one, i.e. the boys were aware of the prestige that their wish and expected jobs carry and the way in which these differ in this respect from their fathers' jobs. Secondly, in their vocational expectations and wishes, grammar school boys, especially of the working class, show a marked social striving. Sixty-three per cent of the lower working-class boys intended to take up at least lower middle-class occupations; while 75 per cent of the upper working-class boys chose occupations from Hall-Jones grades 1–3 (middle middle class) which would certainly require attaining the school-leaving certificate and other formal educational qualifications. On this reckoning, the lower middle class proves rather less striving since only 28 per cent expect to move up by two or more grades, 45 per cent by one grade and 17 per cent to retain their social *status quo*. It is difficult to reconcile these figures with recent reports that a considerable number of school-leavers from grammar schools take up manual work. It may of course be that the nearer the boy comes to leaving school, the more he chooses the immediate and considerable financial return obtained by taking up manual work. It is hoped to follow up the careers of the boys in the sample in order to see how far they live up to their vocational expectations.

Summary and Conclusions

Data obtained from seven hundred young adolescents from grammar and secondary modern schools in the Greater London area showed that, while the upper working class is more adequately represented in the grammar schools since 1944, the lower working class continues to be under-represented. It is unlikely that this is due to differences in 'innate ability', and there is suggestive evidence that working-class children do relatively less well on the tests of attainment which comprise 66 per cent of the selection examination. Further, only among the working-class boys in the grammar school is there an unduly large percentage of chil-

158

dren belonging to one or two child families, and a disproportionately / high number of eldest sons. It may well be that children from small families and the eldest son in families of all sizes receive more parental support and are, therefore, more highly motivated to do well at school.

Success within the grammar school is also partly determined by the boy's social class membership. The working-class boy's academic record is less good than that of his middle-class co-pupil, despite equal measured intelligence. Working-class boys receive lower ratings from their form masters on personality characteristics associated with positive scholastic progress and with integration into the school. This group as a whole expresses less concern about its progress at school. Asked at what age they would like to leave school, working-class boys prefer to leave at an age which would preclude training for further education. Moreover, the boys described their desire to leave early as being in accord with that of their parents.

The attitudes of the thirteen to fourteen-year-old boys suggest that the change since the Education Act of 1944 has not yet made itself felt in the climate of the school. The working-class boys are not as concerned as the middle-class boys to achieve high marks in examinations or to take part in the extra-curricular activities of the school.

And yet, in answers to a variety of questions, the working-class boys seemed aware of the significance of a grammar school education for upward movement in social status, and in their vocational expectations and aspirations they showed themselves the most upwardly mobile group. There is thus a discrepancy between hopes for the future and the extent to which the boys, while they are at school, work to fulfil those hopes.

While the study was not designed to cover a random sample of schools the results are consistent for the various schools examined. Further inquiry is needed, first into the attitudes and aspirations of the parents of the boys, and secondly into the attitudes of teachers to the educational changes and their consequences. It may well be found that the more effective use of the grammar schools by working-class boys will require substantially different teacher-pupil and teacher-parent relations.

VII

An Inquiry into Parents' Preferences in Secondary Education

F. M. MARTIN

THIS chapter deals with one aspect of the many-sided problem of ambitions and aspirations: the attitudes of parents towards different types of post-primary education. Some information on the preferences of a sample of adults in respect of their children's length of school career and ultimate occupation had been obtained in the course of an earlier inquiry.[1] But the value of these findings was limited by the lack of detailed questioning and by the heterogeneity of the sample; the need for a further and more systematic investigation seemed obvious. The present study, which is confined to a single area, forms part of an inquiry into some of the social factors associated with selection for, and success in, secondary education. One section of the project is concerned with the performance of the fifteen hundred-odd children who, in this area,[2] were to sit in 1952 for the Local Education Authority's 'County Entrance Examination', and who would on the basis of that examination be allocated either to a secondary modern or to a secondary grammar school. In order to secure information on the basis of which the children might be classified in terms of status background, it was necessary to interview the parents of those children; and at the same time the opportunity was taken to ask a number of additional questions mainly bearing upon interest in, and attitude towards, secondary education. Almost all these interviews were carried out in March and April 1952, when the entrance examination was still in progress.

In the final report of the investigation,[3] parental attitudes will be

[1] See Chapter III.

[2] The South-west Division of Hertfordshire (Watford and its environs).

[3] J. E. Floud, F. M. Martin and A. H. Halsey: *Secondary Education and Social Mobility* (in preparation). We are very greatly indebted to the Hertfordshire Education Authority for their help at all stages of the investigation.

160

analysed in relation to the examination performance and subsequent placement of the children. Here, however, we are concerned only with attitude differences between occupational groups, and with some of the correlates of those differences.

Early in 1952 each of the primary schools in south-west Hertfordshire was asked to submit a list of the names and addresses of all children who were eligible to enter for the county entrance examination in that year. To these were added the names of the other examination candidates who were then attending private or preparatory schools. Of the 1,575 names sent in, 21 were removed from the sample; these were children who were either orphaned or for some reason were not living with their parents, and who were in the care of the Hertfordshire County Council. One hundred and eight parents could not be traced, could not be interviewed, or refused to be interviewed. The effective sample thus amounted to 1,446, 91·8 per cent of the age group.

Table 1

OCCUPATIONAL COMPOSITION OF SAMPLE

Occupations	No. of Cases	Percentage of Sample
Members of Professions; managers; medium and large business owners	104	7·19
Clerks of all grades	104	7·19
Foremen and supervisors; commercial travellers; shopkeepers and small business owners	255	17·64
Skilled manual workers	630	43·57
Semi-skilled and unskilled manual workers	309	21·37
Information missing or inadequate	44	3·04
Total	1446	100·00

The occupational composition of the sample is given in Table 1. For the purposes of the present analysis, those families for which no adequate occupational data was available were excluded, and some of the status categories were grouped together—managers and business owners with members of the professions; clerks of all grades; and commercial travellers and shopkeepers with foremen and supervisors. It would of

161

course be of great interest to consider separately some of these components, but the numbers are unfortunately too small to permit adequate statistical analysis. Manual workers make up two-thirds of the
sample; the high ratio of skilled to semi-skilled and unskilled manual
workers reflects the industrial structure of the area, in which printing and precision engineering play an important part, and heavy
industry is virtually non-existent. It is, too, a relatively prosperous and
well-housed group. In only one-third of the families was the net income
of the senior wage-earner below £7 10s. per week, and in one family out
of four his net weekly income was about £10. 7·7 per cent of the sample
lived in detached houses, 59·6 per cent in semi-detached houses, and
22·7 per cent in terraced houses; 87·9 per cent of the families included in
this investigation had at their disposal at least as many rooms as there
were members of the family.

Table 2

CONCERN WITH SECONDARY EDUCATION

Father's Occupational Grade	N	Percentage who: Have thought a lot about child's secondary education	Have thought a little about child's secondary education	Have not thought about child's secondary education
Professional	104	82·7	9·6	7·7
Clerical	104	70·2	23·1	6·7
Supervisory	255	62·0	23·2	14·8
Skilled	630	50·5	27·1	22·3
Unskilled	309	35·3	30·7	33·9
Total	1402	53·1	25·6	21·4

Tables 2, 3 and 4 summarize the replies of the five groups to three
questions dealing with attitudes to secondary education, and each reveals
marked differences between occupational groups. Asked, by way of
introduction, whether they had given much thought recently to their
children's secondary education, more than four out of five in the group
of highest status claimed to have thought a good deal about the subject.
This figure falls to 70 per cent among the clerks and 62 per cent among
the foremen; one-half of the skilled manual workers come into the same
category, and just over one-third of the semi-skilled and unskilled
workers. Another third of the non-skilled workers admitted that they had
not thought about their children's secondary education at all; this compares with one-fifth of the skilled workers, one in seven of the supervisors, and only one in fourteen among the 'white-collar' groups.

PARENTS' PREFERENCES IN SECONDARY EDUCATION

In a more direct, and perhaps more revealing question, parents were asked which type of secondary school they would prefer their children to attend—grammar, modern or technical.[1]

Table 3

PREFERRED TYPES OF SECONDARY SCHOOL

Father's Occupational Grade	N	Percentage expressing preference for:				Don't know No Preference
		Secondary Modern	Secondary Grammar	Secondary Technical	Other	
Professional	104	1·9	81·7	3·8	10·6	1·9
Clerical	104	4·8	77·8	9·6	2·8	4·8
Supervisory	255	9·1	60·7	19·2	2·7	8·2
Skilled	630	16·9	48·2	23·0	0·8	10·9
Unskilled	309	23·9	43·4	19·4	1·0	12·3
Total	1402	16·0	54·1	19·1	2·1	9·6

The occupational distribution of preferences for the secondary grammar school is not unlike the distribution of claims to have been much concerned about the child's secondary education in general. Just over four-fifths of the professional, and three-quarters of the clerical group, expressed a preference for the grammar school, as did three-fifths of the supervisory group, 48 per cent of the skilled workers, and 43 per cent of the other manual workers. Another 10 per cent of the professional group would like their children to remain outside the publicly provided system of education altogether, but this preference is shared by very few parents in any other group. The technical school, however, enjoys some popularity among present and former manual workers, but a good deal less in the other groups. Nearly one in four of the skilled workers would rather their children went to a technical than to any other type of secondary school, as would just under one in five of the foremen and of the unskilled workers; fewer than one in ten of the clerks and one in twenty-five of the professionals have a similar preference. It is only among the unskilled and semi-skilled workers that there are more preferences expressed for the secondary modern than for the secondary technical school (23·9 per cent); the corresponding figure for the skilled workers is 16·9 per cent, and this falls away rapidly to less than 2 per cent in the professional group. In no occupational group is there more than a small minority which has no positive preference. 9·6 per cent of the entire sample fall into this

[1] Children in this area could not in fact go to a secondary technical school at age 11, but might be re-allocated at 13+.

163

category; one in fifty of the professional group and one in twenty of the clerks contribute to their number, as compared with one-twelfth of the foremen, one-ninth of the skilled workers, and one-eighth of the non-skilled workers.

Table 4

IMPORTANCE ATTACHED TO MOVE TO SECONDARY SCHOOL

Father's Occupational Grade	N	Percentage who think that:		
		Move will make a lot of difference in child's life	Move will make little or no difference in child's life	Don't know
Professional	104	70·2	25·0	4·8
Clerical	104	62·5	27·8	9·6
Supervisory	255	52·9	33·3	12·9
Skilled	630	45·5	42·7	11·9
Unskilled	309	40·8	37·2	22·0
Total	1402	48·9	37·3	13·8

It may be of interest, finally, to consider the replies of parents to the question of what difference they thought the move to the secondary school would make in the child's life. Seven-tenths of the professional group thought the move would make a lot of difference, and one-quarter that it would make little or no difference. 62·5 per cent of the clerks and 52·9 per cent of the supervisors also thought transfer marked an important stage in the child's life. 45·5 per cent of the skilled and 40·8 per cent of the non-skilled manual workers expressed similar expectations, but within these occupational groups the proportions attaching little or no importance to the transition became almost as large. Again, only a small minority has no opinions on this subject, but it is a minority which is at its smallest in the non-manual groups (7·2 per cent for clerks

Table 5

PREFERRED TYPE OF SECONDARY SCHOOL IN RELATION TO CONCERN WITH SECONDARY EDUCATION

Father's Occupational Grade	Preferred Secondary School	N	Percentage who:		
			Have thought a lot about child's secondary education	Have thought a little about child's secondary education	Have not though about child's secondary education
Supervisory	Grammar	155	74·8	16·8	8·4
Supervisory	Other	100	42·0	33·0	25·0
Skilled	Grammar	303	69·6	20·5	10·0
Skilled	Other	327	32·7	33·3	33·9
Unskilled	Grammar	134	51·5	29·8	18·7
Unskilled	Other	175	22·9	31·4	45·7

and professionals combined). Uncertainty is least uncommon among the non-skilled manual workers, and accounts for 22 per cent of their number; for the skilled workers and supervisors, the figures are respectively 11·9 per cent and 12·9 per cent.

Before going on to an analysis of the social correlates of educational preference, it may be as well to justify the use of an expressed preference for grammar school education as the principal dependent variable. As Tables 5 and 6 show, this preference is not a mere fortuitous judgement, but is in fact quite closely related to the other two variables discussed above. The professional and clerical grades are excluded from these analyses, as the numbers here who do *not* prefer the grammar school are statistically quite inadequate; only the three remaining groups, which

Table 6

PREFERRED TYPE OF SECONDARY SCHOOL IN RELATION TO IMPORTANCE
ATTACHED TO MOVE TO SECONDARY SCHOOL

Father's Occupational Grade	Preferred Secondary School	N	Percentage who think that: Move will make a lot of difference in child's life	Move will make little or no difference in child's life	Don't know
Supervisory	Grammar	155	66·4	22·6	11·0
Supervisory	Other	100	32·0	50·0	18·0
Skilled	Grammar	303	59·7	32·3	7·9
Skilled	Other	327	32·4	52·3	15·3
Unskilled	Grammar	134	54·5	26·1	19·4
Unskilled	Other	175	30·3	45·7	24·0

are both larger and more evenly divided in their views, are considered. Table 5 compares, within each of these three occupational groups, those parents preferring the grammar school with all other parents in respect of their expressed concern with secondary education. There is at each occupational level a significant difference between the two sub-groups, the proportion of those who claim to have thought a lot about their children's secondary education being greater by about 30 percentage points among the parents who would prefer their children to go to the grammar school. It is noteworthy, however, that even when educational preference is held constant, an appreciable difference between occupational groups persists. If we consider only parents who wish to see their children go to a grammar school, we see that the proportion who have thought a good deal about secondary education drops as we descend the occupational scale—at first slowly, from 74·8 per cent among the supervisors to 69·6 per cent of the skilled manual workers, and then move steeply to 51·5 per cent of the semi-skilled and unskilled manual workers. Similar relationships appear in Table 6, in which educational preferences are cross-tabulated with the degree of importance attached to the transfer to the secondary school. In this case the differences between subgroups vary from 24 to 34 percentage points, while the independent differences between occupational groups are far less marked, accounting for fewer than 12 points between the supervisors and the unskilled workers.

Prima facie, it seems very doubtful whether the distribution of educational preferences within specific occupational groups can be explained by reference to any single factor; in all probability, a multiplicity of social and psychological influences is involved. We have at present no direct information concerning the psychological characteristics of the parents in our sample—although such data may be secured if, as seems probable, case studies are undertaken in the near future—but the distribution of a series of social characteristics has been analysed in relation to educational preferences, and the results are summarized in Tables 7 to 11.

Table 7

PREFERRED TYPE OF SECONDARY SCHOOL IN RELATION TO INCOME OF SENIOR WAGE-EARNER

Father's Occupational Grade	School Preferred	N	Percentage having:		
			Weekly income below £7 10s.	Weekly income above £7 10s.	No Information
Supervisory	Grammar	155	12·3	71·0	16·7
Supervisory	Other	100	12·0	68·0	20·0
Skilled	Grammar	303	30·0	66·9	3·0
Skilled	Other	327	36·7	53·5	9·7
Unskilled	Grammar	134	70·8	24·6	4·4
Unskilled	Other	175	67·4	27·4	5·1

One form of attempted explanation might be couched in simple economic terms; within each group, it may be suggested, it is the parents with higher incomes who can most readily contemplate the cost of maintaining the child at a grammar school and forgoing his potential earnings over a number of years. Table 7, which shows, within each of the six sub-groups, the proportion of families the weekly income of whose senior wage-earner exceeds £7 10s., lends little support to this hypothesis. Among the foremen and supervisors the proportion of weekly incomes exceeding £7 10s. is indeed greater in the group of parents who have expressed a preference for the grammar school, but by only 3 percentage points. It should be noted, too, that for an appreciable propor-

166

tion of each group no information as to income distributions can reliably be drawn. The facts about the other two occupational groups are less ambiguous. 66·9 per cent of the skilled manual workers who prefer the grammar school earn more than £7 10s. per week, as against 53·5 per cent of those who have expressed other or no preference. This difference is statistically significant, and although it might well be reduced if the undeclared incomes were known—as their proportion is greater, by 6·7 per cent, among the group that seems to be the poorer of the two—a distinct difference would still remain. On the other hand, this relationship is not confirmed by the income distribution of the semi-skilled and unskilled manual workers; at this level, the proportion of 'high' incomes is in fact slightly less among the parents who prefer the grammar school —although the differences are below the level of statistical significance. We may conclude, in short, that only one of our three occupational groups provides any evidence in favour of a simple economic explanation of educational attitudes.

Table 8

PREFERRED TYPE OF SECONDARY SCHOOL IN RELATION TO FATHER'S FURTHER EDUCATION

Father's Occupational Grade	Preferred Secondary School	N	Percentage of fathers having received: Full-time or part-time further education	No further education
Supervisory	Grammar	155	46·5	53·5
Supervisory	Other	100	31·0	69·0
Skilled	Grammar	303	30·4	69·6
Skilled	Other	327	20·5	79·5
Unskilled	Grammar	134	9·7	90·3
Unskilled	Other	175	7·4	92·6

Any attempt to estimate the importance of parents' own education as an independent determinant of their aspirations for their children's education is likely to encounter the practical difficulty that, as a consequence of the high correlation of educational with occupational status, groups which have been selected on the basis of occupational level will tend to be relatively homogeneous in respect of educational experience. The great majority of fathers in the three groups under consideration had attended senior elementary schools or their equivalent; those who had not, formed a group too small to permit of statistical comparison. In nearly one-third of the families, however, the father had received some form of further education, either full-time or—more commonly—part-time. As Table 8 shows, this additional educational experience does affect aspirations to a significant extent. Of the foremen and supervisors who would prefer their children to be educated at a grammar school, 46·5 per cent have themselves had some form of further education, as compared with 31 per cent of those who, at the same occupational level, do not express a preference for the grammar school. The comparable proportions for the two corresponding groups of skilled workers are respectively 30·4 per cent and 20·5 per cent; among the other manual workers, only one in twelve of whom has received any further education at all, the difference, although still in the expected direction, is negligible. These relations can be expressed somewhat differently if the sample is reconstructed in such a way as to allow a direct comparison between all families in which the father has received further education, and all the families in which he has not. There are 288 in the former category, and of these 62·8 per cent prefer the grammar school for their children; the latter group amounts to 906, 45·8 per cent of whom have similar views. Although this is a convenient form in which to express relations shown in Table 8, it should be borne in mind that it has the disadvantage of obscuring those differences between occupational groups which persist when variations in educational experience are held constant.

Table 9

PREFERRED TYPE OF SECONDARY SCHOOL IN RELATION TO MOTHER'S EDUCATION

Father's Occupational Grade	School Preferred	N	Mother's Education	
			Elementary	Other than Elementary
			%	%
Supervisory	Grammar	155	63·9	35·7
Supervisory	Other	100	74·0	24·0
Skilled	Grammar	303	77·2	18·7
Skilled	Other	327	85·9	13·4
Unskilled	Grammar	134	88·0	11·8
Unskilled	Other	175	87·4	11·4

The educational histories of the mothers of families in the occupational categories included in this analysis seem to be rather more varied than those of their husbands; nearly one in five had attended a central school, a trade or commercial school, or a grammar school. 59·3 per cent of these fall into the 'grammar school preference' group, as against 48·5 per cent of the families in which the mother had received only elementary education. If the three occupational grades are examined separately, as in Table 9, the post-primary education of the mothers is seen to be, at each occupational level, a less discriminative variable than

168

the further education, whether full-time or part-time, of the fathers. It accounts for a difference of 11·7 percentage points among the supervisors, 5·3 points among skilled workers, and less than one point among semi-skilled and unskilled workers.

Mother's occupation before marriage, however, provides a more effective discriminant. Within each sub-group, families have been divided, in Table 10, into those in which the mother had been engaged

Table 10

PREFERRED TYPE OF SECONDARY SCHOOL IN RELATION TO MOTHER'S OCCUPATION BEFORE MARRIAGE

Father's Occupational Grade	Preferred Secondary School	N	Mother's Occupation:		
			Manual %	Non-manual %	Not known %
Supervisory	Grammar	155	50·2	42·1	7·7
Supervisory	Other	100	64·0	27·0	9·0
Skilled	Grammar	303	70·6	25·8	3·6
Skilled	Other	327	84·1	11·3	4·6
Unskilled	Grammar	134	76·8	16·5	6·7
Unskilled	Other	175	86·3	9·1	4·6

in manual work before marriage, and those in which her occupation before marriage was non-manual. Taking the three categories in descending order of status, the proportion of mothers who have not been manual workers, in the groups which have expressed a preference for the grammar school, exceeds their incidence in the other groups by 15·1, 14·5 and 7·4 percentage points respectively. If we adopt the procedure of grouping together, irrespective of father's occupation, all the cases in which the mother had been a manual worker, and all those in which she had not, we find that of 885 in the first category, 44·6 per cent choose the grammar school, which may be compared with 67·3 per cent of the 245 cases in the second category.

The findings of a recent inquiry[1] suggest that the likelihood of reaching a grammar school, in the case of working-class boys, depends in some degree upon the size of the boy's family (i.e. the number of his siblings). When the analysis of the material of the Watford survey has been completed, it will be possible to say whether similar relationships exist within our cohort; but meanwhile it may be noted that there is a definite connection between family size and the educational aspirations of parents, and a connection which persists at each of the three occupational levels. The semi-skilled and unskilled manual workers who want

[1] A. H. Halsey and L. Gardner, 'Social Mobility and Achievement in Four Grammar Schools', *Brit. J. Sociology*, March 1953.

one of their children to go to a grammar school have an average of 3·21 children, as against 3·41 in the families where no such preference is expressed. The difference between the mean family sizes is greater among the foremen and supervisors (2·51 as compared with 2·84), and greatest in the case of the skilled manual workers, where the parents who aim at a grammar school education have an average of 2·79 children, and those parents who do not express that wish have an average of 3·28. We may postulate either that, as a consequence of having smaller families, certain families find themselves in a position from which the direct and indirect cost of a grammar school education can be more readily contemplated; or, more plausibly perhaps, that the smaller families and the educational preferences are both expressions of an underlying concern with social status and aspirations towards social mobility.

Table 11

PREFERRED TYPE OF SECONDARY SCHOOL IN RELATION TO SIZE OF FAMILY

Father's Occupational Grade	School Preferred	N	Mean No. of Children
Supervisory	Grammar	155	2·51
Supervisory	Other	100	2·84
Skilled	Grammar	303	2·79
Skilled	Other	327	3·28
Unskilled	Grammar	134	3·21
Unskilled	Other	175	3·41

It must be admitted that, although the social factors examined above explain some part of the differences within occupational groups, they are far from providing a complete explanation. There is clearly a strong case for the investigation of the psychological correlates of educational and occupational aspirations, whether personal or vicarious, particularly in the study of individuals whose attitudes do not conform to the characteristic pattern of their social groups.

Although it has been shown that an expressed preference for grammar school education for one's children is a fairly good index of a general concern with education, it cannot be assumed that members of diverse occupational grades are to be regarded as directly comparable in their educational aspirations merely by virtue of the fact that they have this preference in common. Tables 12, 13, 14 and 15 summarize the replies given to a series of questions which were asked of this group of parents, and indicate the existence of marked differences between occupational grades. They were asked, for example, whether they felt strongly about the importance of a grammar school education, or whether they simply had a preference, without feeling particularly strongly about it. While the semi-skilled and unskilled manual workers were evenly divided between these two categories, the parents in the highest status group were divided in the ratio of four to one. Among the skilled manual workers, the proportion who feel strongly about the importance of going to a grammar school rises to 58·5 per cent; and the proportion is slightly higher—though not significantly so—among the foremen (70·3 per cent) than among the clerks (64·2 per cent).

Table 12

STRENGTH OF FEELING ABOUT IMPORTANCE OF GRAMMAR SCHOOL EDUCATION

(Asked only of those parents expressing preference for grammar school)

Father's Occupational Grade	N	Percentage who:		
		Feel strongly about importance of going to Grammar School	Prefer Grammar School, but do not feel strongly	Are vague
Professional	85	80·0	18·8	1·2
Clerical	81	64·2	32·1	3·7
Supervisory	155	70·3	25·8	3·9
Skilled	304	58·5	38·8	2·7
Unskilled	134	47·0	48·5	4·5
Total	759	61·9	34·9	3·2

Table 13

READINESS TO ACCEPT PLACE IN SECONDARY MODERN SCHOOL IN EVENT OF CHILD'S FAILING TO REACH GRAMMAR SCHOOL

(Asked only of those expressing preference for grammar school)

Father's Occupational Grade	N	Percentage who:		
		Would accept place in Modern School	Would send child elsewhere	N.R. D.K.
Professional	85	43·5	49·4	7·0
Clerical	81	64·3	25·9	9·8
Supervisory	155	75·5	20·0	4·5
Skilled	304	89·4	6·6	3·9
Unskilled	134	94·7	1·5	3·7
Total	759	79·8	15·3	5·0

Parents who hoped to see their children attend a grammar school were further asked whether, in the event of the child's failing to secure a place in a grammar school, they would accept the alternative of the secondary modern school, or 'send the child elsewhere'—that is, to a school out-side the State educational system. Answers to such a question must inevitably reflect economic differences, but it is still of interest to see that one in two of the parents in the highest status group, and one in four of the clerks, were not prepared to consider sending their children to a secondary modern school. Among the manual workers the correspond-ing proportion is negligible, but rises to one in five among the super-visors.

Table 14

PREFERRED SCHOOL-LEAVING AGE

(Asked only of those expressing preference for grammar school)

Father's Occupational Grade	N	15	16	17	18+	D.K. N.R.	Mean Age
			Percentage preferring:				
Professional	85	2·4	15·3	15·3	67·1	—	17·47
Clerical	81	8·6	32·1	16·1	40·7	2·5	16·91
Supervisory	155	12·9	29·0	12·3	44·5	1·3	16·90
Skilled	303	19·1	35·6	8·9	34·6	1·6	16·49
Unskilled	134	29·9	38·1	4·5	26·1	1·4	16·27

Table 15

PREFERRED POST-SECONDARY EDUCATION OR TRAINING

(Asked only of those parents expressing preference for grammar school)

	Father's Occupational Grade:				
	Professional	Clerical	Supervisory	Skilled	Unskilled
N	81	85	155	304	134
Percentage preferring:					
University or Professional Training	44·8	58·8	38·0	23·0	14·2
Teacher's Training College	4·9	4·7	7·1	8·2	3·0
Technical College	7·4	2·4	14·2	9·5	17·1
Apprenticeship	2·5	4·7	7·1	8·2	7·5
Other forms of education or training	3·7	2·4	4·5	6·2	6·7
No further education or training	6·2	3·5	5·7	6·2	6·0
Doubtful, undecided	48·5	26·2	30·3	42·7	47·7

(Percentages add to more than 100.)

In two additional questions, parents were asked to say up to what age they would prefer the child under discussion to remain at a grammar school, and whether they had yet formed any preferences concerning subsequent education or training. Their answers throw some light, at

172

any rate, upon the problem of early leaving. Fully two-thirds of the unskilled and semi-skilled workers suggested a school-leaving age of 15 or 16, and only 34·3 per cent expressed a desire for their children to attend a university, a teachers' training college, or a technical college, or to enter upon some other form of professional training; one-half of these latter choices, incidentally, were for the technical college. 54·7 per cent of the skilled manual workers were in favour of an early leaving age, and two-fifths mentioned one or other of the forms of post-secondary education and training which might be expected to lead to entry into one of the professions. Not surprisingly, substantial minorities of both these groups were reluctant, as yet, to express any definite preference as to subsequent education. Among the clerks and the supervisors there was a greater readiness to specify a choice, 26 per cent to 30 per cent falling into the 'undecided' category, as compared with 42 per cent to 47 per cent of the manual workers. These two groups are also very much alike in their views about the school-leaving age, two-fifths of both supervisors and clerks specifying 16 or less. Two-thirds of the clerks and three-fifths of the supervisors would like their children to attend university, training college, but preferences for university education are more common, by 20 percentage points, among the clerks, while preferences for technical college, training are expressed by 14·2 per cent of the supervisors, as against 2·4 per cent of the clerks. The group of managers, business owners, and members of the professions is the least divided in its beliefs about the most desirable school-leaving age. 67·1 per cent and 15·3 per cent respectively mention the ages of 18 and 17, with only 17·7 per cent in favour of 15 or 16. Nearly one-half of this group is undecided as to further education; but almost all the remainder choose university education or some form of professional training.

Summary

In the course of an inquiry, carried out in the South-west Division of Hertfordshire, into social and cultural aspects of educational selection and achievement, 1,446 parents, whose children were candidates in the county entrance examination, were interviewed in March–April 1952. Some of the information obtained in these interviews has been presented in this chapter, in a form which allows the educational aspirations of parents of different occupational levels to be compared. Preferences for different types of secondary education were analysed, together with certain associated attitudes, and the importance of some of the social factors which determine educational ambitions within occupational grades was

173

estimated. Finally, those parents, at each occupational level, who wished their children to attend a grammar school, were compared in respect of the importance they attached to this form of education, and of their preferences as to school-leaving age and subsequent training.

The findings of socio-psychological inquiries of this kind cannot lay claim to a validity which transcends the limitations of time and place. The results presented should be interpreted in the light of the dominant characteristics of south-west Hertfordshire—its varied social composition, its present prosperity, the absence of any serious history of unemployment—and of the high reputation of its grammar schools. Nevertheless, the results are of interest in themselves and they also complement the findings of Dr. Himmelweit's study, carried out among children in secondary schools in London, as reported in the previous chapter.

PART III

VIII

Social Mobility in Great Britain: A Study of Inter-Generation Changes in Status

D. V. GLASS AND J. R. HALL

Introduction[1]

ONE of the main objects of the sample inquiry described in Chapter IV was to make possible an assessment of the amount and direction of social mobility in Great Britain since the end of the nineteenth century. And it is on this question that the present chapter is focused. It should, however, be emphasized that given the information now available and the techniques of analysis so far developed, the assessment is a somewhat limited one. Though both more precise and more comprehensive than earlier estimates, the assessment is still a second, if not a first, approximation. In large part the limitations of the present study are due to the fact that there are no previous comparable investigations to serve as a background. But technical difficulties also arise, as will be seen in the discussion of the actual results. Before turning to that discussion, however, it is necessary to describe how the concept of social mobility is used in the subsequent analysis.

It should be explained, first, that throughout the present chapter we are concerned with occupational achievement, and with the relationship between fathers and sons with reference to that kind of achievement. Obviously, there are other aspects of social mobility which are entirely excluded from such an analysis, though one of them, social mobility in marriage, is examined in a later chapter. We also exclude any criterion of the social status of an individual other than his occupation. Some of the reasons for concentrating upon this single factor have already been

[1] We wish to acknowledge our indebtedness to Miss Betty Roxburgh for her work in connection with this analysis. Unfortunately she resigned before the analysis was completed, but she contributed most valuably to the earlier stages of the study.

given—the belief, supported by other material contained in this volume, that in Great Britain occupation is probably the most important single criterion of status; and also the desire to measure the behaviour of other variables against this particular variable. In Chapters XIII and XIV, for example, an attempt is made to see how far the status hierarchy derived from an analysis of occupational prestige coincides with the allocation of status within voluntary organizations, while other chapters examine the relationship between occupational status and attitudes towards education, interest in the school activities of children and aspirations for children.

Secondly, in allocating an individual to a specific category in the social status hierarchy, the modified sevenfold classification, described in Chapter II, is used. This means, in effect, that in comparing father and son we apply a single status scale, based upon attitudes expressed in 1949. Though this may be regarded as a valid approach—in the same sense as it is valid to examine changes in the cost of living in terms of the expenditure patterns prevailing in the most recent year of the series of years considered—it is clearly a restrictive one. But this restriction can only be fully overcome by taking samples of attitudes at regular intervals in the future. A further restriction involved here is that the status scale relates to men's occupations, and that the present study is indeed confined to men. This limitation has been imposed because a prestige scale for women's occupations would not be directly comparable. In our society, in which women have relatively little opportunity to take up occupations of high social status, and where, in any case, most married women give up paid work after the birth of their first child,[1] the occupations held by women tend to be of lower status than those which men of comparable background and education would be willing to accept. Hence in the chapter on intermarriage, the status of a single woman has been measured by the occupation of her father. Similarly, the status of a married woman tends to be regarded as that of her husband. Because of these difficulties, the present analysis is confined to the male subjects included in the sample inquiry.

A third point which should be mentioned here is that in the present study, social mobility is examined on a rather foreshortened time-scale. Ideally, it would be desirable to measure social mobility by examining the changes in status of an individual throughout his particular generation. The study would take as the starting-point the birth year, when the individual's status was equated with that of his father, and trace the

[1] See Chapter XII (pp. 322–3).

changes in achieved status throughout the active life of the individual. Applying this method to successive cohorts would yield a series of comparable status profiles, showing both the nature of intra-generation movement and its end result in the final social status distribution of the cohorts. With such an analysis, the change between the beginning and end of a generation would also be a measure of inter-generation movement in status. The sample inquiry did not, however, provide information on the occupation of the father at the time of birth of the subject; indeed, unless both subject and father were alive, it is doubtful whether a request for such information would yield reliable results. Instead, the last main occupation of the subject's father was ascertained. Hence the analysis is in general confined to a comparison of the last main status of the father with the status of the son as ascertained in 1949. Some use has been made of status profiles of the subject but the profiles derived from our investigation begin at the first occupations taken up by the subjects and not at their birth. The analysis thus tends to be static rather than dynamic, though it still yields much information on the fluidity or rigidity of the social structure.

Another type of foreshortening of the time-scale also arises, and one which only time itself can overcome. In order to have valid information on changes in status between parental and filial generations, it is necessary to know (or to be reasonably certain) that the sons are old enough to have achieved their last main status. This means, however, confining the analysis to persons aged 50 years or more in 1949, since an examination of the profiles shows that, at least until that age, there is still some movement between the various status categories. And because there is no previous comparable inquiry, the true span of comparison, if based on material so circumscribed, would be very narrow. It would also mean excluding those cohorts of individuals who had their education when the national system of secondary schools was expanding fairly rapidly, and when the ladder from the secondary schools to the universities was being built. To some extent the first point is dealt with in the following chapter. By analysing separately the data for subjects whose eldest sons were at least 20 years old in 1949, it is possible to survey three generations instead of two—grandfathers, fathers, and sons—and to push back the initial point of the analysis further into the nineteenth century. On the second point, however, there is no satisfactory solution. One possible approach is to use the status profiles to see if there are measurable differences between cohorts at, say, age 30. This is equivalent to fertility analysis which compares the total family size attained by, say, ten years' marriage duration for successive cohorts and thereby tries to gauge if completed fertility (the total family size achieved by the end of the reproductive period) is changing. In the study of fertility, however, the demographer is greatly helped by the fact that the length of the childbearing period has not been increasing. On the contrary, the effective period of childbearing has been contracting systematically, so that it is now safer to infer completed fertility from fertility at ten years' duration of marriage than would have been the case for the marriages of fifty years ago. For social mobility, however, the reverse is likely to apply, the increase in the expectation of life being accompanied by some increase in the length of working life. Hence it may now be more speculative to infer a man's last main status from his achieved status at, say, the age of 30 years than would have been true at the beginning of the century. This also applies to the second possible method, that of attempting to project from measured status at one particular age or from a series of ages. For this is only another way of putting the first method. In sum, therefore, the results given for the more recent cohorts —generations born after World War I—must be treated with caution. It must remain for later investigators, repeating this kind of inquiry in fifteen or twenty years' time, to establish how far the ultimate chances of mobility have been influenced by educational and other developments during the inter-war period, while the net results of the 1944 Education Act will not be fully ascertainable for another forty or fifty years.

The problems discussed so far do not exhaust the list of questions which need to be considered in measuring social mobility. Other questions, especially those relating to indices of mobility and to the testing of statistical significance, are treated in technical appendices to this chapter. And the question of the concept of 'perfect mobility', basic to the statistical analysis applied, is also considered later in the text of the present chapter, in the section dealing with some of the new measurements of changes in social status. For the moment, however, enough of the background has been given to make it possible to proceed to the first stages of analysis of the material obtained from the sample inquiry.

Changes in Status between Two Generations

The main analysis is based upon those of the male subjects covered by the sample inquiry who were resident in England and Wales, the subjects being classified by decades of birth in order to throw into relief changes over time. The numbers of subjects and their distribution by period of birth are shown in Table 1. Information on occupation was lacking for relatively few individuals, so that the subsequent tables are based on 94·5 per cent of the men interviewed.

Table 1

MALE SUBJECTS CLASSIFIED BY YEAR OF BIRTH

Date of birth	Number of subjects in sample	Father's or subject's occupation not known	Number of subjects included in study
1889 or earlier	713	34	679
1890–99	556	16	540
1900–09	777	26	751
1910–19	802	30	772
1920–29	794	39	755
1930 or later	58	1	all excluded
Total	3700	146	3497

The inquiry also covered Scotland, but the material for that country is less comprehensive. Because of the different educational system of Scotland, a separate and more extensive list of questions would have been needed to produce results which could meaningfully be compared with those for England and Wales. But in a compromise questionnaire serving the needs of three different investigations, this was not practicable. In order to ensure a direct comparison between the chapters on mobility, education and on the relation between education and social status, the data for Scotland have therefore been analysed separately and the results are given in a later section of this chapter.

The general statistics for England and Wales are shown in Table 2, which compares the social status of the subjects interviewed with that of their fathers. The type of analysis applied in the first stage is similar to that used by Professor Ginsberg in his pioneer study,[1] though somewhat more precise methods of measurement are involved here. The data in Table 2 are given in two forms. The percentages in the horizontal rows (in the top right-hand corner of each cell) show the extent to which sons have the same status as their fathers. The series of cells in the first row, for example, shows that among the sons whose fathers were in status category 1, 38·8 per cent are themselves in category 1, 14·6 per cent in category 2, etc. Of the sons whose fathers were in category 7, none has himself achieved category 1, while 27·4 per cent are still in category 7. By looking along the diagonal in the table (distinguished by heavy lines), the extent to which status has remained constant as between fathers and

[1] 'Interchange between social classes' in M. Ginsberg, *Studies in Sociology*, London, 1932 (also in *Economic Journal*, December 1929).

181

sons will be seen. This appears most marked for category 5 and least for category 3—that is, 47·3 per cent of the men whose fathers were in category 5, are themselves in category 5, while only 18·8 per cent of the men whose fathers were in category 3 are themselves in category 3. Referring to the description of the categories, given below for reference, self-recruitment appears to be highest among the skilled manual and routine non-manual workers. The kind of association between parental and filial status is also visible: the higher the status of the fathers, the smaller the proportions of sons in category 5 or lower categories.

STATUS CATEGORIES

No.	Description
1	Professional and high administrative.
2	Managerial and executive.
3	Inspectional, supervisory and other non-manual (higher grade).
4	Inspectional, supervisory and other non-manual (lower grade).
5	Skilled manual and routine grades of non-manual.
6	Semi-skilled manual.
7	Unskilled manual.

The information provided by the vertical columns (in the bottom left-hand corner of each cell) relates to the parental status of men found in given categories in 1949. Thus, of the men found to be in category 1, 48·5 per cent had fathers who were of the same status. This, too, is an indication of self-recruitment, and it will again be seen, by looking along the diagonal, that the maintenance of parental status appears most evident in category 5 and least in category 3. At the same time, there are considerable changes in status between the successive generations. The horizontal rows indicate, for example, that for men whose fathers were in category 1, over 60 per cent were found in lower categories, while for men whose fathers were in category 7, over 70 per cent were found in higher status categories than their fathers. The meaning of such changes will be discussed later.

The material from which Table 2 was compiled is used again, in a somewhat different way, in Tables 3, 4 and 5. The first table shows the proportions of subjects who were of the same status as their fathers, or who had achieved a different status, and the chi-square test shows that the differences, noted in connection with Table 2, are significant. That is also true of the differences between subjects who achieved a higher, as compared with those who were found in a lower, status than that of their

Table 2

DISTRIBUTION OF THE MALE SAMPLE ACCORDING TO SUBJECTS' AND SUBJECTS' FATHERS' STATUS CATEGORY

Subjects' Present Status Category

Fathers' Status Category	1	2	3	4	5	6	7	Total
1	38·8	14·6	20·2	6·2	14·0	4·7	1·5	100·0
	48·5	11·9	7·9	1·7	1·3	1·0	0·5	(129)
2	10·7	26·7	22·7	12·0	20·6	5·3	2·0	100·0
	15·5	25·2	10·3	3·9	2·2	1·4	0·7	(150)
3	3·5	10·1	18·8	19·1	35·7	6·7	6·1	100·0
	11·7	22·0	19·7	14·4	8·6	3·9	5·0	(345)
4	2·1	3·9	11·2	21·2	43·0	12·4	6·2	100·0
	10·7	12·6	17·6	24·0	15·6	10·8	7·5	(518)
5	0·9	2·4	7·5	12·3	47·3	17·1	12·5	100·0
	13·6	22·6	34·5	40·3	50·0	43·5	44·6	(1510)
6	0·0	1·3	4·1	8·8	39·1	31·2	15·5	100·0
	0·0	3·8	5·8	8·7	12·5	24·1	16·7	(458)
7	0·0	0·8	3·6	8·3	36·4	23·5	27·4	100·0
	0·0	1·9	4·2	7·0	9·8	15·3	25·0	(387)
Total	100·0	100·0	100·0	100·0	100·0	100·0	100·0	100·0
	(103)	(159)	(330)	(459)	(1429)	(593)	(424)	(3497)

183

fathers where parental status is not maintained. The tendency to rise appears more marked among men whose fathers were in the lower status categories (leaving aside categories 1 and 7 from which movement in one direction only is possible); but the distance traversed when

Table 3

MALE SUBJECTS WHOSE STATUS CATEGORY IS THE SAME AS, OR DIFFERENT FROM, THAT OF THEIR FATHERS

Subjects' Fathers' Status Category	Subjects' Status Category			% Col. 1 to Col. 3
	Same (1)	Different (2)	Total (3)	
1	50	79	129	38·8
2	40	110	150	26·7
3	65	280	345	18·8
4	110	408	518	21·2
5	714	796	1510	47·3
6	143	315	458	31·2
7	106	281	387	27·4
Total	1228	2269	3497	35·1

changes in status occur is not very great. An attempt is made in Table 5 to express this quantitatively, by assuming that the distance between any two adjacent categories is equal to one unit. This assumption is an extremely dubious one and to validate any assumption would need a new inquiry into the prestige hierarchy of occupations. Here, however,

Table 4

MALE SUBJECTS WHOSE STATUS CATEGORY IS HIGHER OR LOWER THAN THAT OF THEIR FATHERS

Subjects' Fathers' Status Category	Subjects' Status Category			% Col. 1 to Col. 3
	Higher (1)	Lower (2)	Total (3)	
1	—	—	—	—
2	16	94	110	14·5
3	47	233	280	16·8
4	89	319	408	21·8
5	349	447	796	43·8
6	244	71	315	77·5
7	—	—	—	—
Total	745	1164	1909	39·0

we are concerned only to see if the number of categories involved in the shift in status is large, and whether there are significant differences in this respect between the various groups of subjects. An analysis of variance shows that the differences are significant—that the higher the parental status, the further the fall below it, which is hardly surprising since there is then a greater number of categories through which the fall can proceed. But at the same time the shifts upward or downward tend to be of a short-distance variety; where men have a status different from their fathers, they still tend to cluster round the parental category. In brief, therefore, summarizing the discussion, we may say that there is an

Table 5

MEAN DISTANCE BETWEEN FATHERS AND SONS IN THE HIERARCHICAL SCALE (DISTANCE MEASURED IN TERMS OF NUMBER OF CATEGORIES)

Father's Status Category	Son's Position relative to Father	
	Higher Mean and S.E.	Lower Mean and S.E.
1	—	$2 \cdot 46 \pm 0 \cdot 16$ (85)
2	$1 \cdot 00 \pm 0 \cdot 00$ (16)	$2 \cdot 10 \pm 0 \cdot 13$ (94)
3	$1 \cdot 26 \pm 0 \cdot 06$ (47)	$2 \cdot 00 \pm 0 \cdot 06$ (233)
4	$1 \cdot 47 \pm 0 \cdot 08$ (89)	$1 \cdot 40 \pm 0 \cdot 03$ (319)
5	$1 \cdot 65 \pm 0 \cdot 05$ (304)	$1 \cdot 42 \pm 0 \cdot 03$ (447)
6	$1 \cdot 40 \pm 0 \cdot 05$ (246)	$1 \cdot 00 \pm 0 \cdot 00$ (71)
7	$1 \cdot 90 \pm 0 \cdot 06$ (281)	—
	$1 \cdot 62 \pm 0 \cdot 03$ (983)	$1 \cdot 62 \pm 0 \cdot 02$ (1249)

evident association between the status of fathers and sons, seemingly especially marked where the fathers were skilled manual workers or were in the professional or administrative category; that the degree of association differs significantly as between the various categories; and that where there are changes in status between fathers and sons, the sons still tend to be fairly close to their fathers' level.

The Element of Time Considered

To ascertain whether the association between parental and filial status has changed over time, and in what direction, the statistics derived from the sample inquiry were reclassified and grouped by decade of birth of the subjects interviewed. Because this analysis by decades greatly reduces the numbers in each cell, the status categories were recombined, categories 1 and 2 being grouped together and categories 6 and 7 also being treated as a single unit. The basic information is contained in Tables 6 and 7, which together form the equivalent of Table 2. The only difference is that because of the volume of data presented, the rows and columns are listed separately instead of being shown in the same cells, as in the earlier table.

Once again the diagonals, marked by heavy lines, show the extent of self-recruitment, but this time by decades as well as by separate categories. Taking all categories together, as in Table 8, there appears to be no significant change in the proportion of subjects found to have the same status as their fathers, the percentage for each decade being very close to the 35·1 per cent for the whole sample shown in Table 3.

For subjects differing in status from their fathers, there are significant differences between those with a higher and those with a lower status, explained primarily by the behaviour of two cohorts, the earliest and the most recent. Since, however, the most recent cohort is also the most

Table 6

PERCENTAGE DISTRIBUTION OF SUBJECTS ACCORDING TO THEIR FATHERS' AND THEIR OWN STATUS CATEGORIES AND DATE OF BIRTH

Father's Status Category	Date of Birth	Subject's Status Category					Total	
		1 and 2	3	4	5	6 and 7	%	Nos.
1 and 2	Before 1890	**39·7**	23·5	10·3	14·7	11·8	100·0	68
	1890–1899	**48·9**	19·2	12·8	10·6	8·5	100·0	47
	1900–1909	**53·7**	20·4	9·3	11·1	5·5	100·0	54
	1910–1919	**42·9**	26·8	8·9	14·3	7·1	100·0	56
	1920–1929	**40·7**	16·7	5·6	37·0	0·0	100·0	54
3	Before 1890	11·5	**14·1**	17·9	39·8	16·7	100·0	78
	1890–1899	18·8	**25·0**	17·2	26·5	12·5	100·0	64
	1900–1909	16·2	**19·1**	29·4	26·5	8·8	100·0	68
	1910–1919	16·5	**20·2**	20·3	32·9	10·1	100·0	79
	1920–1929	3·6	**16·1**	8·9	55·3	16·1	100·0	56
4	Before 1890	3·8	7·8	**25·0**	39·4	24·0	100·0	104
	1890–1899	7·6	17·7	**20·3**	34·2	20·2	100·0	79
	1900–1909	8·0	14·3	**17·5**	40·0	20·2	100·0	125
	1910–1919	4·7	10·3	**28·0**	43·0	14·0	100·0	107
	1920–1929	5·8	6·8	**15·5**	57·3	14·6	100·0	103
5	Before 1890	3·9	6·4	12·0	**42·4**	35·3	100·0	283
	1890–1899	2·3	11·9	13·7	**42·9**	29·2	100·0	219
	1900–1909	5·6	8·5	13·8	**45·3**	26·8	100·0	340
	1910–1919	3·2	7·8	14·4	**47·8**	26·8	100·0	347
	1920–1929	1·2	4·4	7·5	**56·1**	30·8	100·0	321
6 and 7	Before 1890	0·7	3·4	5·5	32·9	**57·5**	100.0	146
	1890–1899	0·8	2·2	10·7	34·4	**51·9**	100·0	131
	1900–1909	1·8	6·1	14·6	30·5	**47·0**	100·0	164
	1910–1919	1·1	3·8	8·8	39·3	**47·0**	100·0	183
	1920–1929	0·9	3·6	4·5	47·5	**43·5**	100·0	221

curtailed in its exposure to the chances of equalling or surpassing parental status, it is only for the earliest cohort that the proportion of sons surpassing their fathers can really be regarded as unusually low. Apart from this, however, the statistics do not suggest any important change over time, and a similar conclusion must be drawn from an analysis of the material for the separate status categories. Measured by chi-square tests there are some—though not many—significant differences between the apparent degree of self-recruitment (or maintenance of

Table 7

PERCENTAGE DISTRIBUTION OF THE FATHERS OF SUBJECTS ACCORDING TO THE SUBJECTS' STATUS CATEGORY AND DATE OF BIRTH

Subject's Status Category	Date of Birth	Father's Status Category					Total	
		1 and 2	3	4	5	6 and 7	%	Nos.
1 and 2	Before 1890	51·9	17·3	7·7	21·2	1·9	100·0	52
	1890–1899	48·9	25·5	12·8	10·6	2·2	100·0	47
	1900–1909	40·3	15·3	13·8	26·4	4·2	100·0	72
	1910–1919	43·6	23·6	9·2	20·0	3·6	100·0	55
	1920–1929	61·1	5·5	16·7	11·1	5·6	100·0	36
3	Before 1890	27·6	19·0	13·8	31·0	8·6	100·0	58
	1890–1899	13·2	23·5	20·6	38·3	4·4	100·0	68
	1900–1909	13·6	16·0	22·3	35·8	12·3	100·0	81
	1910–1919	19·7	21·1	14·5	35·5	9·2	100·0	76
	1920–1929	19·2	19·1	14·9	29·8	17·0	100·0	47
4	Before 1890	7·9	15·7	29·2	38·2	9·0	100·0	89
	1890–1899	7·8	14·2	20·8	39·0	18·2	100·0	77
	1900–1909	4·3	16·9	18·6	39·8	20·4	100·0	118
	1910–1919	4·3	13·7	25·6	42·7	13·7	100·0	117
	1920–1929	5·2	8·6	27·6	41·4	17·2	100·0	58
5	Before 1890	4·0	12·4	16·4	48·0	19·2	100·0	250
	1890–1899	2·7	9·0	14·4	50·0	23·9	100·0	188
	1900–1909	2·2	6·5	18·0	55·3	18·0	100·0	278
	1910–1919	2·5	8·2	14·5	52·2	22·6	100·0	318
	1920–1929	5·1	7·8	14·9	45·6	26·6	100·0	395
6 and 7	Before 1890	3·5	5·7	10·8	43·5	36·5	100·0	230
	1890–1899	2·5	5·0	10·0	40·0	42·5	100·0	160
	1900–1909	1·5	3·0	12·4	45·0	38·1	100·0	202
	1910–1919	1·9	3·9	7·3	45·2	41·7	100·0	206
	1920–1929	—	4·2	6·8	45·2	43·8	100·0	219

parental status) in the various cohorts, but those di: ·rences are explained primarily by the deviations of the 1920 cohort. Anu as has been noted, these may well be transient features. Nor does the ly of the number of categories involved in changes in status add appreciably to the picture. The application of analysis of variance and of t tests show some significant differences for men whose fathers were in status categories 1 and 5. But in general the picture of rather high stability over time is confirmed.

Table 8

RELATION BETWEEN STATUS OF SUBJECTS AND FATHERS

Date of birth of subjects	Percentage of subjects with same status as their fathers	Of subjects differing in status from their fathers, percentage with higher status than their fathers
Before 1890	33·4	31·8
1890–99	33·9	43·1
1900–09	34·4	44·1
1910–19	36·4	42·7
1920–29	37·0	33·7

The Concept of 'Perfect' Mobility[1]

So far the term 'social mobility' has been used to indicate changes in status between fathers and sons, irrespective of the cause of these changes. And though some indication has been given of differences in the extent to which men with parental backgrounds of specific status have themselves achieved particular status levels, no attempt has been made to measure these differences on any scale or, with reference to such a scale, to estimate if some groups have 'too high' or 'too low' a chance of reaching the top status categories. In terms of everyday reality, there is justification for the relatively simple approach adopted in the preceding discussion. For the man in the street what matters is whether he is 'getting on in the world' as compared with his father. It is less important to him whether his higher status is due to a general increase in the proportion of 'white collar' jobs in the community, or to a redistribution of personnel between the various status categories, a redistribution which may occur at the same time as, or independently of, changes in the overall occupational structure of the community. He does not himself necessarily experience, as a matter of personal sensation, the differ-

[1] It is suggested, in Appendix 1, that the term 'mobility' be used for full intra-generation movement, and that for the parental-filial relationship in status the term 'association' be used. In dealing with the general concept, however, it will not cause confusion to refer to 'perfect' mobility as if it applied either to mobility so defined or to 'association'.

188

ences between these two methods of social mobility. And indeed he may well feel a greater sense of upward mobility with a change in the total occupational structure and a relatively low chance (as compared with an individual whose father had a higher status) of achieving high status, than if with a stationary occupational structure dominated by low prestige jobs, he has a chance of rising equal to that of any other person in his generation, whatever the status of his father. This may be illustrated by a hypothetical case. Suppose there are 100 sons, of whom 20 are the sons of non-manual and 80 the sons of manual workers. Suppose also that in the sons' generation the job availabilities also provide 20 non-manual and 80 manual jobs. Then even if every non-manual job goes to the sons of manual workers, only 20 out of the 80 sons of manual workers can achieve non-manual status. Let us assume now, however, that there is a total structural change, such that in the sons' generation there are 50 non-manual and 50 manual jobs. Then even if only 30 out of the 50 non-manual jobs go to the sons of manual workers (that is, conversely, even if every son of a non-manual worker achieves non-manual status), the ratio of non-manual jobs to the sons of manual workers will be 30 : 80, higher than in the first case. Hence when, because a society is an expanding one, there are increased status opportunities for all, differences in opportunity between individuals of different status origins may scarcely be felt or considered.

For the social scientist, however, the *means* of achieving high status are as important as the end product. The question of *relative* mobility, of the different opportunities of gaining high status available to individuals of different social origin, is part of the problem of the recruitment of *élites*. And the knowledge that, to take an example, there are now more sons of manual workers in the medical profession than there were a generation ago is not a sufficient answer to the question of recruitment. It needs to be supplemented by reference to the changing numbers of medical practitioners in the community as a whole. Alternatively, the index of mobility should take as its basis the number of medical practitioners in the sons' generation as constituting the total opportunities then available for the practice of that particular profession.

Of course, both approaches may be followed. The sample survey results may be used to provide some indication of the changes over time in the total distribution of status opportunities, using the single standard based upon the 1949 inquiry into the prestige of occupations. The results are shown in Tables 9 and 10, the first giving the distribution of status for subjects by their decades of birth, and the second the distribution of status for fathers of subjects by decades of birth of the subjects themselves. Leaving aside the pre-1890 cohort, which covers an undefined period of years, the data still suggest a slight decline in the opportunities for high status over time, a decline which appears in the data for subjects' fathers as well as for the subjects themselves. This is not in conflict with the known fact that certain specific types of white-collar occupations have greatly expanded over the past fifty years. It would mean, however, that other occupations of comparable status have contracted to an even greater extent.[1] But since the development suggested by the statistics in Tables 9 and 10 may seem somewhat unexpected, it is worth seeing how far the trends they appear to reflect are confirmed by the results of the successive censuses of England and Wales.

Table 9

SUBJECTS CLASSIFIED ACCORDING TO THEIR OWN SOCIAL STATUS

(Percentage distribution)

Date ot Birth of Subjects	Subjects' Social Status							
	1	2	3	4	5	6	7	All
Before 1890	4·3	3·4	8·5	13·1	36·8	15·9	18·0	100·0
1890–99	2·8	5·9	12·6	14·3	34·8	16·3	13·3	100·0
1900–09	2·8	6·8	10·8	15·8	37·0	16·6	10·3	100·1
1910–19	2·9	4·3	9·8	15·2	41·2	16·1	10·6	100·1
1920–29	2·1	2·6	6·2	7·7	52·3	19·6	9·4	99·9

It should at once be emphasized that the percentages in Table 9 have a different validity from those in Table 10. The percentages in the former table would agree with the census results, assuming the classification of occupations to be identical, provided that the sample survey was designed correctly and carried out effectively. But the percentages in Table 10 are bound to be biased in one sense. Since they are derived

Table 10

SUBJECTS CLASSIFIED ACCORDING TO THE SOCIAL STATUS OF THEIR FATHERS

(Percentage distribution)

Date of Birth of Subjects	Fathers' Social Status							
	1	2	3	4	5	6	7	All
Before 1890	5·2	4·9	11·5	15·3	41·7	14·3	7·2	100·1
1890–99	3·7	5·0	11·9	14·6	40·6	13·0	11·3	100·1
1900–09	3·5	3·7	9·1	16·6	45·3	10·8	11·1	100·1
1910–19	3·1	4·1	10·2	13·9	44·9	12·2	11·5	99·9
1920–29	3·2	4·0	7·4	13·6	42·5	15·4	13·9	100·0

[1] And also that the expanded opportunities in certain 'white-collar' occupations have been taken over by women.

from information supplied by living sons or daughters, the percentages will not include those individuals of the previous generation who had no children, or whose children did not survive. And, conversely, the larger the number of children born and surviving to a man of the parental generation, the greater the probability of that man being included in the population on which Table 10 is based. Mortality is correlated negatively with social status, but so is fertility, so that the two factors will tend to counteract one another. It is unlikely, however, that they will completely cancel each other. Having regard to the historical development of social status differences in fertility, it is more probable that, relatively, the bias towards the representation of 'manual' fathers will be greater in the more recent than in the earlier cohorts of Table 10. It is because of this kind of bias that the analysis of mobility in the present symposium proceeds generally from son to father—which is a valid approach—and not from father to son.

Comparison of the results in Tables 9 and 10 with the most nearly equivalent census data is still, however, worthwhile. And for this purpose it is necessary to make use of the Registrar General's analysis of occupations. Five 'social classes' are used in the official statistics and they do not compare precisely with any combination of the status categories adopted in the present studies. Nor is the occupational content of each 'social class' exactly the same for each census. A rough approximation may be made by combining the five 'social classes' into two groups, 'manual' (classes 3, 4 and 5) and 'non-manual' (the remainder), and by producing a similar division of the seven status categories. As the Registrar General's class 3 contains subordinate inspectional and supervisory grades, the 'manual' division of the seven status categories must consist of categories 4 to 7 inclusive, though even then the match is by no means exact. In order to select men likely to have achieved their final status, the age-group of 45–54 years has been taken from the census statistics, and the men in this group have been compared with the fathers of the subjects in the sample inquiry. The comparison here is again necessarily rough; it has been made by dividing the subjects into decades of birth and by taking, for a given decade, the census which would most nearly match the fathers of that particular group of subjects.[1] The results are given in Table 11. Two sets of percentages are given for the census

[1] The sample inquiry subjects born, say, in 1890–99 would be 11–20 years old in 1911. Hence their fathers would be 45–54 years old in 1911 if they were 34 years of age at the birth of their mid-child. Though this is not correct in fact, it is not far from reality since the mean age at marriage of men in England and Wales ranged from 28 to 29 years during the period covered by the statistics.

comparison. The first (unadjusted) set is based simply on the men aged 45–54 years in the Registrar General's classes 1 and 2, as a proportion of all active and retired men in the same age-group. But these percentages are particularly lacking in internal comparability, because typists and general clerks were included in the 'non-manual' group in 1911 and 1921, but in the 'manual' group in 1931 and 1951. In the second set of percentages (adjusted), therefore, this specific difficulty has been dealt with by transferring all clerks and typists to the non-manual group in 1931 and 1951. A suppositious figure for 1941 has been obtained by interpolating between the percentages for these two years.

Table 11

COMPARISON OF CENSUS STATISTICS WITH STATISTICS OF SUBJECTS' FATHERS

| Decade of Birth of Subjects | Equivalent Census date for age-group 45–54 years | Percentage of men in 'manual' categories | | |
		(a) Sample Inquiry	(b)[2] Unadjusted Census	(c) Adjusted Census
1890–99	1911	79·5	71·5	71·5
1900–09	1921	83·8	74·7	74·7
1910–19	1931	82·5	78·6	75·1
1920–29	(1941)[1]	85·4	(78·7)	(75·1)

The adjustment of the Registrar General's 'social classes' reduces somewhat the incomparability over time of the census data, though it does not greatly help to overcome the other type of incomparability. Nevertheless the trends of all three sets of percentages are similar, suggesting some increase in the proportion of 'manual' as compared with 'non-manual' occupations. Putting the element of comparability at its lowest, and taking into account the bias in the sample survey data relating to the fathers of the subjects interviewed, the most likely conclusion is that there was no important change between 1911 and 1941 in the proportion of 'non-manual' employment for the men concerned.[3]

[1] There was no census in 1941, but a suppositious percentage is entered, the percentage being the average of the percentages for 1931 and 1951: 78·6 and 78·8 unadjusted, and 75·1 and 75·0 adjusted.

[2] The sources of the census data for England and Wales are: R.G.'s *Decennial Supplements* for 1911, Part 4, pp. 3 ff.; for 1921, Part 2, pp. 3–5; for 1931, Part 2a, pp. 217 ff. Census 1931, *Occupation Tables*, Table 2. Census 1951, *One per cent Sample Tables*, Part 1, p. 83.

[3] The changes of occupational classification in successive censuses make it impossible to construct a completely comparable series of estimates of development of 'non-manual' or 'middle-class' employment over the past fifty years. Attempts have been made, however, probably the most systematic being that of Professor

A comparison on the same lines may also be made between the subjects in the sample inquiry (Table 9) and the men enumerated in the 1951 census. Because the proportion of men in the 'manual' categories alters systematically with age, and because we are here dealing with a series of different age-groups, it is necessary to make the age comparison somewhat more precise. Thus subjects born in 1910–19 were approximately 30–40 years old when interviewed in 1949. As the census data are not given for that age-group but for the groups of 25–34 and 35–44 years, the arithmetic mean of the percentages for these two age-groups has been taken as a reasonable equivalent, this kind of averaging also being used for the other age-groups. The results, which are summarized in Table 12, show a much greater similarity both as between the specific percentages and between the trends. Hence, so far as the subjects themselves are concerned, we may say that the increase in the proportions of

---

Sir A. L. Bowley, in *Wages and Income in the United Kingdom since 1860*, Cambridge, 1937, pp. 127–36. Bowley constructed his estimates by selecting, at each census, the specific occupations which, in his view, came within the 'non-manual' category. There are again important elements of non-comparability here, but linked percentages may be used to provide an indication of the change between 1911 and 1931. Thus for males, Bowley gives a series of percentages of occupied males (excluding the retired) of all ages in 'middle-class' occupations in England and Wales, and this series has been extended to 1951 by taking the occupations in the 1951 census (1 per cent sample) most nearly equivalent to those selected by Bowley from the 1931 census. The percentages in parentheses were obtained by multiplying the percentages in the bottom row by the ratio (23·1/24·5) in order to obtain comparability with the estimate for 1911. The results do not suggest that, in 1951, the proportion was very different from that in 1911.

1911	1921	1931	1951
24·7	23·1	(24·4)	(25·4)
—	24·5	25·9	26·9

For women, however, the corresponding figures indicate a very considerable expansion of 'non-manual' employment, as may be seen below. Although it cannot be assumed that the percentages are fully comparable over the whole period, there is no reason to doubt the reality of the extremely substantial increase, especially between 1921 and 1951.

1911	1921	1931	1951
24·5	31·4	(31·6)	(45·5)
—	31·1	31·3	45·1

If 1931 is taken as the basis of comparison instead of 1911, the percentages for men and women would naturally be slightly different, as is shown below.

	1911	1921	1931	1951
Men	(26·2)	24·5	25·9	26·9
Women	(24·3)	31·1	31·3	45·1

It should, of course, be emphasized that, within the 'manual' group, there have been changes in the distribution between the grades of skilled, semi-skilled and unskilled over time.

'manual' occupations—and therefore of occupations of relatively low rank in the prestige hierarchy—as the more recent decades of birth are approached, is genuine and not due to bias in the sample inquiry. But the increase is also a function of youth and allowance for this might counterbalance the apparent, though not statistically significant, increase in the degree of self-recruitment shown in Table 8. In sum, discounting changes in the overall occupational structure, the degree of self-recruitment would seem to have been practically constant over the whole period.

Table 12

COMPARISON OF 1951 CENSUS WITH THE STATISTICS OF SUBJECTS

Decade of Birth of Subjects	Percentage of men in 'manual' categories	
	(a) In Sample Inquiry, 1940	(b) In Census, 1951 (unadjusted)
1890–99	78·7	78·4
1900–09	79·7	79·2
1910–19	83·1	81·5
1920–29	89·0	87·7

The analysis given above is rather imprecise, and it has been used here more because there is an interest in examining, on its own, the change in the overall occupational structure of England and Wales than because the method itself is of particular value. For the remainder of this chapter, as well as in the subsequent chapters, mobility will be treated in terms of the alternative approach which we must now discuss.

Diagram A

Status of Fathers	No. of sons in each status category					
	Category 1		Category 2		Totals	
Category 1	J	20	K	10	b_1	30
Category 2	L	30	M	40	b_2	70
Totals	c_1	50	c_2	50	d	100

Consider the hypothetical example given in Diagram A of the relation between parental and filial social status. Of the 100 sons observed in the present generation (c_1, c_2), 50 are in category 1 and 50 in category 2 (it is assumed that category 1 is of higher status than category 2), while of the fathers (b_1, b_2) of these sons 30 were in category 1 and 70 in category 2. There has thus been a considerable change in the distribution of status opportunities between the generations. Now consider the generation of sons and assume that there is no association between the status of father and son—that each son has the same chance as any other son of arriving in category 1. Such a situation we describe as representing 'random' or 'perfect' mobility, meaning that there is no link between parental and filial status. In Diagram A, 30 per cent of the sons had fathers in category 1, and in conditions of 'perfect' mobility these sons should in their generation take 30 per cent of the jobs available in each status category. In formal terms this is equal to $(b_1 \times c_1)/d$, or $(30 \times 50)/100$, for category 1 jobs, and $(b_1 \times c_2)/d$, or $(30 \times 50)/100$, for category 2 jobs, the answer in both cases being 15. These, then, are the expected values and may be used as reference points or standards with which to compare the actual values in the diagram. In the diagram, the actual number of sons (J) of category 1 background who themselves arrive in category 1 is 20, and the ratio of 20/15, or 1·3, may be called the 'Index of Association'. The ratio of the actual to the expected number of sons who, having category 1 fathers, arrived in category 2 jobs (K), is 10/15, or 0·67, and may be termed the 'Index of Dissociation'. When the expected values equal the actual values, both indices will be 1·0. The higher the degree of self-recruitment, or of maintenance of parental status, the higher will be the Index of Association and the lower the Index of Dissociation, though the upper and lower limits of both indices in practice depend upon the actual numbers in the cohorts, marginal totals and cells covered by a table. The Index of Association may also, of course, give a result of less than 1·0—though this is rarely likely to be seen in practice—indicative of less self-recruitment than would be expected on a random basis. This would mean that there is reverse association between parental and filial status, and in Western society this would be very unusual. It would occur if there were, between two generations, an overturning of the processes of selection of *élites*—if, to take a hypothetical case, the sons of doctors were prohibited by law or custom from taking up a career in medicine!

Four points should be emphasized in connection with the use of these indices. First, the general approach itself is not original to the present study. The problem of random association was considered by a number of Italian statisticians, including Benini,[1] Livio Livi[2] and Chessa, while the method of taking into account generation changes in the total occupational structure of the communtity was put forward by Goldhamer and applied extensively by Rogoff.[3] In the present study, how-

---

[1] See Appendix 2 of the present chapter.

[2] Livio Livi, 'Sur la mesure de la mobilité sociale', *Population*, January–March 1950.

[3] N. Rogoff, 'Recent trends in urban occupational mobility', in P. K. Hatt and A. J. Reiss, Jr., *Reader in Urban Sociology*, Glencoe, Illinois, 1951. It may perhaps

ever, the method has been developed systematically, as will be seen from the technical appendices to this chapter. Measures of association have been applied to intra-generation as well as inter-generation change, while measures of dissociation have been split so as to indicate separately movement upward and movement downward in status. Tests of significance have also been devised, and these are an essential in using in an objective way the indices of Association and of Dissociation. For it is necessary, for example, to ascertain first that a given Index of Association differs significantly from 1·0 before it can be taken to show a higher or lower degree of status inertia than would be expected on a basis of equal probabilities. And if two indices differ significantly from 1·0 it is still necessary to ascertain that they differ significantly from each other before one can be said to indicate a closer or looser association than the other. Even so, the data available to us do not make it possible to say, within specified limits of confidence, that one index, differing significantly from another, is precisely n times another in size. The most we can say is that the ratio of the indices will give an approximate indication of relative size.[1]

The second point is that the assumption of 'perfect' mobility, or of the existence of equal probabilities of movement for persons of all social origins, does not assume any value system, any claim of social justice, or any basis in fact. It is, indeed, most unlikely that 'perfect' mobility would be attainable in our society or in any other, for there will probably always be some premium (if only in the sense of encouragement or stimulus) on a given parental background. Hence the fact that an index differs significantly from 1·0 means no more than that the given index has a particular statistical value.[2] The sole purpose of the concept of 'perfect' mobility is to provide a common standard which makes it possible to see the *relative* chances of status change of different generations and of men of different status backgrounds. What is important, therefore, is the *difference* between the indices for those generations or groups of men.

Thirdly, in saying that the indices of Association and Dissociation abstract from changes in the total availability of occupations of various levels of prestige, it should be noted that this also means abstracting from

---

be noted, though it is not of great interest, that the method was developed here independently of Rogoff's work.

[1] On the grounds that the best estimate of the ratio is the ratio of the best estimates of the two indices.

[2] That is, the difference between actual and expected frequencies is greater than can be accounted for by sampling fluctuations.

the influence of demographic factors. A constant distribution of available opportunities for the whole adult male population over two generations may, if there is differential fertility, be equivalent to an increase in the available opportunities for part of that population. This may be illustrated by another hypothetical example. Let us assume a stationary total population and distribution of status opportunities, with 300 category 1 and 700 category 2 jobs in each generation. If the categories are taken to represent 'non-manual' and 'manual' groups of occupations, the assumed distribution is not far from the real position in England and Wales.[1] Let us also assume that looking at the picture from the parental generation, each father in category 1 is replaced by 0·84 adult sons, and each father in category 2 by 1·069 adult sons, the ratio of 'manual' to 'non-manual' replacement being 1·27. Again the assumed *ratio* is not very unreal (leaving aside the question of marriage), for the results of the Family Census showed a corresponding ratio of about 1·4 for the average number of live births per marriage of completed fertility,[2] and there would be some reduction in that figure if allowance were made for differential mortality. Given these assumptions regarding differential replacement, the 300 category 1 fathers would be replaced by 252 adult sons and the 700 category 2 fathers by 748 adult sons, making a total of 1,000 males in the filial generation. If we now look at the filial generation and calculate the status distributions of the sons on the assumption of 'perfect' mobility, we shall have the position given in Diagram B.

Diagram B

Status of Fathers	No. of sons in each status category					
	Category 1		Category 2		Totals	
Category 1	J	76	K	176	b_1	252
Category 2	L	224	M	524	b_2	748
Totals	c_1	300	c_2	700	d	1000

Knowing c_1 and c_2, and also b_1 and b_2, we can fill in the cells of the diagram. On the assumption of 'perfect' mobility, L, equal to $(b_2 \times c_1)/d$ must be approximately 224, whence the diagram may be completed as shown. But given 300 category 1 jobs and only 252 adult sons of category 1 fathers, 48 of the men in L—of the 224 sons who arrive in category 1 although their fathers were in category 2—must move there as a

---

[1] See Tables 11 and 12. The 'manual' group in those tables actually includes a number of non-manual occupations, so that a 30/70 division would not be unrealistic.

[2] Royal Commission on Population, *Report*, London, 1949, p. 29.

result of differential replacement, even if every son of a category 1 father maintained his parental status. In consquence, if the total distribution of status opportunities over generations is independent of diffential fertility, then the greater the differential the greater the likelihood that, in the filial generation, manual workers' sons will obtain nonmanual jobs. Yet looking simply at the diagram as presented above, and without taking into account the explanation given—equivalent, therefore, to looking at status change only from the viewpoint of the filial generation—one would infer that there had been an increase in the proportion of jobs of higher status instead of, as is the case, a difference in the net replacement rates of the two categories of fathers.

Finally, it should be stressed that differences between indices of Association or Dissociation, assuming those differences to be statistically significant, are not self-explanatory. They do not say why a differential exists. And clearly the explanation may be very complex, compounded of differences in 'innate' intelligence, in cultural background, in parental stimulus and personal aspirations as well as in more purely economic circumstances. Such factors require separate study, which is why many of the chapters in the present volume are concerned with the nature and causes of differences between people in the different status categories.

The Application of Indices of Association and Dissociation

Taking the whole group of males covered by the sample inquiry, and disregarding date of birth, the indices of Association and Dissociation are respectively 1·440 and 0·858, both being significantly different from unity. As has been explained, however, these facts are not of interest in themselves. The pertinent question is that of the differences between the indices for the sons of different status background, and these are shown in Tables 11A and 11B. In the first table the various indices are shown separately for each status category, the degree of dissociation being looked at from two points of view, from the parental generation and from the filial generation, and also in terms of whether the sons achieved a higher or lower status than their fathers. The indices of Association and Dissociation are all significantly different from unity, and the extent to which the separate indices of Association looked at from the filial generation differ from each other is shown by the significance matrix in Table 11B. In reading this latter table, both the columns and the rows need to be looked at. Thus in the case of category 5, the Index of Association is seen to be 1·157. Looking along the row, to the left, it will be seen that this index is very significantly different from the indices for cate-

198

gories 1 to 4, while looking downwards along the column it will be noticed that the index is also very significantly different from the indices for categories 6 and 7. Using the matrix in this way, the highest degree of differentiation among the indices is found for categories 1, 2 and 5, which differ very significantly from each other and from the indices for all other categories.

Summarizing the meaning of the matrix, we may say that the highest intensity of association between parental and filial status is found among subjects in categories 1 and 2, and the lowest among subjects in category 5. Subjects in other categories show an intermediate position, with category 7 showing the next highest intensity after categories 1 and 2, though

Table 11A

INDICES OF ASSOCIATION AND DISSOCIATION

Status Category	Indices of Association	Fathers' Status	Subjects' Status	Indices of Dissociation			
				Based on Fathers' Status		Based on Subjects' Status	
				Higher	Lower	Higher	Lower
(1)	(2)	(3)	(4)	(5)	(6)	(7)	(8)
1	13·158	0·631	0·534	—	—	—	—
2	5·865	0·768	0·782	3·621	0·677	3·239	0·683
3	1·997	0·896	0·891	1·818	0·813	1·627	0·756
4	1·618	0·907	0·893	1·015	0·880	1·123	0·831
5	1·157	0·891	0·881	1·161	0·950	0·846	0·927
6	1·841	0·828	0·873	0·228	1·279	0·798	1·387
7	2·259	0·826	0·843	—	—	—	—

being of about the same order as categories 3 and 6. Knowing the occupational contents of the various categories, category 7 would seem to have something of a residual character, while in categories 1 and 2 the intensity of association would appear to be more of an exclusivist variety. The indices of Dissociation, also given in Table 11A, have not been tested for significant differences, but show the kind of gradation which would, in the circumstances, be expected. This is also the case of the specific indices of Dissociation given in columns 5 to 8 of the table. They show that subjects with a higher status background are particularly likely to achieve a status higher than their fathers, with the converse applying to subjects of lower status background.

In all, then, the relative chances of alterations in status between fathers and sons, as measured in Table 11A, are rather different from those suggested by the crude figures in Table 2. In the latter table, the highest degree of self-recruitment appeared to be shown among skilled manual and routine non-manual workers. But this appearance was largely a product of the dominant weight of category 5 in both the parental and filial generations.[1] That is, we should necessarily find a large proportion of the sons of skilled manual and routine non-manual workers to be themselves in the same category as their fathers because in both generations that category contains a very large proportion of all occupied males. When we apply the concept of 'perfect' mobility, we look at the

Table 11B

SIGNIFICANT DIFFERENCES BETWEEN INDICES OF ASSOCIATION FOR
TOTAL MALE SAMPLE

Fathers' Status Category	(1)	(2)	(3)	(4)	(5)	(6)	(7)
			Subjects' Status Category				
1	13·158						
2	*	5·865					
3	*	*	1·997				
4	*	*	‡	1·618			
5	*	*	*	*	1·157		
6	*	*	‡	‡	*	1·841	
7	*	*	‡	†	*	‡	2·259

Notes: * significant at 1 per cent level.
† significant at 5 per cent level.
‡ not significant.

situation from a different point of view and ask: How far is the actual level of self-recruitment in the category greater than would obtain if there were no direct correlation between parental and filial status— if the only determinants were the proportion of all subjects who are the sons of skilled manual workers, and the proportion of all jobs now available which come within the skilled manual category? In answer to this kind of question the indices of Association show the smallest excess of actual over expected, and hence the highest relative mobility, for the skilled manual and routine non-manual workers. If, in such terms, we were to draw a profile over the whole status hierarchy, we should find that the category of skilled manual and routine non-manual workers constitutes a kind of valley, with the really important peaks rising on the upper status side, culminating in the professional and high administra-

[1] See Appendix 2, R. Mukherjee, 'Further note on the analysis of data on social mobility'.

tive occupations, which show the highest ratios of actual to expected self-recruitment.

Differences between Cohorts

Variations in the degree of self-recruitment between cohorts have already been considered in crude terms in an earlier section, the material

Table 12A

INDICES OF ASSOCIATION AND DISSOCIATION FOR SEPARATE COHORTS

Date of Birth of Subjects	Status Category	Index of Association	Based on Fathers' Status	Based on Subjects' Status	Indices of Dissociation Based on Fathers' Status Higher	Based on Fathers' Status Lower	Based on Subjects' Status Higher	Based on Subjects' Status Lower
Before 1890	1	10·70	0·57	0·47	—	—	—	—
	2	5·37	0·85	0·78	1·419	0·820	2·530	0·676
	3	1·65	0·94	0·92	1·507	0·887	2·755	0·681
	4	1·91	0·85	0·84	0·712	0·898	1·097	0·747
	5	1·15	0·91	0·89	0·760	1·043	0·891	0·893
	6	1·94	0·82	0·84	0·655	1·434	0·790	1·411
	7	2·05	0·77	0·92	—	—	—	—
1890–99	1	12·59	0·67	0·55	—	—	—	—
	2	4·38	0·79	0·82	4·000	0·690	5·063	0·650
	3	1·99[1]	0·86[1]	0·87[1]	2·154	0·715	1·521	0·796
	4	1·42	0·93	0·93	1·189	0·845	1·074	0·882
	5	1·23	0·88	0·88	0·783	0·986	0·741	0·987
	6	1·93	0·82	0·82	0·711	1·393	0·810	1·207
	7	2·58	0·76	0·76	—	—	—	—
1900–09	1	15·13	0·59	0·49	—	—	—	—
	2	6·48	0·58	0·77	2·554	0·514	1·699	0·739
	3	1·77	0·91	0·92	1·687	0·813	1·889	0·840
	4	1·12	0·98	0·98	1·100	0·939	1·304	0·897
	5	1·22	0·87	0·82	0·774	0·995	0·809	0·824
	6	1·71	0·86	0·92	0·811	1·204	0·819	1·592
	7	2·59	0·82	0·80	—	—	—	—
1910–19	1	13·16	0·64	0·61	—	—	—	—
	2	5·12	0·82	0·82	5·483	0·673	2·924	0·751
	3	2·06	0·86	0·88	2·310	0·762	2·721	0·718
	4	1·85	0·85	0·86	0·881	0·840	1·026	0·822
	5	1·16	0·89	0·87	0·759	1·004	0·803	0·955
	6	1·86	0·84	0·88	0·784	1·202	0·793	1·469
	7	2·65	0·81	0·79	—	—	—	—
1920–29	1	13·75	0·72	0·58	—	—	—	—
	2	8·81	0·79	0·67	6·292	0·665	6·289	0·485
	3	2·58	0·90	0·87	0·749	0·903	2·677	0·722
	4	2·02	0·92	0·84	1·148	0·883	0·947	0·817
	5	1·07[1]	0·92[1]	0·95[1]	0·701	1·063	0·987	0·908
	6	1·76	0·82	0·86	0·789	1·005	0·793	1·215
	7	2·03	0·89	0·83	—	—	—	—

[1] Not significantly greater or less than 1.

201

Table 12ʙ

SIGNIFICANCE OF DIFFERENCES BETWEEN INDICES OF ASSOCIATION FOR STATUS CATEGORIES, ACCORDING TO SUBJECTS' DATE OF BIRTH

Subjects' Fathers' Status Category	Subjects' Status Category						
	1	2	3	4	5	6	7
Subjects born before 1890							
1	10·70						
2	‡	5·37					
3	*	†	1·65‖				
4	*	†	‡	1·91			
5	*	*	‡	†	1·15		
6	*	*	‡	‡	*	1·94	
7	*	†	‡	‡	†	‡	2·05
Subjects born 1890–9							
1	12·59						
2	‡	4·38					
3	*	†	1·99				
4	*	†	‡	1·42			
5	*	*	‡	†	1·23		
6	*	*	‡	‡	*	1·93	
7	*	†	‡	‡	†	‡	2·58
Subjects born 1900–9							
1	15·13						
2	‡	6·48					
3	*	*	1·77				
4	*	*	‡	1·12			
5	*	*	‡	‡	1·22		
6	*	*	‡	‡	‡	1·71	
7	*	*	‡	*	*	‡	2·59

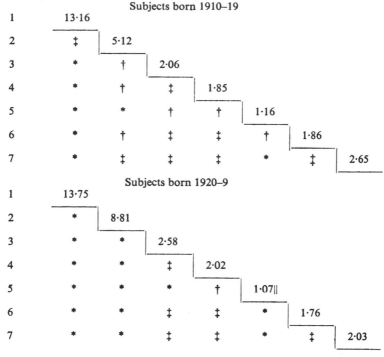

Subjects born 1910–19

1	13·16
2	‡	5·12
3	*	†	2·06
4	*	†	‡	1·85
5	*	*	†	†	1·16
6	*	†	‡	‡	†	1·86
7	*	‡	‡	‡	*	‡	2·65

Subjects born 1920–9

1	13·75
2	*	8·81
3	*	*	2·58
4	*	*	‡	2·02
5	*	*	*	†	1·07‖
6	*	*	‡	‡	*	1·76
7	*	*	‡	‡	*	‡	2·03

* Significantly different at 1 per cent level.
† Significantly different at 5 per cent level.
‡ No significant difference.
‖ Not significantly different from 1·0.

obtained from the sample inquiry having been summarized in Tables 9 and 10. Indices of Association and Dissociation have been constructed from the same material and are given in Tables 12A and 12B. With two exceptions, all the indices of Association are significantly different from unity and show the same kind of ranking in intensity as was visible in Tables 11A and 11B. Categories 1 and 2 differ from all other categories, while categories 3, 4, 6, and 7 tend to bunch together. Once again, save for the 1900–9 cohort, category 5 shows the lowest association between parental and filial status. The one general difference shown by the cohort tables is that the indices for categories 1 and 2 do not differ significantly from each other for any single cohort, though the small numbers should be borne in mind here.

But though the analysis shows a similar ranking of self-recruitment within each cohort, there is still the question of possible differences between cohorts in the association between parental and filial status. To answer this question in detail, a second significance matrix was constructed. It is not reproduced here, but it showed no significant differences between cohorts in the degree of self-recruitment. The same general picture is also obtained if the successive cohorts are looked at as total entities, without regard to the inter-category relations within them. Thus the overall cohort indices of Association and Dissociation, brought together in Table 12c, show a fairly high and consistent degree of self-recruitment. The absence of trend, inferred from Table 8, is thus confirmed, though the precise meaning of the indices for the most recent cohort is still open to doubt for reasons discussed earlier in the chapter.

Table 12c

TOTAL INDICES OF ASSOCIATION AND DISSOCIATION

Decade of Birth of Subjects	Index of Association	Index of Dissociation
Before 1890	1·419	0·851
1890–99	1·495	0·826
1900–09	1·388	0·856
1910–19	1·399	0·844
1920–29	1·280	0·868

Notes: (1) All indices are significantly different from 1·0.
(2) Differences between indices of Association are not significant.
(3) Significance of differences between indices of Dissociation not tested.

The Rôle of Age in the Relation between Parental and Filial Status

One of the special features of the sample inquiry was that the subjects were asked to give information concerning each change—during their working life—of occupation, grade within occupation, industry or town in which they were employed. From this information it is possible to construct various occupational and industrial profiles which may be used for a number of purposes. For the present analysis, the main occupations held at certain specified periods of life were extracted and translated into status categories. It is therefore possible to see the extent to which sons are, at a series of points in their lifetime, in the same status categories as their fathers. Because, however, in some stages of the tabulation the numbers in the cells are greatly reduced, it has been necessary to combine categories 1 and 2, and 6 and 7, to make two groups.[1]

The initial results of this form of analysis are summarized in Table 13,

---

[1] The time analysis in the previous section showed no significant differences in the indices of Association between categories 1 and 2, or between categories 6 and 7. In the statistical sense, therefore, the combination is justified.

which shows, for each status category of fathers, the extent to which sons had achieved that status at five points of their life. The percentages do little more, perhaps, than confirm common observation, but they do it systematically for the first time. It is scarcely startling to learn that, among the sons of manual workers, almost half are in the same status category as their fathers by the age of 20. What is of interest, however, is that parental status has also been achieved by the age of 25 years for a quite substantial proportion of the sons of category 1 and 2 fathers.

Table 13

PROPORTION OF SUBJECTS IN THE SAME STATUS CATEGORIES AS THEIR FATHERS, AT SELECTED AGES OF SUBJECTS

	Subjects' Age	*Fathers' Status Category*				
		1 and 2	*3*	*4*	*5*	*6 and 7*
Percentage of Subjects	20	(11·3)[1]	7·6	2·9	43·8	48·7
in same category as	25	20·3	13·1	7·8	47·6	47·0
father	30	23·0	17·2	12·3	50·1	48·7
	35	32·1	17·3	15·4	48·8	49·7
	40	36·4	18·1	16·5	48·5	51·2

In terms of indices of Association, however, the picture looks somewhat different. Once again, as Table 14 shows, there is at each age selected a systematic pattern of differences in the degree of association between status categories. But there seems also to be a distinction in the trend with increasing age as between categories 1, 2 and 3 on the one hand, and the remaining categories on the other. For the group of higher categories, the indices decline consistently with age; for the lower categories they rise. Part of the apparent trend is caused by the fact that, in Table 14, decade of birth is not taken into account. Thus the indices at age 20 relate to all men in the sample, while those at age 40 refer only to the earlier cohorts. When the statistics are reclassified by date of birth of subjects into two broad groups—subjects born before, and subjects born after, 1910[2]—some of the differences diminish. Nevertheless, the general distinction between the groups at the two ends of the status scale remains valid. For categories 1 and 2, and for categories 6 and 7, there are significant differences between the indices at the age of 20 and at the ages of 35 and 40, the degree of self-recruitment falling with age.

[1] Inferred, in the case of university and professional students.
[2] For the latter category the analysis cannot be taken beyond the age of 35.

in the first case and rising in the second. Here, too, categories 6 and 7 appear to act as residuals; after an initial rise from that category, some sons appear to fall back again. For categories 1 and 2, however, the indices decline with increasing age, consequent upon the entry of men who rise from lower status backgrounds and whose ultimate higher status is achieved at a greater cost in time.

Table 14

SIGNIFICANCE OF DIFFERENCES BETWEEN INDICES OF ASSOCIATION FOR SUBJECTS AT DIFFERENT AGES

Subjects' Fathers' Status Category	Subjects' Status Category				
	1 and 2	3	4	5	6 and 7
		Age 20			
1 and 2	10·549				
3	*	2·993			
4	*	*	1·120‖		
5	*	*	‡	1·070	
6 and 7	*	*	‡	*	1·375
		Age 25			
1 and 2	8·499				
3	*	2·622			
4	*	*	1·194‖		
5	*	*	‡	1·119	
6 and 7	*	*	‡	*	1·541
		Age 30			
1 and 2	6·603				
3	*	2·435			
4	*	*	1·366		
5	*	*	‡	1·148	
6 and 7	*	†	‡	*	1·746

* Significantly different at 1 per cent level.
† Significantly different at 5 per cent level.
‡ No significant difference.
‖ Index not significantly different from 1·0.

Intra-Generation Mobility

In the introduction to the present chapter it was pointed out that, ideally, the study of social mobility should begin at the birth of a cohort of individuals, at which point of time their status could be equated with that of their fathers, and then follow the successive changes in the achieved status of those individuals throughout their lives. The limitations of the sample inquiry bar such an analysis here. Instead, it has been necessary to examine the status relation between fathers and sons, a relation which is somewhat indefinite on the time scale since we do not know to which precise age the final status of the fathers is linked or whether that age is constant over time or between status categories. Because the study was thereby concerned with association rather than mobility in its dynamic aspect, the indices used were described as indices of Association or Dissociation.

But although most of the analysis is concerned with the degree of association between parental and filial status, it is possible to study the dynamics of mobility in a more limited sense. By using the status profiles of subjects at selected ages, and by comparing the status achieved at successive ages, the process of intra-generation change may be looked

207

at, though the first phase of the generation—the period between birth and the entry into gainful employment—is necessarily excluded. Four points of time have been selected—the ages of 20, 30 and 40 years, and the point of final status or status at the time of interview—and three measures of mobility may be used. The first, the Index of Inertia, is precisely the same as the Index of Association, but has been given a different name in order to make it clear that intra-generation, not inter-generation, maintenance of status is being considered. The other measures are the Index of Exit and the Index of Entry. They are described in detail in the technical appendix to this chapter, but are not used here because of the formidable amount of computation involved in testing the significance of differences between successive indices. Hence the Index of Inertia alone is applied to the intra-generation changes, and may be defined, in its application to, say, the maintenance of status between the ages of 20 and 30 years, as (a_1/e_1), where a_1 is the number of men in category 1 both at age 20 and age 30, and e_1 the number expected to be in category 1 at both ages. The choice of age 20 as the initial point of the study is justified because, as may be seen in Appendix 1, over 97 per cent of all the male subjects had taken up an occupation by that age.

The results of this type of analysis take up a considerable number of tables, of which only three are reproduced here—namely Tables 15 to 17, showing the association between status at successive pairs of ages, 20 and 30 years, 30 and 40 years, and 40 years and final status. Once again the characteristic pattern of differences between status categories is evident, and the data make it possible to distinguish between age patterns and generation effects. The use of strictly comparable ages for successive generations scarcely decreases the significance of the differences between status categories *within* a generation. There is less distinction between category 3 and the proximate categories, and categories 6 and 7 are not so clearly marked in their behaviour. But the general ranking of the categories in order of degree of inertia is still maintained, with categories 1 and 2 at the top and category 5 at the bottom. This is also true of the other comparisons, not set out here, between the ages 20 and 40 years and 20 years and final status. Nor are there, with few exceptions, significant differences in the degree of inertia between subjects at the same age and in the same status category but belonging to different birth cohorts. The only notable exception is that in the comparison between age 20 and final status for successive generations, the subjects born in 1920–9 and having category 1 as their final status (which, in fact, means only that this was their status at interview, when they were under 30 years of age), show a degree of inertia significantly different from similar subjects in earlier birth cohorts. This, in the light of the earlier analysis, confirms the doubts already expressed as to the meaning of the results for the most recent cohort. The analysis of association between parental and filial status has shown that men with high status backgrounds not only tend to a very marked extent to achieve high status themselves, but to do so at an early age. It is at the later ages that men with lower status backgrounds begin to reach the upper categories and to diminish the degree of inertia in those categories. Hence the high inertia shown for category 1 subjects of the 1920–9 cohort in the comparison between initial and final status is merely an indication that only the subjects of high status background are being considered, and over a very short age interval. Promotion from the lower categories had scarcely begun to operate by 1949 for the men of the most recent cohort.[1]

Table 15

INDICES OF INERTIA CALCULATED FOR THE STATUS CATEGORIES HELD AT AGES 20 AND 30, ACCORDING TO THE SUBJECTS' DATE OF BIRTH

Status Category at age 20	Status Category at age 30				
	1 and 2	3	4	5	6 and 7
	Born before 1890				
1 and 2	38·961				
3	‡	17·995			
4	*	*	5·288		
5	*	*	*	1·501	
6 and 7	*	*	*	*	2·028

[1] Tests were also applied to the differences between the indices of Inertia for subjects in a given cohort and status category at different ages. Taking the two earlier cohorts, before 1890 and 1890–9, there were some significant differences but, save for categories 5 and 6 and 7, not of a systematic kind. For category 5, the degree of inertia shown in the comparison of status at ages 30 and 40 and 40 and final status was significantly higher than for most other pairs of ages—indicating, in effect, that the contents of that category tended to be stabilized by the age of 30 years. A similar result was found for categories 6 and 7, and the same type of differences was also visible in the 1900–9 cohort. In the latter cohort one other systematic difference was noticeable—the significantly higher degree of inertia for category 1 between the ages of 20 and 30 than between any other pair of ages. Beyond the age of 30, that is, there is a smaller degree of inertia, consequent upon the promotion to categories 1 and 2 of men with backgrounds of lower status. It should again be noted here that in dealing with status at age 20, inferred status is taken for university and professional students.

INTER-GENERATION CHANGES IN STATUS

Status Category at age 20	Status Category at age 30				
	1 and 2	3	4	5	6 and 7
		Born 1890–9			
1 and 2	33·113				
3	‡	12·950			
4	†	‡	8·130		
5	*	*	*	1·660	
6 and 7	*	*	*	‡	1·975
		Born 1900–9			
1 and 2	29·703				
3	*	7·631			
4	*	‡	6·225		
5	*	*	*	1·513	
6 and 7	*	*	*	*	1·994
		Born 1910–19			
1 and 2	17·778				
3	‡	9·166			
4	*	‡	4·921		
5	*	*	*	1·382	
6 and 7	*	*	*	*	2·020

* Significantly different at 1 per cent level.
† Significantly different at 5 per cent level.
‡ No significant difference.

Table 16

INDICES OF INERTIA CALCULATED FOR THE STATUS CATEGORIES
HELD AT AGES 30 AND 40, ACCORDING TO THE SUBJECTS'
DATE OF BIRTH

Status Category at age 30	Status Category at age 40				
	1 and 2	3	4	5	6 and 7
	Born before 1890				
1 and 2	18·227				
3	‡	11·230			
4	*	*	5·450		
5	*	*	*	1·720	
6 and 7	*	*	*	*	2·736
	Born 1890–9				
1 and 2	17·241				
3	†	7·482			
4	*	‡	6·965		
5	*	*	*	1·960	
6 and 7	*	*	*	*	2·743
	Born 1900–9				
1 and 2	13·460				
3	*	6·027			
4	*	‡	4·488		
5	*	*	*	1·772	
6 and 7	*	*	*	*	2·424

* Significantly different at 1 per cent level.
† Significantly different at 5 per cent level.
‡ No significant difference.

Table 17

INDICES OF INERTIA CALCULATED FOR THE STATUS CATEGORIES HELD AT AGE 40 AND THE FINAL STATUS CATEGORY, ACCORDING TO THE SUBJECTS' DATE OF BIRTH

Status Category at age 40	Final Status Category				
	1 and 2	3	4	5	6 and 7
		Born before 1890			
1 and 2	12·520				
3	‡	8·516			
4	*	†	4·927		
5	*	*	*	1·896	
6 and 7	*	*	*	†	2·476
		Born 1890–9			
1 and 2	12·015				
3	*	6·048			
4	*	‡	5·398		
5	*	*	*	2·027	
6 and 7	*	*	*	†	2·596
		Born 1900–9			
1 and 2	10·603				
3	‡	7·661			
4	*	†	5·330		
5	*	*	*	2·215	
6 and 7	*	*	*	†	3·005

* Significantly different at 1 per cent level.
† Significantly different at 5 per cent level.
‡ No significant difference.

INTER-GENERATION CHANGES IN STATUS

A Comparison between England and Wales and Scotland

It has already been pointed out that the information collected for Scottish subjects was rather more limited than that for English adults; questions on occupational profiles were not, for example, included in the interview schedule. Nevertheless, some comparative analysis is possible and is of interest especially because the educational system in Scotland has long appeared to be a rather open one and because of a fairly widespread belief that this is also true of the social structure in general. The comparison is necessarily confined to a study of the degree of association between parental and filial status, and the absolute numbers in the sample are too small to allow a division into more than two broad groups by date of birth of subjects.

Before discussing the results of the comparison, however, two points of difficulty should be emphasized. First, in allocating subjects and their fathers to various status categories, the sevenfold classification devised for England and Wales was used. But that classification was based upon an inquiry made solely in England and Wales and there is no guarantee that the prestige hierarchy of occupations is identical in Scotland. Indeed, there is reason to believe that the prestige positions of the teacher and preacher, to take two examples, differ somewhat between the two countries, and the validity of the comparison may be affected by such differences. For statistical reasons it was necessary to compress the classification into five divisions instead of the original seven, and this compression may at the same time help to overcome (while, unfortunately, suppressing) some of the more subtle differences between the countries. Whether major differences in the ranking of occupations are still left, however, cannot be ascertained from our material.

The second point is the importance of emigration from Scotland. Clearly, emigration overseas cannot be dealt with, and it is doubtful if there would be justification in attempting to do so. But emigration to England and Wales is also an important factor and it is possible that a significant part of what upward mobility occurs among Scotsmen is associated with this movement. It seemed reasonable to provide the maximum opportunity for such social mobility to show itself in the analysis and, accordingly, those male subjects born and educated in Scotland but interviewed as residents in England and Wales were identified and removed from the English material and added to that for Scotland. There were 54 such subjects, and their number makes very little difference to the English material. They are, however, rather

213

Table 18

INDICES OF ASSOCIATION CALCULATED FOR THE SAMPLE OF ENGLISH AND SCOTTISH MALE SUBJECTS

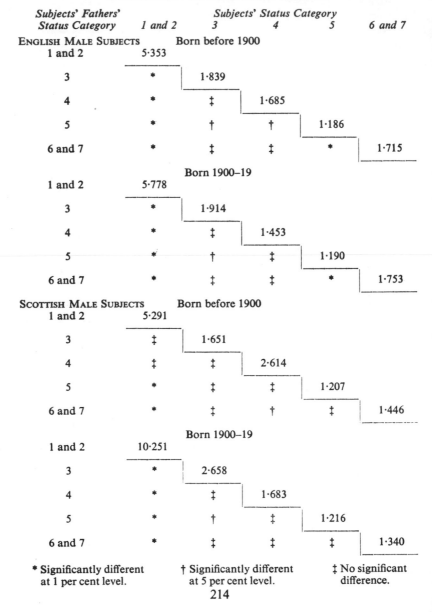

Subjects' Fathers' Status Category	Subjects' Status Category				
	1 and 2	3	4	5	6 and 7
ENGLISH MALE SUBJECTS	Born before 1900				
1 and 2	5·353				
3	*	1·839			
4	*	‡	1·685		
5	*	†	†	1·186	
6 and 7	*	‡	‡	*	1·715
	Born 1900–19				
1 and 2	5·778				
3	*	1·914			
4	*	‡	1·453		
5	*	†	‡	1·190	
6 and 7	*	‡	‡	*	1·753
SCOTTISH MALE SUBJECTS	Born before 1900				
1 and 2	5·291				
3	‡	1·651			
4	‡	‡	2·614		
5	*	‡	‡	1·207	
6 and 7	*	‡	†	‡	1·446
	Born 1900–19				
1 and 2	10·251				
3	*	2·658			
4	*	‡	1·683		
5	*	†	‡	1·216	
6 and 7	*	‡	‡	‡	1·340

* Significantly different at 1 per cent level.   † Significantly different at 5 per cent level.   ‡ No significant difference.

important for the Scottish material which, including these 54, amounts to 471 males who gave information on their own and on their fathers' final occupations or occupations at interview. Only three cases were found of men born in Scotland but brought up and educated in England from an early age, and these were ignored.

The results of the comparative analysis are given in Table 18 and may be looked at in two ways. First, we may consider the results for each country and study the indices of Association for the various status categories and the order in which those categories are ranked in this respect. All the indices differ significantly from 1·0, and for each cohort the ranking is almost exactly the same for both countries. If, however, the results of the tests of significance are examined, certain differences will be seen.

Table 19

COMPARISON OF TOTAL INDICES OF ASSOCIATION AND DISSOCIATION
FOR ENGLAND AND WALES AND SCOTLAND

Area	Date of Birth of Subjects	Indices of	
		Association	Dissociation
Scotland	Before 1900	1·501	0·825
	1900–19	1·435	0·791
England and Wales	Before 1900	1·525	0·814
	1900–19	1·462	0·823

Notes: (1) All the indices differ significantly from 1·0.
(2) There are no significant differences between the indices of Association.
(3) Differences between the indices of Dissociation have not been tested.

For England and Wales, for example, categories 1 and 2 are sharply distinguished from all other categories in each cohort. For Scotland, however, this is not so for the earlier cohort, in which categories 1 and 2 appear to group themselves with categories 3 and 4. Again, in the English material category 5 stands out very significantly from categories 6 and 7, while this is not the case for Scotland in which categories 3 to 7 appear to form a broad group. Of course, the question of small numbers inevitably arises. But so far as the present material is concerned the indices suggest a rather more even distribution of self-recruitment in Scotland, with perhaps some sharpening of the divisions—in terms of the more clear-cut differentiation of categories 1 and 2—in the 1900–19 cohort. Within each country for specific status categories the indices for the two cohorts do not differ significantly from each other. And no significant differences are found in comparing, between the two countries, the indices for a given status category and cohort. In general, therefore,

215

it would seem that there are no major differences in the overall level of the association between parental and filial status in the two countries, but that in Scotland there may be less differentiation between the father-son correlation in the separate status categories and thus a somewhat more even social structure. Table 18 suggests, indeed, that in Scotland there may be a twofold rather than a threefold division in the degree of self-recruitment, while the summary statistics in Table 19 confirm that, so far as our data are concerned and taking all status categories together, the overall indices of Association do not differ significantly between the two countries.

Summary and Conclusion

The discussion of social mobility in this chapter has been rather formal and, because of the frequent use of such terms as 'status category' and 'Index of Association', inevitably somewhat tedious. There is all the more reason, therefore, to summarize as briefly as possible the results of this phase of the investigation and to draw attention to certain doubts and defects which need to be remembered in interpreting these results.

The chief purpose of the study has been to estimate in objective terms the relative chances of men of different social backgrounds reaching various levels of occupational prestige in their own generation. To do this, it was necessary to use, as a standard, the concept of 'perfect' mobility. This is a standard not likely to be realized in fact in present Western society. But whether it is realizable or not is irrelevant here, for the standard has been used only to provide a common basis of comparison, allowing us to say whether one ascertained degree of self-recruitment is greater or less than another.

Using this standard, the study has shown almost throughout an association in status between fathers and sons significantly higher than would be expected on a basis of 'perfect mobility', as well as highly significant differences between the degrees of association for the various strata into which the men covered by the inquiry were classified. So far as our data go, it is these differences which constitute the most outstanding result. It has not been our task to explain the differences; that has been left for other chapters. The second main result is a negative one—the conclusion that, according to our data, there have been no major differences between successive generations in the overall intensity of the status association between fathers and sons. The result here is not definitive, because of differences in the length of the generations and, therefore, in the time available to sons to equal or surpass the status of their fathers.

The indices themselves show no significant differences, but we must allow room for further change in the indices for the youngest generations. If the men born in 1920–9 are investigated again in twenty or thirty years' time, it is by no means unlikely that for their generation the degree of association will then be found significantly different from that for earlier generations. But a difference which is statistically significant is not necessarily a *major* difference. And unless there are very substantial changes in the extent of future promotion among these men, changes which the existing statistics do not and cannot foreshadow, a *major* reduction in the degree of association can scarcely be anticipated. If a major change does occur in the future, it is more likely to be found in the first generation whose education profits fully from the provisions of the 1944 Education Act. But we shall not know if this happens unless later investigators carry out, at some appropriate future date, further studies of the kind reported here.

The discussion in the main text of the chapter has already drawn attention to a number of limitations of, and defects in, the present inquiry. Two further points may, however, be made. First, even within its own limits, the sevenfold status classification is too coarse. In particular, the findings of other studies in this volume show that there are important attitude and behaviour differences between persons in the manual and non-manual sections of category 5, which in our analysis covers routine non-manual as well as skilled manual occupations. Even if recombination had subsequently proved necessary, it would have been better to have begun by treating the manual and non-manual sectors separately.

The second point is that the interest and value of an initial study of this kind, however important it may be in establishing a first stage, is necessarily restricted because it *is* a first study, the results of which cannot be compared with those for other periods or countries.[1] But a start must be made in the hope that other workers will repeat, improve upon and extend the original investigations, and that there will gradually be built up a systematic knowledge of the process of social selection in our various societies.

[1] Some historical reconstruction is possible for Britain, and we hope to return to this in a later study. For comparative material on other countries, see Appendix 3 to the present chapter.

A Note on the Analysis of Data on Social Mobility

RAMKRISHNA MUKHERJEE AND J. R. HALL

Preliminary Consideration

I N studying the social mobility of an individual, the analysis should ideally begin with his birth, his social status then being that of his father, and this birth status should be related to the successive changes in the status the individual himself achieves during his life, until he reaches stability in his final status. In this way the analysis would cover movement in time as well as in, so to speak, space.

In the present studies of social mobility, the range of movement in space is represented by the sevenfold social status hierarchy described in Chapter II. The time co-ordinate is represented by year-units in a generation, thus permitting the study of the movement of an individual within the status hierarchy at fixed points of time. But because of the limitations of the material collected by the samply inquiry, on which the present studies are based (described in Chapter IV), the time scale is inevitably foreshortened.

The inquiry yielded information on the *final* status category of the subject's father, but this is not necessarily the status category of the father at the time when the subject was born. The *movement* of an individual within the social structure cannot therefore be studied from his point of origin, and the major point of reference in the study of social mobility is unknown.

This difficulty has been implicit in previous studies of social mobility. In most cases the problem was assumed to be solved by examining the *association* between the father's and subject's final status categories in a contingency table. But this is to treat the question in a static manner, and to overlook the essentially dynamic character of social mobility. This point is expanded below.

Let P and S represent the father's and the subject's final status categories, and let P_0S_0 be the point at the birth of the child, namely the subject's category of origin. The social mobility of the subject should then be examined with respect to this point, P_0S_0. But, in the course of their respective occupational careers since the birth of the subject, both the father and the subject may have moved up or down the social hierarchy until they attained stability. These possible movements are shown in the following diagram. In it the plus and minus signs refer to the downward or upward movements of the father and the subject in the hierarchical scale with respect to the subject's category of origin at P_0S_0.

$-$		Social Status Scale			$+$	
P_x			P_0		P_y	
S_3	S_2	S_1	S_0	S'_1	S'_2	S'_3

It will be evident from this diagram that for a true measure of the social mobility of an individual, that is, from the category of origin to the final status category of the subject, S_0 represents what may be termed the cell of 'inertia' in the bivariate table. This cell indicates that these subjects had not moved from their father's status category at the time of their birth, and had thus maintained a complete identity in the contingency table.

But in a revised contingency table such as that showing the association between the father's and the subject's final status categories, the cell of complete identity will not only include such individuals as are at the point P_0S_0 in the scale (inertia), but also those at the points, P_xS_2 and $P_yS'_2$ (two other points of equal status, or association). Consequently, the estimate of the number of subjects who were 'inert' may be biased if it is measured solely with respect to equality of status between the final status categories of the subject and his father.

It follows that the estimate of 'mobility' may also be biased if it is measured in terms of differences between the final status categories of the subject and his father. Referring to the above diagram, it will be seen that the 'mobility' of the subject is measured along the scale from the point S_0 to any point shown as S_1, S_2, S_3, S'_1, S'_2, or S'_3. But 'dissociation' between the subject and his father will be measured along the scale from the points P_0, P_x, and P_y to any position other than the position of 'association', that is, excluding only the point P_0S_0 when measured from P_0, the point P_xS_2 when measured from P_x, and the point $P_yS'_2$ when measured from P_y.

Whether any attempt to estimate 'inertia' and 'mobility' from a study of 'association' and 'dissociation' between the subject's and his father's final status categories will produce a bias and whether the bias is positive or negative will evidently depend upon the direction and extent of movement of the subject and his father from the category of origin.

A study of this problem, which is discussed in note 1 on p. 239, based on some relevant models suggests the following conclusions.

(a) If both the subject and his father have equal chances of remaining in the birth category or of moving to any of the remaining six categories (whether these chances are equal or not between the subject and his father), then whether the estimate of:

$$\text{Inertia} \gtreqless \text{Association}$$

depends upon the probability of the subject maintaining 'inertia',

$$P_{s_0} \gtreqless 1/7 \dots\dots\dots\dots\dots\dots\dots\dots \text{(i)}$$

(b) If both the subject and his father have unequal chances of remaining in the birth category or of moving to any of the remaining six categories (whether the corresponding chances of the subject and his father are equal or not), then

$$\text{Inertia} < \text{Association}$$

only if the probability of the subject being 'inert',

$$P_{s_0} \leqslant 1/7 \dots\dots\dots\dots\dots\dots\dots\dots \text{(ii)}$$

But if $P_{s_0} > 1/7$,

$$\text{then Inertia} \gtreqless \text{Association} \dots\dots\dots\dots \text{(iii)}$$

(c) When under conditions noted in (b), the probability of the subject being 'inert' is more than 1/2, then in no circumstances can 'association' exceed 'inertia'. That is, if

$$P_{s_0} > 1/2$$

$$\text{Inertia} > \text{Association} \dots\dots\dots\dots\dots \text{(iv)}$$

But if the probability of the subject being 'inert' is less than 1/2 but more than 1/7, then on condition that both the subject and his father can move only to one of the remaining six categories and to the same category, 'association' will exceed 'inertia'. In other cases no solution can be found. That is, if $1/7 < P_{s_0} < 1/2$,

$$\text{Inertia may be greater or less than Association} \dots\dots \text{(v)}$$

Obviously, unless both the probability of the subject and his father remaining in the birth category, and the probabilities of their moving out to each of the remaining six categories can be ascertained from the available data, it is impossible to find out whether or not the estimate of 'inertia' from the study of 'association' will be biased, and, if so, what is the magnitude and direction of the bias. Unfortunately, such probabilities cannot be calculated from the survey data. Moreover, from empirical evidence, it may be stated that the conditions (*a*) and (*b*) (ii) above are most unlikely to be valid for the society under examination. It follows, therefore, that the estimate of 'association' cannot be equal to, nor can it consistently be an underestimate of, 'inertia'. On the other hand, although it is most unlikely that the probability of the subject being 'inert' will be 1/2 for all the subjects or for all the seven categories, it cannot also be definitely asserted that this probability will always be either greater or less than 1/2. Therefore, the only conclusions which can be drawn from these hypothetical considerations are (i) the estimate of 'association' is not likely to equal the estimate of 'inertia', and (ii) the estimate of 'association' may be either *larger or smaller* than the true estimate of 'inertia'.

Because the relation between 'mobility' and 'dissociation' is always complementary to the relation between 'inertia' and 'association', the above conclusions also apply to the estimation of 'mobility' from the measurement of 'dissociation'. Hence, the *association* between the subject's and his father's final status categories cannot directly provide information on social mobility in terms of movement from the category of origin.

Does it follow, however, that because information is not available on father's status category at the time of the subject's birth, social mobility cannot be assessed at all? It may not be practical for a survey conducted by interviews to collect accurate information on the fathers' social status at the time the subject was born. Many of the persons interviewed may not be able to give the necessary information. Moreover, because the information will relate to a period of which the subject can know only from hearsay, the reliability of such information may be doubtful. If, therefore, the social status at origin is not likely to be ascertainable, either new methods must be developed to approximate the situation required for a comprehensive study of social mobility, or the analysis must be so arranged as to permit the drawing of indirect inferences from the available data.

If the situation can be so approximated, a dynamic study of social mobility can still be made, though of course within definite limitations. Thus, one of the studies included in this symposium examines the movement of subjects in the social status hierarchy at specified ages. The first point in the mobility profile is age 20, by which time most individuals have begun their occupational careers. (A full discussion of this will be found in note 2 on p. 241.) The status of the subjects at specified points may then be studied, such as at ages 25, 30, 35 and 40, and also in relation to the status finally attained in life. Such an analysis cannot, however, take into account changes in status during the first phase of the generation, namely during the period of 0 to 20 years of age. Hence this type of analysis will not assess the full generation movement.

But though full generation *movement* (intra-generation mobility) cannot be examined in this symposium, inter-generation *changes* can be ascertained from the available data. A study of *association* between the father's and the subject's final social status categories, which give the end-points of social mobility in two generations, will furnish a true picture of generation changes. The degree of 'association' or 'dissociation' in social status between the two generations will show the final or net effects of movement in a society, one of the primary objectives of studying social mobility.

Further, differences in the degree of association between status categories in two generations will indicate the relative stability of those categories in the social structure. The amount and the direction of 'dissociation' in each category, and a comparison of the degree of such 'dissociation' between categories, will indicate how the 'unstable' elements in the society have behaved in the final analysis. Finally, the nature of the 'dissociation' in each category can be examined to see if there is a general scatter, or whether there is a tendency to cluster round the final parental status. The degree of rigidity of the social structure can thus be examined. Hence while the approach is static in that it bases itself on the end-results of movement in two generations and not on intra-generation movements as such, a study of the association between father's and subject's final status categories may still lead to fruitful inferences on social mobility.

The Concept of 'Perfect' Mobility

The preceding section has outlined the limits within which the material obtained by the sample inquiry can legitimately be used to study social mobility. The purpose of the present section is to suggest a method of measuring mobility applicable not only to a dynamic analysis of mobility within a hierarchical framework for a given generation (intra-generation mobility), but also to the measurement of the association between the final status categories of the subject and his father (inter-generation change). The method used should be applicable to each separate category within the sevenfold hierarchy as well as to the hierarchy as a whole. Further, the method should make it possible to compare the degree of intra-generation mobility and inter-generation change for subjects born in different periods; it should enable us to see whether there has been a change in the social structure, and also to measure the internal rigidity or fluidity of the structure.

It should be made clear at the outset, however, that the sevenfold status hierarchy is based upon contemporary judgements as to the relative social standing of occupations, subjects being classified according to these judgements no matter what their date of birth. It is possible, however, for shifts in the relative social standing of occupations to have occurred over time, but such changes will not be reflected in our material. The problem was not overlooked in the planning stage of the inquiry, but the difficulties involved in tracing and allowing for social status changes over time, prohibited a practical solution.

Ideally, the problem can be solved only by undertaking successive inquiries, once or twice in each generation, to ascertain the degree and nature of consensus as to the prestige of occupations in the given society. And since the inquiry described in this volume is the first to be undertaken in Britain, only further work in the future can provide this solution. The analysis of prestige ratings given by individuals of various ages is not a satisfactory alternative, since even the judgements of old people will be influenced by the economic and social circumstances of the period in which they give their judgements. Nevertheless it might reasonably be argued that, had there been fundamental changes in the prestige of occupations during the past fifty years, some trace of such changes would very probably be reflected in differences between the prestige scales of old and young subjects. The fact that, as shown in Chapter I, the analysis of ratings by age did not reveal any important differences, tends to suggest that there have not been fundamental changes during the period covered.

Leaving aside these difficulties, however, it is possible to look at the question in a somewhat different way. It is possible, that is, to ask what is the degree of association between the status of fathers and sons, measuring the status of both generations *in terms of a single scale*. Though that way of posing the question is more limited, it is nevertheless valid, in the same way as it is valid, in considering changes in the cost of living, to ask how that cost has changed over time, assuming as constant the expenditure patterns of the most recent period of time

223

studied, though one would also like to look at developments in terms of the patterns of the earliest period covered by the analysis.

Intra-generation Mobility

It will facilitate the explanation of the concept of 'perfect' mobility, the standard by which mobility will be judged, if for the moment the distinctions between the dynamic and static analyses are ignored. 'Perfect' mobility will be discussed in relation to the dynamic analysis of intra-generation mobility for those born in a given period, the equal relevance of the concept to static analysis being indicated at a later stage. This dynamic analysis will relate to the internal fluidity of the social structure.

The material may be presented in the form of bivariate frequency tables as in Table 1 below, which shows for illustrative purposes the status category distributions of a group of individuals at ages 20 and 30 within a sevenfold status hierarchy.

Table 1

STATUS DISTRIBUTION AT AGE 30

Social Status Categories	1	2	3	4	5	6	7	Total
1	$a_{1·1}$	$a_{1·2}$	$a_{1·3}$	$a_{1·4}$	$a_{1·5}$	$a_{1·6}$	$a_{1·7}$	b_1
2	$a_{2·1}$	$a_{2·2}$	$a_{2·3}$	$a_{2·4}$	$a_{2·5}$	$a_{2·6}$	$a_{2·7}$	b_2
3	$a_{3·1}$	$a_{3·2}$	$a_{3·3}$					b_3
4				$a_{4·4}$				b_4
5					$a_{5·5}$			b_5
6						$a_{6·6}$		b_6
7	$a_{7·1}$						$a_{7·7}$	b_7
Total	c_1	c_2	c_3	c_4	c_5	c_6	c_7	d

(Rows 1–7 under the heading "Status Distribution at age 20")

From the above table, the movement of individuals within the status hierarchy between ages 20 and 30 can be examined. In every case, the first numeral following the letter in any cell represents a row of the table (the status category at age 20) and the second numeral a column (status category at age 30). The distributions of subjects by status category at ages 20 and 30 are shown by the marginal distributions. At age 20, b_1 individuals are in category 1, b_2 in category 2 and so on; at age 30, c_1 individuals are in category 1, c_2 in category 2 and so on. Whether or not the individual has moved from the category held at age 20 can be readily seen from the table. Those in the diagonal cells, $a_{1·1}$, $a_{2·2}$, $a_{3·3}$ . . . $a_{7·7}$ have remained in the same category. This is indicated by the numerals following the letter, e.g. $a_{1.1}$. Here, the status category held at age 20 (shown by row 1) is the same as that held at age 30 (shown by column 1). Those in the cells to the right of the diagonal have moved to categories lower than those held at age 20. Again the numerals following the letter illustrate this movement, e.g. $a_{1.2}$, where the status category held at age 20 (shown by row 1) is higher than that held at age 30 (shown by column 2). Those in cells to the left of the diagonal have moved to higher categories. The concept of 'perfect' mobility can be demonstrated within this framework.

'Perfect' mobility may be defined as the condition in which every member of society has an equal chance of reaching a particular status category, so as to produce that social structure evidenced by the status distributions of subjects at the terminal point of time. Thus an individual's chance of reaching a given status category is independent of his category of origin, or of the status he has held at any specified point on his status profile. It is not, however, independent of the marginal distributions, that is, of the distribution of status at the terminal point of time.

Suppose, for example, that for a given group of subjects aged 20, the distributions of categories which will be open to them when they attain age 30 is:

Category	1	2	3	4	5	6	7	Total
Percentage	5	5	10	15	40	10	15	100

Then, in a state of 'perfect' mobility, of those in category 1 at age 20, we should expect 5 per cent to be in category 1 at age 30, 5 per cent to be in category 2, 10 per cent to be in category 3, and so on. Similarly, of those in category 2 at age 20, we should also expect 5 per cent to be in category 1 at age 30, 5 per cent to be in category 2, and 10 per cent to be in category 3 and so on.

Equally, suppose that for a given group of subjects at present aged 30, their distribution by status categories at age 20 was:

Category	1	2	3	4	5	6	7	Total
Percentage	2	4	7	8	49	20	10	100

Then, in conditions of 'perfect' mobility, of those in category 1 at age 30, we would expect 2 per cent to have been in category 1 at age 20, 4 per cent to have been in category 2, and 7 per cent to have been in category 3 and so on. The same applies to individuals in the other categories at age 30.

It follows that if there were 'perfect' mobility, then in a bivariate table such as Table 1 above, the percentage distribution in each column would be the same and equal to that of the pooled total in the marginal *column*, and equally that the percentage distribution in each row would be the same and equal to that of the pooled total in the marginal *row*. If every member in a certain category at a given time moves out of that category, that may be designated *complete mobility*. If, on the other hand, each member of a certain category remains in that category, that may be designated *complete immobility*. Statistically, the concept of 'perfect' mobility makes possible a test of independence of the internal distributions in a contingency table of which the marginal distributions are fixed.

From these fixed marginal distributions it is possible to create a 'model' of 'perfect' mobility, and to derive the numbers expected in each cell of the bivariate table. Taking Table 1 as an example, the 'numbers' expected in each cell may be calculated as follows:

Cell 1/1, i.e. the number in category 1 at age 20 and expected to remain there at age 30. b_1 individuals were in category 1 at age 20, and according to the concept of 'perfect' mobility are expected to be distributed by categories at age 30, in the same proportion as the total distribution of categories at age 30. Hence c_1/d are expected to be in cell 1/1; c_2/d in cell 1/2, c_7/d in cell 1/7. The number in cell 1/1, $a_{1.1}$, is derived

as $b_1 \times \dfrac{c_1}{d}$.

Cell 1/2, i.e. the number in category 1 at age 20, but expected to be in 2 at age 30. From the above reasoning, this is $a_{1.2}$, derived as $b_1 \times \dfrac{c_2}{d}$.

Cell 2/1, i.e. the number in category 2 at age 20, but expected to be in category 1 at age 30. This is $a_{2.1}$ derived as $b_2 \times \dfrac{c_1}{d}$. Equally, it is possible to derive the total number of those in category 1 at age 20, but expected to be in categories other than 1 at age 30, namely $(a_{1.2}, a_{1.3} \ldots a_{1.7})$ or $(b_1 - a_{1.1})$ as $b_1 \times \dfrac{(d - c_1)}{d}$.

To construct this model illustration of 'perfect' mobility the status distributions of the subjects at ages 20 and 30 have been used to create the 'expected' number in each cell, and a similar method is adopted in the *static analysis*, using the present or final status distributions of subjects and their fathers.

For the dynamic analysis, however, contingency tables have been prepared showing the actual distributions of subjects at ages 20 and 30, 20 and 40, 30 and 40, etc., for the five birth cohorts distinguished in the material. In each instance, the marginal distributions have been used to calculate a further contingency table in terms of the concept of 'perfect' mobility, showing the numbers expected to be in each cell. Thus, for each cell in a given contingency table we have an observed and an expected frequency. We can now devise indices measuring the extent to which 'perfect' mobility exists, by comparing the actual frequency with the expected frequency.

In considering the mobility or immobility of one birth cohort as a whole between, say, the ages of 20 and 30, it is possible to construct two indices. Looking first at the diagonal cells of those who have remained in the same category at both ages, by summing the actual numbers remaining in their initial categories, and also the numbers expected to remain, we may calculate the ratio:

$$\frac{\text{Actual numbers in the same categories at ages 20 and 30}}{\text{Numbers expected to be in the same categories at ages 20 and 30}}$$

This we may term the Index of Inertia. Equally, we may design another index, the Index of Mobility, defined as the following ratio:

$$\frac{\text{Actual numbers in different categories at ages 20 and 30}}{\text{Numbers expected to be in different categories at ages 20 and 30}}$$

Where, however, the mobility of a given *category* is being considered, two indices of Mobility may be used, for the movement of subjects from the category held at age 20 into another category at age 30 can be viewed in one of two ways. Subjects in a given status category at age 20 who, now aged 30, are in other categories, may be said to have moved *from* the category held at age 20. Equally, subjects in a given status category at age 30 who, at age 20, were in other categories, may be said to have moved into the category held at age 30. Thus, in Table 1, the total moving out of category 1 at age 20 is $(b_1 - a_{1 \cdot 1})$, the total moving into category 1 at age 30, however, is $(c_1 - a_{1 \cdot 1})$. The number moving *from* the category held at age 20 is the total of the number of cells in the appropriate *row* excluding the cells along the diagonal; while the number moving *into* a category different from that held at age 20 is the total of the number in the cells in the appropriate *column*, excluding the cells along the diagonal. In considering movement *from* a category the Index of Mobility may be defined as:

227

Actual number in a given category at age 20, but not in it at age 30

Number expected to be in a given category at age 20, but not in it at age 30

Conversely, in thinking of movement *into* a category, the Index of Mobility may be defined as:

Actual number in a category at age 30 but not in it at age 20

Number expected to be in a category at age 30 but not in it at age 20

To distinguish between these two indices, the first will be called the Index of *Exit*, the second the Index of *Entry*. The two are not necessarily equal, as they are based upon different totals.

Both these indices of Exit and Entry can be further subdivided. From the Index of Exit, for example, it is possible to create two further indices according to whether the movement from the category held at age 20 is to a higher or a lower category.

Thus an Index of Exit (Higher) for a given category may be defined as:

Actual number in a given category at age 20, but in a higher category at age 30

Number expected to be in a given category at age 20, but in a higher category at age 30

An Index of Exit (Lower) for a given category may be defined as:

Actual number in a given category at age 20, but in a lower category at age 30

Number expected to be in a given category at age 20, but in a lower category at age 30

Indices of Entry (Higher and Lower) may also be defined in parallel terms. Where each of the indices of Inertia, Exit, or Entry equals unity, perfect mobility exists, that is, the number of subjects actually remaining in, moving out of, or into given categories equals the number expected to do so. The practical upper limit of inertia depends upon the cell, marginal and cohort totals, but in the material discussed it rarely exceeds a value of 10, and usually lies between the limits of 1 and 6. Where, in a given cell, the expected numbers exceed the actual, it is possible for the value of the Index of Inertia to lie between 0·0 and 1·0, but in our data this is rarely the case, the Index of Inertia usually being greater than unity. A word of caution is necessary. Differences in the magnitude of indices of Inertia may not always reflect a difference which is statistically significant. Hence it is essential to apply the statistical test described later in this note to all pairs of indices.

Where the Index of Inertia is greater than unity, the indices of Mobility are invariably less than unity, rarely exceeding 0·980 or falling below 0·500. In the few instances where the Index of Inertia is less than unity, the indices of Mobility move in sympathy, but were never, however, observed to exceed a value of 2. Again, differences in the magnitude of indices of Mobility may not reflect differences which are statistically significant. To test for significant differences between indices of Mobility, however, is a complicated and lengthy process, and as a result these indices are calculated in only a few instances.

In the dynamic study of the mobility of a given status category, all these indices: Inertia, Entry and Exit may be used. It has already been noted that five birth cohorts of subjects have been distinguished. By using the marginal distribution at any pair of ages (say 30 and 40) within each of the cohorts to create models of 'perfect' mobility, indices can be calculated which are strictly comparable between cohorts.

The relation between the Index of Exit, the Index of Entry and the Index of Inertia may best be shown in algebraic terms. Suppose that at age 20, b_1 individuals are in a given status category, and that at age 30, c_1 individuals are in that category, that a_1 is the number who were in the category at age 20 and remain there, and e_1 the number expected to be in the category at 20 and to remain there. Then:

1. Index of Inertia $= \dfrac{a_1}{e_1}$

2. Index of Exit $= \dfrac{b_1 - a_1}{b_1 - e_1}$

3. Index of Entry $= \dfrac{c_1 - a_1}{c_1 - e_1}$

It will be seen that in general the greater the Index of Inertia, the greater must a_1 be in relation to e_1, and therefore the smaller the two indices of Mobility.

Inter-Generation Change

We have now to consider how far this concept of 'perfect' mobility is applicable in a static analysis as a measure of the degree of *inter-generation change* between the status categories reached by the subject and his father. Here we are attempting to measure the relative change in the social structure over two generations, and the extent to which the balance of this structure is maintained. The framework of the study is provided by the present or final status distributions of subjects and their fathers, divided into five cohorts according to the date of birth of the subject.

It must be noted at once that 'final status' as applied to subjects and their fathers is a variable, not being fixed in time. As indicated in Chapter IX, final stability in a status category may not be achieved until late in life. Hence, the status category reached by subjects born after 1900 at the time of interview (1949) may not be the category in which they will eventually stabilize. For those born before 1900, we are likely to be studying the association between categories in which both the subject and the subject's father have stabilized. For those born after 1920, though many fathers of subjects may have reached stability, a number may not have done so, while a large proportion of the subjects themselves will not have achieved final stability. In the intermediate birth cohorts, the association is likely to be between one set of categories in which stability has been reached (the fathers), and another set (the subjects) where this is not the case. Nevertheless, the marginal distributions of fathers and subjects will reflect the status opportunities open to them at any one of a number of different points of time, making it possible to calculate expected frequencies and to relate the observed to the expected frequencies.

It is therefore obvious that indices calculated from the relationship between the actual and expected frequencies for the five cohorts will not be strictly comparable. Comparisons between indices for the cohorts born before 1900, where subjects are at least 50, and in consequence likely to have reached their final status, will be valid, and the comparison may be extended to the 1900 cohort with some confidence. Comparisons between indices for the three older and two younger cohorts must be viewed with caution.

Indices of Inertia, Exit and Entry are inappropriate in this context of inter-generation change. We are not here concerned with the movement of a specified generation between two points fixed in time, but with the association between the status levels reached by two generations at different points of time. There can be no estimate of movement out of, or into a category as we have no knowledge of any point of origin. What is being measured is the extent to which fathers and subjects have reached the same status level (association) or the extent to which their status categories are different (dissociation).

'Perfect' association is the condition in which every son has an equal chance of reaching a particular status category of father so as to produce that relationship between the two generations evidenced by the final status distributions of fathers and sons. Thus, a son's chance of reaching a given status category of father is independent of the son's status origin or his status category at any point on his status profile. If all sons are in status categories differing from those of their fathers, this may be designated *complete dissociation*, whilst, on the other hand, *complete association* exists if all sons are in the same categories as their fathers. Statistically, the concept of 'perfect' association makes possible a test of independence of the internal distributions of a contingency table, of which the marginal distributions are fixed. We may, therefore, construct two indices which are calculated in precisely the same manner as the indices of Inertia and Mobility, namely:

1. The Index of Association:

$$\frac{\text{The actual frequency of fathers and subjects in the same status category}}{\text{The expected frequency of fathers and subjects in the same status category}}$$

2. The Index of Dissociation:

$$\frac{\text{The actual frequency of fathers and subjects in different categories}}{\text{The expected frequency of fathers and subjects in different categories}}$$

The theoretical limits for these indices are precisely the same, and the actual limits much the same, as those noted for the indices of Inertia and Mobility. And again, a difference between two indices may not be significant, and needs to be ascertained by applying the statistical test described in the next section. Where, however, the Index of Association is greater than unity, showing more subjects to be in their fathers' status category than would have been expected, the Index of Dissociation is invariably less than unity, and vice versa.

For a given status category, as with the Index of Mobility, the Index of Dissociation can be further split, for the concept of 'dissociation' can be considered from two points of view. First, based upon a given status category of father it is possible to define an Index of Dissociation as follows:

$$\frac{\text{Actual number of subjects in categories different from their fathers}}{\text{Number of subjects expected to be in categories different from their fathers}}$$

Secondly, based upon a given status category of subjects:

$$\frac{\text{Actual number of fathers in categories different from their sons}}{\text{Number of fathers expected to be in categories different from their sons}}$$

231

The first of these indices will be referred to as the Index of Dissociation (fathers' status); and the second as the Index of Dissociation (subjects' status), indicating the point of reference upon which the measure of dissociation is based.

If in Table 1 the subjects' final status distributions are shown in the rows, and the fathers' final status distributions in the columns, then:

Index of Dissociation (fathers' status) category 1

$$= (b_1 - a_{1.1}) \times \frac{d}{b_1 (d - c_1)}$$

Index of Dissociation (subjects' status) category 1

$$= (c_1 - a_{1.1}) \times \frac{d}{c_1 (d - b_1)}$$

The relationship between the indices of Dissociation (fathers' status) and (subjects' status) is similar to that between the indices of Entry and Exit.

Each of these indices can also be subdivided in terms of 'higher' and 'lower'. For example, for a given status category of father it is possible to define two indices according to whether the dissociation is caused by subjects being in categories higher or lower in the status scale than their fathers.

As with the Index of Mobility, however, the test of significant difference between indices of Dissociation is complicated and lengthy. Consequently, the analysis is conducted chiefly in terms of the Index of Association.

The Statistical Validity of the Use of Indices in this Study

Introduction

The analysis of social mobility deals with the movement of a sample of individuals from one social status category to another. At any two points of time between which movement is examined, the final distributions of the individuals in terms of a number of status categories are regarded as fixed. This can be generalized in the following contingency table where, $b_1 \ldots b_k$ and $c_1 \ldots c_k$ are the final distributions of a sample of individuals between k status categories at two points of time; $a_1 - a_k$ are the numbers of individuals who have remained in the same status category; $(b_1 - a_1) \ldots (b_k - a_k)$ the numbers who have moved *out* of a status category and $(c_1 - a_1) \ldots (c_k - a_k)$ the number who have moved *into* a status category; and d is the total sample studied.

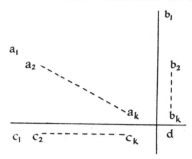

To consider movement in terms of the concept of 'perfect' mobility (or 'perfect' association) a set of indices, viz. Index of Inertia (or Association), Index of Exit or Entry (or Dissociation), was constructed by calculating the ratio of the observed values in the contingency table to the expected value corresponding to it in a test of independence. Thus, referring to the above table, the indices of Inertia (or Association) are:

$$\frac{a_1 \times d}{b_1 \times c_1}, \quad \frac{a_2\, d}{b_2\, c_2} \cdots \frac{a_k\, d}{b_k\, c_k} \qquad \text{............................. (i)}$$

The indices of Exit (or Dissociation) are:

$$\frac{(b_1 - a_1)\, d}{b_1\, (d - c_1)}, \frac{(b_2 - a_2)\, d}{b_2\, (d - c_2)}, \cdots \frac{(b_k - a_k)\, d}{b_k\, (d - c_k)} \qquad \text{.............. (ii)}$$

The indices of Entry Mobility are:

$$\frac{(c_1 - a_1)\, d}{c_1\, (d - b_1)}, \frac{(c_2 - a_2)\, d}{c_2\, (d - b_2)}, \cdots \frac{(c_k - a_k)\, d}{c_k\, (d - b_k)}, \qquad \text{.............. (iii)}$$

This method of analysis, however, raises two important problems which are discussed below

Problem 1. The first problem is to ascertain whether the difference in the values of the numerator and denominator of an index is real or merely due to chance fluctuations. In other words, are these indices truly greater or less than unity?

A simple solution of this problem is to apply a chi-square test as a test of independence to the 2×2 frequency table from which a set of indices is prepared. Thus for the status category 1, the test will show from the contingency table:

	Category 1	*Not 1*	*Total*
Category 1	a_1	$(b_1 - a_1)$	b_1
Not 1	$c_1 - a_1$	$(d - b_1 - c_1 - a_1)$	$d - b_1$
Total	c_1	$(d - c_1)$	d

whether or not the numerator of the Index of Inertia (Association) a_1 is different from the denominator

$$\frac{b_1\, c_1}{d}.$$

The numerator of the Index of Exit (Dissociation) $b_1 - a_1$ is different from the denominator

$$\frac{b_1\, (d - c_1)}{d}.$$

The numerator of the Index of Entry $(c_1 - a_1)$ is different from the denominator

$$\frac{c_1\, (d - b_1)}{d}.$$

In other words, if the chi-square value is significantly large, all the indices constructed from such a table have a *real* meaning, and therefore should be regarded as truly greater or less than unity, as the case may be.

Problem 2. Having thus established the validity of these indices the next problem is to examine whether a group of indices, e.g. the indices of Inertia (Association) for status categories 1 ... k, are significantly different from one another.

Indices of Inertia (Association) between Status Categories

A Specific Case

Assuming $E\,(a_i) = \alpha_i$, where $i = 1, 2, \ldots k$, to test the hypothesis

$$\frac{\alpha_1}{b_1\, c_1} = \frac{\alpha_2}{b_2\, c_2} = \cdots = \frac{\alpha_k}{b_k\, c_k} = \alpha, \text{ a constant} \ldots \text{(iv)}$$

Mr. J. Durbin, of the London School of Economics, has suggested three solutions to this problem. The solutions are given below:

Solution 1

To fit the hypothesis (iv) by minimizing

$$\chi^2 = \sum_1^k \frac{(a_i - \alpha_i)^2}{\alpha_i} = \frac{1}{\alpha} \sum_1^k \frac{(a_i - b_i\, c_i\, \alpha)^2}{b_i\, c_i}$$

$$= \frac{1}{\alpha} \sum_1^k \frac{a_i{}^2}{b_i\, c_i} - 2 \sum_1^k a_i + \alpha \sum_1^k b_i\, c_i.$$

234

$$\frac{\partial x^2}{\partial \alpha} \rightarrow \hat{\alpha}^2 = \frac{\overset{k}{\underset{1}{\Sigma}} (a_i^2/b_i\, c_i)}{\overset{k}{\underset{1}{\Sigma}} b_i\, c_i}.$$

Taking $\hat{\alpha}_i = b_i\, c_i\, \hat{\alpha}$ then

$$\chi^2 = \overset{k}{\underset{1}{\Sigma}} \frac{(a_i - \hat{\alpha}_i)^2}{\hat{\alpha}_i}$$

is approximately distributed as χ^2 with $k-1$ degrees of freedom.

Solution 2

$$\frac{a_1}{b_1\, c_1} \cdots \frac{a_k}{b_k\, c_k} \text{ are unbiased estimators of } \alpha$$

$$\text{with variances } \frac{\alpha_1}{b_1^2\, c_1^2} \cdots \frac{\alpha_k}{b_k^2\, c_k^2},$$

which are proportional to

$$\frac{1}{b_1\, c_1}, \cdots \frac{1}{b_k\, c_k}.$$

Thus the best unbiased linear estimate of α

$$\text{is} \quad \hat{\hat{\alpha}} = \overset{k}{\underset{1}{\Sigma}} a_i / \overset{k}{\underset{1}{\Sigma}} b_i\, c_i.$$

Hence $\quad \hat{\hat{\alpha}}_i = b_i\, c_i\, \hat{\hat{\alpha}}$

and, as before, $\chi^2 = \overset{k}{\underset{1}{\Sigma}} \dfrac{(a_i - \hat{\hat{\alpha}}_i)^2}{\hat{\hat{\alpha}}_i}$ with $k-1$ degrees of freedom.

Solution 3.

By using the Maximum Likelihood method, we have approximately:

$$L = \text{constant} - \tfrac{1}{2} \overset{k}{\underset{1}{\Sigma}} \log \alpha_i - \tfrac{1}{2} \overset{k}{\underset{1}{\Sigma}} \frac{(a_i - \alpha_i)^2}{\alpha_i}$$

$$= \text{constant} - \frac{k}{2} \log \alpha - \frac{1}{2\alpha} \overset{k}{\underset{1}{\Sigma}} \frac{(a_i - b_i\, c_i\, \alpha)^2}{b_i\, c_i}.$$

$$\frac{\partial L}{\partial \alpha} \rightarrow \frac{k}{\alpha} - \frac{1}{\alpha^2} \overset{k}{\underset{1}{\Sigma}} \frac{a_i^2}{b_i\, c_i} + \overset{k}{\underset{1}{\Sigma}} b_i\, c_i = 0.$$

Inserting the 'sensible' solution of this quadratic in

$$\hat{\hat{\chi}}^2 = \overset{k}{\underset{1}{\Sigma}} \frac{(a_i - \hat{\hat{\alpha}}_i)^2}{\hat{\hat{\alpha}}_i},$$

235

with k–1 degrees of freedom, the problem can be solved as in the previous solutions.

While suggesting the above three solutions, Durbin noted that the first solution appeared to be the best because even if either of the others was more accurate, the value of chi-square from the first would always be less than the other two and thus the resultant judgement of the significance of differences between Indices of Inertia (Association) would be a conservative one.

The three solutions were applied experimentally in the main study of social mobility (strictly speaking, the study of 'association'), namely between seven status categories for five birth cohort contingency tables. As will be seen from the following table, the value of α was practically the same for the first and the third solutions, and consistently higher than that of the second. Consequently, the value of chi-square for the same six degrees of freedom was always practically the same for solutions 1 and 3, and smaller than that for solution 2.

Table 2

RESULTS OF TESTING THE SIGNIFICANCE OF DIFFERENCES BETWEEN THE INDICES OF INERTIA (ASSOCIATION) BY THE THREE METHODS FOR FIVE CONTINGENCY TABLES ARRANGED ACCORDING TO THE CLASSIFICATION BY FIVE BIRTH COHORTS

Classification of contingency tables by 5 birth cohorts	Values of α according to solution			Values of chi-square according to solution		
	1	2	3	1	2	3
(1)	(2)	(3)	(4)	(5)	(6)	(7)
Born before 1890	·00269	·00221	·00266	98·663	109·378	98·663
Born 1890–99	·00336	·00289	·00331	59·429	64·253	59·473
Born 1900–09	·00242	·00194	·00240	129·808	145·840	129·850
Born 1910–19	·00219	·00188	·00217	92·598	100·223	92·592
Born 1920–29	·00207	·00173	·00204	106·364	116·696	106·369

Although there was little difference between the results of the three solutions, the first method was finally adopted for reasons mentioned earlier. This method has been used extensively in studies contained in this volume.

Finally, it should be noted that the two conditions assumed for this test—(i) that the frequency values $a_1 \ldots a_k$ are independent and (ii) that the marginal totals $b_1 \ldots b_k$ and $c_1 \ldots c_k$ are fixed—are somewhat contradictory. But even though the marginal totals are fixed, the larger the value of k, the more closely the two conditions will be satisfied. For the present analysis, k = 7, which is not a small number.

Indices of Inertia (Association) between Birth Cohorts for a Fixed Status Category

A Generalized Solution

In the above solutions the sample size, namely d, was not considered, since it could be omitted as a common factor in the numerator of (iv). But one of the main objects of this study is also to test the significance of the differences between corresponding indices derived from analogous contingency tables in which d is also a variable. The situation can be generalized from the following contingency tables.

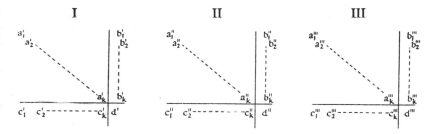

where I, II, III . . . represent different birth cohorts, for each of which a contingency table was prepared to derive the indices based on the concept of 'perfect mobility' (or 'perfect association') at fixed points of time. The problem is to ascertain whether the indices of Inertia (Association) for the same status category differ significantly between the birth cohorts. In other words, using the previous notations, it is required to test the hypothesis:

$$\frac{\alpha'_i \, d'}{b'_i \, c'_i} = \frac{\alpha''_i \, d''}{b''_i \, c''_i} = \ldots = \text{constant}$$

$$\text{that is } \frac{\alpha_i \, d}{b_i \, c_i} = \alpha \text{ say} \quad \ldots\ldots\ldots\ldots\ldots\ldots \quad (v)$$

Following solution 1 given previously,

$$\hat{\alpha}^2 = \sum_1^k (a_i^2 \, d_i/b_i \, c_i) / \sum_1^k (b_i \, c_i/d_i)$$

and then taking

$$\hat{\alpha}_i = \hat{\alpha} \left(\frac{b_i \, c_i}{d_i} \right)$$

the rest will follow as before.

This may be regarded as the generalized solution of which the previous solution was a specific case where d was a constant.

Indices of Mobility (Dissociation)

Using the same methods as were given above for the indices of Inertia (Association), the significance of differences between the indices of Exit (Dissociation) and the indices of Entry may also be tested. Since the solutions for the indices of Exit or Entry would be similar, because the

Index of Exit is $\dfrac{(b_i - a_i)\, d}{b_i\, (d - c_i)}$ and the Index of Entry is $\dfrac{(c_i - a_i)\, d}{c_i\, (d - b_i)}$, only

the solution for the indices of Exit is given below. For reasons noted earlier, only the first solution has been applied in this case. It should be mentioned that we are indebted to Mr. Durbin for this solution, too.

The solution is to fit the hypothesis:

$$\frac{(b_1 - \alpha_1)\, d}{b_1\, (d - c_1)} = \frac{(b_2 - \alpha_2)\, d}{b_2\, (d - c_2)} = \cdots = \frac{(b_k - \alpha_k)\, d}{b_k\, (d - c_k)} = \text{constant}$$

$$\text{that is } \frac{b_i - \alpha_i}{b_i\, (d - c_i)} = \alpha \quad \ldots\ldots\ldots\ldots\ldots\ldots \text{(vi)}$$

$$\text{by minimizing } \chi^2 = \sum_1^k \frac{(a_i - \alpha_i)^2}{\alpha_i},$$

$$\text{where } \alpha_i \text{ from (vi)} = b_i - \alpha\, (b_i\, \overline{d - c_i}).$$

$$\text{Therefore } \chi^2 = \sum_1^k \frac{(a_i - b_i + \alpha\, b_i\, \overline{d - c_i})^2}{(b_i - \alpha\, b_i\, \overline{d - c_i})}.$$

$$-\frac{\partial \chi^2}{\partial \alpha} =$$

$$\sum_1^k \frac{b_i(d - c_i)(a_i - b_i + \alpha\, b_i\overline{d - c_i})^2 + 2(b_i - \alpha\, b_i\overline{d - c_i})\, b_i(d - c_i)(a_i - b_i + \alpha\, b_i\overline{d - c_i})}{b_i^2\, (1 - \alpha\, \overline{d - c_i})^2}$$

$$= 0.$$

Solving for α by successive approximation, then $\chi^2 = \sum_1^k \dfrac{(a_1 - \alpha_i)^2}{\alpha_i}$

is approximately distributed as χ^2 with $k-1$ degrees of freedom.

Because of the enormous amount of computation involved in this test, it has not been extensively used in the present studies, and only some broad inferences have been drawn for seven status categories in five birth cohorts (cf. pp. 199–204). It should, however, be noted that, as is evident from the similar values of the 'Dissociation' indices for all status categories, a detailed comparison by pairs of corresponding indices as undertaken for the indices of Association, is not likely to produce a different result.

Needless to say, a generalized solution to the Mobility indices (or indices of Dissociation) as applied to the indices of Inertia (cf. hypothesis (v)) would also be found by extending the above solution. However, in view of the amount of computation involved, this has not been attempted. It should also be noted that the nature of the data dealt with in this volume does not suggest the need for so elaborate a statistical tool.

From an examination of the indices for different birth cohorts for fixed status categories it will be noticed that except in very few cases they are practically the same, and scarcely warrant the use of a statistical tool to prove their similarity.

This note suggests not only that it is not necessary to confine the study of social mobility to purely subjective inferences from frequency distributions or from apparent differences between indices, but also that the validity of any n-fold social status hierarchy can be statistically verified. Thus from purely empirical considerations a social status hierarchy may be constructed in terms of, say, twelve categories. Tests of significant differences between the indices derived for the twelve categories might, however, indicate that for the sample under consideration a classification of fewer than twelve categories (differing statistically from one another) would have been more appropriate. The composition of a social status hierarchy can thus be derived objectively.

Notes

1. Let the following diagram represent the situation, where 0 at the centre represents the category of origin and the six axes represent mobility to the remaining six categories.

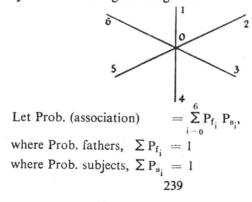

Let Prob. (association) $= \sum_{i=0}^{6} P_{f_i} P_{s_i}$,

where Prob. fathers, $\sum P_{f_i} = 1$

where Prob. subjects, $\sum P_{s_i} = 1$

239

The Problem

To ascertain under what conditions the probability of the subject being 'inert',

$$P_{s_0} \gtreqqless \sum_0^6 P_{f_i} P_{s_i}$$

or $\quad P_{s_0} \gtreqqless P_{s_0} P_{f_0} + \sum_1^6 P_{f_i} P_{s_i}$

or $\quad P_{s_0} \left(1 - P_{f_0}\right) \gtreqqless \sum_1^6 P_{f_i} P_{s_i}$ .... (a)

(a) Now the R.H.S., $\sum_1^6 P_{f_i} P_{s_i}$ will be minimum,

subject to, $\sum_1^6 P_{f_i} = \left(1 - P_{f_0}\right)$

and $\sum_1^6 P_{s_i} = \left(1 - P_{s_0}\right)$,

when $P_{f_i} = \dfrac{1 - P_{f_0}}{6}$ for all i

$$P_{s_i} = \dfrac{1 - P_{s_0}}{6} \text{ for all i}$$

∴ minimum R.H.S. $= 6 \left(\dfrac{1 - P_{f_0}}{6}\right) \left(\dfrac{1 - P_{s_0}}{6}\right)$

$$= \dfrac{\left(1 - P_{f_0}\right)\left(1 - P_{s_0}\right)}{6}$$

And, since the L.H.S. $= P_{s_0} \left(1 - P_{f_0}\right)$

$$P_{s_0} \left(1 - P_{f_0}\right) \gtreqqless \dfrac{\left(1 - P_{f_0}\right)\left(1 - P_{s_0}\right)}{6}$$

if $P_{s_0} \gtreqqless \dfrac{1 - P_{s_0}}{6}$

∴ If all $P_{f_i} P_{s_i}$ are equal (i = 1 ... 6), then Inertia $\gtreqqless$ Association, according as:

$$P_{s_0} \gtreqqless 1/7 \text{ .... solution (i)}$$

Evidently, this solution makes no assumption about the equality of P_{f_0} and P_{s_0}.

240

(b) If all P_{f_i} and P_{s_i} are unequal, then the R.H.S. of (a) will be greater than if they were equal. Therefore,

$$\left. \begin{array}{l} \text{if } P_{s_0} = 1/7 \\ \text{or } P_{s_0} < 1/7 \end{array} \right\} \quad P_{s_0}\left(1 - P_{f_0}\right) < \sum_1^6 P_{f_i} P_{s_i}, \text{ and therefore}$$

Inertia < Association .... solution (ii)

But if $P_{s_0} > 1/7$, $P_{s_0}\left(1 - P_{f_0}\right) \gtreqless \sum_1^6 P_{f_i} P_{s_i}$ ...... solution (iii)

To continue, when $P_{s_0} > 1/7$,

the R.H.S. is maximum, when

$$\left. \begin{array}{l} \text{one } P_{f_i} = 1 - P_{f_0} \\ \textit{and } P_{s_i} = 1 - P_{s_0} \end{array} \right\} \text{ for the same i}$$

and other $P_{f_i} P_{s_i} = 0$

Then R.H.S. $= \left(1 - P_{f_0}\right)\left(1 - P_{s_0}\right)$, and the relation between the L.H.S. and the R.H.S. will be

$$P_{s_0}\left(1 - P_{f_0}\right) \gtreqless \left(1 - P_{f_0}\right)\left(1 - P_{s_0}\right)$$

$$\text{or } P_{s_0} \gtreqless \left(1 - P_{s_0}\right)$$

Hence it follows:

If $P_{s_0} > 1/2$, Inertia > Association .... solution (iv)

If $1/7 < P_{s_0} < 1/2$, Inertia may be greater or less than Association .... solution (v)

We are indebted to Mr. W. Ziegel for his suggestions, and to Mr. A. Stuart of the London School of Economics for his help in preparing this note.

2. An analysis of the data from the sample inquiry shows that 97·6 per cent of the 3,389 male subjects had begun their occupational career by the age of 20. The following table gives the corresponding proportions for the five birth cohorts into which the subjects were divided. It may be noted that there is no significant difference between the five values, as ascertained from a chi-square test.

Birth cohort	Percentage of total subjects beginning their occupational career at (or before) age 20
(1)	(2)
Before 1889	98·0
1890–99	97·7
1900–09	97·4
1910–19	96·7
1920–29	98·5
No. of subjects	3389

APPENDIX 2

A Further Note on the Analysis of Data on Social Mobility

RAMKRISHNA MUKHERJEE

THE purpose of this note is to make a critical appraisal of the methods of analysis employed in the investigation of social mobility in a society,[1] and to interpret the conclusions which may be reached by using different methods.

Studies of social mobility (generally based on sample data collected by interviews), analyse similarity or dissimilarity between social status at two points of reference, such as that of the subject's father and of the subject, of the subject and his son, or of the subject at two age-levels. The structure on which these studies are based can be generalized as follows.

Diagram A

Social Status at Second Point of Reference (1)	Social Status at First Point of Reference, i.e. at the Time of Sample Inquiry (2)				Total (3)
	1	2	. . . .	k	
1	a_1				b_1
2		a_2			b_2
..			..		..
..			..		..
..				..	..
k				a_k	b_k
Total	c_1	c_2	.. .. ..	c_k	d

Assuming that the study is an examination of inter-generation change as between subjects and their fathers, $c_1 \ldots c_k$ represent the affiliation of the sampled individuals, referred to in this note as subjects, to the

[1] In this note the term 'social mobility' has been used in a general sense to express both inter-generation changes and mobility within one generation.

242

k-categories of the social status hierarchy at the time of the inquiry, $b_1 \ldots b_k$ give the affiliation of the subjects' fathers in the parental generation of the society under consideration, and $a_1 \ldots a_k$ refer to those subjects who have maintained the parental social status.

Descriptive Analysis

On the basis of such a classification of sample data, the extent of inertia, the converse of mobility, can be generally measured as:

$$a_1/b_1, \ldots a_k/b_k; \ldots\ldots\ldots\ldots\ldots\ldots\ldots\ldots\ldots\ldots\ldots\ldots \text{(i)}$$

or as

$$a_1/c_1, \ldots a_k/c_k; \ldots\ldots\ldots\ldots\ldots\ldots\ldots\ldots\ldots\ldots\ldots\ldots \text{(ii)}$$

This method of analysis has been described in the present symposium as 'descriptive analysis'.

While there is nothing wrong in using the two forms of descriptive analysis outlined above, the difference in the interpretation of the two sets of results should be borne in mind. The second form of analysis examines social mobility with reference to the social structure at the time of inquiry. But in the first form the point of reference is merely the result of a projection, derived by questioning the subjects, of the parents' status categories, and this projection may not represent the actual form of the social structure in the parental generation. This point is worth stressing because social mobility is often interpreted as representing the *internal changes* in the social structure of a given society between two points of time.

The picture of social structure in the parental generation, obtained indirectly by questioning the subjects, is likely to be incomplete. This may be seen from Diagram B of which Diagram A constitutes a part, comprising only cols. (1)–(3). In Diagram B the data originally summarized in Diagram A have been further subdivided, in each status category, into the groups of autochthones and immigrants. This is particularly necessary if the study of social mobility purports to take into account the changes in the structure of a given society over time, for the immigrant population should then be treated separately.

It will be seen from the next diagram that, as in Diagram A, the recent social structure is represented by $c_1 \ldots c_k$, but that of the parental generation in the society under consideration, by col. (8) which may be obtained by adding cols. (3) to (6) and subtracting col. (7). Col. (4) of this diagram refers to sterile marriages, col. (5) to mortality and col. (6)

Diagram B

(1) Second point of reference, e.g. social status category of the fathers	(2) First point of reference at the time of sample inquiry, e.g. social status category of the sons: 1 2 ... k	(3) First approximation of social structure in parental generation (total of 1...k in Col.(2))	(4) who had no child at all	(5) whose children died before attaining final status	(6) who emigrated with children after attaining final status	(7) Frequency of repetition of the same father because more than one of his sons was drawn in the sample	(8) True composition of the social structure in the parental generation. Cols. (3)+(4)+(5)+(6)−(7)
1 { A		B_1 } b_1	o_1	m_1	e_1	f_1 } F_1	b'_1
{ I			X	X	X		X
2 { A		B_2 } b_2	o_2	m_2	e_2	f_2 } F_2	b'_2
{ I			X	X	X		X
... { A		...	...	...	...	$f...$	...
{ I			X	X	X		X
... { A		...	...	...	...		...
{ I			X	X	X		X
k { A		B_k } b_k	o_k	m_k	e_k	f_k } F_k	b'_k
{ I			X	X	X		X
Present Social Structure	A { $C_1 C_2 ... C_k$ } I { $c_1 c_2 ... c_k$	d	o	m	e	f	d'

A = Those who were in this society in the parental generation.

Th... who ... have immigrated into this society.

to old-age emigration of the complete family. It will also be realized that col. (7) of the diagram refers essentially to fertility habits of the categories. The probability of two or more subjects having the same father increases with the size of families in the parental generation. This column therefore refers to differential fertility in the parental generation, just as cols. (4), (5) and (6) respectively refer to differential incidence of sterility, mortality and old-age emigration of complete families for different categories.

Evidently, therefore, if there were no difference between categories with regard to these attributes, col. (3) would have correctly represented the form of the social structure in the parental generation, and in that case the first form of analysis, $a_1/b_1 \ldots a_k/b_k$, would refer to the social structure in the parental generation.

It is, however, generally known that the various social strata are affected differently by these factors. Nevertheless, the final effect produced by them may not seriously influence the analysis of social mobility because (a) cases of old-age emigration of complete families (col. (6)) and of the complete extinction of families by differential mortality (col. (5)) are likely to be rare in any stable society, and (b) the effects of differential fertility (col. (4) minus col. (7)) would be somewhat counteracted by differential mortality, these two factors affecting the upper and lower social categories in opposite directions. Consequently in a stable society the social structure obtained by projecting the sample data may be regarded as a fair approximation of the true composition.

If, however, the study is restricted to a part of a society—for instance, to the urban community only—or if the society under consideration is rather unstable or 'open' in the sense that it is markedly affected by differential fertility, mortality and emigration, there may not be the same justification for assuming a priori that the data in col. (3) of the Diagram B, namely, $b_1 \ldots b_k$ will give a true representation of the social structure at the second point of reference which is correctly given by col. (8) as $b_1' \ldots b_k'$.

The problem can, of course, be solved by reconstructing the true composition of the social structure in the period in question by giving due 'weights' to the attributes for different categories, the 'weights' being obtained from demographic studies relating to that period. But if such a reconstruction is not feasible, or even if it is found that $b_1 \ldots b_k$ do not properly represent the form of the social structure given by $b_1' \ldots b_k'$, social mobility may still be examined as $(a_1/b_1) \ldots (a_k/b_k)$. Referring to the illustrative case of association or dissociation between the subject's father's and the subject's status categories, this would mean studying social mobility within the framework of familial affiliation of the subjects in the earlier generation of the society. In that case, the extraneous influences which may have a bearing on social mobility (see Chapter VIII) will not be considered at all. This form of analysis will thus examine mobility as due to the two major factors only, namely (i) satisfaction of individual demand, that is, the subject's personal choice of an occupation other than his father's, and (ii) satisfaction of the demand of the society, that is, of the need to expand certain occupational groups and not others at certain phases of development of the society. In a sense, therefore, there may be greater advantage in preparing the structure of analysis according to Diagram A, and not according to Diagram B. This point, which is of special significance in connection with the second form of analysis employed in this symposium, viz. the analysis in terms of the concept of 'perfect mobility' or 'perfect association', will be treated in detail in the following pages.

To sum up the above discussion, social mobility may always be studied on the basis of the generalized structure given in Diagram A, and both the forms of descriptive analysis (i) and (ii) will be valid in all circumstances. But the interpretation of the first form of analysis in relation to the society as a whole, and not simply in relation to the familial affiliation of the subjects, may be somewhat different in different contexts, depending upon the validity of using col. (3) as a reliable substitute for col. (8) of the Diagram B. Hence whether social mobility should be studied on the basis of $c_1 \ldots c_k$ or $b_1 \ldots b_k$, or even $b_1' \ldots b_k'$, or on the basis of all the three standards simultaneously, will essentially depend on the particular standard against which the sociologist intends to examine mobility in the society.

Needless to say, if, within the limits of sampling fluctuations, b_i equals c_i, or b_i' equals c_i, where $i = 1, 2, \ldots k$, the problem is greatly simplified because the two forms of descriptive analysis, viz. (i) and (ii), will lead to the same result.

It should be noted in this connection that the classification of the subjects as autochthones and immigrants, the two sub-groups A and I in Diagram B, is a basic necessity for studying social mobility. These two groups of subjects should be studied separately, because the social structure in the parental generation of the immigrants, or their familial affiliation at that time, lay in societies other than the one under consideration. They may, however, be combined to examine mobility against the standard of the recent social structure, because in that classification all the subjects are legitimate members of the society under consideration.

Limitation of Descriptive Analysis

The descriptive analysis, however, examines social mobility from a particular aspect only. It automatically takes into account the relative importance of the k-categories for whichever standard may be used to classify the data, that is, b's, c's, or b''s. This may be seen from the following consideration.

Considering Diagram A and assuming $E(a_i) = \alpha_i$, where $i = 1$, 2, ... k, suppose that $\bar{P}$ is the total probability of maintaining 'inertia' in the society between the two points of reference. Then $\bar{P} = (\sum_{1}^{k} \alpha_i/d)$, and is the sum of p_i probabilities, where $p_i = \alpha_i/d$. But the probability P_i for each category measured against any standard for the descriptive analysis will be given by, say, α_i/b_i, when the b-values are all fixed.

Now, if $p_1 = p_2$, that is $(\alpha_1/d) = (\alpha_2/d)$,

$$\alpha_1 \text{ must equal } \alpha_2.$$

But even if $\alpha_1 = \alpha_2$,

$$P_1 \gtreqless P_2 \text{ according as } b_2 \gtreqless b_1,$$

because

$$(P_1/P_2) = (\alpha_1 \times b_2)/(\alpha_2 \times b_1).$$

Hence the study of social mobility by the descriptive method of analysis must be affected by the 'size' of the status categories relative to their total distribution. Unless the k-categories are all of equal size, the descriptive analysis cannot give equal importance to the individual categories.

Therefore, if it is required to treat all categories as of equal importance, so that the extent of social mobility in different categories can be duly compared without the *effect* of the relative size of the different categories, a method of analysis different from the one discussed above should be applied.

Livi's Method of Analysis

Livio Livi (1950) attempted to solve the problem by suggesting the range between which the *true* degree of inertia lies if all the categories are treated as of equal importance. Neglecting certain unnecessary complications introduced in the computation of maximum and minimum values, Livi's method consists essentially in suggesting that a_i/b_i and a_i/c_i of Diagram A are the two limits of the range for each category. This, however, does not solve the problem, because Livi's method does not take account of the unequal 'sizes' of b's and c's, which, as explained earlier, is the essential limitation of the descriptive method of analysis. The method is thus not even a partial solution to the problem considered here. In fact, by saying that the *true* degree of inertia lies between the two forms of descriptive analysis referred to earlier as (i) and (ii), Livi is only stating the problem in more precise terms.

From another point of view, however, Livi's method is of importance to social mobility studies. As has already been explained, if mobility is studied on the basis of Diagram A, its final results will be the product of two components; first, changes produced over the period by the creation and cessation of demands for some categories at the expense of others, and secondly, mobility resulting from individual decisions to select occupations, however limited the ability to make such decisions may be in a society. For example, if an agricultural society initiates a rapid industrialization programme, some individuals from, say, category 1 in agriculture have to move into the category 2 in industry, resulting in the depletion of c_1 compared with b_1 and an increment in c_2 compared with b_2 in a 2×2 contingency table of the type shown in Diagram A. Benini (1928) has shown that if $b_1 > c_1$, $b_1 - c_1$ will be included in the cell $(b_1 - a_1)$, and similarly, if $b_2 < c_2$, $c_2 - b_2$ will be included in $(c_2 - a_2)$. Livi, therefore, gives an indication of the method of analysis to be developed in order to examine one component of social mobility irrespective of the size of the categories. But he does not deal with the other component, namely the individual's independent choice of occupations. And, as regards the first component, he offers no precise measure.

Benini's Method

Benini's 'Attraction Index' (1928) deserves attention in this context, although it was developed by him while dealing with problems other than social mobility. This index may be regarded as a step forward in the solution of the problem under consideration.

Benini's index might be used here in the following way. If the members of a society can be divided into two groups, as belonging or not-belonging to a particular category, say 1, at each of the two points of reference, then the following contingency table can be constructed to derive Benini's index on the basis of the notation used in Diagram A.

Diagram C

Second Point of Reference (1)	First Point of Reference 1 (2)	2...k (3)	Total (4)
1	a_1	$(b_1 - a_1)$	b_1
2...k	$(c_1 - a_1)$	(Remainder)	$b_2 - b_k$
Total	c_1	$c_2...c_k$	d

From the above diagram Benini's index is constructed as:

$$\frac{a_1 - \dfrac{b_1 c_1}{d}}{c_1 - \dfrac{b_1 c_1}{d}}, \text{ when } b_1 > c_1,$$

or as,

$$\frac{a_1 - \dfrac{b_1 c_1}{d}}{b_1 - \dfrac{b_1 c_1}{d}}, \text{ when } b_1 < c_1.$$

It will be noticed that Benini's index takes account of the *independent* chance of remaining in the cell 1·1 as $b_1 c_1/d$, and thus attempts to 'neutralize' the effects produced by the unequal sizes of the categories against which social mobility was studied by the descriptive analysis. But because of the nature of its construction, the index becomes somewhat unwieldy and does not measure mobility in very precise terms.

It should be realized from the previous discussion that fully to 'neutralize' the effect of b's and c's in studying mobility or inertia of a's, it is necessary to develop some sort of harmonious relation between p_i, P_i and P_i', where, following the notation used previously, p_i is estimated as a_i/d, P_i as a_i/b_i, and P_i' as a_i/c_i. Benini's index provides a relation between these three sets of probabilities, but the relation is somewhat clumsy. Thus, when $b_i < c_i$, Benini's index,

$$\frac{a_i - \dfrac{b_i c_i}{d}}{b_i - \dfrac{b_i c_i}{d}} \text{ can be written as } \frac{1}{(P_i' - p_i)} \left(P_i' - \frac{p_i}{P_i} \right)$$

by reducing a's, b's and c's into p's, P's, and P''s respectively. Similarly, when $b_i > c_i$, Benini's index,

$$\frac{a_i - \dfrac{b_i c_i}{d}}{c_i - \dfrac{b_i c_i}{d}} \quad \text{can be written as} \quad \frac{1}{(P_i - p_i)}\left(P_i - \frac{p_i}{P_i'}\right)$$

It will be seen when discussing the indices used in the present symposium that a more harmonious relation can be worked out between p_i, P_i, P_i'. Thus Benini's index can be regarded only as a partial solution of the problem.

No less important a reason for rejecting Benini's index is that the range of possible values of the index is rather lop-sided. Because of the method of construction, the value of the index can vary from $+1$ to $-\infty$, as may be shown by taking three hypothetical cases referring to the two limiting stages and to the intermediate one.

(a) In the case of a perfect positive association, for instance, when all the subjects remain in the fathers' status category, the contingency table from which Benini's Attraction Index will have to be derived (cf. Diagram C) will be as follows.

a_1	...	a_1		
...	rest	b_2	...	b_k
a_1	$(c_2...c_k)$	d		

Hence, Benini's index

$$= \frac{a_1 - \dfrac{a_1^2}{d}}{a_1 - \dfrac{a_1^2}{d}} = +1$$

(b) If there is no association at all in the contingency table—that is, if the subjects are equally distributed in the four cells of the contingency table—the table will take the shape of

a_1	a_1	$2a_1$
a_1	a_1	$2a_1$
$2a_1$	$2a_1$	$4a_1$

Hence, Benini's index,

$$\frac{a_1 - \dfrac{4a_1^2}{4a_1}}{2a_1 - \dfrac{4a_1^2}{4a_1}} = \frac{a_1 - a_1}{2a_1 - a_1} = 0$$

(c) Finally, where there is a perfect negative association, the contingency table will take the form

...	b_1	b_1		
c_1	...	b_2	...	b_k
c_1 (c_2.....c_k)	d			

Hence, Benini's index, when $b_1 > c_1$, is

$$\frac{o - \dfrac{b_1 c_1}{d}}{c_1 - \dfrac{b_1 c_1}{d}} = \ldots = -\frac{b_1}{c_1} \quad \ldots\ldots\ldots\ldots\ldots\ldots (i)$$

And when $b_1 < c_1$, Benini's index will be

$$\frac{o - \dfrac{b_1 c_1}{d}}{b_1 - \dfrac{b_1 c_1}{d}} = \ldots = -\frac{c_1}{b_1} \quad \ldots\ldots\ldots\ldots\ldots\ldots (ii)$$

In either case, the index will equal -1 only when $b_1 = c_1$; otherwise it can take any value greater than -1.

Benini's index is also unsatisfactory because the composition of the denominator of the index changes with the relative magnitudes of the b's and c's, as explained on p. 249. It is, therefore, rather laborious to calculate such indices, and, in fact, they refer in different contexts to 'mobility in' and 'mobility out', using the terms followed in the present symposium in connection with the Mobility indices (Appendix 1 of Chapter VIII). This may be shown from a simplified contingency table as follows.

a	b	A
c	d	B
K	L	N

On the basis of the above table, if a' is substituted for $(AK)/N$, Benini's index will be $-(a - a')/(K - a')$ when $A > K$, or as $(a - a')/(A - a')$, when $A < K$.

Now $(a - a') = (b - b') = (c - c')$, and following a similar substitution as in the case of a', $(k - a') = c'$, and $(A - a') = b'$. Therefore, Benini's index can be written either as

$$\frac{\pm (c - c')}{c'} \text{ or as } \frac{\pm (b - b')}{b'},$$

$\pm$ depending upon the relative size of c and c', and b and b'.

That is, as

$$\frac{c}{c'} - 1, \quad \frac{b}{b'} - 1$$

or as

$$1 - \frac{c}{c'}, \quad 1 - \frac{b}{b'}$$

But it has been explained elsewhere (see Appendix 1 to Chapter VIII) that $c/c' = $ Index of Entry Mobility in terms of the concept of 'perfect mobility', $b/b' = $ Index of Exit Mobility in terms of the concept of 'perfect mobility'.

Therefore, if $A < K$,

Benini's index $=$ Index of Exit $- 1$, when $b > b'$,
or $1 -$ Index of Exit, when $b < b'$.

And if $A > K$,

Benini's index $=$ Index of Entry $- 1$, when $c > c'$,
or $1 -$ Index of Entry, when $c < c'$.

Thus, Benini's index is a less efficient method of deriving the mobility indices already discussed in the present symposium.

Indices in Terms of the Concept of 'Perfect' Association or 'Perfect' Mobility

It may be shown that the indices actually used in the present symposium are an improvement on Benini's index, and that they overcome the limitation imposed by the descriptive analysis. Not only are they based on the independent probabilities of maintaining 'inertia' in the society, as attempted by Benini, but they do not suffer from the restrictions involved in Benini's index. Following the notation used on p. 247, the

Index of Association, $\dfrac{\alpha_i \times d}{b_i \times c_i}$, can be written as:

$$\frac{p_i \, d^2}{\dfrac{a_i}{P_i} \times \dfrac{a_i}{P_i'}} = \ldots = \frac{P_i \, P_i'}{p_i}$$

The Index of Association thus takes into account the joint probability of maintaining 'inertia' according to the two forms of descriptive analysis, $a_1/b_1 \ldots a_k/b_k$ and $a_1/c_1 \ldots a_k/c_k$ (as shown by the numerator of the index as $P_i \times P_i'$), and simultaneously expresses the extent of inertia thus measured in terms of the share of this category in the total probability of maintaining 'inertia' in the society, by dividing the product $P_i \times P_i'$ by p_i which equals a_i/d and is thus the share of the category i in the total probability $\bar{P} = (\overset{k}{\underset{1}{\Sigma}} a_i/d)$.

It is thus seen that the indices based on the concept of 'perfect' association or 'perfect' mobility measure social mobility in each category against the same standard scale, taking, as it were, a zero point. An examination, on this basis, of the extent of 'inertia' or of the degree of mobility for different categories will therefore be strictly valid. Furthermore, because these indices can be subjected to statistical tests of significance (see Appendix 1 to Chapter VIII), the conclusions drawn from their analysis will not be based purely on subjective inferences, as is often the case in the study of indices.

These indices were developed at the same time, though independently, at the London School of Economics and also by Professor H. Goldhamer, formerly of the University of Chicago. The equivalent of the Index of Association was first used by a pupil of Goldhamer, Miss Natalie Rogoff, in U.S.A., in her Ph.D. thesis (1950), and later by Marcel Bresard (1950) in France. But in these studies no attempt was made to test the significance of differences between the indices for different status categories. Such tests are, however, indispensable if purely subjective inferences are to be avoided. As will be seen from Appendix 1 to Chapter VIII, such tests have been worked out for this symposium.

Because the concept of 'perfect' association provides a sort of zero point in the scale for measuring social mobility, more than one index can be prepared to examine mobility from different perspectives. This is another improvement upon Benini's index. Such indices have been described in this symposium as Index of Association (or Inertia), Index of Exit Mobility or Entry Mobility, or Index of Dissociation, etc. It may be shown that there is a definite relation between them.

Thus, the indices which, with reference to Diagram C, can be prepared from a 2×2 bivariate contingency table with simple notation as:

a	b	A
c	d	B
K	L	N

will be expressed as follows.

$$\text{Index of Inertia} = a/a', \quad\text{.....................} \quad \text{(i)}$$
$$\text{Index of Exit} = b/b', \quad\text{.....................} \quad \text{(ii)}$$
$$\text{Index of Entry} = c/c', \quad\text{.....................} \quad \text{(iii)}$$

Subtracting 1 from (i), (ii) and (iii) and disregarding $\pm$ signs, the three indices become

$$(a - a')/a', (b - b')/b', \text{ and } (c - c')/c' \quad\text{..............} \quad \text{(iv)}$$

But $(a - a') = (b - b') = (c - c')$; therefore,

$$(1 - \text{Index of Inertia})/(1 - \text{Index of Exit}) = b'/a' \quad\text{.........} \quad \text{(v)}$$

and $\quad (1 - \text{Index of Inertia})/(1 - \text{Index of Entry}) = c'/a' \quad\text{.........} \quad \text{(vi)}$

Hence, (a) when there is 'perfect' association all the three indices are of the same value.

(b) The Index of Inertia cannot be equal to only one of the two mobility indices, because it is impossible that a' should equal b', and not also equal c'.

(c) The Index of Inertia and the two Mobility Indices are complementary in the sense that if the Index of Inertia is an integer, the Mobility Indices are fractions, and conversely. This follows from the fact that if a is greater than a', b must be less than b' and c less than c', because $a + b = a' + b'$ and $a + c = a' + c'$.

(d) Although the two mobility indices may not always be the same, there is a definite relation between them. Referring to the relations in (iv) it is seen that

$$(1 - \text{Index of Exit})/(1 - \text{Index of Entry}) = c'/b'$$

Now referring to the contingency table above, it will be seen that

$$c' = (BK)/N \text{ and } b' = (AL)/N$$

Therefore,

When $K = L$, and $A = B$, $c' = b'$, and therefore Index of Exit = Index of Entry.

254

That is, when both the 'universes' are equally divided between either belonging or not-belonging to the particular social status category, the two mobility indices are the same.

In other circumstances, when $BK \gtrless AL$, $c' \gtrless b'$, and therefore, Index of Exit $\gtrless$ Index of Entry.

Further Analysis of the Index of Association

The concept of 'perfect' association or 'perfect' mobility has further uses in studies of social mobility. Before discussing them, the structure on which the analysis is based should be made clear—that is, whether the indices should be constructed from Diagram A or from Diagram B. It is necessary to decide this before undertaking the analysis because the 'expected' values for association or dissociation in each category will be different for the two forms of analysis, depending upon the difference in the values of b's, b''s and d and d'.

While making the decision on which of the two diagrams the analysis should be based, it should be borne in mind that if, along with the bottom row of Diagram B, col. (8) of the diagram is used to find the 'expected' values for each category, the form of analysis will include the effect produced by the extraneous influences like differential mortality, emigration, fertility, etc. On the other hand, if the analysis is based on Diagram A, it will examine social mobility as the resultant of the two main factors explained on p. 246, namely (i) the obligatory movement of individuals from one category to another as a result of societal planning, and (ii) the voluntary choice of individuals to remain or leave their parental categories.

This point has already been discussed in connection with the descriptive analysis. Its relevance to the analysis in terms of the concept of 'perfect' association follows from Benini's consideration of 'closed' and 'open' groups in a society (1928), and from the logic underlying Livi's method of studying *true* social mobility (1950) discussed on p. 248. In the present context, Benini's concept of 'closed' and 'open' groups may be interpreted as follows. If the relative 'weights' of b''s and c's have changed over the period under consideration, the change measured as $b_i' - c_i$ or $c_i - b_i'$ would be reflected in the mobility in each category to the cells, or cell $(b_i' - a_i)$ if $b_i' > c_i'$, or to $(c_i - a_i)$ if $b_i' < c_i'$. Now, in terms of the concept of 'perfect' association, this change can be examined separately as a contributory element to the Index of Association. This may be seen from the following consideration.

255

Let $b_i' - c_i = \pm \mu_i$

Then, if $b_i' > c_i$, $b_i = c_i + \mu_i$

   if $b_i' < c_i$, $b_i = c_i - \mu_i$

and if $b_i' \doteq c_i$, $\mu_i = 0$

Now, the reciprocal of the Index of Association $= \dfrac{b_i' \times c_i}{a_i \times d'}$

Hence, if $b_i' = c_i$, the reciprocal of the Index $= \dfrac{c_i^2}{a_i \times d'}$,

due only to voluntary choice of subjects to remain in parental status category,

if $b_i' > c_i$, the reciprocal of the Index

$$= \frac{(c_i + \mu_i)\, c_i}{a_i d'} = \frac{c_i^2}{a_i \times d'} + \frac{c_i \mu_i}{a_i d'}$$

if $b_i' < c_i$, the reciprocal of the Index

$$= \frac{(c_i - \mu_i) c_i}{a_i d'} = \frac{c_i^2}{a_i d'} - \frac{c_i \mu_i}{a_i d'}$$

That is, Reciprocal of the Index of Association = Reciprocal of the Index due to voluntary choice of individuals to remain in the same category ($c_i^2/a_i d'$) $\pm$ Reciprocal of the Index due to other factors influencing the individual to remain in the same category.

Evidently, the sign $\pm$ depends upon whether there has been a reduction or increment in the 'size' of the category in the present generation with respect to the parental generation.

It should, however, be remembered that the change effected by the differences in b''s and c's includes several factors which produce mobility directly or indirectly. The direct factor is what has been described as the obligatory movement of individuals, and the indirect factors have also been explained as due to demographic changes. Evidently, therefore, unless it is possible further to separate the effects of the direct and the indirect factors, the study of contributory elements to the Index of Association, prepared on the basis of b''s and c's, would lose much of its value.

Recalling the previous discussion on the relative efficiency of Diagram A and Diagram B as structures for analysing social mobility, it is clear that the two direct factors in social mobility can be best examined if the Index of Association is calculated on the distributions of b's and c's. In this case, following the method of splitting the Index of Association shown in the previous page, ($c_i^2/a_i d$) will account for the voluntary choice of the subjects to remain in their parental category and $\pm (c_i \mu_i'/a_i d)$ for the obligatory movement, where $b_i - c_i = \pm \mu_i$.

Hence, unless it is possible to prepare two sets of indices based on $b_1 \ldots b_k$ and $b_1' \ldots b_k'$, with respect to $c_1 \ldots c_k$ in both cases (so that a measure for mobility due to extraneous influences only can be derived from the two sets of indices as the result of differences in b's and b''s), it would be preferable to construct the indices from Diagram A only.

It should be noted in this connection that the tests of significance for such divisions of the Index of Association have not been worked out. For the studies included in the present symposium it was not particularly necessary because it could be assumed on *a priori* grounds that the society under consideration is fairly stable and is more or less 'closed' in the sense in which Benini used the word (that is, it is not seriously affected by the extraneous influences), and also because the available information showed that the 'sizes' of the categories have not changed appreciably over the last three generations (see Chapter IX). For future studies, however, the possibility of finding real and appreciable differences between b_i, b_i' and c_i, for any value of i, must be borne in mind, and tests of significance should, therefore, be developed in order to make it possible to examine the respective contributions of (i) the obligatory movement and (ii) voluntary movement of the subjects, as well as of (iii) mobility indirectly affected by extraneous influences, to the formation of the Index of Association.

Interpretation of Results of the Descriptive Analysis and of the Analysis in Terms of the Concept of 'Perfect' Association or 'Perfect' Mobility

In examining the studies of social mobility included in the present symposium, it will be noticed that the two types of analysis have led to somewhat contradictory conclusions in regard to one of the major points of study. In Chapters VIII and IX, it is pointed out that, according to the descriptive analysis, of all the seven status categories, category 5 shows the highest association between parental and filial status. But analysing the same data in terms of the concept of 'perfect' association, category 5 gives the lowest value for the Index of Association. On the other hand, category 2, which shows a very low association according to the descriptive analysis, yields a very high value for the Index of Association. There is thus a question of interpreting the results of the two types of analysis. This may best be done by means of the above illustration of apparently contradictory conclusions.

257

Following the terminology used previously, the situation can be generalized as follows.

$$(a_5/b_5) > (a_j/b_j), \text{ where } j \text{ is any category other than 5}$$

and,
$$(a_5/c_5) > (a_j/c_j) \dots\dots\dots\dots\dots\dots\dots \text{ (i)}$$

but, $\dfrac{a_5 \times d}{b_5 \times c_5} < \dfrac{a_j \times d}{b_j \times d}$, where j is the same as above $\dots\dots\dots\dots$ (ii)

Evidently, the above two relations can exist when

$$a_5 > a_j$$
$$b_5 > b_j$$
$$c_5 > c_j$$

Because if

$$\frac{a_5}{b_5} > \frac{a_j}{b_j}, \text{ and } \frac{a_5}{c_5} > \frac{a_j}{c_j}$$

then to satisfy

$$\frac{a_5 \times d}{b_5 \times c_5} < \frac{a_j \times d}{b_j \times c_j},$$

$(1/c_5)$ must be less than $(1/c_j)$,
and $(1/b_5)$ must be less than $(1/b_j)$.

That is,

$$b_5 > b_j$$
$$c_5 > c_j$$

Now, if $a_5 = a_j$, b_5 must be less than b_j,

$a_5 < a_j$, b_5 must be less than b_j,

$a_5 > a_j$, b_5 can be $\gtrless b_j$.

But b_5 is always greater than b_j.

Therefore, a_5 is always greater than a_j.

The above illustration thus shows how the analysis in terms of the concept of 'perfect' association counteracts the 'weighting' produced by the unequal sizes of $b_1 \dots b_7$ or $c_1 \dots c_7$ in the descriptive analysis by the reverse 'weighting' of $d/c_1 \dots d/c_7$ or $d/b_1 \dots d/b_7$. It thus reduces all the categories to equal importance.

The apparent contradiction in the behaviour of category 5 according to the two methods of analysis should not therefore cause confusion in the interpretation of the results of the analyses. While the descriptive analysis shows that, with reference to the total structure of the society, category 5 has the highest stability, the other method brings to light the important fact that, as compared with the other categories, the extent of 'inertia' in this category is the lowest of all. The two methods thus examine social mobility from two different aspects, both of which should be relevant to a sociologist.

If the purpose of the study is to estimate the *effect of mobility in the society as a whole* and if therefore the total make-up of the social status hierarchy, of which the categories form different segments, should be taken into account, the descriptive method of analysis should be employed. On the other hand, if the object is to see whether the *rates of mobility in the different categories* are different, the analysis in terms of 'perfect' association will provide the answer.

In the practical application of the sociological data the two methods would also be of equal importance, provided they are used in the light of the sociological implications of the problems involved. In general, the descriptive analysis will furnish data bearing upon the problems of overall planning of the society, while the analysis in terms of the concept of 'perfect' association may suggest policies for the different categories.

Finally, the methods of analysis discussed here would be equally applicable to any other socio-economic classification of individuals, provided that the classification conforms to the conditions noted above.

REFERENCES

BENINI, RODOLFO, 1928: 'Gruppi chiusi e gruppi aperti in alcuni fatti collecttivi di cominazioni', *Bulletin of International Institute of Statistics*, Vol. XXIII, Nos. 1–2, pp. 362–83.

BRESARD, MARCEL, 1950: 'Mobilité sociale et dimension de la famille', *Population*, Paris, Vol. V, No. 3, July–September 1950, pp. 533–66.

LIVI, LIVIO, 1950: 'Sur la mesure de la mobilité sociale', *Population*, Paris, Vol. V, No. 1, January–March 1950, pp. 65–76.

ROGOFF, NATALIE, 1950: 'Recent trends in occupational mobility', in P. K. Hatt and A. J. Reiss, Jr., *Reader in Urban Sociology*. Glencoe, Illinois, 1951.

A Comparison of Social Mobility Data for England and Wales, Italy, France and the U.S.A.

J. R. HALL AND W. ZIEGEL

REFERENCE has been made in Chapter VIII to previous studies of social differentiation and mobility in Italy, France and the U.S.A. The reports of these investigations give information upon the occupations both of men interviewed during the inquiries and of their fathers, grouped in certain categories, and a comparative study of social mobility in these three countries, and in England and Wales, based upon this information, was attempted. It was realized, however, that the results would be only roughly comparable, as there are considerable differences between the various inquiries.

All the inquiries were directly concerned with aspects of social or occupational mobility, but with different approaches to the subject. Further, the three papers on mobility in Italy, France and the U.S.A. were principally concerned with the presentation of results. The reasons for the nature of the samples used and the bases of the occupational social status classifications used in grading the material were only briefly discussed, the problem of selecting data which are strictly comparable thus being increased.

Let us look at the available material more closely. The French study[1] is based upon a sample taken in 1948 of occupied males aged 18–50. Subjects were asked to state their own and their fathers' occupations at the date of interview. The Italian study[2] concerned a sample of males aged 18 and over in 1948, but the information upon the occupations of subjects and fathers differed from that of the French inquiry; for although each subject was asked to state the occupation he held at the time of interview, the father's occupation recorded was that held *when*

---

[1] Bresard, *op. cit.*   [2] Livio Livi, *op. cit.*

Table 1

OCCUPATIONAL/SOCIAL STATUS CLASSIFICATIONS DEVISED FOR THE STUDY OF SOCIAL MOBILITY

	England and Wales			Italy			France			U.S.A.	
	Standard Classification	%disn. of subj.		Occupational Classification	%disn. of subj.		Occupational Classification	%disn. of subj.		Occupational Classification	%disn. of subj.
1	Professional and high admin.	3·1	1	Managers and owners: large businesses, high admin.	0·9	1	Industrialists: liberal professions	3·9	1	Managers and owners: large businesses	7·2
2	Managerial and executive	4·4	2	Managers and owners: medium businesses, large agric. owners	5·8	2	Admin. officers: teachers: 'higher' employees in industry	4·6	2	'Liberal' professions	8·9
3	Higher supervisory	8·9	3	Semi-professionals, accountants, clerks, students upper-class families	6·6	3	Tradesmen and artisans	15·1	3	Managers and owners: small businesses	13·7
4	Lower supervisory	12·9	4	Employees in public and private concerns. Skilled tradesmen employing personnel	15·3	4	Farmers	25·8	4	Clerks	20·3
5	Skilled manual and routine non-manual	42·5	5	Agricultural foremen: skilled tradesmen	43·6	5	Subordinate officials: clerks	17·1	5	Skilled manual	18·2
6	Semi-skilled manual	15·0	6	Agricultural workers, unskilled workers	27·8	6	Semi-skilled: unskilled workers	23·8	6	Semi-skilled manual	19·2
7	Unskilled manual	13·2				7	Agricultural labourers	9·8	7	Unskilled manual	7·5
									8	Farmers	3·9
									9	Agricultural labourers	1·1

of the same age as the subject. This was an attempt to avoid, in assessing the degree of inter-generation change in status between fathers and sons, the difficulty caused when the son is not of an age to have achieved occupational stability. Finally, the American sample[1] was of males aged 21 + in *urban* communities, taken in 1945, the occupations both of fathers and sons being recorded. However, all sons whose fathers were farmers or farm workers had been excluded from the sample prior to the original analysis. This was done because there was not sufficient information on which to classify the various grades within these occupations.

A common feature of all the inquiries is that the occupational material was graded according to classifications of occupational–social status. But the classifications show considerable variation; and it is this feature which provides a major obstacle to a satisfactory comparative study. The gradings used in each of the studies are shown in Table 1, together with the distributions of subjects in each of the samples. It will be seen that certain of the categories reflect 'industrial' groups rather than differences in social standing. For instance, the Standard Classification used in this symposium differentiates between farmers according to the size of their holding, but neither the French nor the American classifications do so.

Table 2

TOTAL INDICES OF ASSOCIATION

	England	*Italy*	*France*	*U.S.A.*
England	1·45			
Italy	*	1·92		
France	*	‡	1·86	
U.S.A.	†	‡	‡	1·69

To calculate for France, Italy and the U.S.A. indices of association comparable to those for England and Wales, it would be necessary to delineate broad occupational strata of equal social standing capable of being applied to each country. This involves a major assumption, namely that the strata selected do reflect equal social status in the different countries, and such an assumption is not justified. Indeed it has already been suggested in this symposium that the Standard Classification itself would probably not reflect status differences in Scotland as accurately

[1] R. Centers, 'Occupational mobility of urban occupational strata', *American Sociological Review*, April 1948, Vol. 13, No. 2.

as for England and Wales, even though these two areas are so closely akin. Hence, the only reasonable approach is to use a broad functional classification, based upon the nature of the occupation. Such a classification may not represent equivalent status categories, but it should at least reflect equivalent occupational types.

Table 3

INDICES OF ASSOCIATION CALCULATED FOR CERTAIN
OCCUPATIONAL/SOCIAL STATUS CATEGORIES

Non-manual grades (other than routine)

	England	Italy	France	U.S.A.
England	1·74			
Italy	*	2·29		
France	‡	‡	1·86	
U.S.A.	‡	‡	‡	1·91

Skilled manual and routine non-manual

	England	Italy	France	U.S.A.
England	1·19			
Italy	†	1·57		
France	*	‡	1·82	
U.S.A.	‡	‡	‡	1·30

Semi-skilled and unskilled manual

	England	Italy	France	U.S.A.
England	1·75			
Italy	†	2·30		
France	‡	‡	1·90	
U.S.A.	‡	‡	‡	2·01

Note: * = Significant at 1 per cent level.　　　‡ = Not significant.
† = Significant at 5 per cent level.

A comparison of the four classifications and distributions of subjects in Table 1 indicates a number of differences. The distributions for Italy and England and Wales are alike, but both differ from the French classification. Compared with the other three distributions, however, higher grades of non-manual employment are over-represented, and unskilled and rural workers heavily under-represented in the American sample. This is due partly to the fact that the sample is an urban one. The deliberate omission of subjects whose fathers were farmers or farm workers, already noted, also contributes to bias in the sample.

Despite variations in the nature of the methods of classifying the material according to social standing it was possible to differentiate three broad occupational, if not social status, groupings, namely:

1. Non-manual grades (other than routine non-manual), farmers owning or renting land.
2. Skilled manual and routine grades of non-manual.
3. Semi-skilled and unskilled manual.

These were made up as follows:

	Classifications[1]			
	England	Italy	France	U.S.A.[2]
Non-manual grades	1–4	1–4	1, 2 and 4	1–3
Skilled manual and routine non-manual	5	5	3 and 5	4 and 5
Semi-skilled and unskilled manual	6–7	6	6–7	6–7

It is realized that the above grading is only partially satisfactory. Nevertheless it represents an approximation, and despite the limitations both of the grading and of the respective samples, indices of Association were calculated for each country. The results are shown in Tables 2 and 3. All the indices were found to be significantly different from unity.

The overall indices in Table 2 show England to have a lower degree of self-recruitment than the other three countries, though the difference from the U.S.A. is significant only at the 5 per cent level. An explanation of this may lie in the fact that the English classification was designed to reflect social status differences, while the groupings for the other countries are in greater or lesser degree industrial (e.g. farmers who form 25 per cent of the French sample).

When the indices within a given occupational category are compared, however (Table 3), few significant differences were found, though we should take into consideration the possibility that a threefold classification, as used here, will reduce the likelihood of detecting significant differences in the degree of association. In the skilled manual-routine non-manual category, the index for England and Wales is below that for

[1] The numbers refer to the occupational/social status categories set out in Table 1.
[2] Subjects who were farmers or agricultural labourers have been omitted.

France and in all three occupational groups the indices for England and Italy differ, the former always showing a lower degree of association.

It may be that the high measure of association between the occupational categories of fathers and sons in the Italian sample is caused partly by the fact that the relationship is between fathers and sons at the same age. But if indices of Association for subjects born before 1900 in England and Wales, for whom the status relationship between father and son is likely to be stabilized, are compared with the Italian indices, the same characteristic appears, namely that the Italian indices are significantly higher.

The final stage of analysis was to compare within a given country the indices of Association between the three occupational categories distinguished. No significant differences were found in the case of France, but in the other three instances the index for the skilled manual and routine non-manual category always showed a lower degree of association than the other two.

Three conclusions are therefore to be drawn from this analysis :

1. The overall association between the occupational categories of father and son in England is lower than that in Italy or France. So far as the present data are concerned, the overall index for England and Wales also appears to be lower than that for the U.S.A. But the sample for the U.S.A. is not representative, and the biases almost certainly produce an artificially high index of association for that country.

2. Within all three occupational categories, the degree of association differs between England and Italy, and in the skilled manual and routine non-manual category between England and France.

3. Within each country, the Index of Association for the skilled manual and routine non-manual grade is lower than for the other two categories.

IX

A Study of Social Mobility Between Three Generations

RAMKRISHNA MUKHERJEE

Introductory

Object

IN the preceding chapter, which examined the association between the social status of an individual in 1949 and the final status attained by his father, an attempt was made to assess the effect of *time* on inter-generation changes. This was done by dividing the subjects of the inquiry into decennial birth cohorts and then measuring the significance of the differences in the father—son status association for the separate birth cohorts. One of the two points of reference used, namely the end point, was fixed at the year 1949 and referred to the status category reached by the subjects in that year. The initial point, however, remained a variable quantity and referred to the time when the fathers of the subjects attained their final status category. In order to keep the accounting period constant over the cohorts studied, it was assumed that the difference between the age at which a father has a son and the age at which the father attains his final status category is roughly the same for all cohorts. In that case, it is possible to study the effect of *time* on inter-generation change in status.

The assumption of a fixed relation between the birth of *any* child (the first, second or subsequent) and the age at which the final status category is attained may not be entirely justified. Hence, in order to assess more closely the trend of inter-generation changes, a supplementary study was undertaken, focused on three generations, grandfathers, fathers and sons. The grandfather's generation relates to the male subject's father and the female subject's father-in-law; the father's generation to the male subject and the female subject's husband; and the son's generation to the subject's first-born male child.

Sample

The present study is based on two sub-samples drawn from the total sample of 7,939 individuals in England and Wales (see Chapter IV) who were selected at random from the total population, and interviewed in 1949. Of the two samples, one comprises those male subjects whose first-born sons had taken up an occupational career by 1949. The other sample comprises those female subjects who were married once only and were living with their husbands in 1949, and whose first-born sons had taken up some occupation by 1949.

Limitations of the Study

The present study has three main limitations.

(i) The combination of the two sub-samples may not be justified unless the distributions of individuals between status categories are similar in each sample.

(ii) The information obtained from the female subjects on the occupations followed by their husbands and first-born sons in 1949 and on the final occupation of their husbands' fathers may be less accurate than the data obtained from the male subjects in regard to their own, their first-born sons' and their fathers' occupations. Here, again, therefore, it may not be appropriate to combine the two samples.

(iii) The somewhat loose definition of the three generation levels is likely to affect the precision of the study. The survey data referred strictly to the present or the last occupation of the grandfather, father and the sons. But many of the fathers and sons will not have achieved their final status by the date of the survey.

It will, however, be shown below that these limitations are not very serious, and are not likely to affect the reliability of the study.

From Table 1 it is possible to show that there is no serious objection to combining the two sub-samples for the present analysis.

Only in the grandfather's generation is there a slight difference in the two sample distributions, caused entirely by the relatively large proportion of sub-sample (*a*) in category 1. Otherwise, the two sub-samples do not exhibit any significant difference. A chi-square test for categories 2 to 7 gave a value of only 5·819 for 5 degrees of freedom. It is, therefore, legitimate to combine the two sub-samples for the present study.

Considering the second limitation, while it is not improbable that information collected from female subjects about their husbands is less reliable than the corresponding information obtained directly from male subjects, the data obtained from the former may be as satisfactory as any obtained from a first-class proxy. The information required is only

Table 1

TESTING THE SIGNIFICANCE OF DIFFERENCES IN THE DISTRIBUTIONS BY SOCIAL STATUS CATEGORIES OF THE TWO SUB-SAMPLES, (a) MALE SUBJECTS AND (b) FEMALE SUBJECTS' HUSBANDS

Social Status Category (1)	Grand-father's generation				Father's generation				Son's generation			
	Sub-sample (a)		Sub-sample (b)		Sub-sample (a)		Sub-sample (b)		Sub-sample (a)		Sub-sample (b)	
	No. (2)	% (3)	No. (4)	% (5)	No. (6)	% (7)	No. (8)	% (9)	No. (10)	% (11)	No. (12)	% (13)
1	22	4	7	1	14	3	8	1	16	3	18	3
2	21	4	19	4	24	5	24	4	12	2	16	3
3	43	8	46	9	52	10	50	8	34	7	55	9
4	84	16	65	13	80	16	80	13	50	10	48	8
5	230	45	247	48	182	36	243	40	246	50	274	46
6	70	15	69	13	79	15	106	17	94	19	122	21
7	43	8	60	12	81	15	99	17	45	9	57	10
Total	513	100	513	100	512	100	610	100	497	100	590	100
χ^2(d.f.=6)	13·858				7·669				4·307			
P=	>·05<·02				>·30<·20				>·70<·50			

a general description of the occupations pursued by their sons, husbands and fathers-in-law, and not a detailed inquiry into their job characteristics. Female subjects should, therefore, be able to furnish reasonably reliable data. Even so, to avoid chances of error from this source, the two sub-samples will be combined only when a larger sample is needed to substantiate any inference drawn from the sample of male subjects. Otherwise, the present study will be based on the latter sample only.

As regards the third limitation, it will be evident from the following that the points of reference in the grandfather's and the father's generations are in fact comparable. Adjustment can also be made for the son's generation so as to make the situation reasonably comparable with the two earlier generations.

Taking, first, the father's generation, fathers in 1949 might theoretically have been of any age from 18 upwards. But because the sub-samples cover only those subjects whose first-born sons were of an age to take up an occupation, both the male subjects and the female subjects' husbands were very substantially older. The mean ages for the two sub-samples were 58 ± 0.5 for the male subjects and 61 ± 0.6 for the husbands of female subjects. It may therefore reasonably be assumed that all the men in question had attained their final status category by the time of the survey.

It follows from the above that if, because of the character of the sub-samples, the fathers were over 50 years of age, the grandfathers would have certainly reached their final status category. It is true that some grandfathers may have died at relatively young ages and in their case the last status category may be different from the one they might have finally reached if they had lived longer. But this limitation is part of the real framework within which movements in status occur and cannot be eliminated, though it should be borne in mind when interpreting the results of the analysis.

For the sons' generation, the problem is more complex. Their mean age in 1949 was 30 ± 0.5 for sub-sample (a) and 31 ± 0.5 for sub-sample (b). In many cases, therefore, the sons were too young to have reached their final status category. Hence, in order to ascertain whether this truncated accounting period seriously affects the study, part of the analysis will be based on samples covering only those sons who were not less than 50 years of age in 1949 and who may therefore be regarded as having reached their final status categories by that date. Since this adjustment will considerably reduce the size of the total sample it will only be used as a 'control' to test the validity of certain conclusions drawn from the general analyses.

Analysis of the Data

The analysis has been divided into two parts:

(a) A descriptive analysis of the sample material and

(b) An attempt to interpret inter-generation changes in terms of the concept of 'perfect' mobility.

Both analyses will be based on the main Table I given in the Appendix.

269

Sons and Fathers

Descriptive Analysis

Table 2 gives the frequency distribution of the sons by status categories, showing whether sons and fathers were in the same or different status categories.

Table 2

Social Status Category	Son's Social Status Category			Percentage of Col. 2 to Col. 4
	Same as Father's	Different from Father's	Total	
(1)	(2)	(3)	(4)	(5)
1	7	8	15	47
2	3	21	24	13
3	9	42	51	18
4	14	65	79	17
5	104	81	185	56
6	28	48	76	37
7	19	64	83	23
Total	184	329	513	36

Note: Sample (*a*) only.

The percentages of sons who were in the same status category as their fathers (column 5 of the table) show some variation as between categories. A chi-square test applied to the above frequency distribution indicates that these differences are real and not due to chance. Category 5 exhibits the highest agreement and category 1 stands next to it, while the lowest degree of agreement is recorded by category 2.

Bearing in mind the fact that in the above table the sons' status categories may not always be their final status, it is necessary to see how the above analysis may have been affected by the truncated accounting periods referred to earlier. For this purpose a small sample of the first-born sons, aged 50 and over, has been drawn from the two sub-samples (*a*) and (*b*). In this sample the proportion of sons whose status category was the same as that of their fathers was 33·3 per cent. (22 out of 66), the corresponding figure in Table 2 being 36 per cent. A chi-square test indicates that the difference between these two percentages is not significant and suggests, therefore, that the validity of the above table is not affected by the difference in accounting periods.

Taking only those sons who are in a different category from that of their fathers, it is of interest to see whether they have attained a higher or lower status. Table 3 has therefore been prepared, relating only to those sons who were in a different status category from that of their fathers. The first and the last status categories have been omitted from

270

the table because they can register either only a 'lower' or only a 'higher' position. They would not, therefore, have a significant bearing on this analysis.

A chi-square test applied to the above frequency distribution gives a very high value, due primarily to a very large shift to a higher status from category 6. It will be noticed that, of those sons who have moved at all from their fathers' category 6, 85 per cent have moved to a higher

Table 3

Father's social status category	Son's status category in the social status hierarchy with respect to father's			Percentage of Col. 2 to Col. 4
(1)	Higher (2)	Lower (3)	Total (4)	(5)
2	4	17	21	19
3	4	38	42	9
4	10	55	65	15
5	33	48	81	41
6	41	7	48	85
Total	92	165	257	36

Note: Sample (*a*) only.

status, while the corresponding figures for the other categories is 41 per cent maximum. This behaviour of category 6, as distinct from other categories, is due to the fact that out of the 48 sons who belong to a category other than the parental category 6, 29 are in category 5; only 12 have moved to still higher categories, and only 7 are placed in category 7. Thus, a slight disagreement between the father's and the son's status categories (category 6 and category 5) has considerably inflated the proportion of those who have moved to a higher position.

In all other categories the sons were mainly found in a 'lower' position in the scale as compared with their fathers. The rates were, however, different between categories as indicated by the chi-square test. It was highest in category 3 (91 per cent) and lowest in category 5 (59 per cent) (leaving out category 6 for reasons noted above), with categories 2 and 4 behaving similarly (81 per cent and 85 per cent respectively) and remaining in between categories 3 and 5.

The 'lower' position of the sons in the hierarchical scale may partly be due to the fact that they have not yet had the time to reach their fathers' final status categories. To that extent, Table 3 cannot be regarded as showing more than that in a large number of cases the sons began their occupational career from a position lower than that finally achieved by their fathers. An analysis of the data for sons aged 50 and over supports the above suggestion. Out of the 37 sons in categories 2 to 6 who

271

occupied a position in the social status hierarchy different from that of their fathers, 20 (or 54 per cent) were in a 'higher' position (compared with the corresponding figure of 36 per cent in the above table). A chi-square test indicates that this difference is significant at the 5 per cent point.

An attempt was made to measure, though very roughly, the distance between the sons and the fathers who were found in different status categories. For this analysis it has been assumed that the categories are equi-distant from their neighbours, that is, that there is a distance of one unit between categories 1 and 2, 2 and 3, 3 and 4, and so on. The results are shown in Table 4 below.

Table 4

Father's social status category	Mean distance between father's and son's categories in the hierarchical scale Son's position relative to father's			
	Higher		Lower	
(1)	(2)		(3)	
1	—	—	(8)	3·25
2	(4)	1·00	(17)	2·94
3	(4)	1·50	(38)	2·08
4	(10)	1·50	(55)	1·36
5	(33)	1·94	(48)	1·31
6	(41)	1·46	(7)	1·00
7	(64)	1·81	—	—
Total	(156)	1·70 ± 0·06	(173)	1·73 ± 0·07

Note: Sample (a) only.

(Number of sons concerned are given in brackets.)

The table shows that, taking all categories together, regardless of whether the son achieved a higher or a lower category than that of his father, the 'distance' between the fathers and the sons is practically the same. The values are $1·70 \pm 0·06$ and $1·73 \pm 0·07$, respectively. There is no significant difference between these two values as evidenced from a 't' test. It may, therefore, be said that, by and large, inter-generation changes are restricted to movement through one or two categories.

The above conclusion does not apply to the sample of sons aged 50 and over. In their case, taking all the categories together, the mean 'distance' between fathers and sons was $1·85 \pm 0·11$ (N = 27), where the sons had moved upwards, and $1·47 \pm 0·15$ (N = 17) where they had moved downwards, the difference between the two mean values being significant at the 1 per cent level. For these sons, therefore, the 'distance' moved up appears to be greater than the 'distance' moved down. It should, however, be noted that even for this sub-sample the 'distance'

272

moved is restricted to the next one or two status categories, suggesting a tendency for the fathers and sons to 'cluster' round the same or similar social status.

A comparison of the results obtained for sons aged 50 and over with those shown in Table 4 provides further interesting conclusions. Taking only the sons who were in a lower status category than their fathers, the average 'distance' between the fathers and sons is 1·47 ± 0·15 for sons aged 50 and over, but 1·73 ± 0·07 for all sons. On a 't' test the difference between the two mean values is significant at the 5 per cent level. For those sons who were higher in status than their fathers, the corresponding mean values are 1·85 ± 0·11 and 1·70 ± 0·06, but these two mean values are not significantly different. On the whole, therefore, this analysis supports the earlier suggestion that Table 3 understates the proportion of sons who reach or pass the status categories of their fathers.

Analysis in Terms of 'Perfect' Mobility or Association

Following the method of approach used in the preceding chapter, an attempt has been made to ascertain whether the inter-generation changes between the fathers and sons are greater or smaller than would be expected in a system of 'perfect' mobility or association. The results are given in Table 5 below.

Table 5

Association between sons

1. Index of Association	1·471
2. Index of Dissociation for a higher position of the son	0·842
3. Index of Dissociation for a lower position of the son	0·854
4. Index of Total Dissociation	0·848

Note: (i) Sample (*a*) only.
(ii) In the construction of all the indices the 'expected' values were found to be significantly different from the 'observed' values. Their ratios, therefore, represent *valid* indices.

Two conclusions may be drawn from the above table. First, there is less change of status between fathers and sons than would have been expected in conditions of 'perfect' association, and secondly, whether the sons moved up or down in status as compared with their fathers, the indices of 'Dissociation' were of the same order.

An analysis of the sample of sons aged 50 and over gives a similar

273

result. The Index of Association is 1·161, not significantly different from the corresponding value of 1·471 for the sub-sample (a) shown in the table above. The corresponding indices of 'Dissociation' also appear to be similar to those in the above table. They were 0·925, 0·952 and 0·935, respectively.

Table 6 gives the indices of Association and Dissociation for each of the seven status categories. In order to obtain sufficiently large frequencies in the individual cells of the contingency table for the construction of these indices, samples (a) and (b) were combined.

Table 6

Social status category	Index of Association	Index of Dissociation Son's position in the social status hierarchy relative to father's		
		Higher	Lower	Total
(1)	(2)	(3)	(4)	(5)
1	13·316	—	0·584	0·584
2	6·472	4·563	0·723	0·852
3	2·971	1·714	0·764	0·825
4	2·551	0·958	0·831	0·850
5	1·225	0·768	0·818	0·796
6	1·937	0·746	0·899	0·764
7	2·785	0·814	—	0·814
Total	1·584	0·817	0·791	0·804

Note: (i) Sample (a) and Sample (b).
(ii) Chi-square test showed that all the indices are valid except 0·958 (category 4 in col. 3) and 0·899 (category 6 in col. 4).

In all the status categories 'total dissociation' is less marked than would be expected in conditions of 'perfect' association, and it is of about the same order in all the categories save perhaps in category 1 (cf. col. 5 of the table).

On the other hand, columns 3 and 4 of the table show that the indices of 'Dissociation' constructed by taking into account the sons' position in the scale as higher or lower than that of their fathers, form a distinct order in the hierarchical scale. For the sons who are placed higher, the indices are in a descending order down the scale, and they are in an ascending order for sons placed lower than their fathers. These tendencies suggest that for fathers placed higher in the social status hierarchy, more sons went further up the scale than down, and the reverse was the position with regard to the sons of fathers placed lower in the hierarchy. For reasons mentioned in Appendix 1 to Chapter VIII, no statistical tests were applied to examine the significance of differences between the indices of Dissociation. The above suggestion, therefore,

274

needs verification. But it is an important point to note that for categories 2 and 3 the values of the Index of 'Dissociation' for a higher position of the son than of the father are appreciably greater than unity. Such values are likely to be statistically different from the rest which are always less than unity. This rather confirms the contrasting behaviour of the upper and lower status categories in the hierarchy. It suggests that of those men whose fathers were placed in the upper status categories, a large number of sons have further improved their position than would have been expected in conditions of 'perfect' association, while of those men whose fathers were placed in the lower status categories, larger numbers have gone further down the scale. In other words, improvement and deterioration in the social status hierarchy seem to be associated with the higher and lower positions of the parents respectively.

Table 7

THE SIGNIFICANCE OF DIFFERENCES BETWEEN
THE INDICES OF ASSOCIATION

Father's Social Status Category	Son's Social Status Category						
	1	2	3	4	5	6	7
(1)	(2)	(3)	(4)	(5)	(6)	(7)	(8)
1	13·316						
2	‡	6·472					
3	*	‡	2·971				
4	*	†	‡	2·551			
5	*	*	*	*	1·225		
6	*	*	‖	‡	*	1·937	
7	*	†	‡	‡	*	‖	2·785

Note: (i) Sample (a) and sample (b).
(ii) The indices are shown in the diagonal cells.

* Significant at 1 per cent probability level.
† Significant at 5 per cent probability level.
‡ Not significant.   ‖ Almost significant at 5 per cent probability level.

Table 7 gives the results of testing the significance of the differences between the indices of Association for the seven status categories by pairs.

The table shows that the highest association between the father's and the son's social status is found in categories 1 and 2. It is the least marked in category 5. The other categories behave similarly and lie in between category 5 and category 2.

Fathers and Grandfathers

A set of tables (Tables 8–13) is given below to explain inter-generation changes between fathers (i.e. male subjects or female subjects' husbands) and grandfathers (i.e. male subjects' fathers and female subjects' fathers-in-law). These tables are similar to the Tables 2–7, and they lead to conclusions very similar to those noted in the earlier analysis of inter-generation changes between sons and fathers. A brief account of the main conclusions which may be drawn from the tables is given below.

Descriptive Analysis

More than one-third of the fathers remained in the same final status categories as the grandfathers (cf. Table 8). The tendency to remain in the same status category as that of the grandfathers is most marked in the first and the fifth categories (*ibid*). Where there is dissociation, it is largely shown by fathers who fell in status as compared with grandfathers (cf. Table 9). As in the case of sons (cf. Table 3), the only exception is for category 6 where 20 fathers out of 70 (30 per cent) moved upwards to the next category, with 25 (36 per cent) of the total number remaining in category 6.

This conclusion is slightly different from that drawn for the sons. In the light of the available information, it was conjectured that, given a full generation in which to move, the sons would tend to attain or even pass their fathers' status. For the fathers no such tendency is shown.

As in the father-son generation, the tendency to 'cluster' round the parental status holds also for the grandfather-father generation (cf. Table 10).

Analysis in Terms of 'Perfect' Association or Mobility

In all the status categories there is a higher association between the subject's father's and the subject's status categories than would have been expected in terms of the concept of 'perfect' association or mobility. But there is some difference in the degree of association between the categories (cf. Tables 11 and 13). The highest association is shown in categories 1 and 2 (these two categories behaving similarly) and the least in category 5.

The indices of Dissociation are similar to those presented in the earlier section in examining the association between fathers and sons (cf. Table

12). Although these indices have not been tested for significant differences, it may be noted that the values of the index were greater than unity in the case of categories 2, 3 and 4 for fathers who were higher in status than grandfathers, and also in the case of category 6 for fathers who were lower in status than grandfathers. The indices for categories 2 and 4 cannot be relied upon because these two values might have been obtained by chance fluctuations. Nevertheless, the indices suggest the kind of contrasting behaviour between the upper and lower status categories in the hierarchy of the fathers' and the grandfathers' generation which was previously found in the study of fathers and sons.

Table 8

Social Status Category	Father's Social Status Category			Percentage of Col. 2 to Col. 4
	Same as Grandfather's	Different from Grandfather's	Total	
(1)	(2)	(3)	(4)	(5)
1	9	13	22	41
2	7	14	21	33
3	11	32	43	26
4	21	63	84	25
5	100	130	230	43
6	25	45	70	36
7	26	16	42	62
Total	199	313	512	39

Note: (i) Sample (a) only.
(ii) Chi-square = 22·034, degrees of freedom = 6.

Table 9

Grandfather's Social Status Category	Father's Status Category relative to Grandfather's			
	Higher	Lower	Total	Percentage of Col. 2 to Col. 4
(1)	(2)	(3)	(4)	(5)
2	—	14	14	—
3	5	27	32	16
4	12	51	63	19
5	60	70	130	46
6	33	12	45	73
Total	110	174	284	39

Note: (i) Sample (a) only.
(ii) Chi-square on frequencies in categories 3 to 6 = 42·041, degrees of freedom = 3, significant at 1 per cent level.

Table 10

Grandfather's Social Status Category	Mean Distance between Grandfather's and Father's Categories Father's Position relative to Grandfather's			
	Higher		Lower	
	N	Mean	N	Mean
(1)	(2)	(3)	(4)	(5)
1	—	—	13	3·31
2	0	0·00	14	2·07
3	5	1·60	27	1·74
4	12	1·17	51	1·39
5	60	1·68	70	1·49
6	33	1·61	12	1·00
7	16	2·13	—	—
Total	126	1·67 ± 0·07	187	1·64 ± 0·07

Note: Sample (*a*) only.

Table 11

Association between fathers and grandfathers

(1)	(2)
Index of Association	1·609
Index of Dissociation for a higher position of son	0·743
Index of Dissociation for a lower position of son	0·849
Index of Total Dissociation	0·800

Note: Samples (*a*) and (*b*).

Table 12

Social Status Category	Index of Association	Index of Dissociation Father's Position relative to Grandfather's		
		Higher	Lower	Total
(1)	(2)	(3)	(4)	(5)
1	17·606	—	0·668	0·668
2	7·778	1·277	0·668	0·681
3	3·178	1·760	0·701	0·777
4	1·900	1·065	0·798	0·848
5	1·236	0·730	0·974	0·854
6	1·884	0·719	1·307	0·825
7	3·078	0·634	—	0·634

Note: (i) Samples (*a*) and (*b*).
(ii) Chi-square tests applied to the sets of frequencies prepared to derive the indices showed significant difference, confirming the 'validity' of these indices, except for categories 2 and 4 in col. 3 and for category 5 in col. 4.

278

Table 13

THE SIGNIFICANCE OF DIFFERENCES BETWEEN THE INDICES OF
ASSOCIATION

Grandfather's Status Category (1)	*Father's Status Category*						
	1 (2)	*2* (3)	*3* (4)	*4* (5)	*5* (6)	*6* (7)	*7* (8)
1	17·61						
2	‡	7·78					
3	*	†	3·18				
4	*	*	‡	1·90			
5	*	*	†	‡	1·24		
6	*	*	‡	‡	*	1·88	
7	*	‡	‡	*	*	‖	3·08

Note: Sample (*a,* and (*b*).
  (ii) * Significant at 1 per cent probability level.
     † Significant at 5 per cent probability level.
     ‡ Not significant.
     ‖ Almost significant at 5 per cent probability level.
  (iii) The indices are shown in the diagonal cells.

Sons, Fathers and Grandfathers

In this section, in order to simplify the terminology, the grandfather's generation will be referred to as G_3, the father's generation as G_2 and the son's generation as G_1.

Descriptive Analysis

Table 14 gives the number and proportions of individuals in the separate status categories in the three generations.

The table shows that the proportionate representation of the status categories in the total sample remained the same in each generation for categories 1, 2, 3 and 6. For categories 4, 5 and 7 there were significant differences. In the three generations as a whole these three categories accounted for 70, 67 and 68 per cent of the total individuals. Between generations G_2 and G_1 there was a fall in the proportions in categories 4 and 7, but this was compensated by the corresponding increase in category 5. Between generation G_3 and G_2 also there was a fall in cate-

279

gory 5 but this was again compensated by a proportionate rise in category 7.

Table 14

Social Status Category	Number of Individuals				Percentage of Total			Chi-square for each Category $(d.f.=3)$
	G_3	G_2	G_1	Total	G_3	G_2	G_1	
(1)	(2)	(3)	(4)	(5)	(6)	(7)	(8)	(9)
1	22	14	18	54	4	3	3	2·059
2	21	24	13	58	4	5	3	3·432
3	43	52	35	130	8	10	7	3·654
4	84	80	49	213	17	16	10	12·033*
5	230	182	251	663	45	35	49	19·747*
6	70	79	100	249	14	15	19	6·669
7	42	81	47	170	8	16	9	17·808*
Total	512	512	513	1537	100	100	100	—

Note: (1) Sample (a) only.
(ii) * Significant at 1 per cent probability level.

Although Table 14 does not suggest any appreciable change in the final composition of the social status hierarchy in the three generations, there are substantial shifts of individuals between status categories. This may be seen from Table 15 which depicts the changes in social status in

Table 15

CHARACTER OF SOCIAL MOBILITY IN THREE GENERATIONS

Type of Movement	Grandfather– Father	Father– Son	Number of Individuals	Percentage of Total
(1)	(2)	(3)	(4)	(5)
Unidirectional in three	Inertia	Inertia	179	18
generations	Ascent	Ascent	30	3
	Descent	Descent	74	8
No movement in G_3–G_2;	Inertia	Ascent	103	10
unidirectional G_2–G_1	Inertia	Descent	113	11
Unidirectional G_3–G_2;	Ascent	Inertia	91	9
No movement G_2–G_1	Descent	Inertia	123	13
Bidirectional in three	Ascent	Descent	131	13
generations	Descent	Ascent	147	15
	Total		991	100

Note: Samples (a) and (b).

three generations between grandfathers, fathers and sons. In this table, 'inertia' refers to the maintenance of the same final status category between two successive generations. 'Ascent' refers to a higher position of the later generation than the previous one in the hierarchical scale, that is, of fathers with respect to the grandfathers in G_3–G_2 and sons with respect to fathers in G_2–G_1. 'Descent' refers to a lower position of the later generation than the previous one.

A chi-square test applied to the above frequencies gave a significantly large value, so that the shift of individuals shown in the above table is not merely due to sampling fluctuation. It will be noticed from the table that only 18 per cent of all individuals have remained in the same status category in the three generations, only 3 per cent have consistently improved their social status, and 8 per cent have registered consistent demotion in successive generations. This higher rate of 'descent' than 'ascent' is worthy of note. It may further be seen that while the other pairs of complementary movements, such as Inertia G_3–G_2 and Ascent or Descent G_2–G_1, or Ascent G_3–G_2/Descent G_2–G_1 and Descent G_3–G_2/Ascent G_2–G_1, are of the same magnitudes, the cases of Ascent or Descent in G_3–G_2 with no movement in G_2–G_1 are of different magnitudes. The table thus suggests that there has been a tendency for a larger movement downwards than upwards. The magnitude of such movement was not, however, greater than the tendency for inertia in all the three generations, and it is this latter tendency which is the essential characteristic of the society under consideration. This is shown in Table 16 below, which has been derived from the above table.

Table 16

CHARACTER OF SOCIAL MOBILITY IN THREE GENERATIONS

Type of Movement (1)		Number (2)	Percentage (3)
At least in one generation	Inertia	609	62
	Descent	588	59
	Ascent	502	51
Total sample		991	100

A chi-square test shows the three proportions to be significantly different.

Inter-generation changes in the three generations for different status categories are shown in Table 17. This table has been summarized from Table 2 in the Appendix.

Looking at the separate status categories, it will be seen from the table that 62 per cent of the sons in categories of 1 and 2, and 50 per cent of those in category 3 have risen in status as compared with their fathers and grandfathers and only 34 per cent in both cases have remained in the status categories of their fathers or grandfathers or of both. On the other hand, of the sons in category 5, 70 per cent have the same status as their fathers or grandfathers or both. In categories 4, 6 and 7 the proportions

281

SOCIAL MOBILITY BETWEEN THREE GENERATIONS

Table 17

Affiliation of the son to the status category of (1)		Status Category of the Sons						Chi-square D.f.=5
		1 and 2 (2)	3 (3)	4 (4)	5 (5)	6 and 7 (6)	Total (7)	(8)
Number								
Father and Grandfather		8	7	8	129	27	179	51·400*
Father but not of Grandfather		8	13	25	95	73	214	6·471
Grandfather but not of Father		3	8	11	112	19	153	49·538*
Neither Father's nor Grandfather's	But higher than both Father and Grandfather	35	42	28	50	15	170	199·643*
	Other possibility	2	13	18	93	149	275	
	Total	37	55	46	143	164	445	81·240*
Sample total		56	83	90	479	283	991	
Percentage								
Father and Grandfather		14	8	9	27	10	18	
Father but not of Grandfather		14	16	28	20	26	22	
Grandfather but not of Father		6	10	12	23	7	15	
Neither Father's nor Grandfather's	Higher than both Father and Grandfather	62	50	30	10	5	17	
	Other possibility	4	16	21	20	52	28	
	Total	66	66	51	30	57	45	
Sample total		100	100	100	100	100	100	

Note: (i) Samples (*a*) and (*b*).

(ii) * Significant at 1 per cent probability level.

(iii) Categories 1–2 and 6–7 were combined to produce as far as possible a frequency of at least 5 in each cell. In the light of previous analyses this is not likely to distort the picture of the social hierarchy.

(iv) Chi-square tests applied to the data in the above table showed that this frequency distribution is not merely due to chance.

of sons remaining in or moving out of their fathers' and/or grandfathers' categories are nearly equal. But here again, of those who possess a status category different from their fathers and grandfathers, those in category 4 are seen to have improved their position in the main, while in category 6 and 7 they have fallen in the scale. Such movements between the categories in the three generations are reflected in the overall 'ascent' by 3 per cent and the overall 'descent' by 8 per cent in successive generations, the downward movement being more marked in the lower than in the higher categories.

It may also be seen from the table that, as in the study of two generations at a time, the sons belonging to category 5 show the highest agreement with their father's and also with their grandfather's social status. In all categories, where there is a difference between the status of father and grandfather, it is to the status of their fathers that sons tend to adhere (cf. rows 2 and 3 of the table). In only about 18 per cent of all cases is the same status maintained through three generations (col. 7 of the table).

Table 18

Social status category of the previous generation	Mean distances between the grandfather's and father's and the father's and son's categories in the hierarchical scale with respect to the position of the later generation	
	$G_3 - G_2$ Mean $\pm$ s.e.	$G_2 - G_1$ Mean $\pm$ s.e.
(1)	(2)	(3)
	Higher	
1	—	—
2	(0) 0·00 $\pm$ 0·00	(4) 1·00 $\pm$ 0·00
3	(5) 1·60 $\pm$ 0·24	(4) 1·50 $\pm$ 0·29
4	(12) 1·17 $\pm$ 0·17	(10) 1·50 $\pm$ 0·22
5	(60) 1·68 $\pm$ 0·10	(33) 1·94 $\pm$ 0·18
6	(33) 1·61 $\pm$ 0·17	(41) 1·46 $\pm$ 0·13
7	(16) 2·13 $\pm$ 0·20	(64) 1·81 $\pm$ 0·07
Total	(126) 1·67 $\pm$ 0·07	(156) 1·70 $\pm$ 0·06
	Lower	
	(4)	(5)
1	(13) 3·31 $\pm$ 0·50	(8) 3·25 $\pm$ 0·41
2	(14) 2·07 $\pm$ 0·34	(17) 2·94 $\pm$ 0·23
3	(27) 1·74 $\pm$ 0·17	(38) 2·08 $\pm$ 0·10
4	(51) 1·39 $\pm$ 0·09	(55) 1·36 $\pm$ 0·08
5	(70) 1·49 $\pm$ 0·06	(48) 1·31 $\pm$ 0·00
6	(12) 1·00 $\pm$ 0·00	(7) 1·00 $\pm$ 0·00
7	—	—
Total	(187) 1·64 $\pm$ 0·07	(173) 1·73 $\pm$ 0·07

Note: Sample (*a*) only.
(Numbers of individuals are given in brackets.)

Table 18 provides a rough indication of the 'distance' between the three generations in the social status hierarchy, the results being shown separately according to the relative status of the later generation. This table is based upon the data previously given in Tables 4 and 10 with the addition of the standard errors of the mean values for the different status categories. These have been given because the mean values for the two generation changes (G_3–G_2 and G_2–G_1) would now be strictly comparable for the same status category and for the same relative status of the later generations.

The application of analysis of variance to the above data showed that there is no significant difference between the two generation changes for any status category in either of the two scales. 't' tests applied to the individual pairs of means showed a significant difference at the 5 per cent level of significance for only two cases, viz. in categories 2 and 5 in the 'lower' position of the later generation. In regard to the 'distance' moved, inter-generational changes have, therefore, remained practically the same between the last three generations. Once again the material suggests that there is a strong tendency among the members of the society to cluster around the parental status.

Analysis in Terms of 'Perfect' Association or Mobility

Table 19 has been prepared from the Tables 6 and 12 in order to compare the indices of Association and Dissociation in the two generation changes, viz. G_3–G_2 and G_2–G_1.

Table 19

Social Status Category	Indices of Association		Indices of Dissociation						
			Position of the later generation in the social status hierarchy relative to the previous one						
			Higher		Lower		Total	
	G_3–G_2	G_2–G_1	G_3–G_2	G_2–G_1	G_3–G_2	G_2–G_1	G_3–G_2	G_2–G_1
(1)	(2)	(3)	(4)	(5)	(6)	(7)	(8)	(9)
1	17·61	13·32	—	—	0·67	0·58	0·67	0·58
2	7·78	6·47	1·28	4·56	0·67	0·72	0·68	0·85
3	3·18	2·97	1·76	1·71	0·70	0·76	0·78	0·83
4	1·90	2·55	1·07	0·96	0·80	0·83	0·85	0·85
5	1·24	1·23	0·73	0·77	0·97	0·82	0·85	0·80
6	1·88	1·94	0·72	0·75	1·31	0·90	0·83	0·76
7	3·08	2·79	0·63	0·81	—	—	0·63	0·81
Total	1·61	1·58	0·74	0·82	0·85	0·79	0·80	0·80

There are no significant differences between the pairs of indices of Association for G_3–G_2 and G_2–G_1, and other pairs of indices also appear to be the same in all cases. The available data thus suggest that the inter-generation position with regard to the status hierarchy remained the same over the three generations considered.

Social mobility between three generations may, however, be examined from a slightly different point of view by looking into the internal character of the mobility. Extending the concept of 'perfect' association to this analysis, we may ask whether inter-generation changes were greater or smaller than would have been expected if the final results of changes, viz. 'Ascent', 'Inertia' or 'Descent', in the two successive generations remained fixed in the society but if, at the same time, there were equal chances to 'ascend' or 'descend' or to remain fixed in status. In other words, if we take as given the fact that within the society 252 and 280 individuals out of 991 would in any case have improved their status between G_3–G_2 and G_2–G_1 respectively, how many should we expect to have a *continuous* movement in social status, that is, 'Ascent' in both G_3–G_2 and G_2–G_1, and similarly for the other two end results of social mobility, namely 'Inertia' and 'Descent'. Table 20 gives the outlines of this form of analysis. The expected value corresponding to each observed value is shown in brackets, the expected values being derived by dividing the product of the corresponding marginal totals of the table by the grand total. Thus for Ascent both in G_3–G_2 and G_2–G_1 the expected value is $(252 \times 280)/991 = 71 \cdot 20$, whereas the observed value is 30.

Table 20

OBSERVED AND EXPECTED NUMBERS INVOLVED IN INTER-GENERATION
CHANGES, G_3–G_2 AND G_2–G_1

G_3–G_2 (1)	Ascent (2)	G_2–G_1 Inertia (3)	Descent (4)	Total (5)
Ascent	30 (71·20)	91 (99·94)	131 (80·86)	252
Inertia	103 (111·60)	179 (156·64)	113 (126·76)	395
Descent	147 (97·20)	123 (136·42)	74 (110·38)	344
Total	280	393	318	991

Note: Expected numbers are given in brackets.

It will be seen from the table that only in the case of complete inertia in three generations or opposite movements in the two successive generations (that is, Descent–Ascent, and Ascent–Descent in G_3–G_2/G_2–G_1) is the ratio of the observed to the expected value

285

greater than unity. In all other cases the observed values are lower than the expected values.

The above analysis suggests three important features of social mobility in England and Wales. First, for some families, there is a greater tendency to remain stationary in the social hierarchy than would have been expected if the three final results of the changes had equal importance. Secondly, for others the tendency is to be involved in sharp changes from one direction to another (Ascent–Descent or Descent–Ascent), and in their case also the tendency is greater than would have been expected. Finally, the remaining families shift from one position to another (Inertia–Ascent/Descent or vice versa) or may show a continuous rise or fall in status (Ascent–Ascent or Descent–Descent). But in these cases the observed numbers are smaller than the expected values.

Putting these results together with the earlier evidence regarding the stability of English social structure over three generations, the present analysis suggests that the society contains both a solid core of 'stable elements' and, at the same time, a group of 'unstable elements'. The latter may perhaps comprise only a small proportion of the total members of the society, but they are so unstable as to be involved in reverse shifts in status in successive generations, and to a greater extent than would be 'expected' if there were equal chances of moving up or down or of remaining stationary in status.

The above inferences are based on rather slender evidence and need to be confirmed by a detailed examination on these lines of each status category. The present sample is too small to allow this to be done. It may, however, be appropriate to suggest that, to gain more comprehensive knowledge of social mobility, attention should in future be paid particularly to this group of 'unstable elements' with the object of ascertaining whether they come from all or from a few status categories and why they are unstable.

Attention should also be drawn to the second main conclusion of the present study, regarding the contradictory behaviour of the higher and lower status categories. For elements in the upper categories there is a tendency for continued upward movement in the status scale, while in the lower categories the tendency is rather for descent in the scale. Moreover, over the three generations the tendency is for a larger shift downwards than upwards. These trends have not yet become sufficiently well established to produce an appreciable change in the structural arrangement of the status categories. Nevertheless it would be relevant to ascertain why mobility is being influenced in opposite directions as between the higher and lower status categories.

Finally, it may be noted that, looking at the situation on the assumption that each status category is of equal importance in the social structure, the analysis in terms of 'perfect' association or mobility showed that the highest 'inertia' was in categories 1 and 2 and the least in category 5. That is, in all the three generations the highest stratum in the society was found to be the most stable, while the skilled labourers and the routine non-manual workers showed the greatest instability. If, however, the relative size of the status categories in the social structure is taken into account—as is done in the descriptive analysis (cf. Chapter VIII, Appendix 2)—with category 5 accounting for about one-third of the total members of the society and categories 1 and 2 hardly one-twelfth, 'inertia' is found to be most marked in category 5. This suggests that even though, as a group, category 5 is not very stable, its instability does not produce a serious effect on the structure of the society as a whole. Although there have been internal changes in the successive generations, the social structure has retained its characteristic form.

APPENDIX 1

Table 1

SONS AND FATHERS

Sample (a)

| Status category of male subject (1) | Status category of male subject's first-born son | | | | | | | Total |
	1 (2)	2 (3)	3 (4)	4 (5)	5 (6)	6 (7)	7 (8)	(9)
1	7	—	3	1	3	1	—	15
2	4	3	1	4	8	3	1	24
3	2	2	9	5	26	6	1	51
4	1	3	6	14	39	12	4	79
5	4	4	11	14	104	33	15	185
6	—	1	5	6	29	28	7	76
7	—	—	—	5	42	17	19	83
Total	18	13	35	49	251	100	47	513

Sample (b)

| Status category of female subject's husband (1) | Status category of female subject's first-born son | | | | | | | Total |
	1 (2)	2 (3)	3 (4)	4 (5)	5 (6)	6 (7)	7 (8)	(9)
1	3	1	1	—	2	1	—	8
2	3	5	8	1	5	1	—	23
3	3	3	15	1	19	6	1	48
4	2	2	7	21	33	9	3	77
5	5	3	17	16	142	37	17	237
6	—	—	6	8	38	41	8	101
7	2	2	1	1	35	27	28	96
Total	18	16	55	48	274	122	57	590

SOCIAL MOBILITY BETWEEN THREE GENERATIONS

GRANDFATHERS AND FATHERS

Sample (a)

Status category of father of male subject (1)	Status category of male subject							Total
	1 (2)	2 (3)	3 (4)	4 (5)	5 (6)	6 (7)	7 (8)	(9)
1	9	3	2	2	2	2	2	22
2	—	7	6	3	4	—	1	21
3	3	2	11	12	12	1	2	43
4	1	—	11	21	35	12	4	84
5	—	11	19	30	100	36	34	230
6	1	1	2	9	20	25	12	70
7	—	—	1	3	9	3	26	42
Total	14	24	52	80	182	79	81	512

Sample (b)

Status category of female subject's father-in-law (1)	Status category of female subject's husband							Total
	1 (2)	2 (3)	3 (4)	4 (5)	5 (6)	6 (7)	7 (8)	(9)
1	1	1	2	—	2	1	—	7
2	1	7	2	3	4	1	1	19
3	1	4	15	7	13	3	2	45
4	1	3	9	20	21	6	5	65
5	2	5	13	25	125	48	28	246
6	—	2	1	9	23	18	15	68
7	—	—	1	4	21	13	21	60
Total	6	22	43	68	209	90	72	510

SOCIAL MOBILITY BETWEEN THREE GENERATIONS

TABLE 2

Affiliation of the son to the status category (1)		Number of sons in status category					Total
		1 and 2 (2)	*3* (3)	*4* (4)	*5* (5)	*6 and 7* (6)	(7)
Of Father and Grandfather		8	7	8	129	27	179
Of Father but	Better than of Gf.	—	2	6	57	67	132
	Worse than of Gf.	8	11	19	38	6	82
	Not of Grandfather	8	13	25	95	73	214
Of Grand-father but	Better than Father	—	2	1	48	16	67
	Worse than Father	3	6	10	64	3	86
	Not of Father	3	8	11	112	19	153
Of neither Father nor Gf.	Better than of F. and Grandfather	35	42	28	50	15	170
	Better than of F. but worse than Grandfather	1	4	6	15	17	43
	Worse than of F. but better than Grandfather	1	4	6	12	7	30
	Worse than of F. and Grandfather	—	5	6	66	125	202
	Sub-total	37	55	46	143	164	445
	Sample total	56	83	90	479	283	991

Note: Samples (*a*) and (*b*).

X

Education and Social Mobility

J. R. HALL AND D. V. GLASS

THE analysis of the information collected by the sample investigation into social mobility in Great Britain has so far led to two broad conclusions. First, the type and level of education attained by the subjects who co-operated in the investigation depended very heavily upon the social status (as measured in terms of occupation) of the subjects' fathers. Secondly, taking male subjects only, the relation between parental and filial status was seen to be positive and significant at all levels of the status hierarchy, and especially high at the upper levels. Moreover, a similar and powerful relationship was found in studying movements over three generations.

The aim of the present chapter is to supplement these two general conclusions by examining one aspect of the relationship between them —or, rather, of the mechanism through which that relationship is brought into being. The question to be answered is, what rôle has the education of an individual played in producing a powerful association between parental and filial status; and, conversely, how far is upward or downward movement in relation to parental social status influenced by an individual's education? The answers to these questions are scarcely likely to be startling; indeed, in large part the answers are implied in the two general conclusions referred to in the previous paragraph. But it is neither the intention nor the justification of this chapter —or, for that matter, of the previous chapters—to produce conclusions which are startling in their novelty. What is far more important is that the results should be relevant to the problems studied, and that those results should be arrived at objectively so that other research workers may, if they wish, test and verify them.

The Material

Because the chapter examines the rôle of education in the relationship between the status of father and son, the analysis is confined to the male subjects—resident in England and Wales—covered by the sample inquiry. These subjects have been classified in terms, first, of their primary and post-primary schooling and, secondly, of their combined post-primary school and further education. Three categories were constructed under the first head:

1. 'Senior elementary'—implying elementary or private primary school, followed by senior elementary, junior technical or central school. Of the total male sample, 86·6 per cent fall within this category.
2. 'Elementary primary and grammar'—that is, elementary primary school (not private), followed by a grammar school. This category covers 9·7 per cent of the sample.
3. 'Private primary and grammar'—that is, private primary school followed by a secondary grammar school or its equivalent. The small remainder of the sample—4·6 per cent—falls within this category.

For the second heading—combined post-primary school and further education—four categories have been used:

1. 'Senior elementary: none', meaning category 1 above, with no further education, covering 64·7 per cent of the sample.
2. 'Senior elementary: some', namely, category 1 with the addition of further education, 21·2 per cent of the sample being within this category.
3. 'Grammar: none'—categories 2 and 3 above, with no further education; 5·5 per cent of the sample.
4. 'Grammar: some'—categories 2 and 3 above, with the addition of further education, 8·6 per cent of the sample.

The categories used under both headings are far from ideal for studying the relation between education and social mobility. Under the heading of grammar schools, for example, no distinction has been made between independent public shools and other secondary schools, using the term secondary in its pre-1944 Act sense. And in the groupings relating to further education there is an additional blurring of distinctions between full-time and part-time education and, so far as the former is concerned, between university and other full-time further education.

292

This excessive compression of categories was, however, inevitable in view of the size of the sample and the number of cross-tabulations needed. There were, for example, only 101 male subjects who had obtained university qualifications. The number of men who had attended independent public schools was also very small. In neither case could the categories have been extended to deal satisfactorily with these small groups. Hence the treatment which follows is bound to be broad and unsubtle, tending perhaps to under-estimate the rôle of education as a specific factor in the achievement of social status.

Descriptive Analysis

The results of the first stage of the analysis are summarized in Tables 1 and 2, which show the influence of schooling, and of the combination of post-primary and further education, upon the degree of association between the social status of father and son. It should be noted here that the problem of 'random' movement or 'perfect' mobility does not arise in the same way as in Chapter VIII. For in Tables 1 and 2 it is not the degree of self-recruitment of the status categories which is being considered as such, but the rôle of education *within* each status category. Hence though indices of association can be applied—and they are applied later in the chapter—the descriptive analysis may justifiably be used in the present discussion.

If we look first at the totals percentages in the bottom rows of Tables 1 and 2 (the (*b*) columns) the overall importance of education for the status achieved by the subjects is clearly indicated. Thus in Table 1, of the subjects who attended a grammar school or its equivalent, 33·7 per cent achieved status categories 1 or 2,[1] while only 3·2 per cent of those whose schooling was 'senior elementary' achieved that status. The rôle of the grammar school is again shown in Table 2, and also the influence of further education. which, whatever the primary and post-primary schooling, increases the proportion of subjects found in status categories 1 and 2.

But these percentages do not distinguish the separate effects of education and of parental status on the status attained by the subjects. To treat education separately, we must examine its influence *within* each parental status category. Given the overall results mentioned above, we should expect, where the fathers were in the upper status categories, the status affiliation between father and son to be greatest if the sons had been to grammar schools or their equivalents, and that the converse

[1] i.e. the weighted average of 25·2 per cent and 51·6 per cent.

Table 1

PERCENTAGE DISTRIBUTION OF THE MALE SAMPLE ACCORDING TO SUBJECT'S AND SUBJECT'S FATHER'S PRESENT OR FINAL STATUS CATEGORY AND SCHOOLS ATTENDED BY SUBJECT

Subject's Father's Status Category	Schools Attended by Subjects	Subject's Present Status Category											
		(a) 1 & 2 (b)		(a) 3 (b)		(a) 4 (b)		(a) 5 (b)		(a) 6 & 7 (b)		(a)	(b) Totals
1 & 2	Elem/Sen. Elem	24·2	26·3	47·4	23·7	52·0	11·4	59·2	25·4	78·9	13·2	42·0	100·0 (114)
	Elem/Gram	25·8	48·5	26·3	22·7	20·0	7·5	20·4	15·2	21·1	6·1	24·4	100·0 (66)
	Private/Gram	50·0	66·0	26·3	16·0	28·0	7·5	20·4	10·5	0·0	0·0	33·6	100·0 (94)
	Total	100·0 (124)		100·0 (57)		100·0 (25)		100·0 (49)		100·0 (19)		100·0 (274)	
3	Elem/Sen. Elem	39·1	7·2	60·9	15·7	74·2	19·7	82·8	40·6	95·5	16·8	72·8	100·0 (249)
	Elem/Gram	41·3	28·4	26·6	25·4	18·2	17·9	15·6	28·3	0·0	0·0	19·6	100·0 (67)
	Private/Gram	19·6	34·6	12·5	30·8	7·6	19·2	1·6	7·7	4·5	7·7	7·6	100·0 (26)
	Total	100·0 (46)		100·0 (64)		100·0 (66)		100·0 (122)		100·0 (44)		100·0 (342)	
4	Elem/Sen. Elem	41·9	3·1	83·0	10·4	70·6	18·2	89·5	46·6	93·9	21·7	82·8	100·0 (423)
	Elem/Gram	45·2	19·4	17·0	12·5	22·0	33·3	9·6	29·2	4·1	5·6	14·1	100·0 (72)
	Private/Gram	12·9	25·0	0·0	0·0	7·4	50·0	0·9	12·5	2·0	12·5	3·1	100·0 (16)
	Total	100·0 (31)		100·0 (53)		100·0 (109)		100·0 (220)		100·0 (98)		100·0 (511)	

5												
Elem/Sen. Elem	62·0	2·3	87·5	7·1	94·5	12·5	93·3	47·3	96·1	30·8	92·8	100·0 (1371)
Elem/Gram	26·0	14·1	10·7	13·0	4·9	9·8	6·0	45·7	3·6	17·4	6·2	100·0 (92)
Private/Gram	12·0	40·0	1·3	13·3	0·6	6·7	0·7	33·3	0·2	6·7	1·0	100·0 (15)
Total	100·0 (50)		100·0 (112)		100·0 (182)		100·0 (695)		100·0 (439)		100·0 (1478)	
6 & 7												
Elem/Sen. Elem	37·5	0·4	84·8	3·6	100·0	8·7	93·3	37·3	98·0	50·0	95·3	100·0 (786)
Elem/Gram	62·5	15·2	15·2	15·2	0·0	0·0	5·4	51·4	1·5	18·2	4·0	100·0 (33)
Private/Gram	0·0	0·0	0·0	0·0	0·0	0·0	1·3	66·7	0·5	33·3	0·7	100·0 (6)
Total	100·0 (8)		100·0 (33)		100·0 (69)		100·0 (314)		100·0 (401)		100·0 (825)	
Totals												
Elem/Sen. Elem	36·7	3·2	74·0	8·0	84·2	12·9	90·6	43·1	96·4	32·8	86·6	100·0 (2943)
Elem/Gram	32·0	25·2	18·2	17·5	11·1	15·2	7·8	33·0	3·0	9·1	9·7	100·0 (330)
Private/Gram	31·3	51·6	7·8	15·9	4·7	13·4	1·6	14·6	0·6	4·5	4·6	100·0 (157)
Grand Total	100·0 (259)		100·0 (319)		100·0 (451)		100·0 (1400)		100·0 (1001)		100·0 (3430)	

(a) The proportions on the left-hand side of each cell indicate the distribution according to educational background of subjects in that cell. The number upon which the proportions are based is shown in brackets.

(b) The proportions on the right-hand side of each cell indicate the status distribution of subjects with a given educational background and status category of fathers. The number upon which the proportions are based is shown in brackets in the 'Totals' columns at the extreme right-hand side of the table.

295

Table 2

PERCENTAGE DISTRIBUTION OF THE MALE SAMPLE ACCORDING TO SUBJECT'S AND SUBJECT'S FATHER'S PRESENT OR FINAL STATUS CATEGORY AND SCHOOLS ATTENDED BY SUBJECT

Subject's Father's Status Category	Subject's Post-primary School and Further Educ.	Subject's Present Status Category											
		1 & 2 (a)	(b)	3 (a)	(b)	4 (a)	(b)	5 (a)	(b)	6 & 7 (a)	(b)	Total (a)	(b)
1 & 2	Sen. Elem/None	14·5	24·3	23·7	18·9	40·0	13·5	42·9	28·4	57·8	14·9	26·8	100·0 (74)
	Sen. Elem/Some	9·7	30·0	22·0	32·5	12·0	7·5	16·3	20·0	21·1	10·0	14·5	100·0 (40)
	Gram/None	25·8	54·2	15·3	15·3	20·0	8·5	20·4	16·9	15·8	5·1	21·4	100·0 (59)
	Gram/Some	50·0	60·2	39·0	22·3	28·0	6·8	20·4	9·7	5·3	1·0	37·3	100·0 (103)
	Total	100·0 (124)		100·0 (59)		100·0 (25)		100·0 (49)		100·0 (19)		100·0 (276)	
3	Sen. Elem/None	21·7	6·0	42·2	16·2	34·8	13·6	60·7	44·0	77·3	20·2	49·1	100·0 (168)
	Sen. Elem/Some	17·4	9·8	18·8	14·6	39·4	31·7	23·0	34·1	18·2	9·8	24·0	100·0 (82)
	Gram/None	15·2	17·1	20·2	31·7	16·7	26·8	6·6	19·5	4·5	4·9	12·0	100·0 (41)
	Gram/Some	45·7	41·2	18·8	23·5	9·1	11·8	9·7	23·5	0·0	0·0	14·9	100·0 (51)
	Total	100·0 (46)		100·0 (64)		100·0 (66)		100·0 (122)		100·0 (44)		100·0 (342)	
4	Sen. Elem/None	22·6	2·3	37·5	6·9	50·9	18·1	65·4	47·4	80·2	25·3	59·5	100·0 (304)
	Sen. Elem/Some	19·4	5·0	42·8	20·0	20·4	18·3	24·1	44·2	15·6	12·5	23·5	100·0 (120)
	Gram/None	9·6	10·7	3·6	7·1	9·3	35·8	5·0	39·3	2·1	7·1	5·5	100·0 (28)
	Gram/Some	48·4	25·4	16·1	15·3	19·4	35·6	5·5	20·3	2·1	3·4	11·5	100·0 (59)
	Total	100·0 (31)		100·0 (56)		100·0 (108)		100·0 (220)		100·0 (96)		100·0 (511)	

296

5	Sen. Elem/None	19·1	0·9	40·2	4·4	59·3	10·5	68·4	47·0	85·6	37·2	68·7	100·0 (1022)
	Sen. Elem/Some	46·8	6·1	46·4	14·5	34·7	17·5	24·9	48·7	10·6	13·1	24·2	100·0 (359)
	Gram/None	10·6	11·9	0·9	2·4	1·6	7·1	3·0	50·0	2·7	28·6	2·8	100·0 (42)
	Gram/Some	23·5	17·2	12·5	21·9	4·4	12·5	3·7	40·6	1·1	7·8	4·3	100·0 (64)
	Total	100·0 (47)		100·0 (112)		100·0 (182)		100·0 (702)		100·0 (444)		100·0	100·0 (1487)
6 & 7	Sen. Elem/None	11·1	0·2	51·6	2·6	66·7	6·8	74·1	35·2	90·2	55·2	79·7	100·0 (665)
	Sen. Elem/Some	33·3	2·3	33·3	8·4	33·3	17·6	19·3	46·5	8·1	25·2	15·7	100·0 (131)
	Gram/None	0·0	0·0	3·0	5·3	0·0	0·0	3·8	63·2	1·5	31·5	2·3	100·0 (19)
	Gram/Some	55·6	26·3	12·1	21·1	0·0	0·0	2·8	47·3	0·2	5·3	2·3	100·0 (19)
	Total	100·0 (9)		100·0 (33)		100·0 (69)		100·0 (316)		100·0 (407)		100·0	100·0 (834)
Totals	Sen. Elem/None	17·5	2·0	38·3	5·6	53·9	10·8	67·6	42·7	86·0	38·9	64·7	100·0 (2233)
	Sen. Elem/Some	19·8	7·0	34·6	15·3	30·4	18·7	23·1	44·4	10·6	14·6	21·2	100·0 (732)
	Gram/None	18·3	24·9	8·0	13·8	6·4	15·3	4·4	32·8	2·5	13·2	5·5	100·0 (189)
	Gram/Some	44·4	38·5	19·1	20·9	9·3	14·3	4·9	23·3	0·9	3·0	8·6	100·0 (296)
	Grand Total	100·0 (257)		100·0 (324)		100·0 (450)		100·0 (1409)		100·0 (1010)		100·0	100·0 (3450)

(a) The proportions on the left-hand side of each cell indicate the distribution according to educational background of subjects in that cell. The number upon which the proportions are based is shown in brackets.

(b) The proportions on the right-hand side of each cell indicate the status distribution of subjects with a given educational background and status category of father. The number upon which the proportions are based is shown in brackets in the 'Totals' columns at the extreme right-hand side of the table.

General note to Tables 1 and 2: The slight differences in the cell numbers between Tables 1 and 2 are caused by (1) the exclusion from Table 1 of subjects not stating the type of primary school they attended, and (2) the exclusion from the statistics of subjects in status categories 1 and 2 of three subjects not giving information on further education.

would apply to the men whose fathers were in the lower status categories. The percentages in the (*a*) columns in the diagonal cells, bounded by heavy lines, show this to be the case. For those subjects in categories 1 and 2 whose fathers were also at that level of status, 75·8 per cent attended grammar schools and only 24·2 per cent had a 'senior elementary' schooling. And the proportion of subjects who attended grammar schools falls steadily as the status scale is descended. For subjects in categories 6 and 7, whose fathers were in the same categories, only 2 per cent attended grammar schools.

A similar, though not quite the same, picture is seen by examining the (*b*) columns in the diagonal cells. The statistics here indicate the extent to which subjects with a given status background and a given schooling have the same social status as their fathers. The importance of the grammar school is shown here, too, but not with the same consistency. If we take the 'elementary primary and grammar' category, for example, the percentages decline steadily as between subjects whose fathers were in categories 1 and 2 (48·5 per cent), 4 (33·3 per cent) and 6 and 7 (18·2 per cent). But where the fathers were in categories 3 and 5, the influence of schooling is not statistically significant.[1]

The data in Table 2 are given in the same order as those in Table 1, the material now referring to the combined influence of post-primary and further education. Here the distinctions appear to be less sharp. It is not that there is less evidence of the rôle of the grammar school in maintaining at the parental level the status of those subjects whose fathers were in the upper status categories, but that, given this grammar school background, the additional contribution of further education is not, as seen by chi-square tests, generally significant. The point to be remembered here is that status categories 1 and 2 cover not only the professions but also the higher ranks of management in commerce and industry, and that it is for the professions that further education is critical. For the other high status occupations, parental status as such—apart from further education—is important in providing opportunities, while a public school background may have been more important than a university degree. Where, however, it is not a question of achieving the same status as that of their fathers, but of moving up or down in the prestige hierarchy in relation to parental status, the additional contribution of

[1] Chi-square tests were applied here, the material being rearranged to show whether, for a given status of fathers, sons differentiated according to schooling were in the same category as, or in a different category from, that of their fathers. The term 'significant' is used with reference to differences which are significant at the 5 per cent level or above.

further education *is* significant, save for subjects whose fathers were in status category 5. Further education is also important here for those subjects with only a 'senior elementary' school background. Thus where the subjects' fathers were in status categories 3, 4, 6 and 7, those subjects with further education in addition to 'senior elementary' school rose in the status scale to an extent almost equal to that of subjects who had been at grammar schools but had had no further education.

The general discussion in the preceding paragraphs may be made somewhat more explicit by the direct measurement of the number of categories ascended or descended, with reference to the status of their fathers, by subjects with various degrees of educational attainment.[1] It should again be emphasized that the measurement is crude, for it assumes that the distance between any two contiguous categories is the same and equal to one unit. Nevertheless the results, given in Tables 3 and 4, are fairly consistent and are in keeping with the earlier analysis. Thus in Table 3, the mean number of categories of ascent—whatever the status of the fathers—is greater for those subjects with a grammar school education than for those who were at 'senior elementary' schools, the rôle of private primary education being significant in only one case. A similar, though not quite so consistent a picture, is given for descent in status—that is, the mean number of categories descended is smaller, whatever the status of the fathers, for subjects with a grammar school or equivalent education. Again, Table 4 displays a fairly regular pattern of ascent and descent in relation to further education, though there are some deviations. In general, the educational requirements for social ascent seem to be more stringent than those necessary to minimize the degree of social descent. Thus, whatever the status of their fathers, the mean number of categories ascended is greatest for subjects with a combination of grammar school and further education. Except for subjects whose fathers were in categories 6 or 7, the differences in the amount of ascent as between sons with other educational backgrounds are not significant. But for descent, though the fall is generally least for subjects who have had both grammar school and further education, a braking influence is exercised by further education coupled with other primary and post-primary schooling. Save in the case of subjects whose fathers were in categories 1 or 2—and here the distinction is between grammar

---

[1] These measurements apply, of course, only to subjects who did not have the same social status as their fathers—i.e. the number of categories ascended applies to those subjects who achieved higher status than their father, and conversely for the number of categories descended.

school plus further education as against all other educational backgrounds—subjects with 'senior elementary' backgrounds fall a shorter distance if, in addition, they have had some further education.

It has already been explained that, because of the relatively small size of the total sample, the rôle of completed university training cannot be distinguished in the analysis. Nevertheless it is of some interest to take the whole group of those men, numbering 99, who were born before 1929 and who had such education, and to consider them separately.

Table 3

THE INFLUENCE OF THE SUBJECT'S SCHOOLING UPON THE MEAN NUMBER OF CATEGORIES ASCENDED OR DESCENDED BY SUBJECTS FROM GIVEN STATUS CATEGORIES OF FATHERS, TOGETHER WITH THE RESULTS OF 'T' TESTS BETWEEN PAIRS OF MEANS

ASCENT

Subject's Schooling	Father's Category 4		
Elem.: Sen. Elem.	$1 \cdot 228 \pm 0 \cdot 55$		
Elem.: Grammar	*	$1 \cdot 609 \pm 0 \cdot 105$	
Priv.: Grammar	*	†	$2 \cdot 000 \pm 0 \cdot 000$

Subject's Schooling	Father's Category 5		
Elem.: Sen. Elem.	$1 \cdot 532 \pm 0 \cdot 045$		
Elem: Grammar.	*	$2 \cdot 118 \pm 0 \cdot 138$	
Priv.: Grammar	*	‡	$2 \cdot 556 \pm 0 \cdot 243$

Subject's Schooling	Father's Categories 6 and 7		
Elem.: Sen. Elem.	$1 \cdot 341 \pm 0 \cdot 010$		
Elem.: Grammar	†	$1 \cdot 926 \pm 0 \cdot 245$	
Priv.: Grammar	†	†	$1 \cdot 000 \pm 0 \cdot 000$

DESCENT

Subject's Schooling	Father's Categories 1 and 2		
Elem.: Sen. Elem.	$2 \cdot 381 \pm 0 \cdot 122$		
Elem.: Grammar	‡	$2 \cdot 088 \pm 0 \cdot 190$	
Priv.: Grammar	*	‡	$1 \cdot 844 \pm 0 \cdot 155$

Subject's Schooling	Father's Category 3		
Elem.: Sen. Elem.	$1 \cdot 964 \pm 0 \cdot 045$		
Elem.: Grammar	*	$1 \cdot 613 \pm 0 \cdot 089$	
Priv.: Grammar	‡	‡	$1 \cdot 667 \pm 0 \cdot 288$

Subject's Schooling	Father's Category 4		
Elem.: Sen. Elem.	$1 \cdot 318 \pm 0 \cdot 032$		
Elem.: Grammar	*	$1 \cdot 160 \pm 0 \cdot 032$	
Priv.: Grammar	‡	‡	$1 \cdot 500 \pm 0 \cdot 288$

* Significantly different at 1 per cent.
† Significantly different at 5 per cent.
‡ No significant difference.

Table 4

THE INFLUENCE OF THE SUBJECT'S POST-PRIMARY SCHOOLING AND
FURTHER EDUCATION UPON THE MEAN NUMBER OF CATEGORIES
ASCENDED OR DESCENDED BY SUBJECTS FROM GIVEN STATUS
CATEGORIES OF FATHER, TOGETHER WITH THE RESULTS OF 'T'
TESTS BETWEEN PAIRS OF MEANS

ASCENT

Subject's Post-primary Schooling and Further Education — *Father's Category 4*

School	Further Ed.				
Sen. Elem.:	None	1·250 ± 0·084			
Sen. Elem.:	Some	‡	1·200 ± 0·077		
Grammar:	None	‡	‡	1·600 ± 0·600	
Grammar:	Some	*	*	‡	1·625 ± 0·100

Father's Category 5

School	Further Ed.				
Sen. Elem.:	None	1·759 ± 0·045			
Sen. Elem.:	Some	‡	1·701 ± 0·063		
Grammar:	None	‡	‡	2·222 ± 0·324	
Grammar:	Some	†	*	‡	2·091 ± 0·134

Father's Categories 6 and 7

School	Further Ed.				
Sen. Elem.:	None	1·279 ± 0·032			
Sen. Elem.:	Some	*	1·551 ± 0·084		
Grammar:	None	‡	†	1·154 ± 0·155	
Grammar:	Some	*	†	*	2·278 ± 0·320

DESCENT

Father's Categories 1 and 2

School	Further Ed.				
Sen. Elem.:	None	2·518 ± 0·145			
Sen. Elem.:	Some	‡	2·107 ± 0·221		
Grammar:	None	‡	‡	2·259 ± 0·205	
Grammar:	Some	*	‡	‡	1·732 ± 0·145

Father's Category 3

School	Further Ed.				
Sen. Elem.:	None	2·084 ± 0·054			
Sen. Elem.:	Some	*	1·710 ± 0·089		
Grammar:	None	*	‡	1·571 ± 0·148	
Grammar:	Some	*	‡	‡	1·667 ± 0·114

Father's Category 4

School	Further Ed.				
Sen. Elem.:	None	1·636 ± 0·045			
Sen. Elem.:	6ome	*	1·221 ± 0·055		
Grammar:	None	‡	*	1·692 ±0·105	
Grammar:	Some	*	‡	*	1·143 ± 0·063

* Significantly different at 1 per cent.
† Significantly different at 5 per cent.
‡ No significant difference.

The main information regarding these subjects is given in Table 5 below.

Table 5

PARENTAL AND OWN STATUS OF MALE SUBJECTS WITH
UNIVERSITY QUALIFICATIONS

	Percentages	
Status Category	*Father's Status*	*Subject's Final Status*
1 and 2	41·1	60·0
3 and 4	31·6	25·6
5	21·0	14·4
6 and 7	6·3	0·0
	100·0	100·0

Taking the whole group, just over one-quarter had a 'senior elementary' school background. Of the rest, all of whom went to grammar schools or the equivalent, two-thirds began at elementary and the remainder at private primary schools. The ratios of these subjects to the school populations from which they derived were given in Chapter V, where attention was drawn to the differing extent to which boys with different school backgrounds obtained a university education. Here, however, it is relevant to add that while 60 per cent of the whole group of subjects with a university education reached status categories 1 and 2, that proportion is not constant irrespective of the social status of the subjects' fathers. Of those subjects whose fathers were in categories 1 and 2, over four-fifths achieved the same status as their fathers. Where the fathers were in categories 3 and 4, about half of the subjects attained categories 1 and 2. And of subjects whose fathers were in category 5, only two-fifths attained categories 1 and 2.[1]

It should, of course, be emphasized that the differences between these percentages are the result of a combination of factors, and cannot be attributed to the influence of parental social status alone. Differences in 'measured intelligence' and in examination ability will undoubtedly have played their part. But since, in pre-World War II days, the sons of fathers in lower status categories will have largely reached the universities by scholarships and have therefore to a large extent been selected for some attribute or attributes correlated with 'measured intelligence', it is difficult to believe that differences in parental social status as such did not have a substantial effect upon the final status achieved by the subjects.

[1] The differences between these proportions of subjects attaining status categories 1 and 2 are, as shown by chi-square tests, significant at the 1 per cent level.

The Application of the Concept of 'Perfect' Mobility or Association

The relevance of the concept of 'perfect' mobility is rather different in the present context from what it was in preceding chapters. In discussing overall social mobility, the concept was of importance for discounting the change in the distribution of status opportunities between the parental and filial generations, and also as a means of eliminating the effect on measurement of the unequal numbers of individuals in the various status categories. Here, however, movement *within* categories of parental origin is being considered; differences *between* categories of origin are not at issue. Hence the value of the concept of 'perfect' mobility here is to give a greater precision in partialling out the influence of education within given status categories of fathers, rather than to present a picture different from that yielded by the descriptive analysis. For that reason, relatively few indices of Association are presented here. Since in this connection more than one method of applying the concept is possible, the actual method employed will be illustrated with reference to Figure 1 below.

Figure 1

Status Category of Subjects' Fathers	Subjects' Education	Status Category of Subjects		
		1	*Not 1*	*Total*
1	Senior Elementary	a_1	$(b_1 - a_1)$	b_1
	Grammar	a_2	$(b_2 - a_2)$	b_2
Not 1	Senior Elementary		a_3	b_3
	Grammar		a_4	b_4
Total		c_1	c_2	d

In the explanation of the Index of Association given in Appendix 1 to Chapter VIII, the marginal status distributions were taken as fixed—that is, the distributions in the parental and filial generations. The actual number in a given cell—say, $(a_1 + a_2)$ for cell 1/1—was then related to the number expected to be in that cell—say, $(\alpha_1 + \alpha_2)$—on the assumption that the sons of a given category of fathers—say, $(b_1 + b_2)$—are distributed in terms of the existing overall status distribution of subjects, namely in accordance with the ratio (c_1/d). The calculation of indices of Association in the present chapter is based on similar assumptions and methods. Each category of fathers was divided up into the specific educational background of the sons. Expected values for given cells in the matrix were calculated for given educational backgrounds of sons and status categories of fathers. Thus the expected number to be compared with the observed number a_1 in Figure 1 would be $d(b_1/c_1)$. The use of the full status matrix, covering the status distributions of fathers and sons, thus ensures that the entire range of status opportunities represented by the distribution of subjects is taken into account in calculating the indices of Association. The indices so derived were tested for validity —that is, to ascertain if they were significantly different from unity— and tests of the significance of differences between pairs of indices were applied.

The results of these calculations are summarized in Tables 6 and 7, which examine the extent to which the parental-filial association is influenced by the education of the subjects. It is clear, to begin with, that the

Table 6

TESTS OF SIGNIFICANT DIFFERENCES FOR INDICES OF ASSOCIATION BETWEEN STATUS CATEGORIES FOR THE TOTAL MALE SAMPLE, ACCORDING TO THE PRIMARY AND POST-PRIMARY SCHOOLING OF THE SUBJECT

Status Category	Indices of Association Subject's schooling				
(a) Elementary Primary: Senior Elementary School					
1 and 2	3·923				
3	*	1·669			
4	*	‡	1·372		
5	*	†	‡	1·148	
6 and 7	*	‡	‡	*	1·698
(b) Elementary Primary: Secondary Grammar School					
1 and 2	7·228				
3	.*	2·704			
4	*	‡	2·512		
5	*	*	*	1·108	
6 and 7	*	*	*	‡	0·617‖
(c) Private Primary: Secondary Grammar School					
1 and 2	7·336				
3	†	3·279			
4	‡	‡	3·768		
5	*	†	*	0·809‖	
6 and 7	Cell numbers too small to permit statistical test.				

* Significantly different at 1 per cent level.
† Significantly different at 5 per cent level.
‡ No significant difference.
‖ Index not valid—i.e. not significantly different from 1·0.

general conclusions of Chapter VIII tend to apply, whatever the educational background of the subjects. That is, the highest degree of association is found in categories 1 and 2, and the lowest in category 5. The rôle of education, regarded in a positive way, is to intensify the association for the upper categories and to weaken it for the lower categories. In Table 6, for example, the indices for categories 1 and 2, and 3 and 4 rise consistently in passing from 'senior elementary' to 'private primary and grammar' schooling, while for categories 5, 6 and 7 they appear to

Table 7

TESTS OF SIGNIFICANT DIFFERENCES FOR INDICES OF ASSOCIATION BETWEEN STATUS CATEGORIES FOR THE TOTAL MALE SAMPLE, ACCORDING TO THE POST-PRIMARY SCHOOLING AND FURTHER EDUCATION OF THE SUBJECT

Status Category	Indices of Association Subjects' Post-primary and Further Education				
(a) Senior Elementary School: No Further Education					
1 and 2	3·265				
3	†	1·711			
4	*	‡	1·387		
5	*	†	‡	1·150	
6 and 7	*	‡	†	†	1·885
(b) Senior Elementary School: Some Further Education					
1 and 2	4·027				
3	†	1·558			
4	*	‡	1·406		
5	*	‡	‡	1·104	
6 and 7	*	†	‡	‡	1·079
(c) Grammar School: No Further Education					
1 and 2	2·281				
3	†	3·376			
4	*	‡	2·738		
5	*	*	†	1·224	
6 and 7	*	†	†	‡	0·860‖
(d) Grammar School: Some Further Education					
1 and 2	8·081				
3	*	2·505			
4	*	‡	2·729		
5	*	*	*	0·995‖	
6 and 7	Cell numbers too small to permit statistical test.				

* Significantly different at 1 per cent level.
† Significantly different at 5 per cent level.
‡ No significant difference.
‖ Index not valid.

fall with equal consistency. A similar pattern with respect to the influence of post-primary and further education emerges from Table 7. Not all the apparent differences between the indices for a given status category with different educational backgrounds are significant. Indeed, a matrix constructed to test such differences shows that for categories 3 and 5, differences in educational background do not significantly influence the size of the indices of Association. For the remaining categories, however, the indices divide significantly at the grammar school line, and are in keeping with the general pattern described.[1] The same kind of results are obtained when the subjects are divided into two cohorts—those born before 1900 and those born in the period 1900–29. Moreover, the indices do not differ significantly as between cohorts for any status category or educational group, thus supporting the conclusions of Chapters VIII and IX, that in the period from the end of the nineteenth century until World War II the social structure in Britain was a very stable one.

Conclusion

The analysis has shown that education acts in two ways to influence the relation between the status of the subjects and their fathers. In the first place, the type of secondary schooling affects the degree of association between parental and filial status. From this point of view it is the effect of the grammar school (or its equivalent) which stands out sharply. Given a grammar school background, there is a high parental-filial association for subjects whose fathers were in the upper status categories and a low association for subjects whose fathers were in the lower status categories. For the latter group of subjects, a grammar school education increases the distance ascended in the status scale; for the former group, it reduces the distance descended. Secondly, further education appears generally as a reinforcing rather than as a critical agent. The decisive stage in the educational background is the grammar school or its equivalent. If that stage is attained, further education intensifies the parental-filial association for the sons of upper status fathers and still further increases the social ascent of the sons of lower status fathers.[2] For sub-

[1] As in the case of the descriptive analysis, the tests of the indices of Association show that, for status categories 6 and 7, the effect of senior elementary schooling plus further education is to lower very significantly the Index of Association as compared with that shown for senior elementary schooling alone.

[2] An examination of the indices of Association for successive ages of subjects—not reported in the text—shows that, for a given educational background, the characteristic parental-filial status association is established early in the sons' careers.

jects coming from the lower half of the status scale—excluding category 5—further education in itself helps to promote the ascent of those individuals whose secondary education ceased at the 'senior elementary' school level.

In weighing up the meaning of these results, however, it is necessary to remember that, in the period covered by the data, the type of education attained by the subjects is itself heavily dependent upon the social status of their fathers. Hence parental social status and child's education tend to reinforce each other in determining filial social status. Moreover, even though, for those subjects who attain it, grammar school and further education are important in the maintenance or achievement of relatively high social status, the characteristic parental-filial association found in Chapters VIII and IX still tends to apply, whatever the educational background of the subjects. For any given educational background the indices of Association are still highest when the subjects' fathers are professional men or occupy the upper ranks of administration or management, and they are still generally lowest when the fathers are skilled manual workers or routine non-manual workers. Education as such appears to modify, but not to destroy, the characteristic association between the social status of fathers and sons.

XI

Self-recruitment in Four Professions

R. K. KELSALL

T HE discussion of social mobility contained in Chapters VIII and IX related to movement between a small number of very broad strata constructed from groups of occupations. This was inevitable, for the number of persons covered by the sample survey is far too small to allow specific occupations, or even narrow occupational groups, to be examined. As was pointed out earlier, this limitation of the analysis may result in an under-estimate of the frequency of movement between generations. It may also hide differences in social mobility as between Scotland and England and Wales.

With the information now available, no really comprehensive study of recruitment to sub-sections of the various status categories can be undertaken. Indeed, it is not possible at present to say how, in terms of social origins, the members of any one profession have been recruited. There are, however, data which throw some light on entry to the professions. The data are not 'representative' in a full sense. They do not, for example, relate to all universities or all professions, and they omit those entrants to the legal profession who do not proceed via a university. Nevertheless, they afford some indication of the degree of professional self-recruitment, and they show up differences between certain universities.

In two articles in the *Sociological Review* for 1938 Collier showed, for Glasgow University in the period 1926–35, the extent of self-recruitment in teaching, Medicine, the Church and the Law, and also the numerical importance of the children of fathers in these four professions amongst students of that University (other than those taking degrees in Science or Engineering).[1] Collier's conclusions may now be looked at in the light of material relating to certain other British universities at different dates,

[1] Adam Collier, 'Social origins of a sample of entrants to Glasgow University', *Sociological Review*, Vol. 30, 1938.

as a result of four further inquiries which have been undertaken during the last few years.

1. In 1945 a committee appointed by the Cambridge University Appointments Board reported the results of an inquiry into the posts obtained by Cambridge graduates of 1937 and 1938.[1]
2. Student entry records of one Scottish and a number of English universities and colleges for 1947–8 formed the basis of a P.E.P. broadsheet, 'University students', issued in March 1950.[2]
3. An article on Cambridge alumni in the period 1750–1900 appeared in the *British Journal of Sociology* in June 1950.[3]
4. For the purpose of the present study, an analysis was made of the printed records relating to the 4,500 students graduating from Aberdeen University between 1901 and 1925. As those responsible for two of the other three studies were kind enough to allow the present writer access to the original data on which their reports were compiled, it was possible to make statistical tabulations on a broadly comparable basis.

With the aid of this material an attempt may be made to answer two questions.

1. To what extent did the student or graduate children of fathers in the four specified professions follow in their fathers' footsteps?
2. What proportion of those entering any of these professions had fathers either in the particular profession concerned or in one of the other three?

Table 1

NUMBER OF CASES EXAMINED

Cambridge 1850–99	502	Random sample of all Cambridge alumni of the period.
Cambridge 1937 and 1938	2295	Tutors' reports on all men going down from Cambridge in those years.
Aberdeen 1901–25	4532	All graduates (the figures in tables 6 and 8 relate to males only).
Glasgow 1926–35	6911	[4]All students in law, medicine, theology and arts with occupied fathers whose occupation was known.
'A Scottish University', 1947–8	578	All students entering a Scottish University in that session; they specified their intended careers.

[1] Cambridge University Appointments Board: *University Education and Business*.
[2] P.E.P., 'University Students', *Planning*, Vol. XVI, No. 310, 13 March 1950.
[3] Hester Jenkins and D. Caradog Jones, 'Social class of Cambridge University alumni of the eighteenth and nineteenth centuries', *Brit. J. Sociology*, Vol. I, No. 2, June 1950.
[4] See footnote on next page.

Table 2

THE PERCENTAGE OF ALL STUDENTS OR GRADUATES HAVING FATHERS IN CERTAIN PROFESSIONS, WHO CHOSE THE SAME PROFESSIONS AS THEIR FATHERS

University	Teaching		Medicine		Church		Law		All 4 professions	
	Sons	Children	Sons	Children	Sons	Children	Sons	Children	Sons	Children
Cambridge 1850–99	20		29		55		33		43	
Cambridge 1937 & 1938	36		56		33		48		44	
Aberdeen 1901–25	34	50	84	76	24	15	52	35	44	42
[1] Glasgow 1926–35	37	69	82	68	21	16	74	62	52	58
'A Scottish University' 1947–8	30	36	57	50	22	14	40	20	37	33

Table 3

THE PERCENTAGE OF ALL STUDENTS OR GRADUATES HAVING FATHERS IN CERTAIN PROFESSIONS, WHO CHOSE ONE OF THE OTHER THREE PROFESSIONS

University	Teaching		Medicine		Church		Law	
	Sons	Children	Sons	Children	Sons	Children	Sons	Children
Cambridge 1850–99	47		40		20		37	
Cambridge 1937 and 1938	11		20		35		16	
Aberdeen 1901–25	45	32	6	11	67	71	33	45
[1] Glasgow 1926–35	63	31	18	32	79	84	26	38
'A Scottish University' 1947–8	30	25	7	10	11	36	40	50

1. To what extent did the student or graduate children of fathers in these four professions follow in their fathers' footsteps?

(a) *Teaching:* It is clear from Table 2 that teaching was held in comparatively low regard by the sons of teachers at Cambridge in the latter half of the nineteenth century; only one in five of them followed his father's profession. Nearly half of them (as can be seen from Table 3) chose one of the other three professions in preference to teaching: and their choice was most commonly

[1] Attention should be drawn to the fact that Collier's Glasgow material differs in three important respects from the data for other universities used in the present study. (1) His inquiry was restricted to students in four faculties only—Law, Medicine, Theology and Arts. (2) Collier worked on the assumption that all these students intended to follow one of our four professions. This explains why the Glasgow percentages in each column in Tables 2 and 3 add up to 100. (3) His figures only include those with occupied fathers whose occupations were known.

Provided that small differences are ignored, the Glasgow percentages can, however, be compared with the others. In Tables 2 and 3 they represent a slight overestimate of the proportions intending to follow these four professions.

the Church. By 1937 and 1938 a marked change had occurred in their attitude. For one thing, 36 per cent of them now became teachers. For another, only one in ten now chose one of the other three professions in preference to teaching; and of those who did, there was a fairly even distribution among the Church, Medicine and the Law, though the first of these still held the lead.

The position at Aberdeen in the first quarter of the present century was similar to that in pre-war Cambridge. But for Aberdeen there is also information about graduate daughters; and their much greater tendency to go in for teaching (because of lack of alternative opportunities) raises the proportion, for the graduate *children* of teachers, to half. When the propensity to enter the other three professions is examined, the initial resemblance between the Aberdeen and Cambridge cases disappears. For not very much less than half of the Aberdeen sons (and a third of the Aberdeen children) of teachers went in for Medicine, the Church or the Law, while there was a much wider occupational dispersion of the Cambridge counterparts.

Collier's pre-war data for Glasgow show a similar tendency on the part of teachers' student sons to aim at becoming teachers; but a much greater tendency even than in the earlier Aberdeen case for daughters to do so. The natural explanation of this would be that the large increase in the demand for women teachers that took place in the intervening years was catered for more by the daughters of teachers than by daughters in general because the former had, as it were, inside knowledge of the improved opportunities, and were probably given more parental encouragement and help in grasping these opportunities. With the sons of teachers, the position was different. As in the earlier Aberdeen case (but to an even more marked extent), Medicine attracted overwhelmingly more recruits from the ranks of teachers' student sons than did the Law or the Church, and also more than teaching itself succeeded in attracting. This may well have been because the financial rewards of success in the medical profession greatly exceeded those in teaching, and more than compensated for the longer and more expensive training required. It may also support Collier's view that, as the first tremendous increase in the number of teachers had necessarily been achieved by drawing heavily upon the lower social strata, the urge towards still further upward social mobility for their sons was correspondingly strong. The

311

post-war data on student entry to a Scottish University rather suggest that these forces may have worked themselves out. One year's entry at one university does clearly not permit of generalization. But as far as the data go, Medicine and teaching appear to have an equal appeal to the student sons of teachers, but an appeal substantially less than in earlier Scottish experience. A very marked decline in teaching as an occupation for the daughters of teachers is also suggested.

(b) *Medicine:* In the latter part of the nineteenth century, rather less than a third of the Cambridge sons of doctors became doctors themselves; and a further 40 per cent of them entered one of the other three professions. In total, more than two-thirds of them took up one of the four professions, a proportion similar to that for the Cambridge sons of teachers. As in the case of teachers' sons, the Church had a strong appeal, stronger than that of their fathers' own professions, and very much stronger than that of either of the other two vocations. But the change that had taken place by 1937 and 1938 was even more striking than in the case of teaching. Fifty-six per cent of doctors' sons now took up Medicine, and only 1 in 5 was attracted by the other three professions.

The entry of Aberdeen graduate sons of doctors into their fathers' profession was, however, still stronger; nearly seven-eighths of them took medical degrees. The other three professions were almost out of the running so far as they were concerned, and even the inclusion of doctors' daughters only reduces the self-recruitment ratio to a little less than four-fifths. That this position obtained in Scotland generally during most of the pre-war period seems probable from the evidence of the Glasgow material, the main difference in the latter case being the greater tendency of doctors' daughters (like teachers' daughters) to go in for teaching. Even if, as the student entry data for a Scottish university in 1947–8 might suggest, there has since been some decline in the extent of self-recruitment in the medical profession, it appears to be still, at 57 per cent for student sons and 50 per cent for sons and daughters, very much higher than in any of the other three professions. The ability to hand on a practice to a son, or to take him into partnership, is no doubt an important factor in this self-recruitment.

(c) *The Church:* In Cambridge at the earlier period the Church had by far the highest rate of self-recruitment amongst the four professions; no fewer than 55 per cent of the graduate sons of clergymen followed in their fathers' footsteps. A further 20 per cent took up one of the other three professions, teaching being the most popular. The decline in the popularity of the Church as a career, which was noticed in the case of teachers' and doctors' sons at Cambridge, also affected clergymen's sons, only a third of whom entered their fathers' profession in 1937 and 1938. Another third went in for the other three professions, of which teaching, as in the earlier period, was the most popular.

In Scotland the Church seems to have had less appeal to the graduate or student sons of ministers as a profession during the periods for which information is available, and less than a quarter of them chose to follow their fathers. Before the war a very high proportion, of the order of 70 or 80 per cent, chose one of the other three professions. In Aberdeen Medicine had much the greater attraction, and in Glasgow it was teaching that held this position. In both these universities, teaching was the occupation followed by the bulk of ministers' daughters with a university training. The student entry material for 1947–8 shows a wider range of prospective occupations amongst ministers' sons, and only a third of them proposed to enter any of the four professions concerned.

(d) *The Law:* The general trend in the popularity of the legal profession seems to have been similar to that of Medicine. In the second half of the nineteenth century, less than a third of the Cambridge sons of barristers and lawyers chose a legal career; the other three professions taken together were more popular, with the Church or teaching as the commonest choice after the Law itself. By 1937 and 1938, however, nearly half of the graduate sons of fathers in the legal profession were following the Law; and a further 16 per cent were engaged in one of the other three professions.

In Scotland, too, the rate of self-recruitment among the graduate or student sons of advocates and solicitors was high in the pre-war period—52 per cent in Aberdeen and 74 per cent in Glasgow. In both cases Medicine was the next most popular career for such sons, apart from the Law itself; teaching once again claimed the majority of daughters. The Church was virtually excluded as a career by the sons of lawyers and doctors in pre-war Scotland; and apparently still is, if the limited post-war student entry data are representative. But, as in the case of both Medicine and

313

teaching, this post-war material suggests a decline in the rate of self-recruitment in the legal profession too.

2. What proportion of students or graduates taking up a profession had fathers either in that particular profession or in one of the other three?

(a) *Teaching:* The answer to the first part of this question in the case of the teaching profession is that the proportion, as can be seen from Table 4, has always tended to be small. For sons, the range is from 14 per cent in pre-war Cambridge experience to 2 per cent in pre-war Glasgow; though when daughters as well as sons are considered, the proportion does not fall below 6 per cent. In Scotland for some time past, less than 10 per cent of those taking up teaching as a career appear themselves to have been the children of teachers. In England the high proportion of non-graduates

Table 4

THE PERCENTAGE OF ALL STUDENTS OR GRADUATES CHOOSING CERTAIN PROFESSIONS, WHOSE FATHERS WERE MEMBERS OF THOSE PROFESSIONS

University	Teaching Sons	Teaching Children	Medicine Sons	Medicine Children	Church Sons	Church Children	Law Sons	Law Children	All 4 professions Sons	All 4 professions Children
Cambridge 1850–99	6		33		37		15		27	
Cambridge 1937 & 1938	14		34		33		26		25	
Aberdeen 1901–25	9	9	9	9	18	18	33	32	11	11
Glasgow 1926–35	2	6	9	10	16	17	16	17	6	8
'A Scottish University' 1947–8	6	6	10	10	14	14	14	13	9	9

entering the teaching profession makes it difficult to generalize from the Cambridge figures alone. An examination of the 900 student entry registration forms for 1949 for the training colleges within the area covered by Bristol University Institute of Education shows that, though 19 per cent of the graduate entrants had fathers who were teachers, the proportion of entrants generally who had such fathers was only 6 per cent.[1] It may well be, therefore, that the position in England is not very different from that in Scotland. Turning to the second part of the question, the sons of fathers of all four professions taken together clearly made a much greater contribution to the total number of Cambridge

[1] This analysis was undertaken for the purpose of the present study, thanks to the co-operation of Bristol University Institute of Education.

graduates who became teachers at both periods. That as many as a quarter (or, at the earlier period, a third) of the graduates who became teachers should themselves be the sons of members of the four professions seems a remarkably high proportion; the corresponding figure from the 1949 Bristol material (including non-graduates) is 15 per cent, though this relates to daughters as well as sons. The Scottish evidence suggests that between 10 and 16 per cent of the student or graduate children, and a somewhat smaller proportion of the sons, who went in for teaching had fathers in one of the four professions.

Table 5

THE PERCENTAGE OF ALL STUDENTS OR GRADUATES CHOOSING CERTAIN PROFESSIONS, WHOSE FATHERS WERE MEMBERS OF ANY OF THE FOUR PROFESSIONS

University	Teaching		Medicine		Church		Law		All 4 professions	
	Sons	Children	Sons	Children	Sons	Children	Sons	Children	Sons	Children
Cambridge 1850–99	37		57		50		32		45	
Cambridge 1937 & 1938	27		46		44		36		36	
Aberdeen 1901–25	14	16	25	26	23	23	48	49	22	21
Glasgow 1926–35	6	10	19	22	23	24	24	26	12	14
'A Scottish University' 1947–8	9	12	21	22	14	14	14	13	14	15

(b) Medicine: At both periods about a third of the doctors graduating from Cambridge were themselves the sons of doctors; in Scotland, on the other hand, the proportion was as low as 10 per cent. For the country as a whole the proportion probably lay somewhere between these two extremes. Confirmation of this guess is provided by the results of two 1944 inquiries, among doctors and medical students respectively, undertaken by the British Institute of Public Opinion. A provisional and unpublished analysis of a sample of doctors' replies to the first of these inquiries showed that 19 per cent of them were the children of doctors. In the medical student inquiry the proportion was 21 per cent. These proportions are, of course, greatly increased when account is taken of the children of members of the other three professions. Thus for pre-war Cambridge not much less than half of the entrants to Medicine had fathers in one or other of the four professions, while in Scotland less than a quarter were in that position. Unfortunately the form in which the questions were asked in the two 1944 inquiries does not enable us to say where, between these two extremes, the ratio for doctors or medical students as a whole lay; but it seems reasonable, on the analogy of the previous case, to expect that the national proportion fell somewhere between the percentages for Cambridge and for Scotland.

(c) *The Church:* Although the Church has appeared to offer a weak and declining appeal as a career for clergymen's sons, at Cambridge such sons formed as high a proportion of all entrants to the Church as did doctors' sons of all entrants to the medical profession; and in Scotland they formed a higher proportion than did their counterparts in teaching or in Medicine. The explanation is, of course, that the total recruitment to the Church was not very substantial, so that even a small proportion of clergymen's sons formed an important element in the total. (The higher proportion of teachers' sons becoming teachers was swamped by the large number of other people's sons going in for teaching.) This accounts for the otherwise surprising fact that in Scotland the Church (widely regarded as being a calling rather than a profession) had a larger proportion of entrants whose fathers had followed that vocation than any of the other specified professions except the Law. Of Cambridge men making the Church their career before the war, one in three were the sons of parsons, and two out of five had fathers in one of the four professions. In Scotland, however, the sons of doctors, advocates and solicitors looked askance on the Church as a profession, as we have seen; but ministers' and teachers' sons between them accounted for a little less than a quarter of those going into the Ministry. Latterly even teachers' sons have chosen other careers in preference to the Church, if the 1947–8 student entry material is typical; so that (as can be seen by comparing Tables 4 and 5) the recruitment of ministers has come to be about one-seventh from sons of the manse, none at all from the sons of fathers in teaching, Medicine and Law, and the rest from other occupations.

(d) *The Law:* In Scotland, sons of men in the legal profession formed a higher proportion of those making a career in law than their counterparts in teaching and Medicine. The proportion was similar to that of the Church; unlike that case, however, there was substantial additional recruitment from the sons of men in the other three professions. Thus in Aberdeen nearly half of those who, after a university training, became solicitors and advocates, were the children of fathers in one of the four professions. Even in pre-war Glasgow the proportion was as high as a quarter, though it may have fallen substantially since then.

The available evidence all suggests, then, that recruitment to the four professions considered was relatively much greater from families already engaged in those occupations than from other families. In half a century or so, as may be seen from Table 5, the proportion of Cambridge men taking up these careers whose fathers were teachers, doctors, clergy or lawyers had fallen only from 45 per cent to 36 per cent. The opening of these careers to a wider recruitment has clearly been a slow process, and is still very far from being complete. Even in Scotland, where traditionally a greater opportunity has been given to the 'lad o' pairts' to rise to the top, about one in seven of the entrants to these professions has had the advantage of being born into a doctor's, teacher's, minister's, advocate's or solicitor's family.

Table 6

Aberdeen 1901–25

THE NUMBER OF GRADUATE SONS WITH FATHERS IN SPECIFIED PROFESSIONS WHO FOLLOWED CERTAIN PROFESSIONS

Son's Profession	Father's Profession					
	Teaching	Medicine	Church	Law	Other	Total
Teaching	76	4	34	7	738	859
Medicine	85	116	86	15	924	1226
Church	11	0	45	0	188	244
Law	4	4	7	34	54	103
Other	45	13	18	10	396	482
Total	221	137	190	66	2300	2914

Table 7

Cambridge 1937 and 1938

THE NUMBER OF GRADUATE SONS WITH FATHERS IN SPECIFIED PROFESSIONS WHO FOLLOWED CERTAIN PROFESSIONS

Son's Profession	Father's Profession					
	Teaching	Medicine	Church	Law	Other	Total
Teaching	50	13	28	6	267	364
Medicine	5	92	16	11	144	268
Church	6	6	49	4	82	147
Law	4	13	8	63	159	247
Other	73	39	47	48	1062	1269
Total	138	163	148	132	1714	2295

The material so far presented in this chapter has given a broad picture of the intensity of self-recruitment in the specified professions, and has thrown up differences over time and between universities. But to offer a precise measure of the degree of self-recruitment requires a different approach—the approach followed in Chapter VIII in connection with the general analysis of social mobility. Even if a child's profession were chosen at random from all the professions available, *some* children would still in fact take up their fathers' occupations. Hence it is necessary to compare the degree of self-recruitment expected on this random basis with that actually found in practice in order to ascertain exactly how strong is the tendency to professional self-perpetuation. The data for Aberdeen male graduates 1901–25 and for the Cambridge graduates of 1937 and 1938 are particularly amenable to such an analysis. In both cases, and for each of the four professions, the ratio of the actual to the expected number of sons taking up their fathers' professions was calculated and indices of Association obtained. They are given in Table 8. With an index of 1·0, there would be no association—other than a random one—between sons' and fathers' occupations. An index greater than 1·0 indicates an association, the closeness of the association being suggested by the size of the index. It will be seen from Table 8 that all the indices are greater than unity, and that for every profession save the law, the index for the Cambridge graduates is higher than that for the graduates of Aberdeen. Had the material for both universities related to the same period of time, the differences between the universities would most probably have been still more marked.

Table 8

INDICES OF ASSOCIATION CALCULATED AS EXPLAINED IN THE TEXT FROM THE MATERIAL GIVEN IN TABLES 6 AND 7

	Teaching	Medicine	Church	Law
Aberdeen 1901–25	1·17	2·01	2·83	14·57
Cambridge 1937 and 1938	2·28	4·83	5·17	4·43

Before accepting the implication of the indices, it is, of course, necessary to ascertain that they are significantly different from unity, as well as to assess the significance of the differences between pairs of indices. The relevant tests—described in the Appendix to Chapter VIII—were applied and showed, first, a significant difference from unity in all cases except the teaching profession at Aberdeen, and even in that case there is a 90–95 per cent probability that the difference is significant. Secondly, the differences between the indices for the specific professions are signi-

318

ficant both for Cambridge and for Aberdeen graduates. Thirdly, the differences between the Aberdeen and Cambridge indices for the same profession are significant for all the professions.

It may be argued that two factors which cannot easily be measured tend to weaken the value of comparisons of this type. Thus in the first place, though the range of subjects offered by two universities may be superficially similar, the differing reputations of particular faculties in the two cases may lead students of identical inclinations, and open to the same measure of parental influence, to make a different choice. Secondly, the demand for doctors, teachers and the others also differs both between areas and over time, and the choice of a career must often be influenced by these variations as well. Ideally, both these factors ought to be taken into account. But the error involved in not doing so is probably smaller in a study of relative self-recruitment rates than it would be in a broader survey of recruitment.

What this self-recruitment means in terms of the wider universe of employment may be seen—though admittedly in a very imprecise way— by examining the data for Aberdeen. This university draws its students very largely from a well-defined area, and the parental background of the student population may be related to the occupational structure of the population living within that defined area. In the period to which the figures relate, over seven-eighths of the students at Aberdeen University came from an area of Scotland[1] in which (according to the 1921 census) less than 2 per cent of the occupied male population consisted of teachers, doctors, ministers, advocates and solicitors. Yet 21 per cent of all Aberdeen graduates in the period 1901–25 had fathers in one of these professions. That comparison may be taken as a very rough indication of the inequality of entry to the major professions in the north of Scotland at that time.[2] It should be remembered, moreover, that during the whole of this period Scottish students had the advantage of Carnegie help in paying class fees, this help being given without any means test. No doubt part of the inequality of entry is explained by differences in ability and in aspirations. But aspirations themselves are also related to economic and social status. And financial help alone will not throw open the professions to boys of equal talent. As Collier points out, 'it is not the possession of greater wealth which enables the sons of doctors, lawyers,

[1] Comprising the counties of Aberdeen, Banff, Caithness, Elgin, Inverness, Kincardine, Nairn, Ross and Cromarty, and Sutherland.
[2] This comparison inevitably leaves out of account children going from this area of Scotland to other universities, except where they also graduated at Aberdeen.

clergymen, and teachers to secure so large a proportion of the opportunities to enter those professions, but the position of advantage conferred on them by having a father in one of these professions'.[1] Until this problem has been successfully tackled, true equality of opportunity in entering these and other occupations cannot become a reality.

[1] *Sociological Review*, Vol. 30, p. 274.

XII

Social Mobility and Marriage:
A Study of Trends in England and Wales[1]

JERZY BERENT

Introduction

ONE of the tests of the 'openness' of social structure is the extent of marriage between persons of different social origins. It is a test which has not been used very widely, for the information recorded in official marriage returns is rarely sufficient for the kind of analysis required, while to extract details from a sample of marriage certificates—when those certificates contain a fuller range of data—raises difficult practical problems.[2] But the sample investigation of social mobility in Britain provides an opportunity for a study of inter-marriage, a study which is of interest in itself and which supplements the preceding analysis of social mobility as measured by occupational achievement. Because, however, the information collected for Scotland was rather limited, the material dealt with in this chapter is confined to England and Wales.

The present study is made possible because, as was reported in Chapter IV, the questionnaire used in the investigation of social mobility asked certain additional questions when the person drawn in the sample was married, widowed or divorced. Taking these additional questions into account, the relevant information available for each partner of a marriage (whether or not the marriage was still in being at the time of inter-

---

[1] This study was undertaken as part of the research programme of the Population Investigation Committee.

[2] In Great Britain, the marriage certificates record the occupations of bride and groom, bride's father and groom's father. There is some doubt as to the reliability of the information, at least for England and Wales, but it would nevertheless be most desirable to carry out an analysis of the material for samples of a series of marriage cohorts, and it is intended subsequently to undertake such an analysis.

321

view) covered: the education and occupation (wife's occupation at marriage being recorded); the occupation of the father of each partner; date of marriage and age at marriage. Since, in addition, marital status was recorded for each person interviewed, the proportion ever-married can also be calculated for males and females and for the separate status categories. Most of the tabulations derived from this set of data are self-explanatory. It is, however, necessary to explain how the data on occupation have been used, and why this particular method was adopted.

As in the other chapters on social mobility, occupations have been translated into status categories or categories of social prestige, in accordance with the scale described in Chapter II. Because of the limitation of numbers, however, the sevenfold classification has been compressed, and in the present chapter a fourfold classification has largely been used. To avoid confusion we shall refer to this classification as comprising four social groups, in contrast to the seven status categories used in the preceding analysis of social mobility.

The comparison is shown below:

Status Category	Social Group
1. Professional and high administrative	Group I
2. Managerial and executive	
3. Inspectional, supervisory and other non-manual (higher grade)	Group II
4. Inspectional, supervisory and other non-manual (lower grade)	
5. Skilled manual and routine grades of non-manual	Group III
6. Semi-skilled manual	Group IV
7. Unskilled manual	

Broadly speaking, Group I covers the higher and Group II the lower grades of non-manual workers, Group III the skilled manual and Group IV the semi-skilled and unskilled manual workers.

In applying these categories, however, it was not the occupations of the partners of a marriage which were classified, but those of their fathers. There were three main reasons for this decision. First, in Britain, with limited employment opportunities for women (limited in the sense that relatively few women are able to find their way into occupations of high social prestige), occupation of a woman before marriage is not necessarily a reliable index of social status. This is particularly the case in that many women regard paid employment as a temporary measure to be given up at marriage or, at any rate, by the time of the birth of the first child after marriage—and are thus prepared to accept occupations lower in prestige than those taken up by men of the same social origins and educational qualifications.[1] In such circumstances, the occupation of the father of a woman is a more reliable criterion of status. Secondly, if the social origin of the wife rather than her socio-occupational status is taken, it is logical to use the same approach for her husband, and to classify him in terms of the status of his father. This is the more reasonable in that, because of the age factor, occupation at marriage may not be a satisfactory index of the status of the husband *vis-à-vis* that of his father-in-law. In particular, the husband may at marriage have a lower status than that which he can be reasonably certain of attaining during the subsequent ten years or so—this may be especially true of individuals who can reasonably expect to move from Group IV to Group III or from Group II to Group I—and this expectation may in turn be related to his father's status.[2] Thirdly, by taking social origin rather than achieved status at marriage in the case of both husband and wife, it is possible to deal separately with the variable of education. Thus where there are differences in social origin, the gap may be bridged by similarities in educational attainments.

Educational attainment has been classified on lines similar to those used in the main preceding chapters. Because, however, of the desirability of equating the experience of husbands and wives—having regard to the differences in the availability of the various stages of education to boys and girls in the past—it has been necessary to reduce the number of categories used. The fourfold classification given below does not, in

Title	Definition
A. 'Elementary'	Primary and post-primary education if received in Central or L.E.A. schools.
B. 'Secondary'	Grammar, private secondary and public school education.
C. 'Further Education'	Technical, commercial, etc., training *not* resulting in professional qualifications.
D. 'Higher Education'	University or other further education resulting in professional qualifications.

[1] The study, conducted by the Population Investigation Committee and the Royal College of Obstetricians and Gynaecologists, of all women who bore a child during one week in 1946, showed that of married women expecting their first birth, 58·3 per cent were in gainful employment for some period before their confinement. Of the women expecting a second or subsequent child, however, only 8·7 per cent were in gainful employment. See *Maternity in Great Britain*, Oxford University Press, London, 1948, p. 165.

[2] It should be noted, however, that the occupation recorded for the father of a subject is the last main occupation, not that at the birth or at the marriage of the subject.

consequence, allow the lines of demarcation in socio-educational prestige to be as clear-cut as might have been wished, especially with regard
to the rôle of the public schools.

In some sections of the analysis a further compression has been made,
distinguishing only between 'elementary' and 'higher than elementary'
education. For the subjects covered by the inquiry this broad distinction
is, nevertheless, a significant one.

Intermarriage by Social Origin of Brides and Grooms

The first object of the analysis is to obtain a quantitative expression
of the extent to which brides and grooms tend to find their partners in
the same social milieu or, in statistical terminology, to determine the
magnitude of the association between the social origins of husband and
wife in the sample. The higher the association, the greater the propensity to intra-status marriage or 'class endogamy'.

There are in the sample 6,112 ever-married male and female subjects
aged 18 years and over and resident in England and Wales. For a substantial number of these, the full details required in the analysis were not
available.[1] Table 1 shows the distribution of 5,100 couples, for whom
details of social origin and date of marriage were recorded, distinguishing
social origin of the spouses but not distinguishing date of marriage.

The actual numbers of marriages are stated in the centre of each cell.
The figures in the upper right-hand corners, which should be read
horizontally, show the percentages of husbands born in a specified social
group according to the social group into which they married. Thus,
of all husbands born in Group I, 20·6 per cent married wives born in
Group III. The percentages in the lower left-hand corner, which should
be read vertically, give the distribution of wives born in a given social
group, by the social group of origin of their husbands. Thus of wives
born in Group I, 20·9 per cent married husbands who were born in
Group III.

Even a cursory glance at the figures reveals a consistent concentration of numbers along the diagonal, indicating the presence of a positive
association. For example, among the husbands born in Group I 37·4
per cent married in the same group and 36·0 per cent in the adjacent
Group II, while among those born in Group III 53·8 per cent married in
the same group. Similarly, among wives born in Group I 47·4 per cent
chose their husbands from the same group and so on. Altogether, in

---

[1] Insufficient information made it necessary to exclude 1,012 out of the original
6,112 marriages from the analysis.

2,288 marriages out of 5,100, or in 44·9 per cent of the cases reported, husband and wife had come from the same group of origin. This proportion, which is significantly different from what would be expected to occur by chance, may be called the 'diagonal ratio', and is in fact a first

Table 1

DISTRIBUTION OF HUSBANDS AND WIVES BY SOCIAL GROUP OF ORIGIN. ALL MARRIAGE COHORTS

Social group of origin of husbands	Social group of origin of wives				
	I	*II*	*III*	*IV*	*All*
I	37·4 136 47·4	36·0 131 10·9	20·6 75 3·2	6·0 22 1·7	100·0 364 7·2
II	6·4 81 28·2	34·2 434 36·3	41·4 524 22·5	18·0 228 17·8	100·0 1267 24·8
III	2·6 60 20·9	19·8 451 37·6	53·8 1225 52·5	23·8 540 42·1	100·0 2276 44·6
IV	0·8 10 3·5	15·3 182 15·2	42·6 508 21·8	41·3 493 38·4	100·0 1193 23·4
All	5·6 287 100·0	23·5 1198 100·0	45·7 2332 100·0	25·2 1283 100·0	100·0 5100 100·0

Diagonal ratio = 44·9, C = 0·43, r = 0·365
Omissions: Social origin u/k: 890
Date of marriage u/k: 122

All	1012
Included:	5100
Grand Total	6112

approximation to a coefficient of association. It will, of course, vary with the number of cells in the table, but even in the original seven-grade classification it comes to the comparatively high figure of 37·1 per cent. Pearson's coefficient of contingency which, in a 4 × 4 table, may range between 0 and 0·866, takes the value of 0·43 for Table 1. The product-moment correlation coefficient, computed by assigning the numbers

1, 2, 3 and 4 to the four social groups (on the assumption that the distances between each of these groups have the same significance) amounts to 0·37.

None of these indices is altogether satisfactory as a measure of association, but they all point to the same conclusion, namely that among the ever-married persons interviewed in England and Wales in 1949—that is among marriages contracted mainly during the first half of the present century—the degree of 'class' endogamy was significantly greater than would be expected to occur by chance.

Table 2

DISTRIBUTION OF HUSBANDS AND WIVES BY SOCIAL GROUP OF ORIGIN AND BY GROUP INTO WHICH MARRIED

Group into which married	Group of origin									
	I		*II*		*III*		*IV*		*All*	
	H's	*W's*	*H's*	*W's*	*H's*	*W's*	*H's*	*W's*	*H's*	*W's*
2 or 3 groups above	—	—	—	—	2·6	3·2	16·1	19·5	4·9	6·4
	—	—	—	—	(60)	(75)	(192)	(250)	(252)	(325)
1 group above	—	—	6·4	10·9	19·8	22·5	42·6	42·1	20·4	23·4
	—	—	(81)	(131)	(451)	(524)	(508)	(540)	(1040)	(1195)
The same group	37·4	47·4	34·2	36·3	53·8	52·5	41·3	38·4	44·9	44·9
	(136)	(136)	(434)	(434)	(1225)	(1225)	(493)	(493)	(2288)	(2288)
1 group below	36·0	28·2	41·4	37·6	23·8	21·8	—	—	23·4	20·4
	(131)	(81)	(524)	(451)	(540)	(508)	—	—	(1195)	(1040)
2 or 3 groups below	26·6	24·4	18·0	15·2	—	—	—	—	6·4	4·9
	(97)	(70)	(228)	(182)	—	—	—	—	(325)	(252)
All	100·0	100·0	100·0	100·0	100·0	100·0	100·0	100·0	100·0	100·0
	(364)	(287)	(1267)	(1198)	(2276)	(2332)	(1193)	(1283)	(5100)	(5100)

Before this is specifically tested with reference to variations through time and between groups, attention should be drawn to Table 2, which is obtained by rearranging the data in the preceding table. It shows the percentage distributions of husbands and wives by their group of origin and by the direction, so to speak, in which they married. The intention here is to compare the proportions of men and women originating from the same social groups, according to whether they married 'above' or 'below' their group of origin.

Inspection of the last two columns of this table shows that among all husbands, irrespective of origin, 29·8 per cent married 'below' themselves as compared with 25·3 per cent of all women. This difference, though small, is statistically significant at the 1 per cent level, and provides an indication of a slight tendency on the part of men to marry below their group of origin, which is, of course, equivalent to saying that the opposite holds for women. This conclusion is supported if we look at each group of origin separately. In a sense this is a consequence of the fact, which appears from the marginal distributions of Table 1, that the proportion of all husbands coming from the higher social groups was slightly larger than the corresponding proportion of wives. Thus 7·2 per cent of all husbands came from Group I and 24.8 per cent from Group II, as against 5·6 per cent and 23·5 per cent of wives respectively. This particular question should not be confused with the allied problem of variations between social groups in the chances of marriage. The inference to be drawn from the data in Table 2 is simply that among those subjects who did marry, a larger proportion of men than women came from the higher social groups.

Table 3

PROPORTIONS (PERCENTAGE) OF PERSONS EVER-MARRIED BY SEX AND SOCIAL ORIGIN

Sex and age	Group of origin:				
	I	II	III	IV	All
Males	93·6	94·3	92·2	95·4	93·6
(aged 50–59)	(47)	(141)	(218)	(130)	(536)
Females	82·6	85·4	86·2	93·4	87·5
(aged 40–49)	(46)	(206)	(391)	(198)	(841)
Ratio of the proportion of males to females	113	110	107	102	107

The question of the chances of marriage is, however, a relevant one, and the data collected in the sample survey throw some light on it. The approach used cannot be of the type which the demographer would prefer—the calculation of net nuptiality tables for males and females in each social group of origin, showing the combined effect of differences in mortality and in marriage frequency. Instead, the proportions of ever-married men and women may be shown, and are given in Table 3. The age-group 40–49 years is used for women as indicating the proportions marrying by the end of the childbearing period. And since mean age at marriage is higher for men than for women, the age-group 50–59

327

years is used for men. The proportions ever-married are obtained by taking the married, widowed and divorced individuals as a percentage of all individuals in the given age-group and group of origin.

An examination of the table brings out two main points. First, there is no noticeable trend in the proportions ever-married among men in the different social groups. For women, however, the proportions increase consistently with decreasing status, the difference between the highest and the lowest social group being around 10 per cent. Secondly, in each social group and in all groups taken together, the proportions ever-married are higher for men than for women. The ratios of the proportions for men and women indicate that differences in the chances of marriage as between men and women decrease consistently with decreasing social status. These points will be referred to again subsequently.

Returning to the question of inter-group marriage, it should be emphasized that Table 1 presents a static picture of the process. To examine the dynamics, it is necessary to construct similar tables for successive cohorts of marriage. Had the size of the sample permitted, it would have been desirable to use quinquennial or decennial groups of marriages, in order to see in detail the trend over time. But in the given sample size, it was necessary to confine the analysis to three groups of marriages. The dividing lines have been chosen on the assumption that war may be an important factor in the process of social equalization. The three groups of marriage selected for analysis are thus those prior to World War I; those of the inter-war years; and those occurring after the outbreak of World War II.

Table 4

ASSOCIATION BETWEEN SOCIAL ORIGIN OF BRIDE AND GROOM, BY PERIOD OF MARRIAGE

Year of marriage	No. of marriages	Diagonal ratio	C.R.*	Contingency coeff.	Coeff. of correlation	C.R.*
Before 1915	903	48·7%		0·49	0·50	
			2·08			4·09
1915–39	2654	44·7%		0·47	0·37	
			1·13			1·15
1940 and later	1543	42·9%		0·41	0·34	
All	5100	44·9%		0·43	0·37	

* Critical ratio.

The basic data are not reproduced in this chapter, but the results of the first stage of the analysis are summarized in Table 4, which presents the same measures of association as were used in connection with Table 1.

It will be noticed that all three measures show a similar trend. They suggest an increase in what may be called marital social mobility or a fall in the extent of 'class' endogamy. The diagonal ratios and the co-efficients of correlation, which are perhaps more sensitive than the co-efficient of contingency, seem to suggest that, on the whole, the effect of the first world war was stronger than that of the second. It will be seen presently that a similar tendency is found in the analysis of trends for the separate social groups.

Table 5

COMPARISON OF INDICES OF ASSOCIATION, DISTINGUISHING FOUR
SOCIAL GROUPS AND THREE PERIODS OF MARRIAGE

Social Group of Origin	Year of Marriage			
	Before 1915	1915–39	1940–	All Cohorts
I	7·764	6·381	6·558	6·639
II	1·633	1·425	1·406	1·458
III	1·218	1·174	1·156	1·177
IV	1·863	1·678	1·482	1·643

Results of Tests of Significance

A. All indices are significantly different from unity.
B. *Between Marriage Cohorts*
   There are no significant differences.
C. *Between Social Groups*
   Before 1915:   There is no significant difference between Groups II and
                  IV. All others differ.
   1915–39:   All differ significantly.
   Since 1939:   There are no significant differences between Groups II and
                  III and II and IV. All others differ.
   All cohorts: There is no significant difference between Groups II and
                  IV. All others differ.

So far the analysis has been concerned only with measuring the degree of association between the social origin of brides and grooms. But this does not by itself give a clear indication of the extent of assortative mating, or of the degree of social mobility within marriage. The same problem arises here as in the study of mobility in terms of occupational achievement, namely that some concept of 'perfect' mobility or random association must be introduced if the relative intensity of endogamy in different social groups and periods of time is to be ascertained. For this purpose, the measure used in earlier chapters—the Index of Association —is used here, too, and Table 5 shows the indices for the four social groups, and for three periods of time. It should once again be empha-sized that, in using the concept of 'perfect' mobility—or, as it would

329

apply here, of 'random' mating—there is no assumption that such a level of 'perfection' should be or is in fact attainable. The sole purpose of the concept is to provide an objective standard with the help of which the *relative* degrees of mobility in different groups and periods may be compared.

In interpreting the movements in the Index, it must also be remembered that the question of statistical significance arises here, as it did in the earlier chapters. We must first see if the indices differ significantly from unity. If they do, it is still necessary to ascertain whether, for a given cohort of marriages, the indices differ significantly as between social groups; and also if, for a given social group, the indices differ significantly as between marriage cohorts. The results of applying tests of significance—of the kind described in Appendix 1 to Chapter VIII— are given in the notes printed under Table 5.

Looking at both the indices themselves and the results of tests of significance, the picture presented is not unlike that given in Chapter VIII on mobility in terms of occupational achievement. The intensity of assortative mating is greatest in Group I, and least in Group III, the latter covering the skilled manual and routine non-manual workers. Once again, the endogamy of Group I seems to be of an exclusivist, positive variety, while that of Group IV—where there is also a fairly high level of assortative mating—may be more residual in character. As in the case of mobility through occupational achievement, the apparent downward trend of the indices over time is not confirmed statistically, and in this case the question of a curtailed exposure to the chances of mobility of individuals in the more recent cohorts does not arise. Nevertheless, the fact that there are fewer significant differences *between* social groups in the post-1939 cohort than in earlier cohorts suggests that there may have been some genuine reduction in the differentials. And this is confirmed in the next stage of the study, the analysis of the relative educational levels of husbands and wives.

Intermarriage by Educational Level of Brides and Grooms

The methods used in studying the association between the social origins of husbands and wives may equally be applied to their educational background, treating this as a separate variable. The results of the initial stage of the analysis are given in Table 6, which shows the distribution of 5,533 couples by the highest level of education they achieved. In 71·6 per cent of the marriages the standard of education of husband and wife was, broadly speaking, the same. The coefficient of contin-

330

gency has a value of 0·44, also indicating a rather high degree of association. Of all husbands, 23·3 per cent had had some type of post-secondary education, while the corresponding figure for wives is 16·6 per

Table 6

DISTRIBUTIONS OF HUSBANDS AND WIVES BY EDUCATIONAL LEVEL.
ALL MARRIAGE COHORTS

Husband's Education	Wife's Education				
	Elementary	Secondary	Further Ed.	Higher Ed.	All
Elementary	83·3 3475 80·9	2·8 109 31·7	8·6 339 42·0	0·3 11 13·1	100·0 3934 71·1
Secondary	41·6 129 3·0	32·6 101 29·4	21·0 65 8·0	4·8 15 17·8	100·0 310 5·6
Further education	58·0 648 15·1	8·4 94 27·3	31·6 353 43·7	2·0 23 27·4	100·0 1118 20·2
Higher education	26·3 45 1·0	23·4 40 11·6	29·8 51 6·3	20·5 35 41·7	100·0 171 3·1
All	77·7 4297 100·0	6·2 344 100·0	14·6 808 100·0	1·5 84 100·0	100·0 5533 100·0

Diagonal ratio = 71·6 per cent, C = 0·44
Omissions: Education u/k: 458
Date of marriage u/k: 121

	All	579
Included:		5533
	Grand Total	6112

cent.[1] It would therefore be expected that the proportion of men who married women of a lower educational standard is greater than the proportion of women who married men less well educated than themselves. That this is so may be seen from Table 7, in which the percentages of those marrying 'above' and 'below' themselves in terms of educational

[1] The difference is statistically significant at the 1 per cent level.

background are compared for each category of education of husbands and wives.

Thus the last two columns of the table show that 18·2 per cent of all men married below their own educational level, as against 10·2 per cent of all women. The same tendency is noticeable within each educational grade. Among men who had no more than an 'elementary' education, 16·7 per cent married above their own level, while the corresponding figure for women is 19·9 per cent. Again, 41·7 per cent of men with 'secondary' education married below their own level, as compared with 31·7 per cent of women.

Table 7

DISTRIBUTIONS OF HUSBANDS AND WIVES BY EDUCATIONAL LEVEL
AND DIRECTION OF MARRIAGE

Direction of marriage	Educational level									
	Elementary		Secondary		Further Ed.		Higher Ed.		All	
	H's	W's	H's	W's	H's	W's	H's	W's	H's	W's
3 grades above	0·3 (11)	1·0 (45)	—	—	—	—	—	—	0·2 (11)	0·8 (45)
2 grades above	8·6 (339)	15·1 (648)	4·8 (15)	11·6 (40)	—	—	—	—	6·4 (354)	12·4 (688)
1 grade above	2·8 (109)	3·0 (129)	21·0 (65)	27·3 (94)	2·0 (23)	6·3 (51)			3·6 (197)	5·0 (274)
The same grade	83·3 (3475)	80·9 (3475)	32·6 (101)	29·4 (101)	31·6 (353)	43·7 (353)	20·5 (35)	41·7 (35)	71·6 (3964)	71·6 (3964)
1 grade below	—	—	41·6 (129)	31·7 (109)	8·4 (94)	8·0 (65)	29·8 (51)	27·4 (23)	5·0 (274)	3·6 (197)
2 grades below	—	—	—	—	58·0 (648)	42·0 (339)	23·4 (40)	17·8 (15)	12·4 (688)	6·4 (354)
3 grades below	—	—	—	—	—	—	26·3 (45)	13·1 (11)	0·8 (45)	0·2 (11)
All	100·0 (3934)	100·0 (4297)	100·0 (310)	100·0 (344)	100·0 (1118)	100·0 (808)	100·0 (171)	100·0 (84)	100·0 (5533)	100·0 (5533)

Changes over time in the degree of association are summarized in Table 8, where the diagonal ratios and coefficients of contingency are compared for three groups of marriages. Both indices suggest a fall in the propensity to marry partners of the same educational level. And this fall is also visible when the various educational categories are examined separately. Table 9 presents the relevant indices of Association, all of which differ significantly from unity, and also summarizes the results of applying tests of significance to the differences between the

Table 8

ASSOCIATION BETWEEN EDUCATIONAL LEVEL OF BRIDE AND GROOM, DISTINGUISHING THREE PERIODS OF MARRIAGE

Year of Marriage	Number of Marriages	Diagonal Ratio		Standard Error	Coefficient of Contingency
Before 1915	1006	83·6%	±	1·2%	0·49
1915–39	2889	72·9%	±	0·8%	0·45
1940 and later	1638	62·1%	±	1·2%	0·41
All	5533	71·6%		0·6%	0·44

indices. From these results it may be inferred that, save for the 'elementary' education group, there have been significant decreases over time in the propensity of like to marry like. Hence while, for the most recent cohort, there are still significant differences between the various groups (except for the 'secondary' and 'further' education groups), the intensity of assortative mating has changed, though this change was not reflected in the indices for social origins, given in Table 5.

Table 9

COMPARISON OF INDICES OF ASSOCIATION, DISTINGUISHING FOUR EDUCATIONAL CATEGORIES AND THREE PERIODS OF MARRIAGE

Type of Education	Before 1915 (1)	Year of marriage 1915–39 (2)	1940 and later (3)
A. Elementary	1·087	1·124	1·183
B. Secondary	9·776	6·213	2·533
C. Further	4·130	2·220	1·610
D. Higher	30·043	11·928	10·568

Results of applying Tests of Significance:

I. Between marriage cohorts.

Type of education
- A: no significant differences.
- B: (3) differs from (1) and (2).
- C: all three differ significantly.
- D: (1) differs from (2) and (3).

II. Between types of education.
- Cohort (1): all four types differ significantly.
- Cohort (2): all four types differ significantly.
- Cohort (3): no significant differences between B and C; all others differ significantly.

333

Education and Social Origin of Brides and Grooms

In the preceding sections of this chapter, the social origins of individuals and their educational background have been treated as separate variables. The analysis of assortative mating in terms of these two variables yielded similar results, and this is hardly surprising since the two variables are known to be positively correlated. But the correlation is not a perfect one, and it is therefore of interest to see whether differences between husband and wife with regard to one variable are compensated by similarities with regard to the other. Some information bearing upon this question is given in Table 10, in which the relative positions of husbands and wives are shown for both social origin and education. To simplify the table, only two levels of education are distinguished— 'elementary' and 'higher than elementary'.

Table 10

DISTRIBUTION (PERCENTAGE) OF MARRIAGES BY EDUCATIONAL LEVEL OF THE PARTNERS AND BY THEIR RELATIVE SOCIAL ORIGIN

Husband's education	Husband's social origin compared with that of wife	Wife's education:					
		Elementary		Higher than Elementary		All	
Elementary	Higher	28·5	(864)	26·3	(105)	28·2	(969)
	Same	46·5	(1411)	43·6	(174)	46·2	(1585)
	Lower	25·0	(758)	30·1	(120)	25·6	(878)
	All	100·0	(3033)	100·0	(399)	100·0	(3432)
Higher than Elementary	Higher	35·9	(267)	31·0	(212)	33·7	(479)
	Same	40·5	(301)	44·2	(302)	42·3	(603)
	Lower	23·6	(175)	24·8	(169)	24·1	(344)
	All	100·0	(743)	100·0	(683)	100·0	(1426)
All	Higher	30·0	(1131)	29·3	(317)	29·8	(1448)
	Same	45·3	(1712)	44·0	(476)	45·0	(2188)
	Lower	24·7	(933)	26·7	(289)	25·2	(1222)
	All	100·0	(3776)	100·0	(1082)	100·0	(4858)

Among marriages in which the partners had the same educational level (upper left and lower right-hand cells in Table 10), and also among marriages in which the husband had a higher level of education than his wife, the proportion of husbands coming from a higher social group than their wives is larger than that coming from a lower social group.

The position is reversed in cases where the wife is 'better educated' than her husband. Hence the slight tendency for men to marry women of a lower social origin than their own, described in the first section of this chapter, is also noticeable for marriages in which the partners have the same educational level, and is apparently more marked where the partners have both had a 'higher than elementary' education (6·5 per cent as compared with 3·5 per cent for partners with an 'elementary' education).

Table 11

DISTRIBUTION (PERCENTAGE) OF MARRIAGES, SHOWING THE RELATIVE POSITION OF HUSBAND AND WIFE WITH RESPECT TO EDUCATION AND SOCIAL ORIGIN

Husband's social group of origin as compared with wife's	Husband's educational level as compared with wife's			
	Lower	Same	Higher	All
Lower	**11·0** 134 27·2	**71·5** 874 25·3	**17·5** 214 23·6	**100·0** 1222 25·2
Same	**9·8** 214 43·5	**72·9** 1595 46·1	**17·3** 379 41·7	**100·0** 2188 45·0
Higher	**9·9** 144 29·3	**68·3** 989 28·6	**21·8** 315 34·7	**100·0** 1448 29·8
All	**10·1** 492 100·0	**71·2** 3458 100·0	**18·7** 908 100·0	**100·0** 4858 100·0

The difference is largest for marriages in which the husband is 'better educated' than his wife (12·3 per cent). Where the reverse is the case— where the wife is 'better educated' than her husband—the husband tends to come from a lower rather than from a higher social group than his wife. But marriages in which there is a discrepancy as regards both the social origin *and* educational level of the partners are comparatively few.

This latter point may be seen with greater precision in Table 11, in which the relative positions of husbands and wives are shown with reference to both variables. In constructing the table, the fourfold classification of educational level has been used—instead of the twofold classification given in Table 10—in order to avoid overestimating the intensity of assortative mating. Hence the results will not agree exactly with those derived from the previous table.[1] The broad lines, however, are closely similar and show a high degree of association on both variables between husband and wife. Of the 4,858 marriages covered by the table, in only 134 is the husband lower in both social origin and educational status than his wife, and in only another 315 cases is he above his wife on both counts. Thus in only 449, or 9·2 per cent of the marriages are there deviations in the same direction on both variables. On the other hand, in 83·4 per cent of the marriages the partners were matched at least as regards one variable, while in 32·8 per cent of the marriages they were matched on both education and social origin. This association between educational and social characteristics of partners in marriages may be examined in terms of the concept of 'perfect' mobility, accepting as given the existing relationships between husband and wife on either of the two variables. Taking as given, for example, the fact that among the 4,858 husbands covered by Table 11, 1,222 would have a lower social origin than their wives, and 492 would have a lower educational level, the 'expected' number lower on both characteristics would be (1,222 × 492)/4,858, or 124, and this may be compared with the 134 actually shown in the table. Analysis of this kind shows a significant difference between expected and actual values in two cases. The ratio of actual to expected values is significantly greater than unity in the case in which husbands have both a higher educational level and a higher social origin than their wives (the ratio is 1·16), thus confirming as significant the slight tendency of men to marry 'downwards', and also in the case in which husbands and wives are matched on both characteristics (the ratio is 1·02).

One further point may be noted in Table 11, namely the rôle of education as compared with social origin in assortative mating. The position is shown in Table 12, from which it would appear that, as a single factor, education is more important than social origin. Of the total sample, the education of husband and wife was the same in 71·2 per cent of the cases; while in only 45·0 per cent of cases was social origin the same. That these two proportions are significantly different from each other is confirmed by a chi-square test. In terms of social reality, of course, the characteristics cannot be regarded as independent variables. Moreover, the education of the husband (for a particular social

---

[1] That is so because one-grade differences in education may, in a twofold classification, be classified as 'same education' in Table 10. In Table 11 they would be treated as 'higher' or 'lower'.

origin) is linked to the husband's own achieved social status, so that the relative rôle of social status is probably greater than the figures suggest.[1] Nevertheless, the material in Tables 11 and 12 does, within the limits defined, appear to describe an important social fact. The same fact may also be seen by examining separately the groups in which either education or social origin is matched for husband and wife. Thus, in Table 11, taking the group of marriages in which there is matching on education, a relatively substantial degree of discrepancy in social origin is possible, namely 53·9 per cent. But in the group in which husband and wife have the same social origin, the degree of discrepancy in education is only 27·1 per cent.[2]

Table 12

DISCREPANCY OR AGREEMENT IN EDUCATION AND SOCIAL ORIGINS
IN MARRIAGES COVERED BY TABLE 11

	No. of marriages	Percentage of total
1. Agreement in *either* social origin or educational level	4051	83·4
2. Agreement at least in educational level	3458	71·2
3. Agreement at least in social origin	2188	45·0
4. Either higher *or* lower on *both* characteristics	449	9·3
5. No agreement	358	7·3
Total	4858	

Conclusion

Looking over the material discussed in the preceding pages, the following points emerge from this national sample study of intermarriage. First, whether measured in terms of social origin or educational level, there is a significant amount of assortative mating in England and Wales, the degree of association between husband and wife being greatest in the top and bottom status categories. As in the case of mobility obtained by occupational achievement, the category of skilled manual workers shows the least rigidity. So far as education is concerned, the least marital mobility is found among individuals who have had university or other 'higher' education. Secondly, in those marriages in which

[1] The question of the particular educational classification used is also of great importance.

[2] It should, however, be emphasized that the particular educational grouping used inevitably affects the results, and that the grouping used here is far too broad for the results to be definitive.

the partners differ with respect to one or other of the variables selected, there is a slight tendency for men to marry 'downwards'. Thirdly, over the past fifty years the degree of social endogamy appears to have declined. Although the fall in the indices of Association for status origins is not statistically significant, there is no doubt about the significance of the decline in the indices for all the educational types save elementary education. This is relevant not only to the question of social mobility as such, but also to more general demographic questions. It is not unlikely that the loosening of the degree of educational association in marriage, along with the increase in territorial mobility and the consequent expansion of the geographical area within which individuals meet and marry, have been responsible for part of the increase in the chances of marriage visible since 1911. Social mobility in marriage may, therefore, have an important bearing upon the demographic replacement of the community as a whole.[1]

[1] It is unfortunate that so little systematic work has been done in Britain—or elsewhere, for that matter—on changes in the geographic area within which individuals meet and marry. Because of the limitations of a survey designed to supply material for three inquiries, questions bearing upon this problem could not be included in the present study. Information could be obtained by sampling the local marriage records, but so far as we know, this has been done only for a group of rural parishes in Hertfordshire. The study, undertaken by Mr. V. Pons, has not yet been published. The material shows, however, a fall of some 50 per cent over the past century in the extent to which both partners in a marriage were resident in the same or in an immediately contiguous parish.

Social Mobility and Age at Marriage

RAMKRISHNA MUKHERJEE

T HE object of this note is to see whether there is any relation between the age at marriage of an individual and the social status
of his or her father and father-in-law, social status being defined
in terms of the sevenfold classification discussed previously. The study is
based on the sample inquiry covering individuals aged 18 years and over
in England and Wales in 1949.

Table 1 gives the age at marriage of the male and female subjects
classified by the status of their fathers-in-law in the case of male subjects and of their fathers in the case of female subjects. The classification
by social status hierarchy thus refers to the same affine types of grooms
and brides.

Table 1

Social status category of the groom's father-in-law and the bride's father	Bridegroom		Bride	
	No.	Mean age at marriage	No.	Mean age at marriage
(1)	(2)	(3)	(4)	(5)
1	59	$27 \cdot 81 \pm 0 \cdot 73$	63	$26 \cdot 35 \pm 0 \cdot 76$
2	75	$28 \cdot 07 \pm 0 \cdot 58$	97	$27 \cdot 27 \pm 0 \cdot 80$
3	248	$28 \cdot 37 \pm 0 \cdot 42$	267	$26 \cdot 04 \pm 0 \cdot 45$
4	324	$27 \cdot 32 \pm 0 \cdot 41$	376	$25 \cdot 79 \pm 0 \cdot 39$
5	1093	$26 \cdot 49 \pm 0 \cdot 18$	1243	$24 \cdot 55 \pm 0 \cdot 18$
6	311	$26 \cdot 53 \pm 0 \cdot 38$	337	$24 \cdot 57 \pm 0 \cdot 39$
7	297	$25 \cdot 81 \pm 0 \cdot 34$	343	$23 \cdot 46 \pm 0 \cdot 26$
Total	2407	$26 \cdot 80 \pm 0 \cdot 13$	2726	$24 \cdot 87 \pm 0 \cdot 13$

The application of analysis of variance to the above data yields no
significant difference between the status categories for either the brides
or the grooms. But 't' tests applied to the mean values for different status

339

categories show that the first four categories (1–4) appear to be significantly different from the last three categories (5–7).

In Table 2 the mean ages at marriage of the male and female subjects are shown against the relative social status of their fathers and fathers-in-law.

Table 2

BRIDEGROOMS (NUMBER IN BRACKETS)

Father-in-law's social status category (1)	Age of the groom at marriage whose father's social status in relation to father-in-law's was		
	Higher (2)	Same (3)	Lower (4)
1	—	(23) 28·57 ± 1·13	(36) 27·33 ± 0·96
2	(12) 29·58 ± 1·56	(22) 28·68 ± 1·30	(41) 27·29 ± 0·63
3	(42) 29·36 ± 1·18	(57) 28·72 ± 0·71	(149) 27·95 ± 0·54
4	(68) 27·57 ± 0·90	(70) 27·26 ± 0·97	(186) 27·26 ± 0·53
5	(284) 27·14 ± 0·36	(566) 26·51 ± 0·26	(243) 25·68 ± 0·33
6	(193) 26·67 ± 0·47	(71) 27·44 ± 0·91	(47) 24·57 ± 0·67
7	(225) 25·66 ± 0·36	(72) 26·28 ± 0·84	—
Total	(824) 26·81 ± 0·21	(881) 26·88 ± ·22	(702) 26·69 ± ·23

BRIDES (NUMBER IN BRACKETS)

Father's social status category (1)	Age of the bride at marriage whose father-in-law's social status in relation to father's was:		
	Higher (2)	Same (3)	Lower (4)
1	—	(17) 26·71 ± 1·01	(46) 26·22 ± 0·98
2	(11) 25·64 ± 1·12	(28) 28·36 ± 2·16	(58) 27·05 ± 0·82
3	(34) 26·09 ± 1·04	(54) 27·63 ± 1·24	(179) 25·55 ± 0·53
4	(58) 27·24 ± 1·24	(92) 26·22 ± 0·82	(226) 25·25 ± 0·45
5	(316) 24·74 ± 0·35	(664) 24·55 ± 0·23	(263) 24·34 ± 0·46
6	(231) 24·23 ± 0·43	(70) 25·46 ± 0·95	(36) 25·03 ± 1·48
7	(247) 23·34 ± 0·31	(96) 23·77 ± 0·50	—
Total	(897) 24·45 ± 0·21	(1021) 24·99 ± 0·21	(808) 25·19 ± 0·25

As in Table 1, the above table suggests that the ages at marriage of grooms and brides are different only if the status categories are compressed into two broad groups, viz. 1–4, and 5–7. This was also evident from the 't' tests applied to the mean values. It will further be noticed from the above table that for each status category there is hardly any difference in the mean age at marriage of either the male or female subjects whether or not their fathers and fathers-in-law were of the same social status. Differences between categories are of the same order of significance as in Table 1. Hence, to examine significant associations between social mobility and age at marriage it is necessary to recombine the seven status categories into two broad groups, non-manual and manual.

In Table 3 the social status hierarchy refers to manual and non-manual groups only, but the social status association of the parental generation (that is, between the fathers and the fathers-in-law has been examined in terms of the sevenfold classification as before.

Table 3

BRIDEGROOMS (NUMBER IN BRACKETS)

Father-in-law's social status level (1)	Mean age at marriage of the male subjects whose father's social status in the sevenfold scale in relation to father-in-law's was			Total male subjects
	Higher (2)	Same (3)	Lower (4)	(5)
Non-manual	(122) 28·38±·65	(172) 28·10±·50	(412) 27·52±·33	(706) 27·81±·25
Manual	(702) 26·54±·22	(709) 26·58±·24	(290) 25·50±·31	(1701) 26·38±·15
Total	(824) 26·81±·21	(881) 26·88±·22	(702) 26·69±·23	(2407) 26·80±·13

BRIDES (NUMBER IN BRACKETS)

Father's social status level (1)	Mean age at marriage of the female subjects whose father-in-law's social status in the sevenfold scale in relation to father's was			Total female subjects
	Higher (2)	Same (3)	Lower (4)	(5)
Non-manual	(103) 26·69±·78	(191) 26·98±·62	(509) 25·65±·30	(803) 26·10±·26
Manual	(794) 24·16±·21	(830) 24·54±·21	(299) 24·42±·44	(1923) 24·36±·14
Total	(897) 24·45±·21	(1021) 24·99±·21	(808) 25·19±·25	(2726) 24·87±·13

't' tests applied to the mean values in the table showed that there is a consistent difference between the mean age at marriage for the manual and the non-manual groups, individuals marrying later at the former level than at the latter. But, except in the two cases mentioned below, whether or not the fathers and the fathers-in-law were in the same category of the sevenfold hierarchy, and whether one was placed higher or lower than the other, there is no significant difference in the mean age at marriage for either the manual or the non-manual groups. In the manual group only those male subjects whose fathers were in a lower status category than their fathers-in-law married earlier than the rest. In the total sample of women only those whose father-in-law's social status was higher than that of their fathers married earlier than the rest. Although these are the only two cases for which an association between social mobility and age at marriage has been found, both cases follow a similar pattern. That is, in both cases earlier marriages have taken place when the fathers are lower in status than the fathers-in-law.

Table 4

BRIDEGROOM'S MEAN AGE AT MARRIAGE (NUMBER IN BRACKETS)

Father-in-law's social status level	Father's social status level		Total
	Non-manual	Manual	
(1)	(2)	(3)	(4)
Non-manual	(385) $28 \cdot 40 \pm 0 \cdot 34$	(321) $27 \cdot 10 \pm 0 \cdot 36$	(706) $27 \cdot 81 \pm 0 \cdot 25$
Manual	(409) $27 \cdot 02 \pm 0 \cdot 29$	(1292) $26 \cdot 17 \pm 0 \cdot 17$	(1701) $26 \cdot 38 \pm 0 \cdot 15$
Total	(794) $27 \cdot 69 \pm 0 \cdot 23$	(1613) $26 \cdot 36 \pm 0 \cdot 15$	(2407) $26 \cdot 80 \pm 0 \cdot 13$

BRIDE'S MEAN AGE AT MARRIAGE (NUMBER IN BRACKETS)

Father's social status level	Father-in-law's social status level		Total
	Non-manual	Manual	
(1)	(2)	(3)	(4)
Non-manual	(410) $26 \cdot 79 \pm 0 \cdot 40$	(393) $25 \cdot 37 \pm 0 \cdot 33$	(803) $26 \cdot 10 \pm 0 \cdot 26$
Manual	(441) $24 \cdot 55 \pm 0 \cdot 30$	(1482) $24 \cdot 30 \pm 0 \cdot 16$	(923) $24 \cdot 36 \pm 0 \cdot 14$
Total	(851) $25 \cdot 63 \pm 0 \cdot 25$	(1875) $24 \cdot 52 \pm 0 \cdot 15$	(2726) $24 \cdot 87 \pm 0 \cdot 13$

On the whole the above analysis suggests that even if there is an association between social mobility and the age at marriage, this association is not strong enough to be brought out clearly within the relatively fine gradation of the seven status categories. However, since it was found that in our data only a twofold status classification shows a significant difference in the mean age at marriage, this classification into non-manual and manual was also applied studying the influence of social mobility and Table 4 gives the results of this form of analysis. It should be remembered that in this table discrepancies between the parental status categories can register only a lower position from the non-manual and a higher position from the manual levels.

't' tests applied to the above mean values show that in all the classifications there is a significant difference in the mean ages at marriage between the manual and the non-manual levels. We may therefore conclude that when a man of manual parental background marries into the non-manual group, he is likely to marry later than if he married into his own social group. Conversely, a man of non-manual background is likely to marry earlier if he marries into the manual group than if he marries into his own group. These findings also apply to women.

However, the net difference in age at marriage produced by heterogeneous unions between the manual and non-manual groups is only about a year, which is not likely by itself seriously to influence the fertility of the marriages concerned.

Finally, it should be noted that the association between the age at marriage and the manual and non-manual levels of the social hierarchy reflects only the broad pattern of social differentiation. The use of larger samples would have made possible a greater degree of differentiation. A sevenfold classification, for example, might have revealed a greater degree of association between social mobility and age at marriage than is shown by the division into manual and non-manual groups used in the present analysis.[1]

[1] Just as a larger sample—for example, the annual marriage statistics or the large sample used by the Family Census—would show significant differences between final status categories with reference to mean age at marriage.

A Comparison of the Degree of Social Endogamy in England and Wales and the U.S.A.

J. R. HALL

I N Appendix 3 to Chapter VIII, a comparative study was made of the degree of status association between fathers and sons in four countries, the raw material for countries other than England and Wales being obtained from published data. The U.S. investigation, the results of which were used in the study, asked married male subjects to state not only the occupations of their fathers, but also of their fathers-in-law, and examined the relationship between the social origins of brides and grooms in terms of the occupations of the respective fathers.[1] Using this published material, it was possible to calculate indices of Association for the occupational/social origins of brides and grooms, and an attempt was made to compare the relative intensity of 'class' endogamy in England and Wales and in America, rough though such a comparison must be.

To permit greater comparability with the American material, the analysis for England and Wales was confined to the sample of males who married prior to 1940. The nature of the American sample, and the reasons for adopting the three broad occupational/social categories to which the differing status classifications of the English and American samples have been related, have already been discussed in the Appendix mentioned above.

In the two samples, the distributions of fathers of married male subjects over the three occupational/social groups showed no significant differences. When we consider the distributions of fathers-in-law, however, the skilled manual and routine grades of the non-manual group were slightly larger, and the other two groups slightly smaller, in the

[1] R. Centers, 'Marital selection and occupational strata', *Am. J. of Sociology*, Vol. 54, No. 6.

English sample than in the American. This is probably due mainly to the exclusion from the U.S. sample of subjects whose fathers or fathers-in-law were farmers or farm workers.

Within the two matrices, indices of Association were calculated for each country, the indices, and the results of applying significance tests for the differences between them, being given in Tables 1–3. A¹l the indices were found to be significantly different from unity.

Table 1

TOTAL INDICES OF ASSOCIATION

	England and Wales	America
England and Wales	1·409	
America	*	1·736

Table 2

INDICES OF ASSOCIATION CALCULATED FOR CERTAIN OCCUPATIONAL–SOCIAL STATUS CATEGORIES COMPARED WITHIN EACH COUNTRY

ENGLAND AND WALES

Status group of subject's father	Status group of subject's father-in-law		
	Non-manual	Skilled manual and routine non-manual	Semi-skilled and unskilled manual
Non-manual	1·670		
Skilled manual and routine non-manual	*	1·184	
Semi-skilled and unskilled manual	‡	*	1·715

AMERICA

Status group of subject's father	Status group of subject's father-in-law		
	Non manual	Skilled manual and routine non-manual	Semi-skilled and unskilled manual
Non-manual	1·942		
Skilled manual and routine non-manual	†	1·420	
Semi-skilled and unskilled manual	‡	*	2·196

In Table 1, the total Index for the U.S.A. is shown to be significantly higher than that for England and Wales. Because, however, of differences in the representativeness of the samples, it is unlikely that this statistical significance has a genuine social basis. The fact that the U.S.

345

sample is urban and, in addition, excludes those urban subjects whose fathers were employed in agriculture, may well result in an exaggeration of the degree of endogamy. This conclusion is supported by the data in Tables 2 and 3, relating to the separate occupational/social groups. Table 2 suggests that in both countries, the degree of assortative mating is least in the group of skilled manual and routine non-manual workers, while Table 3 finds no significant differences between the indices for the separate groups in England and Wales and in the U.S.A. So far as the basic material permits comparison, therefore, the results of the analysis suggest that the pattern and degree of status association between brides and grooms is probably about the same in the U.S.A. as it is in England and Wales.

Table 3

INDICES OF ASSOCIATION FOR GIVEN OCCUPATIONAL/SOCIAL STATUS CATEGORIES COMPARED BETWEEN COUNTRIES

Status groups	Country	England and Wales	America
Non-manual	England and Wales	1·670	
	America	‡	1·942
Skilled manual and routine non-manual	England and Wales	1·184	
	America	‡	1·420
Semi-skilled and un-skilled manual	England and Wales	1·715	
	America	‡	2·196

* Significantly different at 1 per cent level.
† Significantly different at 5 per cent level.
‡ No significant difference.

PART IV

XIII

Social Stratification in Voluntary Organizations

THOMAS BOTTOMORE

Introduction

THROUGHOUT the series of studies brought together in this volume, there has been a primary focus on the social prestige of the occupations in which men in Britain are engaged. Divided into a series of groups, those occupations have been used as a criterion of social status. Recruitment to the various levels of the status hierarchy has been studied, as well as the behaviour and attitudes of the people within the categories. At no time, however, has it been claimed that occupation is the sole criterion or determinant of social status; on the contrary, there are clearly other criteria and elements to be taken into account. But one of the reasons for choosing a single, though powerful, criterion, is to make it possible to examine the behaviour of other variables in relation to that selected variable. And it is with this kind of examination, in a particular section of the field of behaviour, that the present study is concerned. The section in question is membership and leadership in voluntary organizations, and the object of the study is to see how far the hierarchy derived from an analysis of the social prestige of occupations is reflected in the structure of such organizations. In other words, what kind of people (in terms primarily of their occupations) belong to voluntary organizations; do people of different occupational status meet there on a footing of equality; and how far is leadership in the organizations distributed among people of different status?

A second study in this volume deals with the same general question on a national basis, examining the structure of three nation-wide associations. In the present study, however, an explicitly local approach has been followed. A small English country town was selected, and within that town two investigations were carried out.[1] The first covered all the

[1] A small town rather than a larger one was chosen not only because the physical

349

voluntary organizations which could be identified and attempted to establish the broad lines of membership and leadership. The second took as its basis a small number of organizations and examined their structure, both formal and informal, in greater detail. But before discussing the results of those investigations, it is necessary to give a brief description of the town itself—referred to by the fictitious name of Squirebridge—in order to help the reader to place the voluntary organizations in their environment.

PART I: THE TOWN

Squirebridge is a small country town having a population of about 15,000 and situated in a predominantly agricultural county. The town has had a varied history, beginning in Saxon times as a military stronghold and subsequently becoming a market town, in which rôle, however, it was steadily eclipsed in the course of the later Middle Ages by neighbouring towns which possessed better communications by road and river. From the end of the eighteenth century up to recent times it has been dominated by rich merchants and manufacturers, who settled in the county for the purpose of acquiring gentility by the purchase of land. The population, consequently, became largely specialized in the provision of goods and services for these local squires, and the principal occupations, other than those connected with agriculture, were shopkeeping and domestic service. There were always a few small-scale industries, but further industrialization was steadily resisted by the gentry in order to preserve the residential character of the town. A change began after the first world war, when a new light industry was established and the principal local industry was allowed to expand. Since the last war the town has increased in importance as an administrative centre, and there has been some further industrialization.

The age composition of the population is shown in Table 1.

During most of the present century the population increased very slowly, but there has been a more rapid increase since 1939.

The principal occupations in the town are now commercial (mainly retail trading) and administrative (public and private). There is, however, an increasing number of industrial occupations, ranging from

task of carrying out the investigation was thereby made easier, but also because it seemed likely that in such a community, with its fairly high level of face-to-face contacts and considerable awareness of the backgrounds and histories of individuals, other elements than occupation might have a higher chance of contributing significantly to social status and to leadership in voluntary organizations. There was certainly no desire to minimize the importance of those other elements.

printing to heavy engineering. The 1931 census showed large numbers, and particularly females, engaged in personal (mainly domestic) service, but this is certainly much less important now.

Table 1

POPULATION BY SEX AND AGE (PERCENTAGES)

Age range	Males	Females	Total
0–14	11·5	12·5	24·0
15–24	6·1	8·6	14·7
25–44	13·9	15·3	29·2
45–64	10·0	11·9	21·9
65 and over	4·1	6·1	10·2
Total	45·6	54·4	100·0

Squirebridge is unusual in several respects. Though it is an administrative centre it has a very much smaller population than a number of other towns in the county. Traditional attitudes and behaviour are still strongly entrenched and this situation gives rise to antagonisms between young and old, and between newcomers and residents of long standing, more marked than is probably the case elsewhere. The town is relatively self-contained, in the sense that the majority of the inhabitants are employed and satisfy the greater part of their leisure interests within its boundaries. As an economic unit it is still predominantly commercial, and in consequence a high proportion of the residents belong to the 'middle class' (defined in terms of occupation). Finally, it contains one locality which can be regarded as a separate neighbourhood. This is a former village in which, although it was incorporated in the borough as long ago as the end of the nineteenth century, local sentiment has remained strong. This is indicated by the existence of local organizations parallel to those in the town, and by the inhabitants almost invariably naming it rather than the town as their place of residence.

PART II: A PRELIMINARY STUDY OF THE VOLUNTARY ORGANIZATIONS

Aims and Method

The first inquiry was carried out between April and August 1950. It was concerned only with voluntary leisure-time organizations for those aged 15 and above. Such organizations were defined as non-statutory, non-commercial organizations, participation in which occurs primarily during leisure time. The term 'organization' is used to indicate that the groups studied had a formal leadership, a routine for appointing the leaders, and a fairly stable membership. Amorphous groups, such as darts clubs and discussion groups, were thus excluded from the scope of the inquiry.

The purpose of the inquiry was to analyse the membership of voluntary organizations in terms of occupational status and to find out what influence such status had upon the relations between members within the organizations, and in particular upon the selection of leaders. It was hoped further to throw some light on the rôle of the organizations themselves in conferring upon their members high social status in the community as a whole. This latter question is of considerable sociological interest, but also exceedingly difficult to study. In so far as voluntary organizations take over important functions which the family, or the community as a whole, no longer performs, they become centres of power and prestige, and the individual's status in the community then comes to depend in a larger degree upon membership of such organizations.[1] More will be said on this aspect of the question in Part III of the present chapter.

In this analysis of the membership by occupational status it was not possible to make use of the Standard Classification, since the members were not individually interviewed. Instead, we used three broad occupational groups: A, professional, technical, managerial and executive occupations; B, other non-manual salaried occupations; and C, manual and routine non-manual weekly paid occupations.[2] The method of obtaining the information was as follows: as each voluntary organization became known an approach was made to one of the officials, usually the secretary, who was asked to estimate the proportion of members in each of the three occupational groups, and also to state the occupations of the

[1] See the comment made by H. Goldhamer, *Some factors affecting participation in voluntary associations* (Ph.D. dissertation, University of Chicago, 1945, p. 6). 'For the la.ter [i.e. voluntary associations] play an increasingly important part in the urban system of social interaction; and thus the social "co-ordinates" that establish the "place" of the individual in the social structure of the community derive increasingly from his affiliation with such groups.' Max Weber (in his essay 'The Protestant Sects and the Spirit of Capitalism') drew attention to the importance of the religious sects, and later, the secular clubs, in America, in conferring prestige and providing economic opportunities; '. . . the badge in the buttonhole meant: I am a gentleman patented after investigation and probation and guaranteed by my membership'. Again this meant in business life above all, tested *credit worthiness*. . . . These associations were especially the typical vehicles of social ascent into the circle of the entrepreneurial middle class.'

[2] These groups, however, are derived from the seven categories of the Standard Classification. Group A corresponds to categories 1 and 2, group B to categories 3 and 4, and group C to categories 5, 6 and 7.

principal officials. Estimates of the proportions in different age-groups and of men and women members were also obtained. The disadvantages of this method are obvious; the accuracy of the information depended upon the knowledge and willingness to co-operate of the officials interviewed. It should be said, however, that in many cases a membership list was available, that most of the organizations are small and the members well known to the officials, and finally, that in almost all cases the information given was checked by additional interviews and by attendance at meetings of the organizations.[1] Nevertheless there remains an unknown margin of error in the basic data and for this reason we have avoided any elaborate statistical treatment.

The Organizations

Altogether 135 organizations, as defined above, were found, and this is probably close to the total number of such organizations in Squirebridge. In two cases the officials would not co-operate in the inquiry, and the following analysis refers, unless otherwise stated, to the remaining 133 organizations.

They were roughly classified according to their principal functions under the following headings:

Table 2

CLASSIFICATION OF THE ORGANIZATIONS BY FUNCTION

	Type of organization	No. of organizations
I	Religious (*a*) Churches	11
	(*b*) Church Organizations	22
II	Political	13
III	Cultural and Educational	9
IV	Social Clubs	9
V	Sports and Hobbies	24
VI	Charitable and Benevolent	17
VII	Trade and Professional	15
VIII	Service and Ex-service	13
		133

An analysis of the membership by sex and age was then made, and the figures were compared with the corresponding population figures.[2] The results of this analysis are shown in the table below, together with estimates of the numbers of active members.[3]

[1] The more detailed study reported in Part III of this chapter provided an additional check. See footnote 1, p. 373.

[2] It should be noted that the membership figures refer to *total membership* and not to the number of individuals concerned. One individual may be a member of several organizations.

[3] The criteria of 'active membership' varied, of course, from one organization to

The table shows several interesting characteristics of the organizations. The total membership is 14,649 which gives an average of 110 members per organization. The total membership is greater than the total population of Squirebridge between the same ages, the ratio being about 1·4 : 1. There is one organization for every 80 residents aged 15

Table 3

MEMBERSHIP OF VOLUNTARY ORGANIZATIONS BY SEX AND AGE

Membership (percentages shown in brackets)

Type of orgn.	No. of orgns.	Men	Women	Total	Active	In age-groups 15–24	25–44	45–64	65 and over
(1)	(2)	(3)	(4)	(5)	(6)	(7)	(8)	(9)	(10)
Ia	11	745 (35·2)	1369 (64·8)	2114 (100)	1435	329 (15·5)	697 (33·0)	778 (36·8)	310 (14·7)
Ib	22	170 (17·3)	815 (82·7)	985 (100)	742	192 (19·5)	342 (34·7)	351 (35·6)	100 (10·2)
II	13	894 (60·5)	584 (39·5)	1478 (100)	441	171 (11·6)	488 (33·0)	703 (47·6)	116 (7·8)
III	9	527 (38·0)	859 (62·0)	1386 (100)	759	163 (11·8)	722 (52·1)	453 (32·7)	48 (3·4)
IV	9	1106 (88·4)	145 (11·6)	1251 (100)	493	223 (17·8)	525 (42·0)	354 (28·3)	149 (11·9)
V	24	1871 (78·9)	501 (21·1)	2372 (100)	1539	385[1] (21·3)	668[1] (36·8)	664[1] (36·6)	95[1] (5·3)
VI	17	468[1] (69·6)	210[1] (31·0)	843 (100)	486	125[1] (21·0)	190[1] (32·0)	234[1] (39·4)	45[1] (7·6)
VII	15	1901 (86·3)	301 (13·7)	2202 (100)	249	219 (10·0)	1100 (50·0)	799 (36·2)	84 (3·8)
VIII	13	1694 (83·9)	324 (16·1)	2018 (100)	462	160 (8·0)	615 (30·5)	1065 (52·7)	178 (8·8)
Totals	133	9376[1]	5108[1]	14649	6606	1967[1]	5347[1]	5401[1]	1125[1]
		14484				13840			
% of totals		64·7	35·3	100·0	45·1	14·2	38·6	39·0	8·2

Ratio of membership to total population in same category

		2·0	0·9	1·4		0·9	1·3	1·8	0·8

another, and ranged from attendance at monthly meetings to active participation on several evenings a week. The figures of active members should therefore be regarded as showing the number of members who do anything more than merely have their names on the membership list.

[1] These figures do not add up to the respective totals in column 5 as information was not available from all organizations. Percentages are of the totals of figures given.

and over in the town. Men predominate in the organizations, accounting for nearly two-thirds of the members; their predominance is most marked in the social clubs, sports clubs, trade and professional associations, and service and ex-service organizations. Women, on the other hand, are in the majority in the religious and cultural organizations, and they predominate very markedly in the church organizations. Memberships in religious organizations (churches and church organizations) in fact account for 43 per cent of all female memberships. We should expect participation in voluntary organizations to be less among old people, and the table shows the lowest ratio of memberships to individuals in the 65 and over age-group. More surprising, perhaps, is the high degree of participation by those in the 45–60 age-group and the low degree of participation by those in the 15–24 group. During the course of the inquiry the comment was frequently heard that it is difficult to attract young people into any kind of organized activity and the figures in the table appear to confirm the truth of the statement. Participation by young people is lowest in the service and ex-service organizations (the latter having as members almost entirely ex-servicemen from the 1914–18 war) and highest in the sports and hobbies and the charitable and benevolent organizations.[1]

[1] Comparatively few studies have as yet been made of the structure and functioning of the smaller social groups (but see G. C. Homans, *The Human Group*), and in particular of voluntary organizations. There are, consequently, few studies with which the present results can be compared. However, an interesting comparison can be made with two American studies, that of Boulder, Colorado, reported by F. A. Bushee, 'Social organizations in a small city' (*Am. J. of Sociology*, November 1945), and the well-known 'Middletown' study. An exact comparison cannot be made in either case; in Boulder the lower age limit was 20 years and the area covered went beyond the town boundaries to include most of the territory from which members were drawn, whilst in Middletown', though the lower age limit was the same, the town was considerably larger. But these differences do not seem to be such as to invalidate a comparison altogether, and the relevant figures are given below:

	Boulder	Middletown
Population	11,985†	27,042*
No. of organizations	268	363
No. of residents per organization	48	74
Total membership:	17,324	23,963
Men	6,499	14,846
Women	10,825	7,576
Average membership per organization	65	66

* 15 years and over   † 20 years and over.

Compared with Boulder, Squirebridge has fewer organizations relative to population, but the average size of the organizations is greater; the ratio of total membership to population is not very different in the two cases—1·4 : 1 in Squirebridge and

The preceding account may have given the impression that this is a highly organized community whose inhabitants spend their time bustling from one voluntary organization to another. In fact, however, the many comments received during the investigation gave the opposite impression, that there is quite inadequate provision for organized leisure activity in the town, and that the inhabitants are for the most part apathetic and uninterested. The truth lies somewhere in between these extremes, but it is a failing of the present study that it does not throw much light on the matter. In order to do so, it would have been necessary to find out what proportion of the inhabitants of Squirebridge belong to no organizations, to one, two, three or more organizations, and further, what amount of time is devoted to such organized activities compared with the time given to other leisure interests.[1] The inquiry did throw some light on the question of multiple memberships by revealing a small number of individuals who are active in numerous organizations, but it needs to be supplemented in this aspect.

Occupational Status and Membership of Voluntary Organizations

The occupational-social composition of the organizations studied is shown in Table 4.

It will be seen that of 125 organizations there are 70 with members from all three occupational groups. These are the organizations, therefore, in which the relations between members of different occupational status could best be studied. In fact, another limitation was discovered, since of the 70 organizations there are 13 in which the members from different occupational groups are never, or seldom, present together. This is notably the case where an organization has vice-presidents who are

---

1·44: 1 in Boulder. The outstanding difference is in the relative numbers of men and women members; whereas in Squirebridge 65 per cent of the membership is male, in Boulder the proportions are almost reversed, 60 per cent of the membership being female. The author in fact comments on this as being unusual, and suggests an explanation in the existence of a university in the town and the predilection of faculty wives for organizations. In 'Middletown' the number of organizations relative to the population is almost the same as in Squirebridge, but again the average size of the organizations is less; thus the ratio of total membership to population is also lower, being 0·88 : 1 as against 1·4 : 1. The proportions of men and women members, however, show a greater similarity, with 67 per cent of the members being men. An interesting feature of these comparisons is that they do not show any greater participation in voluntary organizations in these American towns than in the town we have studied, at any rate so far as memberships are concerned.

[1] A study of this kind, on a sample of the population of Squirebridge, was in fact begun, but had to be abandoned on account of its cost.

chosen partly for their high status and partly for their ability and willingness to contribute financially; very often the vice-presidents take no further part in the affairs of the organization, though some of them attend the annual meeting. In these organizations there are evidently no close relationships between all the members and social distance is maintained between those with high and those with lower occupational status. At the annual meeting, any of the vice-presidents who do attend are treated with some deference, take the chair, appear on the platform, etc.; one club in its annual report tenders to the numerous vice-presidents its thanks and appreciation for their continued support. There are only 57 organizations in which all the members regularly associate, and it was in these organizations primarily that the influence of occupational status upon the intra-group relationships was studied.

Table 4

OCCUPATIONAL–SOCIAL COMPOSITION OF THE ORGANIZATIONS

Type of orgn.	No. of orgns. for which occ. status is known	Number of orgns. with members from occ. groups			No. of organizations in which there are members from occupational groups:						
		A	B	C	A, B and C	AB	AC	BC	A only	B only	C only
Ia	10	9	9	9	8	—	—	1	1	—	—
Ib	19	11	15	18	8	1	2	6	—	—	2
II	12	8	11	9	5	2	—	4	1	—	—
III	9	9	8	5	5	3	—	—	1	—	—
IV	9	7	8	9	6	—	1	2	—	—	—
V	23	23	22	21	20	2	1	—	—	—	—
VI	15	14	10	9	8	2	—	—	4	-	1
VII	15	4	1	12	—	1	1	—	2	—	11
VIII	13	10	12	13	10	—	—	2	—	—	1
Total	125	95	96	105	70	11	5	15	9	—	15

The status system within an organization is to some extent revealed by a study of the leadership. Not all those with high status are formal leaders, but all the leaders have high status; this is implied in their being chosen as leaders. From the point of view of this study the important question was whether these inequalities of status indicated by the distinction between leaders (officials) and ordinary members were related to differences of occupational status. A comparison was, therefore, made between the number and proportion of leaders and members respectively in each of the three occupational groups. The results of this comparison are shown in the following table:

357

Table 5

NUMBERS OF MEMBERS AND OFFICIALS IN OCCUPATIONAL GROUPS A,
B AND C (PERCENTAGES IN BRACKETS)

Type of orgn.	No of orgns. for which occ. status of members is known	Total member- ship	Membership in Occupa- tional Group			Officials in Occupational Group		
			A	B	C	A	B	C
Ia	10	1714	218 (12·7)	250 (14·6)	1246 (72·7)	28 (65·1)	8 (18·6)	7 (16·3)
Ib	19	775	80 (10·3)	203 (26·2)	492 (63·5)	35 (46·7)	32 (42·7)	8 (10·6)
II	12	1278	390 (30·5)	281 (22·0)	607 (47·5)	17 (40·5)	9 (21·4)	16 (38·1)
III	9	1386	389 (28·1)	747 (53·9)	250 (18·0)	25 (75·8)	8 (24·2)	— (0·0)
IV	9	1251	106 (8·5)	155 (12·4)	990 (79·1)	26 (60·5)	5 (11·6)	12 (27·9)
V	23	2298	344 (15·0)	491 (21·4)	1463 (63·7)	63 (67·7)	16 (17·2)	14 (15·1)
VI	15	733	214 (29·2)	155 (21·1)	364 (49·7)	60 (77·9)	7 (9·1)	10 (13·0)
VII	15	2202	238[1]	26[1]	1938[1]	11[1]	1[1]	40[1]
VIII	13	2018	158 (7·8)	349 (17·3)	1511 (74·9)	37 (58·7)	8 (12·7)	18 (28·6)
Total	125	13655	1899 (16·6)	2631 (23·0)	6923 (60·4)	291 (62·0)	93 (19·8)	85 (18·2)

Ratio of number of officials to number of members: 1 : 6   1 : 28   1 : 81

It will be seen that there is a considerable difference in the proportion of members and officials respectively, from each of the occupational groups. The difference is greatest for group A which provides 16·6 per cent of the members, but 62 per cent of the officials, and for group C which provides 60·4 per cent of the members but only 18·2 per cent of the officials. In the case of group B there is more symmetry, with 23 per cent of the members and 19·8 per cent of the officials coming from this

[1] Not included in the totals. Since these organizations are trade unions and professional bodies which recruit their members from a single occupation or a small range of similar occupations and grades, their membership is fairly homogeneous, and there is little, if any, difference in occupational status between members and officials within particular organizations.

group. The ratio between numbers of members and numbers of officials in the three groups provides a further illustration of the differences; in group A one out of every 6 members is an official, in group B one out of every 28 members, and in group C one out of every 81 members. There can be no doubt as to the predominance of the members in group A; they provide a very high proportion of the formal leaders of the organizations. Since the differentia of groups A, B and C are occupational we may justifiably conclude that occupational status is an important factor in establishing the hierarchy within an organization. Other things being equal, a member who is in group A has a 14 : 1 chance of becoming an official compared with a member who is in group C. There may, of of course, be other factors, and a comparison of different types of organization suggests what some of them are; the nearest approach to equality between the three occupational groups in the supply of officials is found in the political organizations, chiefly because there is a conscious effort in some of these organizations to eliminate differences based upon occupational status. The greatest inequality is seen in the cultural and educational organizations, where there are no officials at all from group C (the proportion of members from this group being also relatively small); in this case, evidently, educational standards are relevant, but the table indicates that they probably accord quite closely with occupational status, as would be expected.

Occupational Status and Behaviour in the Organizations

The analysis of the membership, discussed in the previous section, was supplemented by observation of many of the organizations and by information about their activities obtained from members and officials. There is not sufficient space, and it would be tedious, to describe each individual organization, but it seems desirable to outline the main features of the various groups of organizations, illustrating these from the material collected.

Churches and Church Organizations

Some objections might be raised to the inclusion of churches in this study since it is usual to regard them as communities rather than associations. It seems possible, however, that the community element in church membership in modern society has been exaggerated; it is evident that for a large proportion of the members the church is an association with specific aims, to which a definite amount of leisure time is devoted, and which has little connection with, or influence upon, other activities.

The members for whom the church is a community are principally those who also participate fully in the subsidiary church organizations. There are, of course, differences in this respect between the churches, and in two cases (the Roman Catholics and the Brethren) the community element seems particularly strong. The study covers eleven churches (four Church of England, Baptist, Congregational, Methodist, Roman Catholic, Society of Friends, Salvation Army and Brethren), and twenty-two church organizations. There is some difference between the Church of England churches and the others, the former having generally a larger proportion of members from groups A and B. That the social differences were greater in the recent past is indicated by the style of life of the ministers; those of the Church of England live in fairly large houses (which they can no longer afford), similar to the houses of the more wealthy professional men and employers in the town, while the other ministers have much smaller houses, of which the best is a small detached villa. At present only the Roman Catholic Church and the Brethren have memberships drawn almost exclusively from group C.

There are two exceptions to the statement that the Church of England churches have larger proportions of members from the higher occupational groups, and these are important as showing the changes now taking place. One of the free churches has a large proportion of members with high occupational status; thus, of the total membership, 40 per cent is in group A, 27 per cent in group B, and 33 per cent in group C. One reason for this is that members of the church largely control two important and old-established firms in the town; as the firms have prospered and expanded so the status of the individuals employed in them has risen, and at the same time the traditional pattern whereby a man transferred his allegiance to the established church as he rose in the world has ceased to operate. The established church has lost a great deal of its social prestige and political influence, with the result that the other churches are now able to retain the allegiance of their more successful members.

On the other hand, one of the Church of England churches has a very large proportion of members from group C, and at the time of the inquiry had a number of church officers from this group. There is no doubt that this was a consequence of certain events in its recent history. The minister had married a member of his congregation whose social status was very much lower than his own. By this action, he aroused the disapproval of many of his parishioners, alienating in particular those with high social status, who soon left the church. He was urged by friendly parishioners to move to another parish where his wife's family background would not be known, but he took no action, preferring to 'wait and see'; meanwhile the congregation continued to diminish. There is little doubt that the critical attitude towards him centred on his marriage and the repudiation of social distinctions which it implied.

The social distinctions *between* the churches are thus becoming less marked. Besides the factors already mentioned, this is partly due to the declining social status of the leading members of the established church. The squirearchy is disappearing and its place in church affairs is being taken over by tradesmen, minor officials and the like. This results in considerable similarity between the leaders of all the churches (except the Roman Catholics and the Brethren); in every denomination there are to be found in the leading positions shopkeepers, teachers, local government officials and professional men, and the remaining social differences are largely an inheritance from the past in the way of property, or a matter of the proportion of weekly wage-earners in the membership. The disappearance of social distinctions between the churches does not, however, imply that social distinctions have vanished within them. On the contrary, the common pattern is that of leadership exercised by those with higher occupational status, and where there is any deviation from this pattern, as was seen in one case, it is likely to create difficulties within the organization.

Political Organizations

As would be expected in a town of this kind, which is not industrialized, which has been for a long time under the patronage of wealthy county families, and in which the principal occupations are administration and shopkeeping, the political attitude of the majority is Conservative. Of the thirteen organizations studied, seven are Conservative, one Liberal, four Labour and Co-operative, and one a branch of the United Nations Association (the latter very small and ineffective); of the total membership of 1,478, 69·8 per cent is Conservative, 13·5 per cent Liberal and 15·8 per cent Labour and Co-operative. These figures somewhat exaggerate the Conservative predominance, since the Conservative organizations include clubs in which either the members are not necessarily Conservative (Working Men's Club) or they are the same people as make up part of the membership of the political organizations proper (Dinner Club). Excluding the clubs there are four Conservative organizations with 55 per cent of the total membership of political organizations other than clubs. It was impossible to make a comparison between all three main political organizations, because the required information could not be obtained from the Liberal organization. However, the Conservative (excluding clubs) and the Labour and Co-operative organizations were compared and the results are shown in the following table:

Table 6

ANALYSIS OF THE MEMBERSHIP OF POLITICAL ORGANIZATIONS (PERCENTAGES IN BRACKETS)

Organization	Men	Women	In age-groups under 25	25–44	45–64	65 and over	In occupational group A	B	C
Conservative	171	375	40	161	325	20	115	220	211
(excl. clubs)	(31·3)	(68·7)	(7·3)	(29·5)	(59·5)	(3·7)	(21·1)	(40·3)	(38·6)
Labour and	128	105	55	87	71	20	8	29	196
Co-operative	(54·9)	(45·1)	(23·6)	(37·3)	(30·5)	(8·6)	(3·4)	(12·5)	(84·1)

It will be seen that there are marked differences; the Conservative organizations have a larger proportion of women members, a higher average age level (with a majority of members in the 45–64 group), and a larger proportion of members in occupational groups A and B. The relations between members within the organizations are also markedly different. Of the sixteen officials of the Conservative organizations (excluding clubs) twelve are from group A and four from group B; there are none from group C although nearly 40 per cent of the members belong to this group. In the Labour and Co-operative organizations, of eighteen officials there is one from group A, one from group B, and sixteen from group C. These differences are accentuated if account is taken of vice-presidents, who, although not active officials, have a greater influence upon policy than the ordinary members and might therefore be regarded as part of the leadership. Whereas the Labour and Co-operative organizations have no vice-presidents, the Conservative organizations have several (in some cases 'patrons'), and these belong, without exception, to group A, and sometimes, indeed, have very high social status (e.g. minor members of the aristocracy). In considering these distinctions in the matter of leadership, however, it should be observed that the membership of the Labour and Co-operative organizations is much more homogeneous from the point of view of occupational status, and this may be a significant factor in determining the character of the leadership. There is one further point of interest concerning the status of the organizations themselves in the community. The secretary of one of the Conservative organizations mentioned that the most regular attenders at the monthly meetings were the working-class members; the members with higher status were inclined to say, 'You know we are Conservatives, so why should we attend meetings?'. One of the factors in the situation appears to be that the Conservative organizations are regarded as conferring prestige, and those members who have low occupational status seek, by assiduous attendance and whole-hearted participation, to raise themselves in the world. The Labour organizations, on the other hand, do not confer prestige, but rather arouse disapproval. It is not surprising, therefore, to find that these organizations depend to a considerable extent for their leadership upon immigrants into the town. In the case of one organization it was stated that the last four secretaries had been immigrants, and all had come from industrial towns of the Midlands and the North of England.

Cultural and Educational Organizations

These organizations are noteworthy for having the smallest proportion of members from group C. This is hardly surprising, since participation in such organizations is strongly influenced by the individual's level of education, which is closely correlated with his occupational status. The same factor probably accounts also for the fact that there are no members from group C in the leadership of these organizations. This situation may appear more surprising when it is realized that a branch of the Workers' Educational Association is one of the organizations; it has only one weekly wage-earner among its thirty members.

Undoubtedly the most important of these organizations is the Dramatic Society. It is an old-established and flourishing organization with about 500 members and enjoys great prestige in Squirebridge. Because of this prestige, it has become an excellent base for acceptance into the community, for social climbing, and for acquiring a boy or girl friend. The latter feature partly accounts for the high proportion of younger members. Less than 10 per cent of the members belong to group C, whilst 80 per cent belong to group B. The majority of the leaders, as would be expected, are people of high status in group A. An organization only slightly less important is the Townswomen's Guild which has over 200 members. In this case nearly half the members belong to group C, but the leadership is in the hands of members in the higher occupational groups. It is significant that this organization has a very low annual subscription (like one other, which has also a large proportion of members from group C); and it is reasonable to suppose that individuals from the lowest occupational groups are in practice excluded from some of these organizations by the high subscriptions, and not merely self-excluded by never having developed the appropriate cultural interests.

Social Clubs

There is not much to be said about most of the social clubs, which have the typical pattern of leadership of the majority of the voluntary organizations. Whilst nearly 80 per cent of the members belong to group C, 60 per cent of the leaders belong to group A. There are special, as well as general, reasons for this in four of the clubs, which are run in connection with public trading undertakings or services. In these clubs it is the practice (except in one instance) to choose the officials from among the heads of the undertaking, electing the manager (or equivalent) as president. With the occupational hierarchy thus reproduced in the hierarchy of the clubs it is hardly to be expected that the members will be on a footing of equality, and in any case the exact status of each individual is too well known for there to be any blurring of distinctions such as might occur where individuals have to be accepted more at their face value.

One of these organizations, a youth club aided by the Education Authority, is interesting as showing how status differences manifest themselves within an organization. The club caters for young people of both sexes between the ages of 15 and 20, and in its early stages (soon after the end of the war) had a large and very mixed membership, the principal distinction being that between grammar school pupils and the other members who had left school and were at work. This distinction corresponded approximately to differences in the occupational status of the parents and it very soon showed itself in the affairs of the club. The boys mixed fairly well, and there are still grammar school boys in the club, but social distinctions quickly developed among the girls, and a definite technique was used to set the 'tone' of the club. The girls were very enthusiastic about arranging dances, and the grammar school girls took the lead in this, but they established standards which were appropriate to their own situation whilst being too high for the other girls. For instance, the tickets for such dances were marked 'Dress optional', and in practice the grammar school girls always wore evening dress while a number of the other girls could not afford to do so. Furthermore, these regular dances were themselves an expense which some of the girls could not meet. Eventually, as more commercial entertainment facilities returned, the wealthier girls left the club, and today it has a much smaller membership, predominantly working class, and with a considerable majority of boys.[1]

Another club shows very clearly the formation of sub-groups along the lines of occupational status. There are no organized club activities, and the members go there to have a drink and conversation, and to play billiards and darts. The club has 200 members, of whom 25 per cent are in group A, 25 per cent in group B, and 50 per cent in group C. There is practically no contact between the members in group C and the members in the other two groups; they congregate separately whether drinking, talking or playing billiards. The officials of the club belong to group A. So far as could be observed, co-membership does very little to modify the status which members have already outside the club.

Sports and Hobbies Organizations

Leadership in these organizations as a whole shows no very marked deviation from the general pattern, but there are some interesting differences between the various clubs. Several of them are, as in the case of social clubs, connected with a business firm or public undertaking, and like the social clubs, reproduce the occupational hierarchy directly in the status system of the club. This is, in some cases, and to some extent, a customary gesture without much practical significance, the offices which are held by the heads of the undertakings being largely non-active, but in most cases it accurately reflects the balance of power in the organization. This influence of the higher officials is perhaps inevitable, because it is the general practice for the directors of the firm to give financial assistance and to make available other facilities. Doubtless, therefore, it seems desirable that the organization's affairs should be in the hands of responsible officials of some standing. In practice, too, the day-to-day administration of the organization is much easier when

[1] The factor of expense is very important in all the organizations, not only in the selection of members (by excluding those in the low income groups), but in the relations between the members within the organization. Where an organization has a variety of activities, all involving money expenditure, it is clear that, other things being equal, the members with the highest incomes will be able to participate in more of the activities, and in fact they generally do so. As a result of greater participation, they achieve greater prominence and prestige, and tend to form the leadership of the organization. Such differentiation may occur spontaneously, or it may be brought about deliberately by continually proposing expensive activities, and it may be carried so far as to lead to disruption of the organization, as in the case described in the text. There is a good account of a struggle for power within a club along these lines in W. Foote Whyte, *Street Corner Society* (Chicago, 1943; Chapter 2).

it is done by officials who do not have to account rigorously for every minute of their time, who have clerical assistance, the use of the telephone, and easy access to the heads of the firm.

There is a very noticeable difference between the town football and cricket clubs. The cricket club has a large proportion of members who belong to group A, and its leading members are all of high occupational status. Among the working-class population of the town it is generally regarded as an 'upper-class' and rather 'snobbish' organization, but this attitude seems to refer to the past rather than to the contemporary situation since almost half the present members of the club are in group C. The football clubs, of which four were studied, have an overwhelming majority of members from group C. Furthermore, the leadership not only includes a large proportion from group C but is drawn from the lower levels of the other occupational groups. In the case of the bowls clubs there is very obvious segregation. Two of them are connected with working-men's clubs and have members only from group C, whilst the others draw most of their members from group A, and have a negligible minority from the other occupational groups. One small hobbies organization with fewer than twenty members, drawn from all three occupational groups, provided an opportunity to study closely the relationships between the members. There was little formality in the meetings and the majority of the members addressed each other by their first names, though the president was not addressed in this manner. In conversation several of the members insisted very emphatically upon the absence of occupational status distinctions within the organization and suggested that interest and proficiency in the particular hobby were the only matters relevant to the achievement of high status inside it. Nevertheless, the president is the member with the highest social status outside the club, being a company director (and also a J.P.), and it was evident that he was treated with some deference in the meetings, and that he took the lead in proposing and deciding upon future activities. He is also the founder of the club, and it seems probable that his high status in Squirebridge was essential to the formation and successful development of the organization.

Charitable and Benevolent Organizations

These organizations may be divided into various types. First, there are the strictly charitable, of which there are two sub-groups, those whose membership includes only the dispensers of charity, and those whose membership includes both the dispensers and the recipients. In the former, the members are drawn almost entirely from group A. In the latter, the membership naturally includes many individuals from group C, but the relationship between members of high and low occupational status is, by intention, one of inequality. The dispensers of charity are, of course, the leaders of the organizations. It is worth noting that the number of charitable organizations has steadily declined over the past thirty years. Secondly, there are the organizations which whilst not strictly charitable, make available social services not provided by any statutory bodies. Some of these are closely related to statutory authorities (e.g. the Road Safety Committee). The members are principally drawn from the occupational groups A and B.

Thirdly, there are three mutual-aid organizations, all of which have a large majority of members from group C. One of them now has a few members who belong to group A, but this is largely because they have themselves risen in the social scale since they became members. The leadership is, however, exercised by the members with higher occupational status.

Service and Ex-service Organizations[1]

In these organizations there is a rather higher proportion of members from group C in the leadership. This is accounted for by the practice, in the ex-service organizations, of having ex-officers as president and chairman and an ex-N.C.O. (frequently in civilian life a comissionaire) as secretary. The status distinctions in these organizations are outwardly somewhat different from those in other voluntary organizations. The officials (except the secretary) are usually ex-officers, and the members are ex-rankers; but since the ex-officers are usually those with higher occupational status in civilian life (and where regulars are concerned the military differences of rank *are* differences of occupational status), the distinctions are fundamentally identical with those in other organizations. Only here they may appear more 'natural' and seem to be taken more for granted. Nevertheless, the fact that the great majority of members are ex-servicemen of the 1914–18 war may indicate that such 'natural' social distinctions are not favourably regarded by the younger ex-servicemen. Another influence keeping out the ex-servicemen of the last war is that the charitable benefits of membership have not been

---

[1] Consideration of the trade and professional organizations is omitted as irrelevant to the present topic since these organizations are homogeneous in their membership. (See note to Table 5 above.)

needed in conditions of full employment and more comprehensive social services.

Final Remarks

From the material collected in this research and briefly presented in the foregoing pages, it emerges clearly that occupational status is an important influence within the voluntary organizations. In the first place, less than half the total number of organizations have members from all three occupational groups (A, B and C); it is evident that there are strong influences towards segregation in accordance with occupational status. Some of these influences are obvious. For instance, the trade and professional organizations are in principle limited to particular occupations and categories. The charitable organizations are also generally restricted to those who are in a position to dispense charity. But in other cases different factors are involved. Consciously or unconsciously some of the organizations discourage or squeeze out individuals with lower occupational status, either by fixing a high subscription, or by establishing a standard of behaviour which is, or seems to be, unattainable by such individuals (e.g. one which involves frequent 'treating'). From the standpoint of the individual, a voluntary organization is seen not only as a means of satisfying certain of his interest or needs, but also as a group of people of a specific kind with whom he may or may not feel that he could mix freely. His appreciation of this situation may, of course, be erroneous, as it seems to be, to some extent, in the case of the cricket club which is widely regarded as an 'upper-class' organization out of reach of the ordinary working man, whereas in fact it has a considerable number of working-class members. In general, however, cricket seems to have a higher status than some other sports, and notably than football.

The high occupational status of the members of an organization may, on the other hand, be an attraction to the individual whose own status is low if he is anxious to climb. But this is exceptional. Upward social mobility seems to depend chiefly upon educational or occupational advancement, and membership of a particular organization which itself has high status is sought rather as a confirmation of the newly acquired status than as a step towards acquiring higher status.

In the organizations which have members from all three occupational groups, the official leadership is unquestionably concentrated in the hands of those members with high occupational status. But this is not to be regarded as a simple causal relationship. There are two possibilities,

368

either that the leaders are chosen for their high status or that they are chosen for various qualities of character or competence which may also be responsible for their high occupational status. In the case of vice-presidents it is usually occupational status which is the principal factor in their selection, since they take no active part in the affairs of the organization and any personal qualities they may have are largely irrelevant. But in the case of active officials the relationship is more complicated. When a bank manager is appointed treasurer, this may be more for his technical ability than for his status, and in varying degrees the same is true of many officials. They are appointed for their abilities in administration, or for their skill in the activities of the organization, and not merely because they have high occupational status. Nevertheless, it is easy to be misled on this point, and it is worth considering whether ability and skill within an organization may not be, in part, a function of status. W. Foote Whyte has drawn attention to this possibility;[1] he indicates that those individuals with high status, as formal or informal leaders of a group, will tend to perform well in all the main activities of the group, because the members want them to perform well so long as they have high status. A similar situation may exist in the case of high occupational status in relation to the activities of voluntary organizations. Furthermore, it is quite possible for the members of an organization to confuse high status with ability; in a stratified society such as our own the possession of 'natural' abilities of various kinds is frequently claimed by individuals with high status, who may in fact not possess these abilities at all, or not in any greater degree than the generality of men. These difficult questions cannot be decided on the basis of our present material. We can only point out that high occupational status and the exercise of leadership are closely related, without specifying the precise nature of the relationship.

The material acquired from direct observation at meetings made it possible to identify a number of general factors influencing status differences within the organizations. The first of these is the size of the organization. A small organization functions as a whole; the members are in closer contact with each other, learn more about each other, and develop, in relation to the aims of the organization, a common system of values. In the larger organizations sub-groups come into existence, and it was noticeable that these almost always followed the lines of occupational status differences. Such organizations tend to be hierarchies of groups with differing systems of values.

[1] See his *Street Corner Society*, Chicago, 1943, p. 23.

The second important factor is the nature of the activities. There is a marked difference between those organizations which have no pre-scribed activities (e.g. some of the social clubs) and those which have. In the former there is no common interest to unite the members, and the tendency is for small groups to form, composed of members who have something in common outside the organization, which usually means that the groups are distinguished by occupational status. In the organizations which have specific activities, differentiation develops according to the type of activity. This is obvious, for instance, in the charitable organizations which include in their membership both the dispensers and the recipients of charity, and in which, consequently, inequality of status is implied from the beginning. Where there is an activity requiring skill, and in which most of the members take part, prestige will be gained by possessing such skill, and this may produce a status system differing from that based on occupations.[1] It may not always be reflected in the leadership, but may significantly affect be-haviour within the organization, as appears to be the case in the hobbies club mentioned earlier, where the meetings are very informal and where, except for the status of the president, there is no sign of differential treatment according to occupational status. Similar conditions exist in the football clubs and in one of the youth clubs. It was remarked earlier that financial cost is important in the selection of members. It is just as important within the organizations, as is also cost in terms of time. Where an organization has a variety of optional activities, prestige is acquired by those who participate most fully, and this depends largely upon having sufficient time and money. Thus social differences are emphasized and inequalities based upon them are enhanced.

The frequency and type of meetings, which depend in some degree upon the nature of the activities, are of great significance. A Rotary Club whose members meet once a week to have lunch together is a very different organization from a horticultural society whose members culti-vate their *own* gardens and may meet only once a year at the annual show. And though in the case of the Rotary Club the occupational differences are not great, owing to the prescribed method of selecting members, there are other organizations, in which all the occupational groups are represented, which likewise meet frequently and informally,

---

[1] On the other hand these status systems may coincide if, as is sometimes the case, the skills required within the organization are similar to those required in a business or profession and themselves have a certain social prestige, as being the product of a long and expensive education.

370

and thus, provided they are not too large, tend to create a rough equality in the relations between the members. Where meetings are infrequent and formal in character social distance is much more easily maintained.

Aims and Method

This second inquiry was intended to supplement the first by penetrating behind the formal hierarchy of the organizations to the informal hierarchy, and to the informal relationships between the members both inside and outside the organizations. We wanted to find out, in particular, whether close personal friendships between members were influenced, and to what extent, by the occupational status of these members, and in the case of members who evidently had very high status in an organization, what factors could be considered responsible for their position and what effect this had upon their status in the town.

Four organizations were selected for study, a Rotary club, a cricket club, a dramatic society, and a youth club, and the field work was carried out between February and May 1951. Membership lists were first obtained from the organizations and the members (active members in the case of the dramatic society and the youth club) were then interviewed and graded by occupation according to the Standard Classification.[1] Information about the members' associations with each other, including personal friendships, was obtained from the interviews, observation at meetings, and general conversation with members. The informal hierarchy was likewise studied by observation at meetings, and from the replies to a question which asked the subject to name three members whom he would choose to represent his organization before the townspeople.

Description of the Organizations

The Rotary club is a small, but very active, organization with 39 members (all men) who meet regularly once a week. Membership is restricted, by the rules of the Rotary movement, to men in executive positions, and though the term 'executive' is broadly interpreted, as will be seen from the occupational analysis in Table 7, the members are drawn mainly from the occupational categories 1–3. The financial cost of

[1] In the youth club members were graded according to their father's occupations.

371

membership, which is at least £14 a year, would no doubt, in any case, be a powerful deterrent to individuals in the lower occupational categories.

The cricket club is also small, but is one of the principal organizations in the parish which was referred to in Part I above as forming a distinct neighbourhood within Squirebridge. The club has a president, 18 vice-presidents and 40 ordinary members (all but two being men). It is favoured, from the point of view of financial aid and status in the community, by the fact that one part of the parish is a residential area inhabited by many of the wealthier citizens of Squirebridge, some of whom are vice-presidents of the club. The financial cost of membership is low.

The dramatic society, founded more than thirty years ago, is, without question, the most flourishing and important leisure organization in the town. It is regarded, by most of the townspeople, as a 'middle-class' organization, and this impression is confirmed by the occupational analysis (see Table 7). There are nearly 500 members, of whom three-fifths are women. The financial cost of membership is not high so far as the subscription (7s. 6d. a year) is concerned, but the activities, involving continuous rehearsals in the members' homes during the producing season from September to March, and the conviviality which even an amateur connection with the stage seems to entail, probably raise the cost to a level out of the reach of those in the lower occupational categories.

The youth club is a voluntary organization run by an adult management committee but encouraged and financially aided by the Education Authority. It caters for young people aged 15–20 years and has a membership of 117, of whom 90 are boys. The majority of members are from the lower occupational categories. The principal activities are concerned with sport, particularly football. Members pay an annual subscription of 1s. and a small charge on the weekly club night.

Occupational Status of the Membership

The composition of the organizations is shown in Table 7.

It will be seen that in the Rotary club and the dramatic society the majority of the members come from the higher occupational categories (1–3), while in the cricket club and the youth club the majority is in the lower categories (5 and 6). The lowest category, 7, is hardly represented, and this is a typical feature of participation in voluntary organizations in Squirebridge. The material collected in the course of our two inquiries suggests that individuals in the lowest occupational categories, and especially in category 7, take little part in voluntary organizations other than churches in the case of women, and trade unions and sports clubs in the case of men; and even in these organizations they rarely take an active part.

Table 7

ANALYSIS OF THE MEMBERSHIP BY OCCUPATIONAL CATEGORY[1]

Occupational category	Rotary club	Cricket club		Dramatic society[2]	Youth club[2]
		Number of members in specified category			
		Presidents and vice-presidents	Ordinary members		
1	8	11	—	22	—
2	13	2	—	35	1
3	12	3	5	25	3
4	2	—	6	17	4
5	—	1	18	14	18
6	—	—	3	1	6
7	—	—	—	—	1
Not known	4	2	8	—	—
Total	39	19	40	114	33

In the cricket club we have shown separately the occupational status of the president and vice-presidents and the ordinary members, in order to emphasize the considerable difference between the two groups. This is another common feature of the organizations, and even in the dramatic society, most of whose members have relatively high occupational status, the status of the vice-presidents and honorary members is still higher (including one member of the aristocracy). It needs to be emphasized that, because of these status differences, there is usually very little contact between ordinary members and vice-presidents, etc. The cricket club, for instance, holds an annual party to which all members are invited; in 1951 most of the ordinary members attended,

[1] These results have been compared with the estimates of the proportion of members in occupational groups A, B and C, obtained in the first inquiry, for the same four organizations. The two sets of results agree closely, except in the case of the dramatic society, where it appears that the numbers in group A were underestimated, and the numbers in group B overestimated, in the first inquiry. This difference may, however, be due in part to the fact that in the second inquiry only the most active members of the dramatic society were interviewed.

[2] In these two organizations we decided, for reasons of economy, to interview only the active members, of whom there were, according to the officials, 190 in the dramatic society and 45 in the youth club. Even this proved impossible, particularly in the dramatic society where 47 of the active members lived outside Squirebridge and could only have been interviewed at considerable expense. In the youth club, where interviews were done at the club, it seems that the number of active members was overestimated by the officials.

the president paid a fleeting visit in the best clerical manner (he is the rector of the parish), and only one of the vice-presidents, who happens to be the father-in-law of the chairman of the club, put in an appearance. In the day-to-day life of most organizations the vice-presidents, patrons, etc. take no active part, and limit their interest to an annual donation and sometimes the loan of their names for letter headings. Nevertheless, they should be considered part of the leadership of the organizations, for they undoubtedly have more influence upon policy than do those ordinary members who are not officials.

The Leadership

Each of the organizations studied has a formal leadership elected annually by the members, and we began our study of status within the organizations, as in the previous inquiry, by a comparison of the occupational status of members and officials (excluding any non-active officials).[1] It was possible on this occasion to take into account also the

Table 8

A COMPARISON OF THE OCCUPATIONAL STATUS OF OFFICALS (PRESENT AND PAST) AND MEMBERS

(A = members; B = present officials; C = past officials)

| Occupational category | Percentage of total in the specified category | | | | | | | | | | | |
| | Rotary club | | | Cricket club | | | Dramatic society | | | Youth club | | |
	A	B	C	A	B	C	A	B	C	A	B	C
1	22·9	25·0	15·0	—	—	—	19·3	26·7	31·6	—	—	—
2	37·1	33·3	40·0	—	—	—	30·7	46·7	42·1	3·0	—	—
3	34·3	41·7	40·0	15·7	25·0	9·1	21·9	13·3	15·8	9·1	16·7	33·3
4	5·7	—	5·0	18·7	25·0	18·2	14·9	6·7	5·3	12·1	—	—
5	—	—	—	56·2	50·0	72·7	12·3	6·6	5·2	54·5	83·3	66·7
6	—	—	—	9·4	—	—	0·9	—	—	18·2	—	—
7	—	—	—	—	—	—	—	—	—	3·1	—	—
Total	100·0	100·0	100·0	100·0	100·0	100·0	100·0	100·0	100·0	100·0	100·0	100·0

[1] The principal active officials of the organizations are as follows: *Rotary club:* president, immediate past president, two vice-presidents (in this case they are active officials), secretary, assistant secretary, treasurer, and a council of six members; *Cricket club:* chairman, secretary-treasurer, team secretary, and a general committee of seven members; *Dramatic society:* chairman, vice-chairman, secretary, business manager, and committee of ten members *Youth club:* secretary, and committee of five members (in addition, of course, there is the adult management committee).

past official positions held by the members, and by this means to correct the element of chance selection in the particular year of the inquiry.

Only in the dramatic society is there any clear indication that occupational status is important in the selection of leaders. This is worthy of note, however, since the dramatic society is the only organization, of the four studied, in which there are members from practically all occupational categories. A further point of interest is that the office of president of the society has been left unfilled since the retirement of the last president, a highly respected and wealthy solicitor. There is a strong feeling, expressed by the chairman, that it would be presumptuous for anyone else to take office as long as he is still living in the town. The youth club, which also appears to cover a wide range of occupational categories, in fact has most of its members from categories 5 and 6; only one member is in category 2 and this is a somewhat doubtful classification. It should be remembered also that non-active officials (e.g. vice-presidents) have been excluded from consideration in the case of the cricket club and the dramatic society, and that these officials have very high status. If they were taken into account the correlation between high occupational status and the exercise of leadership would be much more evident.

The situation in the Rotary club and the youth club is quite different. In the former, all members who have belonged to the club for more than five years have been officials at some time or other. The various offices, of course, differ in importance, but if we consider that of president, which is the highest attainable in the club, we find a distribution between occupational categories similar to the distribution of all offices. The picture is changed, however, if we examine the occupational category of all past presidents, whether they are present members of the club or not; of nineteen past presidents whose occupations are known, seven were in category 1 and six in category 2. This may mean either that in the past high occupational status was a more important factor in being elected president than it is now, or that there has been a decline in the status of the membership as a whole. Though there is no exact information about the past membership of the club it seems likely that the latter explanation is correct. Townspeople who know the club well consider that the occupational status of members is less high than it used to be, and there is corroborating evidence in the fact that a number of Squirebridge residents with very high occupational status have belonged to the club in the past but are no longer members. At all events, occupational status is unimportant at the present time. This may well be due to the restriction of membership, which in practice excludes some individuals with exceptionally high status as well as those in occupational categories 5–7. Differences of status within the range of categories 1–4 are perhaps not a serious obstacle to a rough equality of treatment, particularly in an organization which has as its official doctrine the promotion of fellowship. We shall return to this question of the distance between occupational categories at a later stage.

In the youth club, occupational status again appears relatively unimportant in relation to leadership, but the impression given by the analysis in Table 8 is somewhat misleading. We described earlier (p. 364) the evolution of the club leading to the secession of the 'middle-class' members, and leaving the membership predominantly 'working class', as it undoubtedly is at the present time. Although most of the officials are from category 5, the only really effective official, the secretary, is in category 3, and her effectiveness *vis-à-vis* the adult management committee (which is, naturally, the real source of authority) undoubtedly derives largely from her relatively high status.

Having analysed the formal hierarchy of the organizations, we attempted, by asking members to choose three representatives, to discover whether there existed any informal hierarchy, and how it was composed. There was a striking convergence of choices in all the organizations, but the choices were concentrated in every case upon individuals who were, or had recently been, important officials. In the Rotary club, five members received a large number of choices, and of these, four were or had been officials, and one had been a prominent member of a neighbouring club. In the cricket club, the five members receiving most choices were all officials. Similarly, in the dramatic society, eight officials received the largest number of choices, and in the youth club the officials and one member who had been an official. So far as these organizations are concerned there is evidently no informal hierarchy distinct from the formal hierarchy.

Personal Friendships

Friendship may be to the poet the 'peculiar boon of Heaven, the noble mind's delight and pride'—to the sociologist it is something besides. Those who enter into intimate personal relationships, such as friendship or marriage, must be presumed to have some common interests and attitudes, and to regard each other as, in some sense, equals. In a stratified society we should expect friendships to be formed, for the most part, between individuals belonging to the same stratum;

that this happens is a matter of common experience. The importance of occupation as a basis of social status would, therefore, be demonstrated if people invariably chose their friends entirely within their own occupational category. Conversely, if we were to discover that within the voluntary organizations friendships are formed without regard to occupational status, this would indicate that there are other bases of status which counteract the influence of occupation. The problem may also be approached in a different way. We may distinguish the friends people have from the friends they would like to have; if it were found, for example, that actual friends are usually in the same occupational category, whereas 'wished-for' friends are frequently in a higher occupational category, than that of the subject, this would indicate that, in the voluntary organizations, people wish to identify themselves with the members whose occupational status is high, and therefore that occupational status is an important factor in establishing the hierarchy of the organizations.

The present inquiry was mainly concerned with actual friends, but the questions on this topic elicited replies which confused actual and wished-for friends; in other words, people named as personal friends others who did not always name them in return. We were able, by cross-checking the replies, to separate the two categories, and thus to gain information about both. A summary of the friendship *choices* is given in the following table:

Table 9
SUMMARY OF CHOICES OF FRIENDS
(A = number of members; B = choices received per member; C = choices made per member)

Occupational category	Rotary club A	B	C	Cricket club A	B	C	Dramatic society A	B	C	Youth club A	B	C
1	8	1·1	0·4	—	—	—	22	1·0	1·5	—	—	—
2	13	1·2	2·6	—	—	—	35	1·7	1·5	1	—	—
3	12	1·4	1·2	5	2·0	1·4	25	1·3	1·4	3	0·7	1·3
4	2	3·0	2·0	6	2·8	2·2	17	0·6	0·5	4	0·8	0·5
5	—	—	—	18	0·2	0·6	14	0·9	0·6	18	1·1	1·1
6	—	—	—	3	—	0·3	1	—	1·0	6	0·2	0·3
7	—	—	—	—	—	—	—	—	—	1	1·0	—

These results do not show any strong correlation between occupational status and number of choices received, and in this they differ considerably from the results of a similar but more extensive study made by Lundberg in America.[1]

[1] See G. A. Lundberg, 'Social attraction patterns in a rural village', *Sociometry*, Vol. 1, July–October 1937. The person interviewed (any member of each

Only in the cricket club is it clear that those with higher occupational status received more choices than others, and also received more choices than they made. The main feature of the choices is that, except in the Rotary club, members in the higher occupational categories both received and made more choices than those in the lower categories. It is clear from the material, of which Table 9 is a summary, that the choices were by no means confined to the occupational category of the person choosing, and that, except in the cricket club, they were not made predominantly 'upwards'. On the present evidence it seems that membership of a voluntary organization may have some modifying influence on the individual's status based on occupation.

However, an analysis of actual friendships (the choices of wished-for friends having been eliminated) showed the limits of such modifying influences. Although, in the organizations other than the cricket club, friends had been chosen indiscriminately 'upwards' or 'downwards', it was noticeable that, in the great majority of cases, these choices had not extended more than one category immediately above or below the category of the person choosing. It was also apparent, in two of the organizations, that the gap between occupational categories 4 and 5, to which we have already referred in connection with the leadership, was equally important in the sphere of friendships. In the cricket club, no members in category 6 and only one in category 5 were personal friends of members in categories 3 and 4. In the dramatic society, though the division between categories 4 and 5 is less evident in the table, a similar situation obtains. Only four members in category 5 were friends of members in higher categories, and these four were all clerical workers, whereas the rest of the members in category 5, with one exception, were manual workers. This suggests that one of the principal status distinctions in leisure organizations is that between non-manual and manual workers, a distinction corresponding, in most cases, to that between the first four, and the last three, occupational categories. Another form of association between members of the dramatic society provides further evidence of a division of the membership into two basic groups. A number of members, described as the 'very active', and in fact in-

---

family, usually the housewife) was asked to name his/her best friends in the village, which had a population of approximately 1,000. The families were graded according to socio-economic status, using the Chapin scale. It was found that 'the average number of choices *made* by people in different socio-economic groups did not vary significantly. . . . The number of choices *received*, however, increased conspicuously with increasing socio-economic status.'

cluding most of the officials, meet regularly for a drink in one of the town's principal hotels. Twenty-nine of the members are known to associate in this way, and of these seven are in category 1, eleven in category 2, nine in category 3, one in category 4, and one (who is a clerical worker and also an official) in category 5. Thus an inner group has been formed in the society, which virtually excludes the members who are not in occupational categories 1–3.

In the Rotary club, since there are no members in occupational categories below 4, the question of a fundamental division between categories 4 and 5 does not arise. It is worth noting that the greatest similarity of behaviour between different occupational categories in the choice of friends, is to be found in the Rotary club. This is almost certainly due to the restriction of membership to the first four categories, and to the official policy of promoting fellowship.

The youth club is an exception; in this case no barrier exists between categories 4 and 5 so far as friendships are concerned. The most likely explanation of this seems to be that, for young people, status relationships are less clear and less fixed. The members are relatively ignorant of the adult status system, or at least of its more subtle distinctions, and they may also, of course, regard it as unimportant. It should be added that the members were graded in accordance with their father's occupations, and that the facts about these occupations may not be known within the group.

Status in Voluntary Organizations and Status in the Community

It has been suggested, by a number of recent writers, that the individual's status in the community is increasingly affected by the degree of his participation in voluntary organizations.[1] If this were so, and if the degree of participation in voluntary organizations were not itself correlated with occupational status, an important alternative basis of social status would be available. An attempt was made, in this inquiry, to investigate these matters, but it soon became clear that participation in voluntary organizations is in fact correlated with occupational status.

In the Rotary club, where there are no members in the categories below 4, there is little difference between occupational categories in respect of degree of participation in voluntary organizations (the high figures for category 2 are due to the exceptional activities of two members). This appears to be a special characteristic of the Rotary club, as already noticed in connection with leadership and friendships; the

[1] Cf. Goldhamer, cited in footnote 1, p. 352 above.

SOCIAL STRATIFICATION IN VOLUNTARY ORGANIZATIONS

generally high degree of participation in other voluntary organizations is in accordance with the aims of the club, which are to give service to the community. In the dramatic society, there is a decline in the degree of participation from the top to the bottom of the scale, with marked breaks between categories 2 and 3 and between categories 4 and 5. There is a broadly similar decline in the case of the cricket club. On the evidence available we must acknowledge that the degree of participation in voluntary organizations is correlated with occupational status, and cannot, therefore, be regarded, in general, as contributing independently to the determination of social status. There remains, however, the possibility that the social status of some individuals may be affected by their assiduous activity in voluntary organizations. We carefully examined individual cases to see if this were so, but only in one instance did it appear likely. This is the case of a small shopkeeper, in occupational category 4, who is active in numerous organizations, and who has (it seems by this means) considerably enhanced his social status and built up a circle of friends whose occupational status is far higher than his own. But this is exceptional. We have found, as a general rule, that one of the most effective ways of compensating for low occupational status is to acquire formal political authority; of the individuals, in Squirebridge as a whole, whose social status was most elevated in comparison with their occupational status, almost all were, or had been, town or county councillors or aldermen. It may be suggested, therefore, that the most important voluntary organizations, from the point of view of general social status, are the political organizations.

Table 10

MEMBERSHIPS AND OFFICIAL POSITIONS IN OTHER ORGANIZATIONS (EXCLUDING TRADE AND PROFESSIONAL ORGANIZATIONS) OF MEMBERS OF THREE OF THE ORGANIZATIONS STUDIED

(A = number of members; B = memberships per member; C = official positions per member)

Occupational category	Rotary club			Cricket club			Dramatic society		
	A	B	C	A	B	C	A	B	C
1	8	2·9	1·3	—	—	—	22	2·0	0·7
2	13	4·7	3·0	—	—	—	35	2·1	0·7
3	12	2·9	1·8	5	1·6	—	25	1·7	0·6
4	2	3·0	3·0	6	2·1	0·8	17	1·8	0·4
5	—	—	—	18	1·1	0·3	14	1·1	0·4
6	—	—	—	3	0·3	—	1	1·0	—
7	—	—	—	—	—	—	—	—	—

The importance of occupational status is shown in two ways. First, there is a correlation between high occupational status and the exercise of leadership, which involves more *intensive* participation in activities. Secondly, high occupational status is correlated with more *extensive* participation in voluntary organizations.

Final Remarks

This second inquiry has confirmed, in general, that there is a correlation between occupational status and status in voluntary organizations, though this is not so evident when occupations are graded according to the Standard Classification as it is with the broader classification used in the first inquiry. Social differentiation in the voluntary organizations produces three, and not seven, basic status groups. The demarcation line between two of these groups can be represented in terms of the occupational scale; it is that which separates categories 1–4 from categories 5–7, and it has been demonstrated from the patterns of leadership and friendships. The distinction between these groups corresponds broadly to that between non-manual and manual workers. The second demarcation line is at the top of the social hierarchy, and though it is not revealed by an analysis based on the Standard Classification its existence is obvious.[1] It separates the aristocracy, the squirearchy, and the very wealthy from everyone else, including the majority of those who would be classified in category 1 of the occupational scale. In Squirebridge, for instance, there are a few people in this category, principally wealthy business men (one of whom lends the grounds of his house for the summer fêtes of various local organizations). Those who do take any part in voluntary organizations are always presidents, vice-presidents, or patrons, and mix very little, if at all, with the ordinary members. The principal status distinction in many cases is, in fact, that between the ordinary members (including officials) and the vice-presidents or patrons. This has been illustrated from the cricket club and the dramatic society, but it is true of many other organizations in the town.

The distinction between manual workers, non-manual workers, and the aristocracy and the very wealthy corresponds roughly with the traditional distinction between working class, middle class, and upper class. In this sense our inquiries may be said to have confirmed the

---

[1] For this reason the Standard Classification is not entirely satisfactory as an instrument of research, especially in small group and community studies. It would be useful to make further studies of the distances between categories, and of the distinctions within category 1.

validity of the classical analysis of social stratification. There arc almost infinite subtleties of social differentiation in modern society, but the skeleton of the social hierarchy is still constituted by the division into three broad classes. Of course, social distinctions have always existed within the main social strata, as for example within the aristocracy itself or, in the middle class, between an independent professional man and a salaried employee. Our inquiry suggests that today these finer social distinctions are losing some of their importance, at least within the middle-class group. In terms of the Standard Classification, occupational status within the range of categories 1–4, though it has *some* influence upon status inside the voluntary organizations, has usually only a slight influence. Where the influence appears to be strong it will generally be found that the distinction is between individuals whose social status is very high and the rest of the members of categories 1–4. At the other end of the scale, the division between categories 4 and 5 is extremely clear; at the bottom of the hierarchy, the members of the working class play a relatively small part in the voluntary organizations (other than their own particular sport, trade union, and political organizations), and have practically no share in their government.

One final comment should be made on the locality in which the research was done. Since the gentry left their country mansions (many of which are now used as offices or schools), Squirebridge has few inhabitants with very high social status; it is pre-eminently a middle-class town. The range of status positions is probably, therefore, less extensive than it would be in some other communities and this affects both the composition of the organizations and the relations between the members inside them. It may be doubted, for instance, whether the influence of occupational status on the intra-group relations would be so slight in Rotary clubs elsewhere. The small size of Squirebridge is another factor to be considered. On the one hand, there is a local patriotism which tends to diminish status differences, while on the other hand, the exact status of each individual is better known than it would be in a larger and more anonymous community. So far as we could determine, the first influence, together with that of the general middle-class character of the population, is more effective.

XIV

A Study of Three Voluntary Organizations

ROSALIND C. CHAMBERS

THE field of social service and philanthropy is one in which, until recently, social stratification was particularly marked; in no sphere of national life, perhaps, were Disraeli's Two Nations more apparent. The community—in so far as it was concerned with the question at all—fell into two distinct groups, the benefactors and the beneficiaries. Income level, education, social status and even geographical location were similar within each group, and it would be in the highest degree unlikely for a resident in the poorer districts of a town to be a member of the benefactor group.

Such a relationship did not necessarily imply patronage or servility; a division of society into classes below preparing for a hierarchic heaven above was simply an accepted part of the divinely ordered scheme of things, and the very sense of social obligation and responsibility which undoubtedly inspired many of the English upper classes helped to perpetuate it.

During the last part of the nineteenth century recognized standards in some branches of social work were developed, and with the evolution of the qualified woman (for social work was and is a largely feminine profession) the lady bountiful was frequently supplanted. But this did not materially change the situation; nor did the appearance, mostly in rural areas, of the *nouveaux riches*, who often lacked the sense of social responsibility possessed by the older aristocracy, so that personal relationships between the benefactor and beneficiary classes were less satisfactory. Social change in these respects merely meant the substitution of one *élite* for another.

Up to the outbreak of the 1939–45 war, though some change was observable, it would have been almost inconceivable that in a philanthropic organization the relationships of e.g. committee members and

383

clients could be interchangeable, or that members of particular trades or industries or even residents in a 'poor' locality could take part in social service, much less in the control of such service.

In the past ten years this situation has altered, assisted by the effects of the war, the increase in State-controlled or assisted welfare activities and the processes of social and economic change. This study has tried to discover whether there is evidence that for social service, mobility between social groups is increasing, and that members of the lower and lower middle income groups are participating, and to some extent assuming control in various forms of public and social service, while the scope of such work widens and it ceases to be identified with monetary help.

Three organizations have been examined—chiefly composed of women —the Women's Institutes, the Women's Voluntary Services, and the British Red Cross Society. I have personally gathered the information set down here from the W.V.S. and the Women's Institutes by means of interviews at different levels and visits to various localities to observe and participate in the activities of branches and centres. The Red Cross were not able to give such facilities and most of the material concerning this society has been taken from their publications or from information collected by one of their own officers who undertook the inquiry in close consultation with me. Certain deductions have been made from this information but the bulk of it was not secured at first-hand.

These three societies have two characteristics in common; the members of each engage in public service (though in the Women's Institutes this is a secondary aim) and they claim to offer opportunities for all social groups to take part in such service; apart from this their differences are great. In origin, the Red Cross is by far the oldest, having been founded in 1870, and it is also international in character, while both the others are British. The Women's Institutes' movement began in 1917 and arose to some extent out of the 1914–18 war, while the Women's Voluntary Services was formed in preparation for the war of 1939–45. The Charter of the Red Cross Society limits its activities to those bearing upon the promotion of health and the alleviation of sickness, though this is widely interpreted to include a great deal of social service. The Women's Institutes, unlike the other two, is a rural organization, consisting of gatherings of countrywomen whose main purpose is to improve and develop the conditions of life in the country; it is in the first place educational but various forms of public service come a good second. The W.V.S. was originally concerned with Civil Defence and its implications, and the many forms of work which it has since undertaken have developed bit by bit as the need arose.

There are also considerable divergences in control and finance. The British Red Cross Society is governed by a council which appoints the executive committee and formulates policy. The local branches have a good deal of responsibility and freedom both financially and as to work and personnel. They are organized on a county basis, with a county president and county director and committee in control. The county branches raise their own funds through local appeals and activities, while the national headquarters are supported by subscriptions, legacies and accumulated funds. The society also receives grants from the Duke of Gloucester's Red Cross Fund.

The Women's Institutes have an elaborate structure of federations, councils and committees on an elected basis with the ultimate control of policy determined by the general membership at the annual general meeting at which all Institutes are entitled to be represented. They are financed through members' fees and donations, interest from an endowment fund and a Treasury grant for educational work.

The W.V.S. has no committee system and is indeed a virtual dictatorship at all levels. There is a chairman's committee of senior officers at headquarters which makes all executive appointments down to borough organizers; local organizers appoint minor officers in their areas. All expenses are paid from public funds by the Home Office (or local authorities); there are no subscriptions, and no appeals to the community for the W.V.S. as such.

In all these organizations the control and personnel are changing and the activities are widening. Until comparatively recently the leading personage in each Red Cross branch, Women's Institute or W.V.S. centre was almost invariably the most prominent woman in the upper classes; in some cases greatness was thrust upon her, though even then she usually accepted her status without question, and in others she assumed the chief position as an automatic right. Where required by the rules, the constitutional procedure of democratic election was carried out, but the result of ballots and elections was more or less a foregone conclusion. In recent years, however, a change has taken place; more and more officers and leading members are being chosen from the wives or female relatives of farmers, market gardeners, minor public officials, small tradesmen, railway men and unskilled workers.

It is not easy to give statistical evidence of this; it would of course be possible to group members of different branches of national societies according to occupation or income level but it would not present a true picture of national organizations because the social status of such groups varies in different parts of the country. The term 'farming' is variable according to whether the district is one of large or small farms or both. In some parts the wife of a leading tractor driver, stockman or foreman on a large farm who would officially rank as an agricultural worker might, as far as education and income are concerned, stand higher in the scale than the wife of a small independent farmer. In some towns the dominant group may be also the highest income group; in others it may not; and in some parts of the country people in occupations of lower status will be admitted to fields which would be less open to them in other districts. In a manufacturing city in the north, the wives of industrialists and managers will be given higher status than in a cathedral or university city with an *élite* of its own.

In spite of such difficulties there is evidence that in these societies office bearers no longer belong to one social group. The process has not been carried out without pain and heartburnings; both the dispossessed and the new office bearers have sometimes been outraged and alarmed. Some ordinary members have resented 'someone like us' being chosen for or appointed to positions of control. An officer of one organization remarked that the village woman was usually a snob, and would much prefer to follow the squiress or vicaress whom she would regard as the 'natural' leader. Another said that if she wanted to start a new branch or invigorate an old one, she would approach first the 'Big House' if one existed and if it had a woman in it, because if interest could be aroused there the rest of the community would almost certainly follow the example set. It requires a long educational process to get the 'ordinary' woman to accept and exercise responsibility, but it is being accomplished and is assisted by social change, particularly in rural areas. In increasing numbers big houses are being turned into institutions of various kinds and there is no longer a squire or squiress to lead the villages. Both in town and country ecclesiastical parishes are being united so that one parson serves two or even three villages or districts. He can only live in one and in the others the vicarage is empty. Factors in the assumption of positions of control are now most frequently the possession of a telephone or a car or—most important—time to attend meetings. These are sometimes though not always marks of economic superiority, but where such lack of amenities alone constitutes an obstacle to office bearing, there is a change in attitude. The faith in a divinely ordered, graded society is disappearing and particular groups are no longer regarded as inherently incapable of fulfilling particular functions.

The Women's Voluntary Services

The W.V.S. was formed shortly before the last war and worked as a voluntary organization in close touch with the Government and under the orders of local authorities. Its activities were many and they are described in the official History of the War and also in many other publications, newspapers, books and films, for the service has always received excellent publicity. At the end of the war there were over a million members; in the period immediately following, the future of W.V.S. was uncertain and the membership fell off considerably. But now that a permanent place has been given to the service the numbers are increasing again.

The W.V.S. has aroused bitter criticism and enthusiastic admiration, both often equally undiscerning and obscured by prejudice and emotion. One of the main grounds of criticism is the alleged undemocratic structure and organization. There are no committees; senior appointments are made from headquarters, largely on personal grounds rather than on paper qualifications. Since the W.V.S. is a service as distinct from an ordinary voluntary organization, it is contended that government through elected bodies would be impossible. The success of the organization at all levels and in all centres depends on the personality of the organizers, and the whole service from top to bottom is strongly influenced by the very remarkable personality of the chairman, Lady Reading.

The heads of departments at headquarters are chiefly drawn from the middle and some from the upper ranks of society, as are the principal regional officers. There are not very many of these potentates—the country is divided into twelve regions and there are twenty departments at national headquarters; positions of control below this are not as sometimes alleged the preserve of the lady of the manor or her urban equivalent.

Though W.V.S. uniform is marked according to its wearer's 'unit', e.g. headquarters, regional staff, centre organizer, etc., there are no rank badges. In most of those centres observed, the vitally necessary condition for W.V.S. success was fulfilled—the presence of the key woman usually of the middle class, sometimes of the lower middle class, with a group of enthusiastic satellites. The atmosphere was in varying degrees affected by a somewhat naïve heroine worship, and it is perhaps difficult to disentangle devotion to the service of the community from devotion to the personality of Mrs. (or occasionally Lady) X. Where classes in a centre were very mixed, evidence was looked for of that brand of snobbery and emulation which gains glory from working with a social class regarded as superior. Such evidence was not apparent, though it may have been missed owing to the middle-class bias and outlook of the investigator.

A second charge levelled against W.V.S. is that it is not really voluntary—many of its workers are in fact paid from public funds though they are not under Government control. The reply made by the service is that the overwhelming majority of its members are voluntary and are women who by reason of their responsibilities and circumstances could not do full-time work. There are some paid full-time national and regional appointments; their numbers and identity are difficult to discover and this uncertainty has given rise in some quarters to the criticism that the W.V.S. regard paid work as derogatory and despise the worker who has to earn a salary in return for her services. If there is an element of truth in this, there is a more justifiable reason for not disclosing the facts about paid workers. The W.V.S. take the line that the obligations of voluntary workers are quite as strong as those of paid ones; there should be no difference between them in the fulfilment of responsibilities or the quality and regularity of work. To distinguish between the volunteer and the paid worker might be to impair this principle.

The aim of W.V.S., which was almost achieved during the war, is to have a nation-wide organization based on local government units but with representative members in every village and as far as possible in every urban street. It is unlikely that this aim will be fulfilled in time of nominal peace, but the structure with its gradations and its wide range of opportunities offers scope for service and for some measure of control to large numbers of women who had never contemplated doing such work before W.V.S. was formed, and many of whom belonged to the social groups who received help rather than rendered it.

Attendance at any large and representative gathering of W.V.S. makes it clear that the movement contains members drawn from many social groups, and that its members are largely middle-aged or even elderly, though a certain number of young recruits are coming in and may increase with the return of Civil Defence. A rough analysis of age grouping taken from the numbers present at a refresher course open to the whole country, a large general meeting, a county conference of area organizers and the actual members of two London boroughs, six provincial boroughs, and the rural areas of three counties indicates that about 60 per cent of the membership is over 40 and about 10 per cent under 25. One reason for this rather elderly pattern may be that 'crabbed age and youth cannot live together' but it is also likely that most young women, whether married or single, are very fully occupied and cannot given regular service. W.V.S. members are grouped in three categories—A, who give regular and frequent service; B, who help occasionally; and C, who can only be called on in an emergency. A detailed analysis of the age-grouping in these three categories would show a higher percentage of younger women in B and C. But as some centre organizers do not include their C members in their total membership returns while others do, and some are very uncertain about their B women, such an analysis cannot be made.

No W.V.S. member can be fully enrolled, receive a badge and have the right to wear uniform unless she has signed an enrolment form, done sixty hours' work and taken the 'basic training' which consists of three 'talks'; two on general W.V.S. activities and one on some special aspect of the work. There is also special training—i.e. instruction in some field of work where specialized knowledge is required, and 'refresher' courses lasting about three days which take place regularly at headquarters. While the importance of training is emphasized, it is clear that W.V.S. attach a somewhat special meaning to it; it was pointed out at one refresher course that training does not necessarily mean taking a long course or becoming an expert. For most members common sense plus a little extra knowledge is quite enough. These modest qualifications are usually supplemented by one-day schools, discussions, etc. Some centres include a training officer on their centre staff—all did so originally. W.V.S. headquarters at any rate emphasize that they are not trying in any way to rival the expert or professional worker in any of their fields; W.V.S. are ancillary and undertake training simply to equip themselves to be useful co-operators.

A typical course consisted of about twenty-five women, mostly middle-aged or elderly, from all over the country. They were carefully selected by the regions and their expenses were paid. They were drawn from many social groups but there were no industrial workers. The occupational status of students at these courses is not known to the organizers; but there was enough variety of accent, appearance and attitude to make it clear that there was a considerably greater mixture of social class than is seen in many other voluntary women's organizations. The whole atmosphere was outstandingly friendly, courteous and affable. This is not as trivial as it sounds for these women are, in their various fields of work, dealing with all sections of the community, and the standard of manners established at headquarters and in the refresher courses tends to be reproduced in the centres. Sympathetic insight was also shown by speakers on various forms of welfare, and there was no trace of the Lady Bountiful attitude. It is unfortunately true that this example is not invariably achieved in the centres, but a divergence between the standards set by the headquarters of an organization and the practice of some of its local units is certainly not peculiar to the W.V.S. The criticism sometimes heard that the *élite* at the top level sets an example of patronage and condescending benevolence which is followed by the lesser lights throughout the service is not generally justified.

The general purpose of W.V.S. activity as described by one of their leaders is that 'no individual should suffer unnecessarily through lack of a helping hand'. The service works primarily as the handmaid of central and local government departments, but also through individuals and other associations. No instructions as to carrying out a particular job are issued by headquarters; circulars may be sent out suggesting or requesting some service, but the local organizers are free to decide whether it is possible or suitable for their members. It is claimed that this freedom of action disposes effectively of the criticism that W.V.S. is autocratic and imposes a headquarters dictatorship upon its members; but in fact the influence and prestige of the chairman and her committee are so great that it is improbable that requests and suggestions as to forms of service are often turned down. The wide range of W.V.S. work during and since the war is well known; it has become almost a motto that 'W.V.S. never says no'. One noteworthy feature of activities is a tendency to regard as equally valuable the small and the big, the important and the trivial. This may indicate a lack of the sense of proportion but it may also be evidence of an attitude which has to a great extent been lacking in social work organizations—a belief that service to the community can be rendered irrespective of age, status, wealth, intellect, leisure or technical qualifications.

The focal point of W.V.S. activity is the centre in urban districts or the area—which unites a group of villages—in rural districts. The organizers who are appointed from headquarters are responsible for the work done and for the choice and appointment of subordinate officers. Organizers do not work through committees and are virtual dictators in theory; in practice the success of their work depends on their relationships with their fellow workers and with the local authorities and other public bodies with whom they work.

The social status of organizers has changed since the war, though in some centres the same key woman—usually though not invariably a representative of the aristocracy, as indicated by a title, or of the upper professional classes—still holds office. Where there has been a change the new organizer is often of lower social status; she may be the wife of a business man or a schoolmaster or architect or a bookie and is generally younger than her predecessor. As far as these positions of authority go, there is no evidence of great social mobility; it is unusual for a representative of the wage-earning groups to be head of a W.V.S. centre. There is a filtering up of the second grade into what was largely a monopoly of the first grade, but no more than that.

Below the organizer women of all social groups take part in and control W.V.S. activities. In old people's welfare the leaders are in many instances wives of railway workers, small tradesmen or industrial workers. In one borough visited the leader was the wife of an assistant cook in an hotel while her assistant was a colonel's wife; in another, the leader was the wife of a small builder and decorator; in a country town the chief assistants to the centre organizer, each of whom was in charge of some activity, included a municipal official's wife, two or three boarding-house landladies, a waiter's wife, a bank manager's widow and the wife of an industrial worker. In another semi-urban district the assistants to the area organizer were a farmer's wife and the wife of a small shopkeeper.

In rural districts each village has a representative to assist the area organizer. In one area, largely feudal in outlook, the village representatives were a vicar's wife, a squire's wife, various farmers' wives, a policeman's wife and a retired postmistress. An important factor in the appointment of a village representative is the possession of a telephone, for in scattered districts when an urgent job has to be undertaken, rapid contact is a necessity. This rules out agricultural workers to a great extent, as such workers are not usually on the telephone. One organizer, herself an impoverished member of the aristocracy and an outstandingly capable woman, stated that she would prefer to have all her subordinate officers drawn from the working classes because she considered them more reliable than those of higher social groups. It is possible, however, that an unconscious reason for preferring those of lower social status was because they were more ready to recognize the superiority by nature and education of the centre organizer. In all these cases the people con-

391

cerned appeared to work efficiently and in complete harmony. The heroine worship of the leader or leaders is there but this is not a phenomenon peculiar to W.V.S. It is present in many organizations, for example in the Women's Institutes, though the structure of the W.V.S. gives it perhaps more scope.

Apart from holding positions of control, it would be true to say that all classes take part in W.V.S. activity, but that the working class is in a minority, partly owing to lack of time. In some centres only a very few members belong to this social group; in others a considerable number. In one London borough which includes many social classes in its area, about 60 per cent of the W.V.S. membership is drawn from industrial workers, shop assistants or small independent traders; the proportion of working-class members is seldom more than 30 per cent in any centre. The geographical basis of W.V.S. activity is the local government unit and such units vary in the social composition of the population.

Any large and representative gathering of W.V.S. members contains a much larger proportion of lower middle-class and working-class women than is present at the annual meetings of most social service organizations; and there is no doubt that the chairman is right in her contention that women in social groups who never before took part in community services have been enabled to do so through the wide variety of work offered by the W.V.S.

The Women's Institutes

The main purpose of Women's Institutes is to improve and develop the conditions of life in the country; this necessarily involves community and social service, but the W.I. movement is not, as is the W.V.S., primarily an organization for rendering service to the community. An important part of its work is the education of its members through its own institutions, Denman College, and also through week-end and one-day schools, lectures and discussion at W.I. meetings. Such education finds its practical issue in action on matters of common interest, on national and local level.

The Women's Institutes came into being during the First World War, the idea of countrywomen meeting together being derived from Canada where the first Women's Institute was formed in 1897. From the beginning the movement was based on the principle that all members have the same rights and privileges and all may and should take part in the running of their own Institute and in formulating the national policy of the movement. In this, as the official handbook notes, the Institutes have had to combat the long tradition of silence of the countrywoman, who in the early days of Institutes would not talk, vote or serve on committees.

The National Federation of Women's Institutes which now covers England, Wales and the Channel Islands—the movement has assumed a rather different form in Scotland—came into being in 1917. There are at the present time over 7,500 Institutes grouped in county federations with a membership of nearly half a million.

The members, through their Institutes, are responsible for formulating the policy of the movement, by means of their delegates to the annual general meeting. Each Institute elects its own president and committee and takes part in the election of the county committee and most of the national executive committee.

The National Federation of Women's Institutes derives its funds from affiliation fees, donations from county federations, profits from sales of literature and Treasury grants for educational, agricultural and handicrafts work. Individual Institutes get their income from members' subscriptions and money-raising efforts. All Institutes must contribute to a pool for paying the fares of delegates to the annual general meeting and many county federations also pool the expenses of the delegates attending council meetings and pay travelling expenses of county executive and members. The observance or neglect of this practice has some bearing on the social and economic composition of these bodies.

The individual Women's Institute can only be formed in a rural community ordinarily of not more than 4,000 population; the initiative must come from the women of the area and at least twenty-five (or twelve in small hamlets) must express a wish for an Institute. After various preliminaries an officially appointed organizer may start one, a committee and officers will be elected and activities begin. Within the framework of the rules each Institute is free to develop in the direction which seems most helpful to its own village.

The wide range of Women's Institute activities emerge in various directions from the basic aim—that of improving and developing the conditions of country life. This fundamental object is carried out with the assistance of national and county federation sub-committees covering such subjects as agriculture, drama and music, handicrafts, education and public questions, international affairs, marketing and literature.

A high standard is reached in these various branches and the establishment of Denman College with its educational courses is likely to develop these activities still further. In the Women's Institutes' work to keep and improve the rural way of life, there is no trace of that self-conscious rusticity associated sometimes with morris dancers and hand-woven garments. Even a cursory survey of village and county pro-grammes shows an awareness of modern needs; the poster publicizing one county produce sale and show displayed as an added attraction a mannequin parade and an exhibition entitled Beauty for Everyone. The Institutes are not, as are the Red Cross and the W.V.S., a movement whose main objective is fulfilled by public and social service; such service is, however, a necessary part of their work. It may be undertaken by the movement as a whole through resolutions, approaching government departments, representation on national bodies or publications on rural questions; there is also local service such as the membership of local government and other public bodies, old people's welfare, the 'adoption' of children in homes or institutions and other allied work. During the war exceedingly valuable work was done by the Women's Institutes in connection with the evacuation scheme and the food preserving scheme, to name only two of their fields of service.

The Women's Institute is nearly always the most important women's organization in the village and often the only one. Where there are other societies the members, especially the leaders, are the same people in all, and the activities overlap; but the Women's Institute comes first. In some villages almost every eligible woman or girl belongs to it, and members are drawn from all ranks and all age-groups. The social pattern of a village differs widely from that of a town; so to some extent does that of one village from another. The mechanization of agriculture or the erection of factories in a rural area has introduced a class of workers into the village who are more characteristic of industrial areas. While the wives of these mechanics and factory workers often join the Institutes the number of the lowest-paid agricultural workers' wives is still small, and the average age of members as a whole is high. But these charac-teristics show signs of change. The intake of younger women is in-creasing, particularly where the Institutes hold their meetings in the evening, and the proportion of lower wage groups is also increasing. The Institutes whose programmes seem to come nearest to the ideals of the movement are not always those with largest membership but those where the mixture of class and age is greatest. One of the most alive and go-ahead of the Institutes which I have visited was in a small and scattered village where the president was the squire's wife and the officers and members covered all classes; a village moreover to which access was so difficult and where winter storms were so severe that no outside speakers or entertainment could be called upon during the worst months. On the other hand the most parochially minded Institute I have seen was in a largish village with a big membership drawn from small farmers' or farm workers' wives and families.

From the beginning the Women's Institutes have been democratic in conception and have worked through democratic methods: the ordinary member is encouraged to take a full part in shaping policy and there is no reason in theory why she should not assume a position of control on the highest level. At national level there is at present little sign of penetration by the wives of small farmers or agricultural workers. Most of the national executive and county presidents may be assigned unhesitatingly to the upper and professional classes. The county federations vary in their social pattern, which has changed in the last few years and is still changing. Observation at the annual general meeting, discussions with officers and an analysis of membership of some of the county executive committees indicate that a proportion of the members is drawn from the farming groups, and not always the 'large' farming groups. In one case this proportion was put at about 25 per cent; here the remainder of the membership was less obviously aristocratic than usual, and there was a general tendency towards a mixing of social groups. The main hindrance to leadership and control is much more lack of time and difficulty of communication than class 'feeling'; where such feeling does exist it is stronger in the lower social groups than in the higher, and reluctance to take responsibility on one side rather than clinging to office on the other prevents a larger representation of farmers and farm workers.

The chief officers of individual Institutes are much more representative of the lower income groups. Social change is more obvious in rural areas than in urban, as shown in the disappearance of the lord of the manor and the conversion of his house into an approved school or an hotel, and in the amalgamation of parishes resulting in the departure of the vicar and his wife. Even where the latter remains, domestic duties in an inconvenient vicarage have often made it impossible for her to assume her former dominating position. But it is not, of course, only social change that has altered the distribution of power in Women's Institutes: the ideals and the long-continued educational work of the movement itself have been a much more effective agent. In one Institute the former lady of the manor had been duly elected as president every year since its beginning. A few years ago a considerable stir was caused when she was defeated in the ballot and a poultry farmer took her place. The Institute continued to flourish in spite of the prophecies of some of

395

the older members, and after some years' successful tenure of office the poultry farmer was followed by a retired schoolmistress and she in her turn by a policeman's wife. The other officers and committee belong to widely different social groups—the retired maiden lady and equally retired domestic servant, the schoolmistress, the district nurse, the wives of small and large farmers, the publican and the shopkeepers. At the other side of England is an Institute where the president is still the lady of the manor, the secretary is the stationmaster's wife and the committee includes the wives of builders and farmers and a lecturer of the local education authority. In another village there is much less variation; there is no squire, no resident doctor or parson, and the population consists of shopkeepers, small farmers working on their own or employing at most two or three men, and the agricultural workers. These groups are indistinguishable as a 'class' from each other, except that the shopkeepers are the most prosperous. Here, with no élite to draw upon, the Institute almost disappeared because no one could be found to take responsibility. A 'pep' talk from a vigorous county officer resulted in an unwritten law that every member should be willing to serve on the committee. This had an admirable effect and the Institute has now a satisfactory and increasing membership with excellent officers. I have myself seen no Institute where the proceedings and activities were dominated by one social group—except as indicated above. But discussion with officers of the movement shows that some do still exist, where the formalities of democratic procedure have to be followed, but where control is vested in the leading ladies of the village. These are, however, becoming fewer and are in no sense characteristic of the movement as a whole. As with the W.V.S. there is often a strong element of heroine worship but this is not only shown by members of lower social status for those of higher, though it may take this form. The people who inspire affection and veneration of this kind are usually national or local officers and do not always belong to the aristocracy or even the middle class. This is apparently characteristic of many women's organizations and it is a mistake invariably to identify it with snobbishness or 'class feeling' at all.

All members are expected to participate in Institute activities, including public and social service, though the degree to which this expectation is realized varies. The annual general meeting, where public questions are discussed and where the whole movement is represented, shows that countrywomen of all degrees from the nobility and gentry to the wives of agricultural workers and miners are, through their Institutes, taking an active and intelligent part in public affairs. On one occasion eleven resolutions were on the agenda, including such varied subjects as the provision of spectacles under the National Health Service, accidents in the home, open-cast coalmining, women in industry, and accommodation for old people. The proposers and seconders of the resolutions and those taking part in the discussion came from many social groups. This was clear not only from the superficial criteria of appearance and speech, but delegate after delegate in setting forth her reasons for supporting or opposing a resolution explicitly or implicitly indicated the occupational group from which she came, and such groups were as diverse as mentioned above. Many women are taking part in rural government as a result of the interest aroused by Women's Institute lectures and discussion; but the majority belong to the middle classes—retired professional women or the wives of farmers or doctors, etc., and this form of public activity does not show all-class representation to any marked degree. Participation in old people's welfare and activities connected with children and the sick is, as in the W.V.S., spread throughout all groups. It is in fact so general, largely as a result of the Women's Institutes, that it is often forgotten how comparatively recent a development such service is.

There are two more factors, both promoting social mixing in the Women's Institutes, that should be mentioned. The first of these is Denman College at Abingdon which is an educational institution founded in 1948, offering courses to Institute members. Students are selected so that each course is as far as possible representative of different localities and the mixing together tends to break down the isolationism sometimes characteristic of country people. No questions are asked as to the students' social background and as they mostly share rooms and all take part in small groups in household duties there are considerable possibilities for mixing during a course. A country housewives' course which was reasonably typical consisted of about forty women, the majority of whom were farmers' or country tradesmen's wives but including a few teachers, and one or two belonging to the retired gentlewomen group. They were mostly between 35 and 55, five under 30, one or two over 60. During the day which was spent there it was possible to observe the process of mixing at work; barriers to this were much more geographical than social, but by the end of the afternoon the different elements had become a group of students with a bond in the Women's Institutes and a common aim—that of improving the quality of their own Institute and becoming more effective members.

The second and very different development which must be mentioned is the progress of suburbanization, which is affecting the Women's Institutes in several ways. In the home counties, villages which are rural in many respects, serve to a large extent as dormitory areas for workers in London, and the wives of middle-class professional men form an increasingly large proportion of Women's Institute members. This may affect the balance of membership but the population does not usually, at present anyhow, rise beyond the 4,000 limit and the village remains a rural entity with predominantly rural interests, though those may become rather self-conscious.

A different situation arises where the actual town enlarges its limits and absorbs former villages. This is happening not only on the borders of large towns but also in the medium-size provincial towns such as Norwich, Cambridge or Scarborough. Here there is no gap between the former village and the present town; Women's Institutes established in the early days of the movement find themselves with a very large membership functioning in an area with a population well in excess of 4,000 and one which can only by a considerable stretch of imagination be called rural. Apart from problems of size and function, this suburban development has had its effect upon the social status of members. In the villages the population still falls into two or perhaps three main groups— a decreasing number of the landowners, the farmers, tenant or owner, and the farm workers. Professional and trading groups are still a small proportion of the whole. In the suburban districts now encroaching upon the villages the agriculturists and landowners are being supplemented, and even nearly superseded, by an increasing number of minor professional, clerical and shop-working groups, some of whom work in the easily accessible town, some in the scarcely distinguishable village. In these suburban Institutes, therefore, a large proportion of the members belong to the middle and lower middle class and the skilled working class; they form an active and dynamic group, ready and willing to take responsibility and exercise a considerable influence on the character and programmes of their Institutes. One question arising from this situation is whether the Women's Institutes should withdraw from the area and leave an urban organization to function. But the members are generally very unwilling that this should happen as they naturally have a deep affection for their Institute and value the movement as a whole, and they maintain that the originally rural character of their neighbourhood is still sufficiently strong to justify their continuance within the national federation.

From the point of view of social integration, the influx of new types of members, tending often to take the lead, may help to bridge the gulf still sometimes existing between 'leading ladies' and agricultural workers' wives and encourage a greater readiness by the latter to act as officers or committee members. On the other hand it may tend to squeeze them out as they feel the Institute is no place for them. Both these possibilities seem to me to be present in Institutes which I have seen, but it is too soon to say which will be the stronger.

The British Red Cross Society

The British Red Cross Society, the third of the organizations selected for study, differs from the two others in important respects. First, it is considerably older, and though like the W.V.S. it came into being in response to the needs of war, its object under its First Charter was not to help in Civil Defence, but to furnish aid to the sick and wounded on the battlefield and to train its members to operate as recognized auxiliaries to the Army and Navy medical services. By a Supplementary Charter granted in 1919, the work was extended to the promotion of health, the prevention of disease and the mitigation of suffering throughout the world. These objects have been given a wide interpretation and especially since the latter period of the 1939–45 war, have included welfare activities which are in some respects similar to those performed by the W.V.S. and Women's Institutes.

Secondly, the Red Cross, unlike the other two, is an international organization of which the British Society is a leading member, operating throughout the Commonwealth and, if required, outside it.

Thirdly, it consists of both men and women although male members form a comparatively small proportion, and it also has a Junior Branch, consisting of boys and girls, which should be a good recruiting ground for adult membership; but, as with most youth organizations, there is a considerable wastage at 16.

Lastly, full membership of the Red Cross implies submission to training and the acquisition of certain defined qualifications which are tested by examination. While it is certainly not suggested that many W.V.S. or Women's Institute members are 'passengers', the structure and requirements of the Red Cross make it perhaps more difficult to be an inactive member than in either of the other two societies.

The Red Cross is organized on a county basis; the county branches have control over their funds, personnel and property, although they follow the policy laid down by the national council, which also appoints the national executive committee. Each county branch has a president —whose activity varies from place to place—a committee and a director who is responsible for his area. The national council was originally composed of members of the governing bodies of various societies which amalgamated with or were merged in the British Red Cross Society at the beginning of this century. Since that time vacancies occurring on the council have been filled by inviting suitable persons to serve.

The county executive committees, which are the governing bodies for the branches, are composed of the senior officers, representatives of the divisions and detachments, appointed or elected by these groups, and a limited number of co-opted members. The administrative machinery is not therefore democratic at the highest level but is rather more so in the branches.

The lower grades of the county administrative staffs—whether they are members of the society or not—are paid salaries. The highest executive positions are generally speaking all held by voluntary workers though occasionally with an honorarium. There are some posts of a rather less high rank, but carrying considerable responsibility, where small salaries are paid. So far, therefore, as the administrative staffs are concerned this salary structure must to some extent determine the economic status of the hierarchy and in so far as the two are synonymous, the social status also.

The society differs from the other organizations as to its finance, relying to a great extent upon local appeals and money-raising activities, and it has also accumulated funds from legacies and bequests.

There were at the beginning of 1950 nearly 140,000 members and associates in the British Red Cross. These include 8,653 men and 37,941 junior members, both boys and girls. Just over 4,000 of the adults were under 21, and 47,330 were associate members. The Red Cross are a uniformed body, but with a far more elaborate hierarchy of rank than the W.V.S. The rank badges of officers and members correspond to those of the Army and, as is natural in an organization much of whose work is closely linked with the services and with hospitals, there is a rigidly defined relationship between officers and members and a strict code of etiquette and behaviour for all workers. This is necessarily different from anything existing in the W.V.S. or Women's Institutes and combined with a tradition, built up over many years, tends to create a similarity of outlook and atmosphere within branches and detachments.

The Red Cross would claim now to comprise all social groups, both as regards officers and members. In its earlier days it was principally composed of people from the upper and middle sections of society; at the present time the higher grades of the officers still chiefly belong to the upper middle or professional groups and their average age is high. Lack of time and the increase in paid full-time employment among younger middle-class women are considered responsible for this as in the W.V.S. and in the Women's Institutes, and it is further suggested that the demands made upon officers in the Red Cross are great and lack of time is supplemented by lack of desire to fulfil them.

No barriers necessarily prevent the ordinary member from rising to the highest rank; most of the senior officers in fact started as members— the days when the lady of the manor automatically became commandant and the vicar's wife her second-in-command are over in this as in other societies. Members, however, appear reluctant to become officers; most of the younger ones look to matrimony as a full-time occupation in the near future and the rather older women are married already or fully occupied. This reluctance may not be due to any unwillingness to take responsibility. But there is some evidence that the same thing is happening as happened rather earlier in the Women's Institutes—people of lower status are reluctant to assume positions of leadership, with the consequent maintenance in office of older people of a different social grade who would be very ready to retire and who stay on from a sense of duty. It is probable also that the qualifications required by officers, which demand a good deal of specified work such as attendance at lectures and taking examinations, are a contributory factor in the ordinary members' preference to remain as such, and a factor which is not operative to the same extent in the W.V.S. and Women's Institutes.

While 'class consciousness' does not seem to be prevalent in most Red Cross units, rank consciousness is strong; and while many officers do, as indicated, still belong to at least the middle grades of society, the respect and obedience which the structure of the Red Cross requires and which is freely given is not normally a 'class' phenomenon and there are few signs of social emulation. It seems universally accepted that officers of all grades have become so by virtue of efficiency as shown in training and examination and not through social or income status, and that they have accepted a heavy and unenviable task.

The importance of training is emphasized in the Red Cross, and

401

first-aid certificates must be obtained by members as soon as possible after joining, with further qualifications in the shape of either a welfare or home-nursing certificate; a third certificate is urged though not compulsory. The welfare certificate has only been included since the 1939–45 war, when social service, in connection, as the Charter requires, with the sick and suffering, was added to the Red Cross activities. Required qualifications include some knowledge of the development and scope of social services, statutory and voluntary, and of the social agencies working in the field. All training is based on official syllabuses and training manuals and the Society now has a training centre, Barnett Hill, near Guildford, where qualifying courses in each of the three recognized subjects are given at regular intervals. These courses last a week, and as at Denman College are of great value quite apart from their educational usefulness in the narrower sense. They give an opportunity for members from all parts—including overseas—and from many social and economic groups to discuss problems and join in activities of various kinds. Barnett Hill, as the house is called, is an excellent mixing agent, and the atmosphere is considerably less 'rank conscious' than in some other Red Cross meetings and groups. There is less standing to attention on the entry of an officer and less formality in address.

A typical 'welfare' course was composed of about twenty-five women, mostly of the middle or lower middle social groups, with a few representatives from the upper middle or upper ranks and from the farming class—no one representative of the industrial wage-earner.

The emphasis on training, though such training is necessarily and avowedly limited in scope, reinforces the consciousness of and respect for rank and status mentioned earlier. On the whole now, though it may not always have been so, the higher the rank the greater the qualifications required, and qualifications are gained by training. The highly qualified, highly graded officer, therefore, inspires admiration, respect and often affection, partly because of her superior knowledge and attainments, partly no doubt because of her personality and powers of leadership, but not at any rate usually because of her social position. The structure of the Red Cross is, however, a strictly graded hierarchy with some similarity to military ranks, and a long tradition of obedience to and almost a quasi-mystical respect for an officer class as such, apart from the qualifications of those who comprise it, helps to produce something very like the heroine worship observable in other organizations.

In England the Red Cross Charter has been widely interpreted and covers a considerable range of social service; the work is in some respects similar to that undertaken by W.V.S. or occasionally by Women's Institutes, but the demand for such services is great. Generally speaking the organizations mutually agree to divide the work and the area, the W.V.S. usually acting in default of another body, and relationships are quite harmonious. Friction occasionally arises however, both as to the scope of responsibility, the methods employed and the personalities of those doing the job. The range of activities undertaken by the Red Cross is much narrower than that open to W.V.S.; the former makes greater maximum demands upon its members and requires more stereotyped qualifications. The woman with only an odd hour or two to offer is more likely to find opportunities in the W.V.S. than the Red Cross; but the recognized standard qualifications demanded by the latter probably increase the value of its workers in some fields as compared with those in other bodies.

The senior officers in counties and to some extent also in detachments, while they have in most cases 'risen from the ranks', are usually members of the upper or upper middle groups, for reasons already set forth. The members as a whole, however, contain a large proportion of the weekly wage-earning group—shops, offices and factories—either working in this way themselves or having married workers of this kind. An unofficial estimate of the social grouping considers that about 20 per cent of the membership (all ranks) belongs to the upper and upper middle groups (higher professional), 35 per cent to the middle (minor professional and administrative) and 45 per cent to lower-paid wage earners. The members are younger on the whole than the officers and it is suggested that the high proportion of the wage-earning class to be found among them is partly due to the fact that the unmarried daughters in this group are more likely to be living at home and show a greater tendency to 'stay put' than those in the professional grades, who are inclined to take up trainings and careers which may entail leaving home and movement from place to place, and make it more difficult to strike roots. Thus organizations such as the Red Cross, which demand qualifications taking some little time to acquire, gain a larger proportion of young members from the relatively non-mobile young women than from the more nomadic groups. There are many exceptions to this but there is probably a good deal in it. For whatever reasons there is clearly a large number of members (though not officers) in the Red Cross belonging to lower income groups who are distributed over the whole field of activities. It is difficult to discover whether they play an important part in the comparatively new field of social welfare, but if so there is evidence that social service is here as elsewhere widening its boundaries and is no longer a rôle confined to people of higher status. Incidentally, the Red Cross, probably because it is a much older organization, asserts more strongly than either of the other two that in its work the relationships of benefactor and beneficiaries are being reversed; in old people's welfare work and to some extent in other domestic assistance, former Red Cross officers and members are requesting and receiving help in various forms from workers belonging to social groups to which in earlier days they themselves gave help.

Conclusion

The organizations discussed are sometimes criticized by working-class groups on the grounds of the superior social status of their members and particularly their leaders and because of the patronage and condescension which is believed to colour their work. The former assertion was probably true to a great extent ten years ago; it is much less true now, but beliefs of this kind are very difficult to dislodge and many old-established groups are perhaps inclined to retain suspicions which have largely ceased to be valid. Condescending attitudes are difficult to affirm or deny; some groups and some individuals will tend to find what they are looking for though it may not be apparent to those of a different outlook. But patronage and condescension were certainly present in the earlier days of these associations as in many others—exactly the same criticisms were made of the Family Welfare Associations; similar attitudes could probably be found here and there today.

It seems possible that there is another, unconscious, bias behind the hostility with which working-class groups sometimes regard such bodies as W.V.S., Red Cross and even Women's Institutes. Most working-class organizations are predominantly masculine in their leadership and control, while the groups named are entirely feminine in two cases, largely so in the third. It seems possible that criticisms against 'these ladies' are fundamentally directed towards 'these women' and that the old, probably unconscious sex antagonism plays a part.

There is in these three organizations evidence of a changing pattern of membership—one representative of a wider range of social groups. The diversity of activity which they undertake provides opportunity for service to women belonging to social groups which have not been identified with social service in the formal sense and which have certainly not mixed with others, though mixing is not yet apparent to any marked degree in the leadership at headquarters or in the higher provincial or regional positions which are almost exclusively held by women of the upper and professional groups.

Minor positions of authority are, however, held by women of many social levels and participation in community service which was largely a wartime development has been carried on and extended and all social groups take part. Such service is most imaginative and intelligent where there is a substantial mixture of strata, and it is certainly true that women of all groups from the highest—as measured by status and income—to the lowest take part, though the latter are in a minority.

The apparent attitudes of the people involved in the changing pattern are very various. In some cases taking part in work which was formerly, mainly, undertaken by those of higher status confers great satisfaction and is regarded as a social leg-up, and those feelings are heightened if their owner becomes an officer or committee member—in fact her main purpose in joining at all may be to raise her social status. It is seldom, however, that these motives of emulation are the predominant ones, even in ordinary members, and still less frequently in officers. People with this attitude are not often elected or appointed to positions of control and if by some mischance they are, wholesale resignations result and adjustments take place. 'Class-consciousness' is not present at all in a considerable number of women; they join an organization in order to do a job of work and lend a helping hand, and while they may realize that many of their fellow members belong to a different social group the fact does not worry them and they are certainly not conscious of being elevated by association with such a group. Probably the majority have mixed feelings; they are genuinely anxious to offer service to the community, they are also sometimes—though not always—pleased at having an opportunity to use their abilities in positions of minor authority, especially if they belong to the groups which have previously played very little part in control. Many of them probably feel an element of satisfaction also at taking part in activities which have hitherto been so largely the preserve of women of higher social status and which, as already indicated, are still mainly governed by them at the higher levels. The heroine worship which sometimes characterizes local units is a personal attitude and not necessarily an attitude of one group to another.

The women from higher social groups who are becoming less prominent in these organizations also vary in their reactions. In a few instances displaced persons may be seen hovering uncertainly at meetings, rather pathetically trying to exercise their old authority; their attitude is sometimes resented but more often treated with good-tempered tolerance. More frequently the former office bearers have given up their monopoly with resignation and even with pleasure and have adjusted themselves successfully to the new developments. The problem of the woman with a strong desire for power occurs in these organizations as it does in associations of all kinds, but this again is not a social question, though it is true that the woman of lower status with this urge is having a better chance of gratifying it than she has had before.

How far is the situation as set forth here an index of the social mixing in the community? Probably at present not significantly so. The members of the Women's Institutes, the Red Cross and the W.V.S. may work together harmoniously enough in their activities. The policeman's wife may be an official, the doctor's wife an ordinary member; the railwayman's wife may run a club for old people and the general's wife be her subordinate. But they will not invite each other to lunch. Outside the particular field of Women's Institutes, Red Cross or W.V.S. their circumstances are too different and the organizations have not made a sufficient impact upon the community to influence its general social patterns.

But though this is certainly true, one method of promoting social integration is through the acquisition of and participation in the same activities, gradual though this process inevitably is. The organizations studied and to some extent described and analysed offer examples of such common interest in a field where, as suggested at the beginning, social stratification has hitherto been most marked.

It may be objected that social and economic change rather than an alteration in attitudes has been responsible for this. Women of higher social status are no longer available to hold office or play a prominent part, and organizations have merely bowed to the inevitable in opening their ranks to lower social groups. This may be true in some societies; it is not true as far as the Women's Institutes and the W.V.S. are concerned, and I do not think it is true of the Red Cross, though as much of the information about that body was not obtained at first-hand it is difficult to speak certainly.

The primary object of the W.V.S. and the Women's Institutes is not to break down social barriers, but rather to render service to the community in various ways. But both bodies aim at making participation in their activities open to all social groups, and have never divided the community into benefactor and beneficiary classes as did older social service organizations—by implication if not explicitly. Social and economic changes have reinforced existing attitudes and facilitated their expression in action; but the social attitudes are not themselves the result of change.

Index of Persons and Organizations

407

Subject Index

Aberdeen University, 309–19
  catchment area of, 319
Age, as determinant of subjective
  status, 57–8
Age at marriage, and social origins, 339
  and social mobility, 340
Ambitions, 65–75
Association and Dissociation, indices
  of, 18, 195 ff., 318–19
  for England and Wales, at successive
    points in working life, 206; by
    decade of birth only, 204; by status
    category, 199; by status category
    and decade of birth, 201
  for Scotland, by status category and
    decade of birth, 214; for decade of
    birth only, 215
  possible future trend in England and
    Wales, 217

Benini, index of attraction, 248
British Red Cross Society:
  activities, 403–4
  administrative structure, 399–400
  rank consciousness within, 401–2
  social composition of, 400–1, 403
  training, 401–2
Business ownership, 65

Cambridge University, 309–19
  Appointments Board, 309
Carnegie, help to Scottish students, 319
Class identification, 51–75
Church, the, 308–19
Clergymen, 308–20
Continuous registration, systems of, 13

Differential social perspectives, 58–64
Doctors, 309–19

Econcmic depression, between the wars,
  101 108, 110, 122

Education, as criterion of social status,
  30
  attitudes towards, 160 ff.
  classification of (in main sample
    survey), 82
  influence of, upon association be-
    tween fathers and sons, 304–5
Education Act, 1870, 13
  1902, 13, 104
  1944, 4, 10 n., 15 17, 19, 21, 23, 25,
    100, 123
  effect of, 141, 147, 159
Education and social mobility, 99, 123
  descriptive analysis, 293
  educational classification used in
    analysis, 292
  influence of schooling upon son's
    achieved status, 300
  role of further education in relation-
    ship, 298
  role of grammar school in relation-
    ship, 298
Educational, aspirations, 68, 75, 160 ff.
  ladder, 106, 116, 122
  opportunity, social distribution of,
    in relation to previous schooling,
    118–19, 120–1
  selection, 9, 75
Educational Reconstruction, White
  Paper on, 28
Electoral Register, 52
Examination, County Entrance, 160–1
  School Certificate, 103, 112
Extra-curricula school activities, par-
  ticipation in, 151–2

Family Census, results compared with
  main sample survey, 89
Family size, and scholastic performance, 145–6, 159
  and social class, 145–6, 159
Fee paying pupils, 102, 104, 109–10
Fees, abolition of, in 1945, 102

409

The International Library of

Sociology

and Social Reconstruction

Edited by W. J. H. SPROTT
Founded by KARL MANNHEIM

ROUTLEDGE & KEGAN PAUL

BROADWAY HOUSE, CARTER LANE, LONDON, E.C.4

CONTENTS

PRINTED IN GREAT BRITAIN BY HEADLEY BROTHERS LTD
109 KINGSWAY LONDON WC2 AND ASHFORD KENT

GENERAL SOCIOLOGY

Brown, Robert. Explanation in Social Science. *208 pp. 1963. (2nd Impression 1964.) 25s.*

Gibson, Quentin. The Logic of Social Enquiry. *240 pp. 1960. (3rd Impression 1968.) 24s.*

Homans, George C. Sentiments and Activities: Essays in Social Science. *336 pp. 1962. 32s.*

Isajiw, Wseveled W. Causation and Functionalism in Sociology. *165 pp. 1968. 25s.*

Johnson, Harry M. Sociology: a Systematic Introduction. *Foreword by Robert K. Merton. 710 pp. 1961. (5th Impression 1968.) 42s.*

Mannheim, Karl. Essays on Sociology and Social Psychology. *Edited by Paul Keckskemeti. With Editorial Note by Adolph Lowe. 344 pp. 1953. (2nd Impression 1966.) 32s.*

Systematic Sociology: An Introduction to the Study of Society. *Edited by J. S. Erös and Professor W. A. C. Stewart. 220 pp. 1957. (3rd Impression 1967.) 24s.*

Martindale, Don. The Nature and Types of Sociological Theory. *292 pp. 1961. (3rd Impression 1967.) 35s.*

Maus, Heinz. A Short History of Sociology. *234 pp. 1962. (2nd Impression 1965.) 28s.*

Myrdal, Gunnar. Value in Social Theory: A Collection of Essays on Methodology. *Edited by Paul Streeten. 332 pp. 1958. (3rd Impression 1968.) 35s.*

Ogburn, William F., and **Nimkoff, Meyer F.** A Handbook of Sociology. *Preface by Karl Mannheim. 656 pp. 46 figures. 35 tables. 5th edition (revised) 1964. 45s.*

Parsons, Talcott, and **Smelser, Neil J.** Economy and Society: A Study in the Integration of Economic and Social Theory. *362 pp. 1956. (4th Impression 1967.) 35s.*

Rex, John. Key Problems of Sociological Theory. *220 pp. 1961. (4th Impression 1968.) 25s.*

Stark, Werner. The Fundamental Forms of Social Thought. *280 pp. 1962. 32s.*

FOREIGN CLASSICS OF SOCIOLOGY

Durkheim, Emile. Suicide. A Study in Sociology. *Edited and with an Introduction by George Simpson. 404 pp. 1952. (4th Impression 1968.) 35s.*

Professional Ethics and Civic Morals. *Translated by Cornelia Brookfield. 288 pp. 1957. 30s.*

Gerth, H. H., and **Mills, C. Wright.** From Max Weber: Essays in Sociology. *502 pp. 1948. (6th Impression 1967.) 35s.*

Tönnies, Ferdinand. Community and Association. *(Gemeinschaft und Gesellschaft.) Translated and Supplemented by Charles P. Loomis. Foreword by Pitirim A. Sorokin. 334 pp. 1955. 28s.*

3

SOCIAL STRUCTURE

Andreski, Stanislav. Military Organization and Society. *Foreword by Professor A. R. Radcliffe-Brown. 226 pp. 1 folder. 1954. Revised Edition 1968. 35s.*

Cole, G. D. H. Studies in Class Structure. *220 pp. 1955. (3rd Impression 1964.) 21s. Paper 10s. 6d.*

Coontz, Sydney H. Population Theories and the Economic Interpretation. *202 pp. 1957. (3rd Impression 1968.) 28s.*

Coser, Lewis. The Functions of Social Conflict. *204 pp. 1956. (3rd Impression 1968.) 25s.*

Dickie-Clark, H. F. Marginal Situation: A Sociological Study of a Coloured Group. *240 pp. 11 tables. 1966. 40s.*

Glass, D. V. (Ed.). Social Mobility in Britain. *Contributions by J. Berent, T. Bottomore, R. C. Chambers, J. Floud, D. V. Glass, J. R. Hall, H. T. Himmelweit, R. K. Kelsall, F. M. Martin, C. A. Moser, R. Mukherjee, and W. Ziegel. 420 pp. 1954. (4th Impression 1967.) 45s.*

Jones, Garth N. Planned Organizational Change: An Exploratory Study Using an Empirical Approach. *About 268 pp. 1969. 40s.*

Kelsall, R. K. Higher Civil Servants in Britain: From 1870 to the Present Day. *268 pp. 31 tables. 1955. (2nd Impression 1966.) 25s.*

König, René. The Community. *232 pp. Illustrated. 1968. 35s.*

Lawton, Denis. Social Class, Language and Education. *192 pp. 1968. (2nd Impression 1968.) 25s.*

McLeish, John. The Theory of Social Change: Four Views Considered. *About 128 pp. 1969. 21s.*

Marsh, David C. The Changing Social Structure in England and Wales, 1871-1961. *1958. 272 pp. 2nd edition (revised) 1966. (2nd Impression 1967.) 35s.*

Mouzelis, Nicos. Organization and Bureaucracy. An Analysis of Modern Theories. *240 pp. 1967. (2nd Impression 1968.) 28s.*

Ossowski, Stanislaw. Class Structure in the Social Consciousness. *210 pp. 1963. (2nd Impression 1967.) 25s.*

SOCIOLOGY AND POLITICS

Barbu, Zevedei. Democracy and Dictatorship: Their Psychology and Patterns of Life. *300 pp. 1956. 28s.*

Crick, Bernard. The American Science of Politics: Its Origins and Conditions. *284 pp. 1959. 32s.*

Hertz, Frederick. Nationality in History and Politics: A Psychology and Sociology of National Sentiment and Nationalism. *432 pp. 1944. (5th Impression 1966.) 42s.*

Kornhauser, William. The Politics of Mass Society. *272 pp. 20 tables. 1960. (3rd Impression 1968.) 28s.*

Laidler, Harry W. History of Socialism. Social-Economic Movements: An Historical and Comparative Survey of Socialism, Communism, Co-operation, Utopianism; and other Systems of Reform and Reconstruction. *New edition. 992 pp. 1968. 90s.*

Lasswell, Harold D. Analysis of Political Behaviour. An Empirical Approach. *324 pp. 1947. (4th Impression 1966.) 35s.*

Mannheim, Karl. Freedom, Power and Democratic Planning. *Edited by Hans Gerth and Ernest K. Bramstedt. 424 pp. 1951. (3rd Impression 1968.) 42s.*

Mansur, Fatma. Process of Independence. *Foreword by A. H. Hanson. 208 pp. 1962. 25s.*

Martin, David A. Pacificism: an Historical and Sociological Study. *262 pp. 1965. 30s.*

Myrdal, Gunnar. The Political Element in the Development of Economic Theory. *Translated from the German by Paul Streeten. 282 pp. 1953. (4th Impression 1965.) 25s.*

Polanyi, Michael. F.R.S. The Logic of Liberty: Reflections and Rejoinders. *228 pp. 1951. 18s.*

Verney, Douglas V. The Analysis of Political Systems. *264 pp. 1959. (3rd Impression 1966.) 28s.*

Wootton, Graham. The Politics of Influence: British Ex-Servicemen, Cabinet Decisions and Cultural Changes, 1917 to 1957. *316 pp. 1963. 30s.*
Workers, Unions and the State. *188 pp. 1966. (2nd Impression 1967.) 25s.*

FOREIGN AFFAIRS: THEIR SOCIAL, POLITICAL AND ECONOMIC FOUNDATIONS

Baer, Gabriel. Population and Society in the Arab East. *Translated by Hanna Szöke. 288 pp. 10 maps. 1964. 40s.*

Bonné, Alfred. State and Economics in the Middle East: A Society in Transition. *482 pp. 2nd (revised) edition 1955. (2nd Impression 1960.) 40s.*
Studies in Economic Development: with special reference to Conditions in the Under-developed Areas of Western Asia and India. *322 pp. 84 tables. 2nd edition 1960. 32s.*

Mayer, J. P. Political Thought in France from the Revolution to the Fifth Republic. *164 pp. 3rd edition (revised) 1961. 16s.*

CRIMINOLOGY

Ancel, Marc. Social Defence: A Modern Approach to Criminal Problems. *Foreword by Leon Radzinowicz. 240 pp. 1965. 32s.*

Cloward, Richard A., and **Ohlin, Lloyd E.** Delinquency and Opportunity: A Theory of Delinquent Gangs. *248 pp. 1961. 25s.*

5

Downes, David M. The Delinquent Solution. A Study in Subcultural Theory. *296 pp. 1966. 42s.*

Dunlop, A. B., and **McCabe, S.** Young Men in Detention Centres. *192 pp. 1965. 28s.*

Friedländer, Kate. The Psycho-Analytical Approach to Juvenile Delinquency: Theory, Case Studies, Treatment. *320 pp. 1947. (6th Impression 1967). 40s.*

Glueck, Sheldon and **Eleanor.** Family Environment and Delinquency. *With the statistical assistance of Rose W. Kneznek. 340 pp.* **1962.** *(2nd Impression 1966.) 40s.*

Mannheim, Hermann. Comparative Criminology: a Text Book. *Two volumes. 442 pp. and 380 pp. 1965. (2nd Impression with corrections 1966.) 42s. a volume.*

Morris, Terence. The Criminal Area: A Study in Social Ecology. *Foreword by Hermann Mannheim. 232 pp. 25 tables. 4 maps. 1957. (2nd Impression 1966.) 28s.*

Morris, Terence and **Pauline,** assisted by **Barbara Barer.** Pentonville: A Sociological Study of an English Prison. *416 pp. 16 plates. 1963. 50s.*

Spencer, John C. Crime and the Services. *Foreword by Hermann Mannheim. 336 pp. 1954. 28s.*

Trasler, Gordon. The Explanation of Criminality. *144 pp. 1962. (2nd Impression 1967.) 20s.*

SOCIAL PSYCHOLOGY

Barbu, Zevedei. Problems of Historical Psychology. *248 pp. 1960. 25s.*

Blackburn, Julian. Psychology and the Social Pattern. *184 pp. 1945. (7th Impression 1964.) 16s.*

Fleming, C. M. Adolescence: Its Social Psychology: With an Introduction to recent findings from the fields of Anthropology, Physiology, Medicine, Psychometrics and Sociometry. *288 pp. 2nd edition (revised) 1963. (3rd Impression 1967.) 25s. Paper 12s. 6d.*

The Social Psychology of Education: An Introduction and Guide to Its Study. *136 pp. 2nd edition (revised) 1959. (4th Impression 1967.) 14s. Paper 7s. 6d.*

Homans, George C. The Human Group. *Foreword by Bernard DeVoto. Introduction by Robert K. Merton. 526 pp. 1951. (7th Impression 1968.) 35s.*

Social Behaviour: its Elementary Forms. *416 pp. 1961. (3rd Impression 1968.) 35s.*

Klein, Josephine. The Study of Groups. *226 pp. 31 figures. 5 tables. 1956. (5th Impression 1967.) 21s. Paper 9s. 6d.*

Linton, Ralph. The Cultural Background of Personality. *132 pp. 1947. (7th Impression 1968.) 18s.*

Mayo, Elton. The Social Problems of an Industrial Civilization. With an appendix on the Political Problem. *180 pp. 1949. (5th Impression 1966.) 25s.*

Ottaway, A. K. C. Learning Through Group Experience. *176 pp. 1966. (2nd Impression 1968.) 25s.*

Ridder, J. C. de. The Personality of the Urban African in South Africa. A Thematic Apperception Test Study. *196 pp. 12 plates. 1961. 25s.*

Rose, Arnold M. (Ed.). Human Behaviour and Social Processes: an Inter-actionist Approach. *Contributions by Arnold M. Rose, Ralph H. Turner, Anselm Strauss, Everett C. Hughes, E. Franklin Frazier, Howard S. Becker, et al. 696 pp. 1962. (2nd Impression 1968.) 70s.*

Smelser, Neil J. Theory of Collective Behaviour. *448 pp. 1962. (2nd Impression 1967.) 45s.*

Stephenson, Geoffrey M. The Development of Conscience. *128 pp. 1966. 25s.*

Young, Kimball. Handbook of Social Psychology. *658 pp. 16 figures. 10 tables. 2nd edition (revised) 1957. (3rd Impression 1963.) 40s.*

SOCIOLOGY OF THE FAMILY

Banks, J. A. Prosperity and Parenthood: A study of Family Planning among The Victorian Middle Classes. *262 pp. 1954. (3rd Impression 1968.) 28s.*

Bell, Colin R. Middle Class Families: Social and Geographical Mobility. *224 pp. 1969. 35s.*

Burton, Lindy. Vulnerable Children. *272 pp. 1968. 35s.*

Gavron, Hannah. The Captive Wife: Conflicts of Housebound Mothers. *190 pp. 1966. (2nd Impression 1966.) 25s.*

Klein, Josephine. Samples from English Cultures. *1965. (2nd Impression 1967.)*
1. Three Preliminary Studies and Aspects of Adult Life in England. *447 pp. 50s.*
2. Child-Rearing Practices and Index. *247 pp. 35s.*

Klein, Viola. Britain's Married Women Workers. *180 pp. 1965. (2nd Impression 1968.) 28s.*

McWhinnie, Alexina M. Adopted Children. How They Grow Up. *304 pp. 1967. (2nd Impression 1968.) 42s.*

Myrdal, Alva and **Klein, Viola.** Women's Two Roles: Home and Work. *238 pp. 27 tables. 1956. Revised Edition 1967. 30s. Paper 15s.*

Parsons, Talcott and **Bales, Robert F.** Family: Socialization and Interaction Process. *In collaboration with James Olds, Morris Zelditch and Philip E. Slater. 456 pp. 50 figures and tables. 1956. (3rd Impression 1968.) 45s.*

Schücking, L. L. The Puritan Family. *Translated from the German by Brian Battershaw. 212 pp. 1969. About 42s.*

THE SOCIAL SERVICES

Forder, R. A. (Ed.). Penelope Hall's Social Services of Modern England. *288 pp. 1969. 35s.*

George, Victor. Social Security: Beveridge and After. *258 pp. 1968. 35s.*

Goetschius, George W. Working with Community Groups. *256 pp. 1969. 35s.*

Goetschius, George W. and **Tash, Joan.** Working with Unattached Youth. *416 pp. 1967. (2nd Impression 1968.) 40s.*

Hall, M. P., and **Howes, I. V.** The Church in Social Work. A Study of Moral Welfare Work undertaken by the Church of England. *320 pp. 1965. 35s.*

Heywood, Jean S. Children in Care: the Development of the Service for the Deprived Child. *264 pp. 2nd edition (revised) 1965. (2nd Impression 1966.) 32s.*

An Introduction to Teaching Casework Skills. *190 pp. 1964. 28s.*

Jones, Kathleen. Lunacy, Law and Conscience, 1744-1845: the Social History of the Care of the Insane. *268 pp. 1955. 25s.*

Mental Health and Social Policy, 1845-1959. *264 pp. 1960. (2nd Impression 1967.) 32s.*

Jones, Kathleen and **Sidebotham, Roy.** Mental Hospitals at Work. *220 pp. 1962. 30s.*

Kastell, Jean. Casework in Child Care. *Foreword by M. Brooke Willis. 320 pp. 1962. 35s.*

Morris, Pauline. Put Away: A Sociological Study of Institutions for the Mentally Retarded. *Approx. 288 pp. 1969. About 50s.*

Nokes, P. L. The Professional Task in Welfare Practice. *152 pp. 1967. 28s.*

Rooff, Madeline. Voluntary Societies and Social Policy. *350 pp. 15 tables. 1957. 35s.*

Timms, Noel. Psychiatric Social Work in Great Britain (1939-1962). *280 pp. 1964. 32s.*

Social Casework: Principles and Practice. *256 pp. 1964. (2nd Impression 1966.) 25s. Paper 15s.*

Trasler, Gordon. In Place of Parents: A Study in Foster Care. *272 pp. 1960. (2nd Impression 1966.) 30s.*

Young, A. F., and **Ashton, E. T.** British Social Work in the Nineteenth Century. *288 pp. 1956. (2nd Impression 1963.) 28s.*

Young, A. F. Social Services in British Industry. *272 pp. 1968. 40s.*

SOCIOLOGY OF EDUCATION

Banks, Olive. Parity and Prestige in English Secondary Education: a Study in Educational Sociology. *272 pp. 1955. (2nd Impression 1963.) 32s.*

Bentwich, Joseph. Education in Israel. *224 pp. 8 pp. plates. 1965. 24s.*

Blyth, W. A. L. English Primary Education. A Sociological Description. *1965. Revised edition 1967.*
1. Schools. *232 pp. 30s. Paper 12s. 6d.*
2. Background. *168 pp. 25s. Paper 10s. 6d.*

Collier, K. G. The Social Purposes of Education: Personal and Social Values in Education. *268 pp. 1959. (3rd Impression 1965.) 21s.*

Dale, R. R., and **Griffith, S.** Down Stream: Failure in the Grammar School. *108 pp. 1965. 20s.*

Dore, R. P. Education in Tokugawa Japan. *356 pp. 9 pp. plates. 1965. 35s.*

Edmonds, E. L. The School Inspector. *Foreword by Sir William Alexander. 214 pp. 1962. 28s.*

Evans, K. M. Sociometry and Education. *158 pp. 1962. (2nd Impression 1966.) 18s.*

Foster, P. J. Education and Social Change in Ghana. *336 pp. 3 maps. 1965. (2nd Impression 1967.) 36s.*

Fraser, W. R. Education and Society in Modern France. *150 pp. 1963. (2nd Impression 1968.) 25s.*

Hans, Nicholas. New Trends in Education in the Eighteenth Century. *278 pp. 19 tables. 1951. (2nd Impression 1966.) 30s.*
   Comparative Education: A Study of Educational Factors and Traditions. *360 pp. 3rd (revised) edition 1958. (4th Impression 1967.) 25s. Paper 12s. 6d.*

Hargreaves, David. Social Relations in a Secondary School. *240 pp. 1967. (2nd Impression 1968.) 32s.*

Holmes, Brian. Problems in Education. A Comparative Approach. *336 pp. 1965. (2nd Impression 1967.) 32s.*

Mannheim, Karl and **Stewart, W. A. C.** An Introduction to the Sociology of Education. *206 pp. 1962. (2nd Impression 1965.) 21s.*

Morris, Raymond N. The Sixth Form and College Entrance. *231 pp. 1969. 40s.*

Musgrove, F. Youth and the Social Order. *176 pp. 1964. (2nd Impression 1968.) 25s. Paper 12s.*

Ortega y Gasset, José. Mission of the University. *Translated with an Introduction by Howard Lee Nostrand. 86 pp. 1946. (3rd Impression 1963.) 15s.*

Ottaway, A. K. C. Education and Society: An Introduction to the Sociology of Education. *With an Introduction by W. O. Lester Smith. 212 pp. Second edition (revised). 1962. (5th Impression 1968.) 18s. Paper 10s. 6d.*

Peers, Robert. Adult Education: A Comparative Study. *398 pp. 2nd edition 1959. (2nd Impression 1966.) 42s.*

Pritchard, D. G. Education and the Handicapped: 1760 to 1960. *258 pp. 1963. (2nd Impression 1966.) 35s.*

Richardson, Helen. Adolescent Girls in Approved Schools. *Approx. 360 pp. 1969. About 42s.*

Simon, Brian and **Joan** (Eds.). Educational Psychology in the U.S.S.R. *Introduction by Brian and Joan Simon. Translation by Joan Simon. Papers by D. N. Bogoiavlenski and N. A. Menchinskaia, D. B. Elkonin, E. A. Fleshner, Z. I. Kalmykova, G. S. Kostiuk, V. A. Krutetski, A. N. Leontiev, A. R. Luria, E. A. Milerian, R. G. Natadze, B. M. Teplov, L. S. Vygotski, L. V. Zankov. 296 pp. 1963. 40s.*

SOCIOLOGY OF CULTURE

Eppel, E. M., and M. Adolescents and Morality: A Study of some Moral Values and Dilemmas of Working Adolescents in the Context of a changing Climate of Opinion. *Foreword by W. J. H. Sprott. 268 pp. 39 tables. 1966. 30s.*

Fromm, Erich. The Fear of Freedom. *286 pp. 1942. (8th Impression 1960.) 25s. Paper 10s.*

The Sane Society. *400 pp. 1956. (4th Impression 1968.) 28s. Paper 14s.*

Mannheim, Karl. Diagnosis of Our Time: Wartime Essays of a Sociologist. *208 pp. 1943. (8th Impression 1966.) 21s.*

Essays on the Sociology of Culture. *Edited by Ernst Mannheim in co-operation with Paul Kecskemeti. Editorial Note by Adolph Lowe. 280 pp. 1956. (3rd Impression 1967.) 28s.*

Weber, Alfred. Farewell to European History: or The Conquest of Nihilism. *Translated from the German by R. F. C. Hull. 224 pp. 1947. 18s.*

SOCIOLOGY OF RELIGION

Argyle, Michael. Religious Behaviour. *224 pp. 8 figures. 41 tables. 1958. (4th Impression 1968.) 25s.*

Nelson, G. K. Spiritualism and Society. *313 pp. 1969. 42s.*

Stark, Werner. The Sociology of Religion. A Study of Christendom.
Volume I. Established Religion. *248 pp. 1966. 35s.*
Volume II. Sectarian Religion. *368 pp. 1967. 40s.*
Volume III. The Universal Church. *464 pp. 1967. 45s.*

Watt, W. Montgomery. Islam and the Integration of Society. *320 pp. 1961. (3rd Impression 1966.) 35s.*

SOCIOLOGY OF ART AND LITERATURE

Beljame, Alexandre. Men of Letters and the English Public in the Eighteenth Century: 1660-1744, Dryden, Addison, Pope. *Edited with an Introduction and Notes by Bonamy Dobrée. Translated by E. O. Lorimer. 532 pp. 1948. 32s.*

Misch, Georg. A History of Autobiography in Antiquity. *Translated by E. W. Dickes. 2 Volumes. Vol. 1, 364 pp., Vol. 2, 372 pp. 1950. 45s. the set.*

Schücking, L. L. The Sociology of Literary Taste. *112 pp. 2nd (revised) edition 1966. 18s.*

Silbermann, Alphons. The Sociology of Music. *Translated from the German by Corbet Stewart. 222 pp. 1963. 32s.*

SOCIOLOGY OF KNOWLEDGE

Mannheim, Karl. Essays on the Sociology of Knowledge. *Edited by Paul Kecskemeti. Editorial note by Adolph Lowe. 352 pp. 1952. (4th Impression 1967.) 35s.*

Stark, W. America: Ideal and Reality. The United States of 1776 in Contemporary Philosophy. *136 pp. 1947. 12s.*

The Sociology of Knowledge: An Essay in Aid of a Deeper Understanding of the History of Ideas. *384 pp. 1958. (3rd Impression 1967.) 36s.*

Montesquieu: Pioneer of the Sociology of Knowledge. *244 pp. 1960. 25s.*

URBAN SOCIOLOGY

Anderson, Nels. The Urban Community: A World Perspective. *532 pp. 1960. 35s.*

Ashworth, William. The Genesis of Modern British Town Planning: A Study in Economic and Social History of the Nineteenth and Twentieth Centuries. *288 pp. 1954. (3rd Impression 1968.) 32s.*

Bracey, Howard. Neighbours: On New Estates and Subdivisions in England and U.S.A. *220 pp. 1964. 28s.*

Cullingworth, J. B. Housing Needs and Planning Policy: A Restatement of the Problems of Housing Need and "Overspill" in England and Wales. *232 pp. 44 tables. 8 maps. 1960. (2nd Impression 1966.) 28s.*

Dickinson, Robert E. City and Region: A Geographical Interpretation. *608 pp. 125 figures. 1964. (5th Impression 1967.) 60s.*

The West European City: A Geographical Interpretation. *600 pp. 129 maps. 29 plates. 2nd edition 1962. (3rd Impression 1968.) 55s.*

The City Region in Western Europe. *320 pp. Maps. 1967. 30s. Paper 14s.*

Jackson, Brian. Working Class Community: Some General Notions raised by a Series of Studies in Northern England. *192 pp. 1968. (2nd Impression 1968.) 25s.*

Jennings, Hilda. Societies in the Making: a Study of Development and Redevelopment within a County Borough. *Foreword by D. A. Clark. 286 pp. 1962. (2nd Impression 1967.) 32s.*

Kerr, Madeline. The People of Ship Street. *240 pp. 1958. 28s.*

Mann, P. H. An Approach to Urban Sociology. *240 pp. 1965. (2nd Impression 1968.) 30s.*

Morris, R. N., and **Mogey, J.** The Sociology of Housing. Studies at Berinsfield. *232 pp. 4 pp. plates. 1965. 42s.*

Rosser, C., and **Harris, C.** The Family and Social Change. A Study of Family and Kinship in a South Wales Town. *352 pp. 8 maps. 1965. (2nd Impression 1968.) 45s.*

RURAL SOCIOLOGY

Chambers, R. J. H. Settlement Schemes in Africa: A Selective Study. *Approx. 268 pp. 1969. About 50s.*

Haswell, M. R. The Economics of Development in Village India. *120 pp. 1967. 21s.*

Littlejohn, James. Westrigg: the Sociology of a Cheviot Parish. *172 pp. 5 figures. 1963. 25s.*

Williams, W. M. The Country Craftsman: A Study of Some Rural Crafts and the Rural Industries Organization in England. *248 pp. 9 figures. 1958. 25s. (Dartington Hall Studies in Rural Sociology.)*
The Sociology of an English Village: Gosforth. *272 pp. 12 figures. 13 tables. 1956. (3rd Impression 1964.) 25s.*

SOCIOLOGY OF MIGRATION

Humphreys, Alexander J. New Dubliners: Urbanization and the Irish Family. *Foreword by George C. Homans. 304 pp. 1966. 40s.*

SOCIOLOGY OF INDUSTRY AND DISTRIBUTION

Anderson, Nels. Work and Leisure. *280 pp. 1961. 28s.*

Blau, Peter M., and **Scott, W. Richard.** Formal Organizations: a Comparative approach. *Introduction and Additional Bibliography by J. H. Smith. 326 pp. 1963. (4th Impression 1969.) 35s. Paper 15s.*

Eldridge, J. E. T. Industrial Disputes. Essays in the Sociology of Industrial Relations. *288 pp. 1968. 40s.*

Hollowell, Peter G. The Lorry Driver. *272 pp. 1968. 42s.*

Jefferys, Margot, with the assistance of **Winifred Moss.** Mobility in the Labour Market: Employment Changes in Battersea and Dagenham. *Preface by Barbara Wootton. 186 pp. 51 tables. 1954. 15s.*

Levy, A. B. Private Corporations and Their Control. *Two Volumes. Vol. 1, 464 pp., Vol. 2, 432 pp. 1950. 80s. the set.*

Liepmann, Kate. Apprenticeship: An Enquiry into its Adequacy under Modern Conditions. *Foreword by H. D. Dickinson. 232 pp. 6 tables. 1960. (2nd Impression 1960.) 23s.*

Millerson, Geoffrey. The Qualifying Associations: a Study in Professionalization. *320 pp. 1964. 42s.*

Smelser, Neil J. Social Change in the Industrial Revolution: An Application of Theory to the Lancashire Cotton Industry, 1770-1840. *468 pp. 12 figures. 14 tables. 1959. (2nd Impression 1960.) 50s.*

Williams, Gertrude. Recruitment to Skilled Trades. *240 pp. 1957. 23s.*

Young, A. F. Industrial Injuries Insurance: an Examination of British Policy. *192 pp. 1964. 30s.*

ANTHROPOLOGY

Ammar, Hamed. Growing up in an Egyptian Village: Silwa, Province of Aswan. *336 pp. 1954. (2nd Impression 1966.) 35s.*

Crook, David and **Isabel.** Revolution in a Chinese Village: Ten Mile Inn. *230 pp. 8 plates. 1 map. 1959. (2nd Impression 1968.) 21s.*
The First Years of Yangyi Commune. *302 pp. 12 plates. 1966. 42s.*

Dickie-Clark, H. F. The Marginal Situation. A Sociological Study of a Coloured Group. *236 pp. 1966. 40s.*

Dube, S. C. Indian Village. *Foreword by Morris Edward Opler. 276 pp. 4 plates. 1955. (5th Impression 1965.) 25s.*
India's Changing Villages: Human Factors in Community Development. *260 pp. 8 plates. 1 map. 1958. (3rd Impression 1963.) 25s.*

Firth, Raymond. Malay Fishermen. Their Peasant Economy. *420 pp. 17 pp. plates. 2nd edition revised and enlarged 1966. (2nd Impression 1968.) 55s.*

Gulliver, P. H. The Family Herds. A Study of two Pastoral Tribes in East Africa, The Jie and Turkana. *304 pp. 4 plates. 19 figures. 1955. (2nd Impression with new preface and bibliography 1966.) 35s.*
Social Control in an African Society: a Study of the Arusha, Agricultural Masai of Northern Tanganyika. *320 pp. 8 plates. 10 figures. 1963. (2nd Impression 1968.) 42s.*

Ishwaran, K. Shivapur. A South Indian Village. *216 pp. 1968. 35s.*
Tradition and Economy in Village India: An Interactionist Approach. *Foreword by Conrad Arensburg. 176 pp. 1966. (2nd Impression 1968.) 25s.*

Jarvie, Ian C. The Revolution in Anthropology. *268 pp. 1964. (2nd Impression 1967.) 40s.*

Jarvie, Ian C. and **Agassi, Joseph.** Hong Kong. A Society in Transition. *396 pp. Illustrated with plates and maps. 1968. 56s.*

Little, Kenneth L. Mende of Sierra Leone. *308 pp. and folder. 1951. Revised edition 1967. 63s.*

Lowie, Professor Robert H. Social Organization. *494 pp. 1950. (4th Impression 1966.) 50s.*

Mayer, Adrian C. Caste and Kinship in Central India: A Village and its Region. *328 pp. 16 plates. 15 figures. 16 tables. 1960. (2nd Impression 1965.) 35s.*
Peasants in the Pacific: A Study of Fiji Indian Rural Society. *232 pp. 16 plates. 10 figures. 14 tables. 1961. 35s.*

Smith, Raymond T. The Negro Family in British Guiana: Family Structure and Social Status in the Villages. *With a Foreword by Meyer Fortes. 314 pp. 8 plates. 1 figure. 4 maps. 1956. (2nd Impression 1965.) 35s.*

DOCUMENTARY

Meek, Dorothea L. (Ed.). Soviet Youth: Some Achievements and Problems. *Excerpts from the Soviet Press, translated by the editor. 280 pp. 1957. 28s.*

Schlesinger, Rudolf (Ed.). Changing Attitudes in Soviet Russia.
2. The Nationalities Problem and Soviet Administration. Selected Readings on the Development of Soviet Nationalities Policies. *Introduced by the editor. Translated by W. W. Gottlieb. 324 pp. 1956. 30s.*

Reports of the Institute of Community Studies

(Demy 8vo.)

Cartwright, Ann. Human Relations and Hospital Care. *272 pp. 1964. 30s.*
Patients and their Doctors. A Study of General Practice. *304 pp. 1967. 40s.*

Jackson, Brian. Streaming: an Education System in Miniature. *168 pp. 1964. (2nd Impression 1966.) 21s. Paper 10s.*

Jackson, Brian and **Marsden, Dennis.** Education and the Working Class: Some General Themes raised by a Study of 88 Working-class Children in a Northern Industrial City. *268 pp. 2 folders. 1962. (4th Impression 1968.) 32s.*

Marris, Peter. Widows and their Families. *Foreword by Dr. John Bowlby. 184 pp. 18 tables. Statistical Summary. 1958. 18s.*
Family and Social Change in an African City. A Study of Rehousing in Lagos. *196 pp. 1 map. 4 plates. 53 tables. 1961. (2nd Impression 1966.) 30s.*
The Experience of Higher Education. *232 pp. 27 tables. 1964. 25s.*

Marris, Peter and **Rein, Martin.** Dilemmas of Social Reform. Poverty and Community Action in the United States. *256 pp. 1967. 35s.*

Mills, Enid. Living with Mental Illness: a Study in East London. *Foreword by Morris Carstairs. 196 pp. 1962. 28s.*

Runciman, W. G. Relative Deprivation and Social Justice. A Study of Attitudes to Social Inequality in Twentieth Century England. *352 pp. 1966. (2nd Impression 1967.) 40s.*

Townsend, Peter. The Family Life of Old People: An Inquiry in East London. *Foreword by J. H. Sheldon. 300 pp. 3 figures. 63 tables. 1957. (3rd Impression 1967.) 30s.*

Willmott, Peter. Adolescent Boys in East London. *230 pp. 1966. 30s.*
The Evolution of a Community: a study of Dagenham after forty years. *168 pp. 2 maps. 1963. 21s.*

Willmott, Peter and **Young, Michael.** Family and Class in a London Suburb. *202 pp. 47 tables. 1960. (4th Impression 1968.) 25s.*

Young, Michael. Innovation and Research in Education. *192 pp. 1965. 25s. Paper 12s. 6d.*

Young, Michael and **McGeeney, Patrick.** Learning Begins at Home. A Study of a Junior School and its Parents. *About 128 pp. 1968. 21s. Paper 14s.*

Young, Michael and **Willmott, Peter.** Family and Kinship in East London. *Foreword by Richard M. Titmuss. 252 pp. 39 tables. 1957. (3rd Impression 1965.) 28s.*

14

The British Journal of Sociology. *Edited by Terence P. Morris. Vol. 1, No. 1, March 1950 and Quarterly. Roy. 8vo., £3 annually, 15s. a number, post free. (Vols. 1-18, £8 each. Individual parts £2 10s.*

All prices are net and subject to alteration without notice

1268 H.B.